CW00447924

CAMBRIDGE STUDIES IN RUSSIAN LITERATURE

Joseph Brodsky

a poet for our time

CAMBRIDGE STUDIES IN RUSSIAN LITERATURE

General editor MALCOLM JONES

Joseph Brodsky, *c.* 1973

Joseph Brodsky
a poet for our time

VALENTINA POLUKHINA

University of Keele

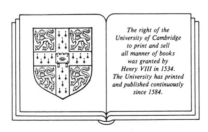

The right of the
University of Cambridge
to print and sell
all manner of books
was granted by
Henry VIII in 1534.
The University has printed
and published continuously
since 1584.

CAMBRIDGE UNIVERSITY PRESS

CAMBRIDGE

NEW YORK   PORT CHESTER   MELBOURNE   SYDNEY

Published by the Press Syndicate of the University of Cambridge
The Pitt Building, Trumpington Street, Cambridge CB2 1RP
40 West 20th Street, New York, NY 10011, USA
10 Stamford Road, Oakleigh, Melbourne 3166, Australia

© Cambridge University Press 1989

First published 1989

Printed in Great Britain by the University Press, Cambridge

British Library cataloguing in publication data
Polukhina, Valentina.
Joseph Brodsky: a poet for our time. –
(Cambridge studies in Russian literature).
1. Poetry in Russian. Brodskii, Iosif, 1940–
I. Title.
891.71'44

Library of Congress cataloguing in publication data
Polukhina, Valentina.
Joseph Brodsky: a poet for our time / Valentina Polukhina.
p.   cm. – (Cambridge studies in Russian literature).
Bibliography.
Includes index.
ISBN 0–521–33484–5
1. Brodsky, Joseph, 1940–   – Criticism and interpretation.
I. Title.
PG3479.4.R64Z84 1989
891.71'44–dc19   89–709 CIP

ISBN 0 521 33484 5

CE

To Lapushka and Osin′ka

Contents

Preface

If a poet has any obligation toward society, it is to write well. Being in the minority, he has no other choice. Failing this duty, he sinks into oblivion. Society, on the other hand, has no obligation toward the poet. A majority by definition, society thinks of itself as having other options than reading verses, no matter how well written. Its failure to do so results in its sinking to the level of locution at which society falls easy prey to a demagogue or a tyrant. This is society's own equivalent of oblivion.[1]

Even before Brodsky was forced out of his country (1972), he acquired the reputation of being the most fastidious and intellectual of contemporary Russian poets. In exile he continues to demonstrate wide erudition, astonishing technical virtuosity, and a profound concern with the problems of our age. His six books of poetry and a collection of essays offer one of the most searching treatments of epistemological themes and an enormous intellectual challenge for his readers.

Brodsky's poetic world is as much a world of ideas as it is of images. It is equally a review of ideas, not so much to resolve them as to perceive and reformulate them in the spirit of our time. His poetic world reveals a paradoxical type of the poet: he is simultaneously solitary and social. Finding himself in conflict with a society which rejected and exiled him, he has retained a deep and treasured link with this society. The theme of Russia nurtures his poetry no less than world culture does. This outcast and exile is as much immersed in the fate of his people as he is in the fate of civilization as a whole. His keen sense of time forces him to see what we prefer to close our eyes to. Apart from such universal themes as life and death, faith and time, Brodsky writes about man at the end of the second millennium of Christianity.

Brodsky's almost obsessive preoccupation with time might in itself justify the title of this book. Like every poet, he 'strives for the

same thing: to regain or hold time past or current time' (*L.* 180).
He does not declare our time to be the best or the worst. He does
not reject it, but he does not accept it either. Like Eugenio
Montale, he believes that 'today all true ideals have been discredi-
ted'[2] and that mass man at the end of the twentieth century needs a
moral alternative which can be provided by poetry. Poetry itself is
seen by Brodsky as a counterbalance to what Montale called the
'massacre of time'.[3] Poetry for Brodsky is a unity of ethics,
aesthetics, and memory. This is the only weapon we have in our
struggle against time. Memory expresses itself in Brodsky's poetry
in numerous allusions, echoes, and direct quotations from the
poetry of different epochs and cultures. This can be seen as
Brodsky's attempt to maintain cultural continuity in our age of
mass culture.

As far as the social duties of a poet are concerned, his main tasks
are: to improve the quality of his language; to inspire in his reader a
desire for self-improvement; and to make society less vulgar. In an
age of mass culture and the collapse of spiritual values, Brodsky
defends the unique individuality of each person, his right to his own
vision of the world, however much it may differ from any *Herr
omnes* of our time. Reading Brodsky, one must bear in mind that
he never gives a definite answer to his endless questioning and that
he is a very uncomfortable poet because he is truthful without
mercy. The emotional neutrality of his tone allows him to preserve
sharpness of vision and depth of focus. A social voice resounds in
the very spirit of his poetry. Like Tsvetaeva, he is convinced that 'in
essence all poets of all times say the same thing. And this same
thing remains on the surface of the world's skin, just as the visible
world itself remains on the surface of the poet's skin.'[4]

I do not pretend to be able to unravel all the hidden references,
echoes, and hints of associations, or to give a full picture of
Brodsky's poetic world. My task is to gain a preliminary insight into
this world, which is complex, striking, and absorbing. My approach
to Brodsky's poetry is neither chronological nor thematic. This
book is an attempt to identify the principles of organization of
Brodsky's poems by discussing his technical resources: the system
of his tropes, his use of vocabulary and syntax; what makes them
aesthetically unified. His syntax is either condensed and twisted or
very simple and prosaic. All kinds of violations of syntagmatic links
abound – inversions, enjambements, parenthetic constructions,

extrapolations of subordinate clauses into principal ones. In his tropes, Brodsky conjures up the most surprising images that linger in the mind. Brodsky has concerned himself with the widening and renewal of poetic language. As a result, his vocabulary reflects all the changes that have taken place in the modern Russian language since the Revolution. Throughout this entire study I hope to show that Brodsky's use of language conveys the poet's perception of certain values through his language. Brodsky's ultimate importance as a poet will undoubtedly rest on this treatment of language and his whole attitude towards language. I also hope to demonstrate that Brodsky's poetry is as much linguistically as philosophically orientated. For this reason, the emphasis in the book is not on the poet's life or his personality, but on the language he uses.

The first chapter is not the poet's biography in the strict sense of the word. Such a biography would be a different task altogether. Besides, among Brodsky's recently published selected essays, *Less Than One*, the reader can find at least three most beautifully written autobiographical pieces. Instead, I have presented only the most essential facts of the poet's life in the hope that the rest will follow from his poems, which are put under intense scrutiny in every chapter: most of them have never been previously discussed by Brodsky's critics. The first three chapters are designed to establish the poet's literary genesis, to trace the poetic tradition which Brodsky continues and to ascertain the extent of his departure from it. For this purpose, all the metaphors in all his published poetic works have been detected, classified, and compared with the metaphors of ten other Russian poets. The choice of the first seven poets was self-evident. Every contemporary Russian poet is forced to live and write under the constant gaze of one, at least, if not all of the 'magnificent seven': Blok, Khlebnikov, Mayakovsky, Mandelstam, Tsvetaeva, Pasternak, and Akhmatova. They also represent the principal poetic systems which existed in Russian poetry at the end of the last and at the beginning of this century: Symbolism, Futurism and Acmeism. In order to gain a more objective picture of the Symbolists' metaphoric system I have included Bal'mont. Derzhavin and Baratynsky were suggested by Brodsky himself as his link with Russian Classicism and Romanticism. The comparative analysis of metaphors is designed to help understand the ways and means whereby Brodsky broke away from established poetic systems. A thorough examination of Brodsky's tropes helps

to relate him to the whole of Russian literature from Derzhavin to
Akhmatova. The second chapter is the first sustained effort to
relate Brodsky's work to English poetry.

In the third and the fourth chapters every one of Brodsky's
metaphors has been considered on three levels: its grammatical
structure, its semantics, and its part in the conceptual model of the
poet's world. Such an approach has provided me with the most
adequate possible account of the correlation between the grammar
and the semantics of metaphor. I shall argue that the originality of
Brodsky's metaphoric system lies not only in the grammar of his
tropes but also in the character of his metaphoric transformations
and the types of interrelations between the real world and the
poetic world. Brodsky's tendency to depict abstraction by abstraction, in order to penetrate into the very essence of things, forced
him to create metaphoric formations in which associations by
similarity give way to relations of cause and effect, of space and
time; in other words, metaphor approximates to metonymy. This is
a part of a poetic conflict between Brodsky's prosaic speech and the
fabric of his verse. The further he moves towards the metonymic
pole of language, the more need there is for compensations,
whether by strict metre and precise rhymes or by saturating his
poems with tropes.

The fourth chapter is mainly concerned with the conceptual
functions of metaphor. The conceptualization of time, things, and
man is achieved by various kinds of alienation of meaning in the
trope. The classical triad, 'Spirit–Man–Thing', is widened by
including number and language as equivalent terms. Language, as
one of the principal characters of Brodsky's poetry, is subjected to
the same semantic transformations in his metaphors as 'thing' and
'man'. The desire to comprehend the ontological essence of language is what motivated these processes. As a result, the traditional
opposition 'man–thing' is neutralized. This new correlation
between 'word–man–thing' constitutes a specific cluster of Brodsky's metaphoric network, which can be seen as the key to
interpretation of his poetic world.

The inquiry into the system of Brodsky's metaphors will bring all
his principal themes into sharp focus. They will be considered in the
last two chapters. The paramount theme of his poetry is the theme
of time. The intricacy of Brodsky's treatment of this theme is due to
the close interrelated connection with other themes such as

Empire, faith, love, creativity, and language. He has a deep
awareness of man's painful existence and its futility. It is the image
of a man in exile, both political and existential, which pervades the
poet's universe. The theme of alienation appears in his poetry not
only as the imaginative centre of meaning (or meaninglessness),
but also as a source of dissociation within language itself – a
disjunction of syntactic and semantic links, which both manifests
the estranged meaning in tropes and serves the needs of rhythm and
rhymes. The device of metonymic representation of man is also
loaded with the function of alienation. The destruction of an
integrated perception is a characteristic feature of our time.

All Brodsky's major themes are also discussed in an unobtrusive
way throughout the book, from the very first chapter, in the context
of the poet's complete works. I have not attempted a close analysis
of Brodsky's versification. Doing him any justice at all would have
led to complexities and detail beyond the scope of my study.
However, I describe briefly the metre and rhyme scheme of every
poem I discuss. I am only too aware that whatever method of
analysis one employs, there will always be something left out which
is beyond our reach, e.g. the poet's sagacity, his gift of foresight, his
acute feeling of orphanhood, or his deep apprehension of the
mediocrity of our dispirited time. Any analysis of poetry is only a
dance around the Spirit. The Spirit in Brodsky's poetry is identified
with the language itself, with the Word. The poetic word puts us in
touch with our inner self, uncomfortable, frightened, intrigued,
and humbled.

Acknowledgements

I should like to acknowledge my gratitude to the British Academy for providing financial support for my research in the USA during my sabbatical in 1979–80, and during the preparation of this book for publication. Many of Brodsky's friends helped me in my research into the poet's life and work. I am most grateful to Igor' and Marina Yefimov, Garry Voskov, Natalya Sharymova, Lev Losev and Diana and Alan Myers for their support and assistance during the writing of my doctoral thesis, 'Joseph Brodsky: A Study of Metaphor' (University of Keele, 1985). I have also benefited from my conversations with Vladimir Vishniak, Tatyana Chambers, Yefim Slavinsky and Nina Stavisky about Brodsky's poetry and his life in Leningrad. My debt to Mila Kuperman, who introduced me to Brodsky, is no less deep.

I am greatly indebted to my colleague Joe Andrew for his help in translating and editing various parts of the manuscript, including some of Brodsky's poems. Special thanks are due to my student Chris Jones for his brave attempt to help me to translate Brodsky's poems into English prose. I should like to express my gratitude to all who have read different chapters of this book, especially Henry Gifford, Peter France, Ann Shukman, Leon Burnett, and Roy Fisher who read the entire typescript and made valuable suggestions.

I owe more than I can say to my friends Joan Heath and Fiona Gaunt for being my most patient listeners. I especially thank Vladimir Maramzin for allowing me to copy Brodsky's early unpublished poems from his *samizdat* four-volume collection of Brodsky's poetry. I also warmly thank Natalya Gorbanevskaya for letting me use Brodsky's letter to her from exile. My deepest gratitude is reserved for Brodsky himself, for patiently answering my numerous queries during the last nine years and for permission to quote his work as much as I need. Finally, I am very grateful to Nicola Pike, who typed the entire manuscript.

Acknowledgement is made to Penguin Books for permission to quote from Brodsky's *Less Than One: Selected Essays*. Some of the material has previously appeared in articles in journals: *Essays in Poetics* (1979, 4/1; 1985, 10/1); *Wiener Slawistischer Almanach* (1985, 17), and in the collection of articles, *Brodsky's Poetics* (1986). In this book, selections from these articles have been modified or substantially changed. I wish to thank the editors and publishers of the above works for permission to re-use some of that material here.

Abbreviations

The following abbreviations are used for those works of Brodsky's repeatedly cited in Russian and in English:

C.   *Stikhotvoreniya i poemy* (Short and Long Poems)
O.   *Ostanovka v pustyne* (A Halt in the Wilderness)
K.   *Konets prekrasnoi epokhi* (The End of a Beautiful Epoch)
Ч.   *Chast' rechi* (A Part of Speech)
H.   *Novye stansy k Avguste* (New Stanzas to Augusta)
У.   *Uriniya* (Urania)
L.   *Less Than One: Selected Essays*

Transliteration

The following system is used: the letters e, ё, ю, я are transliterated as ye, yo, yu, ya at the beginning of the word, after ь, ъ and after vowels; in any other position these letters are transliterated as e, io, iu, ia respectively. Exceptions are made for such well-known names as Tsvetaeva, Mandelstam.

Russian letters	English letters	Example
А, а	a	Akhmatova
Б, б	b	Blok
В, в	v	Vigdorova
Г, г	g	Gorbanevskaya
Д, д	d	Dovlatov
Е, е	e/ye	net, Yevtushenko, pyesa
Ё, ё	io/yo	Piotr, Yolkin
Ж, ж	zh	Zhdanov
З, з	z	Zvezda
И, и	i	Ivanov
Й, й	i/y	Aleksei, Mayakvosky
К, к	k	Kuzminsky
Л, л	l	Losev
М, м	m	Maramzin
Н, н	n	Naiman
О, о	o	Osipov
П, п	p	Pushkin
Р, р	r	Rozanov
С, с	s	samizdat
Т, т	t	Ternovsky
У, у	u	Uraniya
Ф, ф	f	Fiodorov
Х, х	kh	Khlebnikov
Ц, ц	ts	Tsvetaeva
Ч, ч	ch	chast' rechi

Ш, ш	sh	Shestov
Щ, щ	shch	veshch, oveshchestvleniye
Ъ	–	
Ь	'	Bal'mont
Ы	y	my, poemy
Э, э	e	Etkind
Ю, ю	iu/yu	Yury, s liubovyu
Я, я	ia/ya	vremia, yazyk, stikhotvoreniya

1

A stepson of the Empire

A poet's biography is in his vowels and sibilants, in his meters, rhymes, and metaphors . . . With poets, the choice of words is invariably more telling than the story line; that's why the best of them dread the thought of their biographies being written.[1]

The generation of 1956

The time was not exactly out of joint, there was no sense of joint of any kind.[2]

Russian literature, according to Brodsky, was born on the shores of the Neva. The founder of the city, Peter the Great, had not only transferred the capital of Russia to the outskirts of the Empire, but he had also succeeded in transferring world culture in miniature to his city. A child of this 'most premeditated city',[3] Brodsky writes on his life in Leningrad:

from these façades and porticoes – classical, modern, eclectic, with their columns, pilasters, and plastered heads of mythic animals or people – from their ornaments and caryatids holding up balconies, from the torsos in the niches of their entrances, I have learned more about the history of our world than I subsequently have from any book. Greece, Rome, Egypt – all of them were there . . . And from the gray, reflecting river flowing down to the Baltic, with an occasional tugboat in the midst of it struggling against the current, I have learned more about infinity and stoicism than from mathematics and Zeno. (*L*. 5)

In another essay, 'A Guide to a Renamed City', which is also full of nostalgia for 'this most beautiful city on the face of the earth' (*L*. 32), Brodsky argues not only that Russian literature came into existence with the emergence of St Petersburg, but that the city was made real by its fiction.[4]

This most classical of all Russian cities has cultivated respect for tradition and form in every poet who lived and worked there: 'For two and a half centuries this school, from Lomonosov and Derzha-

vin to Pushkin and his pleiad (Baratynsky, Viazemsky, Delvig) to
the Acmeists – Akhmatova and Mandelstam in this century – had
existed under the very sign under which it was conceived: the sign
of classicism' (L. 83–4). Brodsky is the direct heir to this tradition.
As he explained, 'any author, however young and inexperienced, if
he began his writing career in Leningrad, is associated with
Pushkin's school of harmony ... there is also something in the
architecture itself, in the very physical sensation of the city where
the idea of a certain insane order is realized. And when you find
yourself among all these numerous and impeccable avenues, colonnades, pilasters, porticoes etc., you intentionally or unwillingly try
to transfer them into poetry.'[5] The city represents the supreme
fundamental root of a large number of Brodsky's poems.
Moreover, the theme of the city is interlinked with no less important themes which predominate in his works: Russia, memory, and
time.

   The poet's father, Aleksandr Ivanovich Brodsky (1903–84), was
also born and died in this city. He studied in the Geography Faculty
of the University and the School of Red Journalists. Just before the
war, he married Mariya Moiseevna Volpert (1905–83). She and her
son survived the siege of Leningrad (1941–3):

I was luckier than many [said Brodsky] because I had my grandparents to
care for me ... I remember that the church on our block was used as a
bomb shelter and when I was a small boy we had to go there in the night. It
is a Russian custom in the churches to give the priest cards on which are
written the names of people to pray for. These cards are kept in special
boxes which were piled in the cellars and I was put to sleep on them.[6]

   Brodsky's father began the war in Finland in the year of his son's
birth (1940) and ended it in China (1948). During these eight years
he managed to see his family once, in 1945, when his son had already
learned to read. On returning to Leningrad, Aleksandr Ivanovich
worked in the Navy Museum as a head of the Photography
Department. In 1949 he was dismissed from the Navy, as were
most Jewish officers, and he returned to his profession as a
photo-reporter. He toured the whole country under contract to the
All-Union Agricultural Exhibition in Moscow. But his earnings
were irregular. The family often lived on Mariya Moiseevna's
income as a secretary or as an accountant in the office of the local
housing department. It was only just prior to retirement that his
father found regular work on the Leningrad harbour newspaper.

Brodsky has written a remarkable essay about the parents he did not see for the last twelve years of their lives:

They took everything as a matter of course: the system, their powerlessness, their poverty, their wayward son. They simply tried to make the best of everything: to keep food on the table – and whatever that food was, to turn it into morsels; to make ends meet – and although we always lived from pay-day to pay-day, to stash away a few rubles for the kid's movies, museum trips, books, dainties. (*L.* 449)

But meanwhile, having only just dealt with the external enemy, Stalin switched his attention to those within. He organized two attacks against his unloved city, separated by an interval of three years. On 14 August 1946, he despatched to the 'intellectual' attack one of the least well educated of his lieutenants, his cultural boss, Andrei Zhdanov. The latter closed the journal *Leningrad* and expelled Gorky's favourite, the writer Mikhail Zoshchenko, from the Union of Soviet Writers, calling him a 'philistine and vulgarian'; he deprived Akhmatova of the title of poet, supporting his decision on the following 'theoretical' basis: 'The range of her poetry is narrow to the point of poverty: it is the poetry of an infuriated lady, who dashes from boudoir to chapel . . . first a nun, then a harlot, or rather, both harlot and nun, whose fornication is mingled with prayer.'[7] She was expelled from the Union of Soviet Writers.

The Union of Writers, headed by Fadeev, began strenuously to hunt down the 'philistines' and 'nuns' all over the country. '"This was . . . first and foremost, an orgy of annihilation of everything which, in a large or small way, was intellectually superior to the common level", writes one of the victims of *zhdanovshchina*.'[8] The cultural terror gave way to party terror. In 1949, 'The Leningrad Affair' was invented. The entire party leadership of the city was arrested and executed. The third 'crusade' of the Soviet anti-Semites was stopped halfway through by the death of the satrap.[9] On 12 August 1952, on Stalin's orders, all the members of the anti-Fascist committee were shot. In Siberia, in Kazakhstan, in Golodnaya Steppe, barracks were built, planned for the entire Jewish population of the European part of the Soviet Union: 'to redeem with hard labour in remote parts the great harm we had inflicted upon the Russian people' (*L.* 470).

Stalin's death changed the geography of the future places of exile of our poet. On 5 and 6 March 1953, in honour of this non-Russian Tsar who had spent the longest period of all on the Russian throne, the country listened to the everlasting *marche funèbre*: '"My mother cried all the same", Brodsky remembers. "At the moment it was justified because you didn't know what was going to ensue. Besides, the man had been with us for thirty or forty years. He had become a part of nature, he was there like the seasons. So therefore it was something absolutely unexpected."'[10]

As in a provincial tragi-comedy which they themselves had written, staged, and now watched, the brothers-in-arms and heirs of Stalin began to oscillate between fear of any changes in the Empire and fear over their part in his crimes. On the one hand, the party, through the mouth of Khrushchev, unmasks the 'cult of personality' (February 1956), and on the other, through the mouth of Andropov, lures Imre Nagy into the trap of the Soviet Embassy in Budapest (October 1956). One third of the population of Hungary went into the streets, smashed all the statues of Stalin, and forced the Soviet Army to withdraw. This spontaneous uprising was crushed. By 3 November, the Soviet Army had returned and put Janos Kadar on the socialist throne, where he sat during the next thirty-one years. '"The thing about the people of my generation," said Brodsky, "the kids of sixteen and seventeen, was that we couldn't be shocked by anything. We knew about the lies, the duplicity, the callousness all around us; we lied ourselves. It would have taken a lot more than Stalin's death to shock any of us. Actually it took Hungary."'[11] Shock, shame, and a feeling of powerlessness were to be lived through several more times by the generation of 1956. But it was precisely these dramatic events – the disclosures of Khrushchev's speech and the suppression of the Hungarian Revolution – that turned them into adults and forced them to think: 'each in his own way we began to analyse that system. Thus arose our literature, the fate of which also determined the character of our personal destinies.'[12].

Ferment had also begun in the literary world. After a twenty-year interval the second Congress of Soviet Writers was convened in 1954. Akhmatova was reinstated. Ehrenburg published his novel, *The Thaw* (1954), which gave the new epoch its name. In 1956, the annual almanach, *The Day of Poetry*, began to appear. Public performances by poets were permitted again, which gave birth to such Soviet poets as Yevtushenko, Akhmadulina and Voznesensky. In 1956, Fadeev, the Soviet 'almost Tolstoy', who had personally sent dozens of writers to the Gulag, shot himself in his Peredelkino dacha. In the same year, the journal *Novy Mir* published Dudintsev's second-rate novel, *Not by Bread Alone*, and rejected Pasternak's masterpiece, *Doctor Zhivago*. The two volumes of *Literary Moscow* appeared, including poetry by Zabolotsky, who had spent eight years in Stalin's camps, and by Tsvetaeva, who had hanged herself in Yelabuga in 1941. Thousands of Stalin's prisoners, now at liberty, spoke of the scale of the crimes of the Leader of all times and peoples: 'With the sixty million dead in the Civil War, collectivization, the Great Terror and things in between, Russia in this century has produced enough history to keep the literati all over the world busy for several generations.'[13] Russian unofficial literature of the second half of the 1950s is a literature of accusation. From the writer it was demanded that above all else he tell the truth: 'From the possibility of telling it like it is, and not as it should be, literature choked on the accusatory fact. For a time everyone forgot about *belles lettres* . . . and critics began to be engaged in work that was not theirs – the criticism of society instead of literature.'[14] But by the end of the 1950s, literature began to perceive itself not only as a sociological phenomenon, but as a purely aesthetic one too, primarily in the works of the young authors.

Literary societies (*Lito*) for young writers appeared: at the Leningrad Mining Institute such a *Lito* was led by Gleb Semionov; at the club of Labour Reserves there was another society with David Dar at its head; there was a university circle of poets and a group of young poets at the Technological Institute. Brodsky attended them all. A slightly older generation also began to make itself known: Boris Slutsky, Semion Lipkin, David Samoilov, and Naum Korzhavin. This was a generation of 'cultural mutants', as Losev called them,

who had undergone the severest propaganda irradiation. And all the same, we see that the seeds dropped into the souls of these pioneers and *Komsomols* by Khlebnikov, Pasternak, Mandelstam, by the Russian and European classics, had not perished. They lay dormant, and then began to sprout. On occasion the growth was crooked and poor, but all the same the seeds began to blossom as wild, new flowers.[15]

They also prepared the way for Brodsky's arrival. The influence of Boris Slutsky at this stage of Brodsky's evolution as a poet was significant. Much later, Brodsky wrote on the innovative aspects of Slutsky's poetry:

It is Slutsky who almost single-handedly changed the diction of post-war Russian poetry. His verse is a conglomeration of bureaucratese, military lingo, colloquialisms and sloganeering, and it employs with equal ease assonance, dactylic and visual rhymes, sprung rhythm and vernacular cadences. The sense of tragedy that his poems convey frequently extends, almost against his own will, from the concrete and historical to the existential: where every tragedy, in the end, belongs.[16]

We shall see in the following chapters that Brodsky's own poetry 'employs with equal ease' vocabulary from all strata of language and that he himself 'speaks the language of the twentieth century'. As for the 'tragic timbre', it is a birth-mark of his poetry.

The other poet who is much younger than Slutsky and who is still considered by Brodsky as virtually his mentor is Yevgeny Rein. Brodsky has repeated several times that he has learned a great deal from Rein: 'One lesson he gave me simply during our conversation. "Iosif," he said, "a poem should have more nouns than adjectives, more nouns even than verbs. A poem should be written in such a way that if you cover the paper with a magic cloth which would absorb all the adjectives and verbs, and then removed the cloth, the paper still should be dark because the nouns would remain." That was maybe the only lesson on versification which I received in my whole life.'[17]

A year before the events in Hungary, Brodsky left school:

one winter morning, for no apparent reason, I rose up in the middle of the session and made my melodramatic exit through the school gate, knowing clearly that I'd never be back. Of the emotions overpowering me at that moment, I remember only a general disgust with myself for being too young and letting so many things boss me around. Also, there was that vague but happy sensation of escape, of a sunny street without end. (*L.* 10–11)

Later, Brodsky was to consider this his first act of free will. It was not the last time he was to escape the menaces of Fate. He would find himself in and out of the system a dozen more times. Meanwhile, at sixteen, he assumed the *toga virilis*. In 1956, he went to work at the 'Arsenal' plant. Instead of cannon, machine-operator Brodsky produced agricultural machinery and air-compressors: 'It wasn't exactly lovely, but at least I caught up with the working class in the conditions which Mr Marx described. Three shifts of workers were sleeping in the same room, you had to queue for the lavatory, etc., etc. I got to know life quite well.'[18] A year later, he went to work in an even more sombre environment, the morgue of the local hospital. In those years he wanted to become a doctor or a pilot, not a poet. Between 1956 and 1962 he changed his job thirteen times. In 1957 he joined the geologists: 'I had some interest in geology – it gave me an opportunity to travel as widely as I could possibly wish. I covered quite a lot of the ground in the Empire. I saw lots of landscape. Then gradually I began to write.'[19] One day, finding himself in Yakutsk, Brodsky discovered a slim volume of Baratynsky's poetry in a bookshop: 'When I read this book, it became clear to me that I had no business in Yakutsk, or with the expedition, that I knew and understand nothing else, that poetry was the only thing I understood.'[20] Brodsky was attracted by the powerful intellectual character of Baratynsky's poetry and by its deliberately non-civic content. As Brodsky reveals, 'anti-heroic posture was the *idée fixe* of our generation' (*L.* 367). Brodsky's restrained tone, the control of emotions in his poetry, perhaps derives ultimately from Baratynsky. He has also learned from Baratynsky as well as from Dostoevsky that any 'contra' in accurate psychological analysis of man should be no less convincing than the 'pro'. Like Baratynsky's, Brodsky's own poems soon became highly complex and structured.

According to Losev, young Brodsky was aware of the trap of metrical banality, as he understood it then. He experiments in *vers libres* combine traditional metres with *dol'nik*, which considerably extends the length of the poetic line.[21] Most of the poems written at the beginning of the 1960s use consonantal rhymes: *Бах – Бог* ('Bach' – 'God'); *перст – крест* ('finger' – 'cross'); *слову – Голгофу* ('word' – 'Golgotha'). Brodsky did not eschew homonymic rhymes: *засыпали – засыпали* ('fell asleep' – 'covered'); *увядать – увидать* ('to fade' – 'to see'); *аллей – алей* ('avenue' – 'more scarlet'). This period of apprenticeship also saw some losses. His quest for unexpected tropes was not always sufficiently motivated by the semantics of the poem. Certain of Brodsky's juvenilia were not without the Russian tendency to overstatement.

Historical and mythological figures are prominent in his early verse, as is religious imagery. He introduced themes which would become central to his creativity: faith: *каждый перед Богом / наг* (*C.* 23) ('Each one of us is naked before God'); time: *я вижу материю времени, / открытую петухами* (*C.* 28) ('I see the matter of time, / discovered by cockerels'); poetry: *Свои стихи /*

доканчивая кровью (С. 33) ('Their verses / completing with blood'), and language:

> И уходя, как уходят в чужую память,
> мерно ступая от слова к слову,
> всеми своими тремя временами
> глаголы однажды восходят на Голгофу.   (*С.* 72)

And departing, as they depart into another's memory, / in measured step from word to word, / by all their three tenses / verbs are one day ascending Golgotha.

Only later would Brodsky elevate to an aesthetic principle the complete identification of man with the word through his metaphors at the expense of the fusion of the signifier and the signified. In the poem 'Verbs', Soviet citizens are replaced by a part of speech ('hungry verbs', 'naked verbs', 'main verbs', 'deaf verbs') which is, as it were, sociologized:

> Глаголы, которые живут в подвалах,
> говорят – в подвалах, рождаются – в подвалах
> под несколькими этажами
> всеобщего оптимизма.   (*С.* 72)

Verbs which live in cellars, / talk in cellars, are born – in cellars / under several storeys / of universal optimism.

This is one of the very rare poems by Brodsky with a political coloration. Religious verse is far more common. Brodsky is proud of the fact that he restored to Russian poetry the word 'soul' in the sense of man's existence on a metaphysical plane: 'Speak, soul, of how life looked, / of how it looked from a bird's-eye view?' (*C.* 62). This idea would form the basis of 'The Great Elegy to John Donne' (1963).

When Brodsky met Akhmatova in 1962 she almost immediately recognized him as a poet. She had already heard of him from Naiman and Rein. Later on, she repeated several times to her friends that she hadn't read anything like Brodsky's poems since Mandelstam. It took longer for Brodsky to appreciate Akhmatova's work:

I remember that very clearly. A friend of mine, one of those three or four, suggested that we go and see Akhmatova. At that point the name meant little to me. In the first place, I was surprised that she was alive. Then I went to read, beforehand, two or three poems of hers since I was going to see her, but they didn't tell me much ... She was living in a dacha outside the city. When we met, I saw a very attractive, very grand woman, but somehow it didn't make any sense to me. She knew about my poems and I showed her some more, and she said very pleasant things ... The procedure was repeated I think three or four times, before one night, returning from that place in the train, in the carriage full of people, something of a miraculous nature took place ... some lines of hers came across my mind. I remember the line ... And suddenly I realized who I was dealing with ... After that, it was more or less like an addiction, and I saw her whenever it was possible ... One fall I rented a house near her, in Komarovo. I saw her twice a day throughout the entire fall and then an end came to that merely because I got arrested. She felt very guilty, thinking it was because of our close friendship that I had attracted these hounds to me. I don't think that was true. She came greatly to my defence.[22]

In evaluating his relationship with Akhmatova, Brodsky would gratefully recognize that she, so to speak, had pointed him towards the true path, that everything had begun with her. But all the same, Akhmatova's influence on Brodsky was more spiritual and cultural than stylistic. According to Brodsky's own testimony, Akhmatova said to him one day: 'I don't understand what you're doing here, Joseph: you can't like my poetry.'[23] Akhmatova could see nothing of her own in Brodsky's verse, and expressed this in her incomprehension as to why Brodsky should so often be in her house. In her eyes, Brodsky's lyrics lacked simplicity; were turning in the direction of emotional abstraction, were permeated with philosophical reflection. To Akhmatova's terseness of expression he preferred long poems, heavy logical discourse, loaded with inversion and enjambement; to her meagreness of metaphor he opposed a riot of tropes, sometimes constructed entirely on witticisms and paradox. '"I liked her poetry enormously, and still do, but for all that ... for all that," Brodsky has said, carefully choosing his words, "it's not the sort of poetry which interests me."'[24] He described in a similar way her reaction to his newly completed poem, 'The Great Elegy to John Donne' (1963):

'I fear, Joseph, that you do not understand what you have written.' In general terms, I could understand what was going on. But when you write, especially in Russia, then no one, properly, affords it the attention it deserves ... And what was important in Akhmatova was that she looked at it the way it should be looked at ... In the end, this is your civilization, which no one shares.[25]

The profundity of Akhmatova's view, her evaluations, her judgements, always penetrated to the moral core: 'I like to think – maybe

I am deluding myself – but I like to think that in many ways I owe to her my better human qualities; without her they would have taken longer to develop, if ever.'[26] Of Brodsky's long poem 'Shestviye' (1961), she said: 'What depth of loneliness!' '"This, by the way," Brodsky confessed, "is precisely what I had tried to convey at the time." '[27] This poem called to life some literary characters: Harlequin, Columbine, Don Quixote, Hamlet, Prince Myshkin, as well as many nameless characters: the thief, the honest man, the liar, the weary man, the king, and even the devil; to those were joined abstract concepts: love and weeping. All of them declaim a series of monologues about the meaning of life, the nature of love, about good and evil. Each of the monologues receives sceptical commentaries, which are full of aphorisms of the type: 'we are all approaching the time / of immeasurable loneliness of the soul'; 'to pass off loneliness for freedom'.

This 1,880-line *poema* (C. 156–222) is written mainly in iambic pentameter with various rhyme schemes: *aabbcc / abab / aabbb / aaabb / ABAB / aBaB / aBBa / AABB*. The classical meter is interrupted by a four-ictus *dol'nik*, with rhyme scheme *abab / aabb* (parts 4 and 17), as well as by iambic trimeter and trochaic pentameter (parts 22, 23, 28). The length of the stanzas is irregular and the predominance of masculine rhymes is very unusual. We already encounter in it extremely bold metaphors and similes: *Place in the glass on the table a bouquet of evil; like the shadow of people, evil is invulnerable.* The compound rhymes do not yet displace the semantics of the poetic line: *ни в ад – виноват* ('not to hell' – 'guilty'), *о фее – Орфея* ('about the fairy' – 'Orpheus'). By rhyming many times *человек – век* ('man' – 'age'), Brodsky introduces, as yet only peripherally, one of the main themes of his creativity: what time does to a person. It is also highly significant that Brodsky finds several new rhymes for the words 'love' and 'to love': *лови – любви* ('catch' – 'love'), *безумья вы – любви* ('madness you' – 'love'), *люблю – по рублю* ('I love' – 'one ruble'), *любовь – боль* ('love' – 'pain'). He even renews the most worn-out rhyme, *кровь – любовь* ('blood' – 'love'), replacing it by *кровь – нелюбовь* ('blood' – 'nonlove').

From the very beginning of his writing, Brodsky created a language which is highly distinct from the official language of the state, thereby attracting attention to himself and bringing misfortune on himself. Both understanding and accepting this lin-

guistic conflict, the poet foretells his future: 'Thank God for being
deprived of my motherland' (*C.* 84). The gift of foresight is the gift
of many great poets, for which they pay no small price. We also pay
our price for the privilege of being the contemporaries of a great
artist. This price is our blindness. And no nation was, and still is,
more blind than Russia. In Stalin's camps and prisons alone, about
six hundred writers and poets died, and several hundred more
returned as invalids. Brodsky suggested his own explanation for
this thoughtless squandering of talents on the part of the state:

there are two things: the idiom of the state and the language of literature;
and they jar. Simply, if you're a stylist you deplore the banality. And the
state insists it has a monopoly on the language. Any writer who avoids the
jargon of *Pravda* is immediately suspect.[28]

Such writers are either not accepted into the Union of Soviet
Writers at all, or they are 'ejected' from it as an alien body.

A new pre-Gutenberg epoch

Samizdat is a new word that has been coined for a phenomenon that existed all the time. I first read Mandelstam,
Tsvetaeva, much Klyuyev, Yesenin – the best of Russian
poetry – in type-written copies.[29]

Yury Mal'tsev, one of the historians of *samizdat*, suggests that we
consider the first *samizdat* works to be *A Journey from St Petersburg to Moscow* (1790) by Radishchev, Griboyedov's *Woe from Wit*
(1825), and Belinsky's *Letters to Gogol* (1847).[30] Banned by the
censor, these works were distributed in hand-written copies. But
even if we were to add to them some poetry by Pushkin and
Lermontov and some other works banned by the Tsarist censorship, they do not constitute a mass phenomenon. *Samizdat* as an
underground or second literature is only as old as the October
Revolution.

The collection of articles on the Russian Revolution, *Out of the
Depths* (1918), and the works of the Russian religious philosophers
such as Shestov, Berdiayev, and Bulgakov are still not published in
the Soviet Union. But *samizdat* in our present-day understanding
of it is a child of Khrushchev. The name of this 'simple-hearted
tyrant'[31] will forever be inscribed in the history of Russian literature alongside the names of two Russian poets: Pasternak and
Brodsky. He succeeded where Stalin had failed: in dealing with

Pasternak. Protected by the magnanimity of the 'most outstanding mediocrity of the party',[32] Pasternak was subjected to public humiliation by Khrushchev, that less outstanding mediocrity. The trial of Brodsky was the second official outrage against a poet to be organized by Khrushchev's henchmen.

The history of Russian underground literature began with the Soviet refusal to publish *Doctor Zhivago* in 1957. Pasternak's poetry had already blazed the trail for his novel. His poetry, like that of his dead contemporaries Khlebnikov, Mandelstam, and Tsvetaeva, went the rounds of both capitals of the Empire. At the end of the 1950s and in the early 1960s, poetry had a decisive role in the nation's spiritual awakening. It was copied out by hand from faded copies, pages from first editions which had been miraculously preserved were photographed, tape recordings were made of someone's recitals.

The models of Stalin's 'byzantinism' drowned in a torrent of memoirs, novels, stories, and poems. *Samizdat* even produced its own journals: *Sintaksis* (1958), *Boomerang* (1960), *Phoenix* (1961), *Sphinxes* (1965), *The Lamp, Workshop, Russian Word*.[33] In 1968, there appeared the first number of the journal of the Russian democratic movement, *The Chronicle of Current Events*.[34] It contained information about religious, national, and political rights in the Soviet Union. For the West, it was a window into Russia, the most important source for the various aspects of Soviet life. The blossoming of *samizdat* came in the middle of the 1960s. Solzhenitsyn's novels, *The First Circle* and *Cancer Ward*, which had been rejected by the Union of Writers, appeared in *samizdat*. There followed Lidiya Chukovskaya's *Going Under* and *Deserted House*; Nadezhda Mandelstam's *Hope against Hope* and *Hope Abandoned*; Yevgeniya Ginzburg's *Journey into the Whirlwind* and *Within the Whirlwind*; and Varlam Shalamov's *Kolyma Tales*. *Samizdat* has also resurrected several suppressed Russian writers: Bulgakov, Babel', Platonov, Pil'niak, Zoshchenko. Such Western European writers as Proust, Joyce, Beckett, T. S. Eliot, and Robert Frost came to the Russian reader first via *samizdat*. By reading them, Brodsky discovered for himself not only stylistic modernism, but also 'quite a different psyche'.[35] In these years, he read more of the great works of world literature than any Soviet university graduate. Suzanne Massie, who visited his flat in Leningrad, wrote:

In his tiny sanctuary, one feels almost completely cut off from the outside world by the presence of books. They seem everywhere, lined up on shelves on every side, from wall to wall and floor to ceiling, surrounding, protecting, insulating. Dictionaries of many languages, volume after volume of Russian poetry, collections of English poets, books of American poetry, they have the warm look of old friends.[36]

To this list, one should add the works of the Russian religious philosophers, Berdiaev and Shestov, and the Bible, which Brodsky studied at the beginning of the 1960s. The result of this was the long poem 'Isaak and Abraham', which he finished in 1963. While in Central Asia with the geologists, Brodsky came upon a treasure – a new ten-volume edition of Dostoevsky.

What Brodsky has said of the erudition of the young people who surrounded him applies first and foremost to himself: 'In its ethics, this generation was among the most bookish in the history of Russia, and thank God for that . . . Books became the first and only reality, whereas reality itself was regarded as either nonsense or nuisance' (*L.* 28). Brodsky read Mandelstam's poetry when he was nineteen: 'It blew my mind. Really because for the first time, I think, I was reading something which was mentally congenial . . . It was a discovery!'[37] Mandelstam's almost biological hostility towards the regime, the curved spine of his lonely resistance, could not but exert some influence on Brodsky's personality. To understand Mandelstam's poetry, one has to know the epoch, the obliterated chapters of history. *Samizdat* provided this information.

Brodsky has written one of the most penetrating essays on Mandelstam, in which he offers his own interpretation of the poet's tragedy: 'A poet gets into trouble because of his linguistic, and, by implication, his psychological superiority, rather than because of his politics. A song is a form of linguistic disobedience, and its sound casts a doubt on a lot more than a concrete political system: it questions the entire existential order. And the number of its adversaries grows proportionally' (*L.* 136).

Brodsky has emphasized such features of Mandelstam's poetry as economy of poetic means, nobility, spiritual acceleration, marking him out as 'a poet for and of civilization': 'He is kind of taking on the entire civilization in a very unobtrusive way – an absolutely natural way. In a sense he gives you a feeling that Russian literature belongs to civilization – it is not parochial.'[38]

Indeed, Mandelstam possessed an amazing ability to reconstruct an ancient cultural heritage which he interpreted as a living active force in the contemporary world. He did the almost-impossible in order to humanize the twentieth century with a warmth both delicate and theological. In the epoch when Russian literature was condemned to death, Mandelstam saved it almost single-handed, and this makes him profoundly literary. Homer, Ovid, Virgil, and Dante gaze at us from every poem of the early Mandelstam. His poetry is also full of resonances of French and Russian poets, reflecting the Acmeists' 'nostalgic longing for world culture'. World culture is given by Mandelstam its finest representation in the Russian language.

To hold Russian poetry in the channel of world-wide civilization was to be one of the essential tasks of Brodsky himself. In this, too, he is the direct heir of Mandelstam, because, since the times of Mandelstam, Russia has not known a more European poet than Brodsky. Both Pasternak and Akhmatova, for all their high culture, remained to the end of their days attached to Pushkin's umbilical cord. 'Akhmatova completed the line of Pushkin', Brodsky was to say.[39] Pasternak returned to it after the 1930s by beginning to rewrite and correct the poetry of his Futurist period. Since the death of these two poets, Russia has not had a more educated poet than Brodsky. By giving Russian poetry European and American inoculations, he has saved it from the disease of provincialism. Like Mandelstam, he could have said: 'Such poetry does not exist in Russian. Yet it *must* exist in Russian.'[40]

The second poet given to Brodsky by *samizdat* was Marina Tsvetaeva: 'When I read her poetry it stunned me.'[41] And to this day he considers Tsvetaeva the greatest innovator of form in Russian poetry, greater than Khlebnikov and Pasternak. Two essays, the best written about Tsvetaeva, bear witness to Brodsky's profound interest in her poetry and prose: 'In her, Russian letters found a dimension that hitherto had not been intrinsic to it: she demonstrated language's own self-interest in the tragic subject matter' (*L*. 192). In Brodsky's opinion, Tsvetaeva surpassed the Acmeists in precision of detail, and in the power of her aphorism and sarcasm she surpassed everybody. As opposed to the Futurists', all Tsvetaeva's formal achievements, such as root and compound rhymes, sound allusion, enjambement, the energy of the monologue, are identical with her semantics: 'because Tsvetaeva the poet was identical to Tsvetaeva the person; between word and deed, between art and existence, there was neither a comma nor even a dash: Tsvetaeva used an equals sign' (*L.* 219–20). Apart from Tsvetaeva's attitude to language, which is always paramount for Brodsky in his evaluation of a poet, he sees Tsvetaeva's uniqueness in another way:

One of the great features of Tsvetaeva is a kind of sentiment which is not to be found, I think, elsewhere in European poetry or in English poetry. It is the sensibility of the Biblical Job, but with a greater degree of self-rejection. And through that there goes a terrific lyrical *tremolo* very speedy, very fast. She is much more masculine in her poetry than any man.[42]

In Siniavsky's view, which is shared by many, Russia had, at the turn of this century, the finest poetry in the world.[43] Disseminated in *samizdat*, it helped the young generation to perceive and assert its own personality. In the 1950s and 1960s, poetry replaced other forms of spiritual communication and played a greater role than religion or philosophy.

Nobody knew literature and history better than these people, [said Brodsky about his friends] nobody could write in Russian better than they, nobody despised our times more profoundly. For these characters civilization meant more than daily bread and a nightly hug. This wasn't, as it might seem, another lost generation. This was the only generation of Russians that had found itself, for whom Giotto and Mandelstam were more imperative than their own personal destinies. (*L.* 29)

And, meanwhile, Brodsky's own poetry began to appear in *samizdat*. In 1960, in *Sintaksis*, 'A Jewish Cemetery' and 'Pilgrims' were reprinted. Other poems were copied out by hand and even sung ('A Christmas Romance').[44] The poem quoted below dates from 1962. It is a part of Brodsky's first lyrical cycle, recently published in full by Losev.[45] This poem is not only completely free from any influence, but it is also a programmatic poem. It is important to analyse it here in order to understand why Brodsky, among many other talented poets of his generation, attracted the KGB's attention. The apolitical nature of his poetry was seen as more 'dangerous' than some 'anti-Soviet' poems by Yevtushenko.

Огонь, ты слышишь, начал угасать.
А тени по углам – зашевелились.
Уже нельзя в них пальцем указать,
прикрикнуть, чтоб они остановились.

Да, воинство сие не слышит слов.   5.
Построилось в каре, сомкнулось в цепи.
Бесшумно наступает из углов,
и я внезапно оказался в центре.
Всё выше снизу взрывы темноты.
Подобны восклицательному знаку.   10.
Всё гуще тьма слетает с высоты,
до подбородка, комкает бумагу.
Теперь исчезли стрелки на часах.
Не только их не видно, но не слышно.
И здесь остался только блик в глазах,   15.
застывших неподвижно. Неподвижно.
Огонь угас. Ты слышишь: он угас.
Горючий дым под потолком витает.
Но этот блик – не покидает глаз.
Вернее, темноты не покидает.   (*O.* 65)   20.

The fire, you hear, has begun to go out. / And the shadows in the corners have begun to stir. / It is no longer possible to indicate them with your finger, / to shout to them to stop. / Yes, this host does not hear words. / It has been arranged in a square, ranked in close order. / Noiselessly it advances from the corners, / and I have suddenly found myself at the centre. / The bursts of darkness from below are ever higher. / They are like an exclamation mark. / The darkness flies down from on high ever thicker, / to my chin, it crumples the paper. / Now the hands on the clock have vanished. / Not only can they not be seen, but they cannot be heard. / And here only remains a speck in [my] eyes, / which have frozen motionless. Motionless. / The fire has gone out. You hear: it has gone out. / Smouldering smoke swirls beneath the ceiling. / But this speck – does not leave the eyes. / More probably, does not leave the darkness.

Only the mention of such everyday details as 'in the corner', 'under the ceiling', helps us to establish that the 'action' takes place in a house, most probably in the country, as there are no fireplaces in urban Soviet apartment blocks. However, if we read the first line, 'The fire, you hear, has begun to go out', not literally, but metaphorically, then 'fire' can only be seen as a hackneyed metaphor of substitution for 'love' which had begun to be extinguished and which is extinguished after sixteen lines: 'The fire has gone out. You hear: it has gone out.' All that remains of it is the 'smouldering smoke beneath the ceiling'. But such a banal reading of the poem is contradicted by the haunting presence of darkness, which is underlined by such forceful verbs as *зашевелились* ('have begun to stir'), *наступает* ('advances'), *слетает* ('flies down'). The comparison of the shifting shadows with an army is highly effective, since Brodsky is using the slightly archaic word *воинство* instead of the modern *войско*. Arranged in a square, ranked in close order, they noiselessly but irresistibly encroach on the lyrical 'I' from all sides. This army is inexorable because it does not hear words; it is invisible because it fuses with the darkness. It enmeshes the poet, who suddenly turns out to be at the centre, right up to his chin. It is not impossible that the 'attack' takes place during the actual writing, hence it 'crumples the paper'. The reference to the paper explains the comparison of 'the bursts of darkness' with an exclamation mark. All that remains of the lyrical hero is 'only a speck in [the] eyes'. This patch of light can be interpreted as a metaphor of substitution for love, life, or faith. This twice-repeated and concluding line, this 'speck', leaves neither the eyes nor the darkness. This solitary ray of light or, more precisely, its reflection in a human eye, is opposed to the darkness which is so omnipotent that it is capable of cutting off not only light but even time: 'Now the hands on the clock have vanished. / Not only can they not be seen, but they cannot be heard.' Here something more serious than extinguished love is being talked of. It is worth noting that the spiritualizing of the darkness and the shadows by traditional verbal metaphors differs from the usual personification of nature. These non-material forces that are imbued with human qualities remain unamenable to human control or even neutral observation: 'it is not possible to indicate them with your finger', they do not hear words. The supercharging of the negative particle *не* ('not') – *нельзя* ('it is not possible'), *не слышит* ('doesn't hear'), *не слышно* ('cannot be heard'), *не видно* ('cannot be seen'), *неподвижно* ('motionless') underlines human impotence before the darkness which has closed around the poet. The 'speck' that does not leave him is all the more important. From this ray of light that was not defeated by the darkness, another metaphor would be born twenty years later, a metaphor of substitution for faith, *the golden five-kopeck piece*, in the twelfth of the 'Roman Elegies':

> На сетчатке моей – *золотой пятак.*
> Хватит *на всю длину потёмок.*   (*У*, 117)

On my retina is a *gold 5-kopeck piece*. / It will last me *throughout the darkness*.

The metaphor, *throughout the darkness*, substitutes for death. It is highly significant that this metaphor sees the realization of the same type of semantic transformation as the metaphor *the bursts of darkness*,[46] namely, the reification of non-material phenomena. The poet finds himself at the very centre of the dark spot of existence and ascends to a metaphysical level of description of this situation.

Ipso facto, Brodsky emancipates himself from the poetic system he inherited by finding his own style. This poem can be further called programmatic because its stylistic and thematic beams will illuminate many later poems. In particular, the single comparison of 'the bursts of darkness' with an 'exclamation mark' would be repeated in one of his early poems: 'И те же фонари горят над нами, / Как *восклицательные знаки ночи*' ('And the same lamps burn above us, / Like the exclamation marks of night', *C*. 68). There were to follow comparisons with other punctuation marks: lamps with dots ('Sant Pietro'); sails with a question mark ('The New Jules Verne'); human lives with the lines of a text: 'Наши жизни, *как строчки*, достигли точки' ('Our lives, like lines, have reached a full stop', *Ч*. 18). Thus began the inclusion of yet one more aspect of language in the perception and description of the world.

It is no less important to look at the young poet's experiments with metre. According to Losev, it was precisely at this time that Brodsky 'immersed himself in following up the richest possibilities of the iambic pentameter'.[47] The poem discussed above is written in this metre, with alternating masculine and feminine rhymes. However, only in the fifteenth and seventeenth lines is the classical model of the metre realized. The remaining eighteen lines test out the prosodic flexibility of the iambic pentameter. The twelfth, sixteenth, and twentieth lines are rhythmically set apart by having only three stresses. It is noteworthy that it is precisely in these lines that the authorial 'I' is metonymically present: chin, eyes, and the speck in the eyes. Although not separated into stanzas, the poem has a harmonious rhythmic structure, corresponding to the stanza form. Each stanza coincides with the end of a grammatical sentence. There is not a single enjambement. But this does not mean that there is no tension between rhythm and syntax. It merely varies in degree. It will suffice to compare lines fifteen and seventeen which have the full-stressed iambic pentameter: 'И здесь остался только блик в глазах' ('And here only remains a speck in [my] eyes') – the metre fits into a single intonational syntagma, an uninterrupted syntactic unit. Line seventeen: 'Огонь угас. Ты слышишь: он угас.' ('The fire has gone out. You hear: it has gone out.') The three syntactic units create rhythmic and intonational interruptions in the metre, which are intensified by the weakly stressed personal pronouns, 'you' and 'it'. The syntactic parallelism of the first and seventeenth lines is slightly obscured by deviations in the metre and a variety of intonational types in the first syntagma. On the other hand, the ninth and eleventh lines echo each other by their syntactic constructions, the rhythm, and the identical intonation, reinforcing the semantic of *the burst of darkness* and its thickening. This 'collision' of syntax and rhythm, which alternates with the harmony between them, is also achieved either by the introduction of the caesura, or by avoidance of it.

The rhythm in this poem fulfils the function of a control on the emotional state of the lyrical hero: either to repress and hold in passion or to let it go. 'As pitches go,' said Brodsky, 'altitude determines attitude' (*L.* 351). Not only is the metre semantically loaded, so too is the point of view of the authorial 'I'. Finding himself at the centre and almost staring at everything that is happening, the poet is able to abstract himself and find an almost impersonal tone of description.

The department in which Brodsky breaks his own future rules, or, more precisely, where he has not yet formulated them, is rhyme: 'Never rhyme the same parts of speech. Nouns you can, verbs you shouldn't, and rhyming adjectives is taboo' (*L.* 315). Only one pair of masculine rhymes links verb and noun: *угас – глаз* ('gone out' – 'eyes'); all the others consist of identical parts of speech: three pairs of verbal rhymes, five noun rhymes, and one adverbial. But soon Brodsky would discover new possibilities for compound rhymes, of which the Futurists, nurtured on pure phonetics, could only dream. Many of his rhymes assume the function of tropes.

For all its originality, Brodsky's poetry turned out to be unacceptable to Soviet literature. The reason was not political, but metaphysical and linguistic: its language and its spirit were alien to Socialist Realism. But, meanwhile, a compromise was being born inside the 'literature of protest' itself. Those who desire fame or simply well-being sooner or later accept an invitation to dinner with the Leviathan State. And, once they had been published and had been paid for it, these writers lost their spiritual independence. And those who perceived the 'thaw' too literally would, several years later, be obliged to accept the 'invitation' to emigrate. Khrushchev's last liberal gesture was the 1962 publication in *Novy Mir* of Solzhenitsyn's *One Day in the Life of Ivan Denisovich*. *Samizdat* would continue to flourish for a good while yet in Russia, 'achieving the scale of Russian drunkenness',[48] but this round of de-Stalinization was over.

The northern exile

> I just happened to combine the most inviting characteristics in that I was writing poetry and I was a Jew.[49]

The unforgettable decade of the thaw was also over. It ended with the arrest of a poet who so far had been recognized only by experts. Christmas 1963 was approaching. 'It was a cold night', Brodsky remembers:

> I was walking along the street, three men surrounded me. They asked me my name and like an idiot I answered that I was 'the same'. They suggested that I go somewhere with them, they needed to have a talk. I refused – I was going on my way to visit a friend. A struggle began . . . They called up a car and twisted my arms behind my back . . .[50]

This was not the first or the last encounter between the poet and the state.[51] It had been preceded by three other arrests. In 1959, Brodsky was gaoled, questioned, and held without formal charges. As he told John Green, he was betrayed by a friend who was arrested for carrying a gun:[52] 'they tried to threaten me by saying, "We're going to send you far away, where no human foot ever trod." Well, I wasn't terribly impressed because I had already been to many of the regions they were talking about.'[53] In 1961, Brodsky was arrested again and was again soon released. No sufficient grounds were found for imprisoning him in 1962 either. Meanwhile, the decree on 'the struggle against parasites' was passed on 4 May 1961. Immediately it was used for political ends. At first, those who thought unconventionally lost their jobs, and were then exiled as being 'disinclined to take up socially useful work'. Brodsky, who had often changed his job and who 'did not work' for months between geological expeditions, easily fell foul of this law. On the fourth occasion, the decision to arrest and try Brodsky was taken at a high level and enacted on the ground in a very unpleasant way.

On 29 November 1963, the newspaper *Evening Leningrad* printed the feuilleton, 'A Semi-literate Parasite', signed by Lerner, Ionin, and Medvedev. Two weeks later (13 December), Lerner, a former captain of the KGB, paid a visit to the Secretary of the Leningrad Union of Writers, the poet Aleksandr Prokofyev. Lerner showed Prokofyev a vicious epigram against him, allegedly written by Brodsky. A few days later, Brodsky was arrested. He was first imprisoned in the gaol with the highly symbolic name, 'Crosses'.

The year 1963, which had begun for Brodsky with the appearance of his name in the journal *Novy Mir*, under an epigraph taken by Akhmatova from his poem dedicated to her, ended with his name being included in the list of patients of the Kashchenko psychiatric hospital in Moscow, where he remained until 5 January 1964. This 'parasite' had spent 1963, apart from translating the Cuban poet Hernández and the Yugoslav poet Rakic, working on translations of Gałczyński.[54] With a reading of these works, Brodsky made a public appearance at the Mayakovsky house of writers in Etkind's oral almanach 'In Russian – for the first time'. This was one of his rare public appearances in the Soviet Union. Brodsky learned Polish and English on his own, and had negotiations concerning his translations with various publishing houses. But more importantly, Brodsky during that year had written two masterpieces, the long poems 'Isaac and Abraham' and 'The Great Elegy to John Donne'. According to Losev, in 1961–2 alone, Brodsky wrote 'at least 10,000 lines of original poetry'.[55] In Maramzin's *samizdat* four-volume collection of Brodsky's poetry, there are about thirty short and long poems (over 2,000 lines), dated 1963. Most of them have never been published.

Everything he had achieved was ignored, as was the defence of Brodsky by Professor Etkind and the journalist Frida Vigdorova. They succeeded, however, with Akhmatova's assistance, in attracting three Lenin Prize laureates to Brodsky's side: Dmitry Shostakovich, Samuil Marshak, and Kornei Chukovsky. Their letters, telegrams, and phone calls to the administration of the Union of Writers, the Leningrad Party Committee, and even to Khrushchev himself on the Central Committee, remained unanswered. The Leningrad Union of Writers refused to defend Brodsky, having handed him over to the court.

During January and February 1964, Brodsky was in hiding from the militia, on the advice of his friends, moving from town to town, sleeping at friends' dachas. As soon as he returned to Leningrad, on 11 February, he was arrested. On 14 February 1964, the poet's trial took place at 36 Uprising Street, in the Dzerzhinsky district of Leningrad. Thanks to Vigdorova, we have a stenographic record of the hearing:

JUDGE SAVELYEVA: What do you do for a living?

BRODSKY: I write poetry. Translate. I suppose...

JUDGE SAVELYEVA: No 'I suppose'. Stand properly! Don't lean against the wall! Look at the court! Answer the court properly! Do you have regular work?

BRODSKY: I think that it's regular work.

JUDGE: Answer exactly!

BRODSKY: I have been writing poetry. I thought that my poems would be published. I suppose...

JUDGE: We are not interested in 'I suppose...'. What is your special field?

BRODSKY: I'm a poet. A poet-translator.

JUDGE: And who has said you're a poet? Who ranked you a poet?

BRODSKY: No one. [Without defiance] And who ranked me a human being?

JUDGE: And have you studied this?

BRODSKY: What?

JUDGE: To be a poet? Have you tried to do a course where you are prepared ... where you're taught...

BRODSKY: I didn't think that came through education...

JUDGE: Well, how then?

BRODSKY: I think that it [in confusion] comes from God.[56]

In Nadezhda Mandelstam's opinion,

Frida Vigdorova opened a new era by writing down the proceedings at Brodsky's trial, and this first genuine record of its kind had a shattering impact. Even the unspeakable woman judge at the trial realized this could not be permitted, and she forbade Vigdorova to take notes, but only towards the end, when it was already too late. She can scarcely be blamed for not having acted more quickly. It must never have entered her head that a Soviet journalist, a staunch upholder of the powers-that-be and the courts, would dare to hawk her notes, uncensored by her or anyone else, around the editorial offices of the newspapers; here somebody – despite the care in selecting such people – purloined and circulated them in *samizdat*, whence they speedily found their way across the frontier to be published in the pages of the enemy press. Nothing like this had happened in decades.[57]

The court laid down: 'To be sent to judicial-psychiatric specialists who are to consider the question whether Brodsky is suffering from any psychiatric disorder, and whether such a disorder precludes Brodsky being sent to distant places for forced labour.'[58] On 19 February, Brodsky was sent for testing at a Leningrad psychiatric hospital, situated on the river Priazhka, and was declared fit for work. To these three weeks spent among the clinically mad and 'state-mad', we are indebted for the appearance of one of the most brilliant of Brodsky's works – the long philosophical poem 'Gorbunov and Gorchakov', written in the style of his beloved Beckett.

The second trial on 13 March 1964, like the first, the absurd spectacle of the Soviet legal system, was played out with workers and members of the general public called as witnesses. The court passed sentence: 'Brodsky systematically fails to fulfil the obligation of a Soviet man in respect of material values and personal well-being as is evident from his frequent changes of jobs ... Brodsky to be exiled to distant places for a period of five years with the application of obligatory labour.'[59]

When asked what he felt after the sentence, Brodsky replied: 'I tried to divorce myself as much as possible from what was happening. In the first place because, legally speaking, it was absolutely grotesque. And for me it was psychologically somehow already out of date – it was like something one read in books, books already written like Kafka's *Trial*.'[60] Brodsky was again imprisoned in the 'Crosses', and on 22 March, together with real criminals, he was deported to the village of Norinskaya, in the Konoshskii district of Archangel province. Here he lived for eighteen months. During the day he carted manure, chopped wood, and worked in the field with the collective farm-workers.

We can learn about Brodsky's oppressive surroundings and his emotional state from his letter to Natalya Gorbanevskaya. After apologizing for not writing or answering any letters, Brodsky confessed:

It's not at all because of indifference, thoughtlessness, or anything else of that kind. It's quite complicated and unpleasant to write letters in general as there's too much nonsense in my head. I can't explain and I don't feel like explaining. Do believe me: it's not a case of depression, self-absorption, it's not that sort of gloomy egoism. I am ironical enough for such things. It is simply physiologically unpleasant to write, to talk, to dip my pen in the ink-well etc.

For a moment or two I suddenly imagined (a month ago) that someone could help me (indeed, at that time I was hemmed in), but, unfortunately (or it could not be otherwise), nothing came out of it . . . At the time I was very hurt, indignant, but now that's all passed . . .

Then he asks Gorbanevskaya to send him two or three tins of instant coffee and tells her that he misses music terribly: there is no electricity in the village. Brodsky goes on to say that he has been inundated with translation,

but I cannot shift myself, get going: it is very hard here to use one's imagination, and that's what is most important in translations. From time to time I write poems comprehensible only to myself: I am not sending them to anyone. Every day I shift 15–20 tons of grain: that's a fair amount. If I've got any strength left, at the end of the day I wander through some empty, harvested fields, look at sailing clouds, mutter something to myself. To tell you the truth, I'm very weary of my solitude, of this nonsense, of forced thoughts.

Many of those 'forced thoughts' are formulated poetically in 'New Stanzas to Augusta' (1964); some lines of the poem echo the letter: 'Here, buried alive, / I wander through the stubble at dusk . . . Pressing a frozen palm to my hips, / I wander from mound to mound, / without memory, with just some kind of sound.' (*O.* 156). The spiritual emptiness of the peasants, prematurely aged by work, the penetrating, icy, northern wind – these are the main characters of another poem written in exile, 'Autumn in Norenskaya':[61]

> Мы возвращаемся с поля. Ветер   1.
> гремит перевёрнутыми колоколами ведер,
> коверкает голые прутья ветел,
> бросает землю на валуны.
> Лошади бьются среди оглобель
> чёрными корзинами вздутых рёбер,
> обращают оскаленный профиль
> к ржавому зубью бороны.

We are returning from the field. The wind / clangs the upturned bells of the buckets, / mangles the bare twigs of the white willows, / throws up the earth on to the boulders. / The horses, black baskets of swollen ribs, / struggle amid the shafts, / turn a bare-toothed profile / to the rusty tooth of harrow.

The eight-line stanza with its protracted feminine rhyme, *ветер – ведер – ветел* ('wind' – 'bucket' – 'willows'); *оглобель – рёбер –*

профиль ('shaft' – 'ribs' – 'profile'), seems to act as an accompaniment to the wind that always blows in these parts. The enclosing masculine rhyme *валуны* – *бороны* ('boulders' – 'harrow'), allows one to pause and catch breath. All of the five eight-line stanzas are constructed in the scheme *AAAbBBBb*, as monotonous as life itself in this God-forsaken northern village. Literally so: the churches, even if they once existed, have long since fallen into ruin. Only the sounds of the upturned buckets and the cartwheels remind us of the ringing of church bells. The metaphor of comparison, *black baskets of swollen ribs*, conveys the degree of emaciation of the horses who draw the carts and harrows.

> Ветер сучит замерзший щавель,   2.
> пучит платки и косынки, шарит
> в льняных подолах старух, превращает
> их в тряпичные кочаны.
> Каркая, кашляя, глядя долу,
> словно ножницами по подолу,
> бабы стригут сапогами к дому,
> рвутся на свои топчаны.

The wind spins the frost-blighted sorrel, / swells kerchiefs and neckerchiefs, fumbles / in the linen skirts of the old women, transforms / them into ragged cabbage-heads. / Cawing, coughing, glancing downwards, / the old women in topboots cut their way home, / like scissors on the hem, / bursting to get into their plank beds.

Unlike the houses, the old women are protected against the wind by a pile of rags which renders them formless, like cabbage-heads. They, like soldiers, are shod in awkward tarpaulin boots. Exhausted by heavy labour, they do not look up from the road as they hurry home to their beds. There is the same destitution in their houses as in the surrounding autumn scene: the bare, curtainless glass of their windows, wooden cots instead of beds. The metaphor *тряпичные кочаны* ('ragged cabbage-heads'), rhyming with *топчаны* ('wooden beds'), imbues the latter with its own semantics: the wooden beds, most likely, are covered not with blankets, but with old clothes, that is, rags.

All this poverty-stricken world is described metonymically, through the detail: instead of a cart, shafts, in which the horses are trapped, as in a cage; the old harrows are represented by their rusty teeth; the old women by objects of their meagre clothing. This material world is bereft of any inner life, or else it is severely

deformed: *виденья рожиц* ('the vision of crabbed little imps'),
подобья лиц ('the semblance of faces'), the black baskets which
do not exist in nature.

The metaphor *scissors*, which stands for death in Brodsky's
poetry, is repeated in the third stanza: 'В складках мелькают
резинки ножниц' ('Between folds flash the elastic of scissors'). It
rhymes here with *рожиц* – *колхозниц* ('crabbed little imps' –
'female collective farm-workers'), signalling the ominous approach
of the end.

> Эти виденья – последний признак   4.
> внутренней *жизни*, которой близок
> всякий возникший снаружи призрак,
> если его не *спугнёт* вконец
> благове*ст ступицы*, лязг теле*жный*,
> вниз головой в колее колесной
> перевернувшийся мир теле*сный*,
> реющий в тучах *живой скворец*.

These visions are the last sign / of hidden life, to which every / ghost is
akin springing up from the outside / if it is not scared off completely /
by the church-bell ring of the wheel hub, by the wagon clatter, / head
down in a wheel rut / which turns upside down the corporeal world, /
a living starling soaring into the clouds.

The vision of the crabbed little imps is a sign of a dark force that
can't be frightened off by the 'church-bell ring of the wheel hub', as
it is firmly entrenched in those places from which God is banished.
The rhymes *признак* – *близок* – *призрак* ('sign' – 'akin' –
'ghost'), form a metaphor in this context. The whistling gusts of
wind and the creak of the scissors are conveyed on the acoustic level
of the poem by repeating sibilants.

> Дождь панует в просторе нищем,   5.
> и липнут к кирзовым голинищам
> бурые комья родной земли.

Rain lords it over this poor destitute / and to their [the peasants']
tarpaulin boots cling / brown clods of the homeland's earth.

The wind also lords it; it has rolled smooth the boulders, blown
everything off the land, making it barren and brown. Here it is
all-powerful. There is no defence against it, either for animals,
farm-workers, or dead objects. Its destructive activity is conveyed
by the abundance of verbs in the present tense with a variety of

rhythmical patterns: two-syllable *гремит, сучит, шарит, пучит, гонит* ('clangs', 'spins', 'fumbles', 'swells', 'chases'). In their accentuation these verbs are reminiscent of the camp guards' orders. Then three- and four-syllable verbs: *бросает – превращает* ('throws up', 'transforms'), and finally five-syllables, *расшвыривает – разбегаются* ('throws about', 'rush around'), to emphasize the wind's activity.

Brodsky uses a non-classical metre – the four-ictus *dol'nik* – which allows him to get close to natural speech, that is, to include a relatively large number of polysyllabic words which would be rejected by the standard metres: for example, *перевёрнутый, оскаленный, перевернувшийся, вырисовывающейся* ('up-turned', 'bare-toothed', 'reversed', 'become visible'). In distorting the rhythm, these long words arrest the reader's attention, not only by their articulation, but by their almost post-Christian semantics – of dereliction, timelessness, hostility. The poet, placed by the will of the Fates in these parts, seems to be the only person capable of understanding the degree of maimedness of this world which has been overturned by the wind of history. And, at the same time, his presence is hardly felt. He is detached, yet deeply compassionate. He gives us a unique inside view of everyday life on a Soviet collective farm, in which only women, old men, and children remain. The men are either in the army, or working and studying in the town, and the women don't expect them back. This is why the exiled 'parasites' help out in the fields. He has also caught up with the Russian peasants in the conditions that Aleksandr Radishchev described in the eighteenth century. Later Brodsky would say of his own experience of exile: 'If there is any reason for pride in my past, it is that I became a convict not a soldier. Even for having missed out on the military lingo – the thing that worried me most – I was generously reimbursed with the criminal argot' (*L.* 24).

In November 1965, Brodsky was freed at the request of Soviet and foreign writers. He returned to Leningrad, with a world-wide reputation as a poet. While he was in exile his first collection of poems, *Short and Long Poems* (1965), appeared in America. Translations of his works appeared in many European languages, notably 'The Great Elegy to John Donne'.[62] Some of his poems were published in the Soviet Union.[63] He again worked on trans-lations, especially of the Polish poets Caprian Norwid, Zbigniew Herbert, Czesław Miłosz, and Konstanty Gałczyński. According to

Brodsky's American translator George L. Kline, the Polish poets showed Brodsky 'new ways of broaching a subject indirectly, letting the poem follow its own absurd logic through verbal jokes and even intellectual clowning, and at the same time allowing the subject to retain whatever serious implications it might have'.[64]

From English he translated Andrew Marvell and John Donne. Only one of his translations has been published in his own country;[65] the rest were included in his second book, *A Halt in the Wilderness* (1970). His acquaintance with English poetry in the original was no less an influence on the formation of Brodsky's individual style than his discovery of Tsvetaeva had been. He owes to the English metaphysical poets the intellectual discourse, full of wit and paradox, which was well suited to his own inclinations. Although he was prepared to take on board the poetics and ethics of both the Russian religious philosophers and the Russian metaphysical poets, Baratynsky and Tiutchev, Brodsky received his title of metaphysical poet from the English.

The degree of ratiocination with which much of Brodsky's poetry is permeated had never previously been a characteristic of Russian poetry. Never had there been such a contrast between majesty of style and asceticism of feeling. Without discriminating against any of the linguistic sub-systems, Brodsky deftly includes in his poetry mythological, historical, and journalistic material. In his imitations of scientific formulations he even runs the risk of going beyond the bounds of poetry. As will become more evident from the following chapters, Brodsky's poetry, by absorbing such heterogeneous material, becomes a new form of harmony, with an exceptionally dynamic profile. All the structural elements of the verse interact both with each other and with the thematic design of the poem. Humour and irony rescue him from scholasticism and moralizing.

It is hardly surprising that Soviet Russia sensed in Brodsky's poetry something deeply alien to itself and racked its brains long and hard over what to do with him. For a time he was untouched. As before his northern exile, he travelled widely. He spent the summer of 1966 in Moscow, where his friends Naiman and Rein had already moved. Often he wintered in the Crimea: in Yalta, Gurzuf, Koktebel. Even more often, he would visit his beloved Lithuania: Vil'nus, Palanga, Kaunas. He continued writing, and translated Brendan Behan's play *The Quare Fellow* and Stoppard's

Rosencrantz and Guildenstern Are Dead. In 1969, Robert Lowell invited him to participate in the International Festival of Poetry in London. He was not given permission to go. In response to another invitation to the Festival of Two Worlds in Spoleto, the Union of Soviet Writers said: 'There is no such poet in Soviet Russia.' A few more names had been crossed out from the official lists of Russian writers and poets. In 1966, Siniavsky and Daniel were put on trial. Aleksandr Ginzburg, who made a record of their trial, was tried along with Yury Galanskov for publishing it, as the *Belaya kniga*, in the West.[66] In 1968, Solzhenitsyn was expelled from the Union of Soviet Writers.[67] The following year, the poet Natalya Gorbanevskaya was imprisoned in a psychiatric hospital for taking part in the Red Square protest against the Soviet intervention in Czechoslovakia, and for organizing the *Chronicle of Current Events*.[68] The process of repression against those who thought independently was becoming a crescendo. Sentences were increasing. Comparing his own sentence with those that followed, Brodsky said: 'I got off rather easily. I didn't get much of a raw deal. It was unpleasant in so many ways . . . But, on the other hand, it was only two years. By the Soviet standards it's something absolutely homoeopathic.'[69] Later, when the emigration of Soviet Jews was permitted, Brodsky had no desire to abandon Russia. However, in May 1972, Brodsky was given ten days to leave the country: 'when they told you to leave, you go. They simply told me, either that or I was going to have a hard time. I wouldn't have minded that; I know a hard time inside out. But I simply would have been redundant.'[70]

In July 1974, Brodsky's friend, the writer Vladimir Maramzin, was arrested for compiling a *samizdat* collection of Brodsky's poetry. Professor Etkind, too, was reminded of his 'display of political myopia and political illiteracy'. For organizing Brodsky's defence in 1964 he was stripped of all his academic degrees, expelled from the Union of Soviet Writers, and in October 1974 was given a 'visa to Israel'.[71] The Leningrad writer and historian Mikhail Kheifets was tried and sentenced to four years in the camps and two years' exile 'for distributing' a foreword to the collection entitled 'Joseph Brodsky and our Generation', which was never published, however, since the KGB confiscated every copy.[72]

Brodsky was the first Russian poet to be brought to trial by Khrushchev, and one of the first literary figures to be sent abroad by Brezhnev. At the beginning of the 1970s, Brezhnev decided to relieve Russia of some of its finest sons. Brodsky was followed to the West by the poets Galich and Korzhavin, then by Solzhenitsyn and the philosopher Zinovyev, the journalist Dovlatov, the poets Bobyshev and Kuzminsky, the writers Maksimov, Voinovich, Nekrasov, and Vladimov. These are merely some of the names of those whose expulsion bears witness to the triumph of the dictatorship of mediocrity in Brezhnev's Russia. 'The State's fur is certainly rubbed the wrong way by literature,' said Brodsky, 'and it has engaged, from the day of its emergence, in the spiritual and intellectual castration of the populace.'[73]

Brodsky's expulsion from Russia may serve as a convenient marker of the end of his second period of creativity, the beginning of which was also marked by an extra-poetic factor, namely his exile to the Archangel countryside in May 1964. Brodsky himself has given this period the name of his third collection, 'The End of a Beautiful Epoch'. Stylistically, it marked the end of his lyrical period. With the physical journey away from his native city, Brodsky had begun his anti-lyrical journey. The stylistic vector of the poetry he has written abroad is clearly directed towards abstraction, rationalism, and even greater tonal neutrality. Brodsky has done for Russian poetry what Dostoevsky did for Russian prose: he has stripped it of naiveté and innocence. Tying the 'knots between good and evil', he has forced his poetry to discuss the 'accursed' questions in the context of the post-Christian situation. The old themes of time and art, Christianity and culture, have equally been given a new variation.

A change of empires

When a man creates a world of his own, he becomes a foreign body against which all laws are aimed: gravity, compression, rejection, and annihilation.[74]

Having tasted almost every item on the state's menu of arrest – beatings, harassment for being 'unemployed', incarceration in prisons and mental institutions, exile to a remote part of the Empire – Brodsky should have felt happy to find himself in Vienna on 4 June 1972, alive and free. But he felt angry. 'Anger directed partly at myself, because I'd been deluding myself: up till then I thought that no matter what kind of dirt they poured over me, they still felt that I was of some value. I'd been deluding myself, and flattering myself – and by the same token, them, too.'[75]

The manuscripts of all Brodsky's poetry remained in the Moscow Customs House at Sheremetyevo airport, while his parents, whom the state would never allow him to see again, and his four-year-old son remained in the city on the Neva: 'I'm getting used to the role absurdity plays in my life. I rather think this is the way it ought to be. The more weird, the more ridiculous, the better, i.e., the more real.'[76]

The word 'exile' as a sign of reward has been appended to the titles of articles about the poet and interviews with him: 'Joseph Brodsky in Exile' (1973); 'Poet and Language in Exile' (1980); 'Born in Exile' (1981); 'Conjurer in Exile' (1986).[77] The poet himself refuses to dramatize his situation: 'I don't really think that my experiences are so unique . . . first of all you don't want to be a hostage to any moment in your biography, in your life . . . you want to keep moving, keep going.'[78]

The more he has thought through what happened to him, the more benefit he has extracted from it for Russian letters. Six months after crossing the borders of the contemporary Russian Empire, he wrote the poem '1972', in which all the structural and semantic resources fulfil the almost-Calvinistic function of dismissal of pain and loss. The metre (four-ictus $dol'nik$) is accompanied by a very original rhyme scheme, $A'A'A'B'C'C'C'B'$ / $A'A'A'BC'C'C'B$). In the dominance of dactylic rhymes one can distinguish a tone of lamentation which is suppressed by the sustained irony of the poem's semantics.

> Всё, что я мог потерять, утрачено
> начисто. Но и достиг я начерно
> всё, чего было достичь назначено.   (Ч. 25)

All that I could lose has been lost / utterly. But I've also achieved, roughly, / all that I was meant to achieve.

Quotations from Pushkin (*Здравствуй, племя, / младое, незнакомое!*) and from *The Lay of Igor's Campaign* are deliberately surrounded by a pejorative context, which is diluted by scintillating humour:

> Здравствуй, младое и незнакомое
> племя! Жужжащее, как насекомое,
> время нашло, наконец, искомое

> лакомство в твёрдом моём затылке.
> В мыслях разброд и разгром на темени.

Greeting, young and unknown / tribe! The buzzing, insect-like, / time has found, finally, its sought for / delicacy in my resilient occiput. / In my thoughts there is disorder, and rout about my head.

The very fact of the allusion to the finest examples of Russian literature acts as an affirmation of the thought expressed in the tenth stanza:

> Слушай, дружина, враги и братие!
> Всё, что творил я, творил не ради я
> славы в эпоху кино и радио,
> но ради речи родной, словесности.
> За каковое раченье-жречество
> (сказано ж доктору: сам пусть лечится)
> чаши лишившись в пиру Отечества,
> нынче стою в незнакомой местности.

Listen, lads, enemies and brethren! / Everything I've done, I've done not for / fame in the age of movies and radio, / but for my native tongue, for literature. / For this kind of sacrificial zeal / (it is said, physician, heal thyself), / deprived of a cup at the feast of the Fatherland, / I now stand in an unknown locality.

The understatement demonstrates itself by the poet's refusal to be sentimental, an attitude which his Russian readers often mistake for coldness. Brodsky has managed to avoid sentimentality thanks to his prosidic skill. The metre of the poem is brought into intense conflict with its syntax. Semantic and rhythmical units are remorselessly broken up by the poetic line. The flowing syntactic periods erode the boundaries of lines and strophe; this is Brodsky's technique for constructing the poem. This poem also illustrates Brodsky's new strategy: high-style Slavonicisms, à la Khlebnikov: *дружина* ('lads'), *братие* ('brethren'), *глаголаю* ('speak'), intermingled with low-style folk-language expressions: *валял дурака под кожею* ('played with his thing'); bold enjambements, à la Tsvetaeva, which several times deposit the personal pronoun 'I' at the end of the line:

> Брал, что давали. Душа не зарилась
> на не своё. Обладал опорою,
> строил рычаг. И пространству впору я
> звук извлекал, дуя в дудку полую.

I took what I was given. My soul did not covet / what was not its own.
I had support, / I fashioned a lever. And to fit the space I / extracted a
sound, blowing into the hollow pipe.

However strange it may seem at first glance, the extent of the
poet's lack of well-being is more clearly visible in his thoughts for
the future than in his memory of the past:

> Вот оно – то, о чём я глаголаю:
> о превращении тела в голую
> вещь! Ни горé не гляжу, ни долу я,
> но в пустоту – чем её ни высветли.

There it is – what I'm talking about: / about the transformation of the
body into a naked / thing! I'm not looking on high, or below, / but
into emptiness – whatever may illuminate it.

The explanation for this can be found in Brodsky's prose: 'For
some reason, the past doesn't radiate such immense monotony as
the future does. Because of its plenitude, the future is propaganda.
So is grass' (*L.* 7). The future, however unknown it may be, has
one highly distinct characteristic: beyond it stand time, silence, and
death. Thus, at the age of thirty-two, Brodsky began to sing of
growing old:

> Старение! Здравствуй, моё старение!
> Крови медленное струение.

Growing old! Good day, my old age! / The slow flow of blood.

A highly ironic tone and lexicon are found for his poetic self-
depiction. In the next six lines we can easily detect a sentiment of
self-disgust, self-negation, and despair:

> Правильно! Тело в страстях раскаялось.
> Зря оно пело, рыдало, скалилось.
> В полости рта не уступит кариес
> Греции древней, по меньшей мере.
> Смрадно дыша и треща суставами,
> пачкаю зеркало.

Quite right! The body has repented the passions. / In vain did it sing,
sob, grin. / In the mouth's cavity the caries do not give way / to
ancient Greece, at least. / With foul breath, and joints creaking / I
stain the mirror.

The uncomfortable thoughts are very often brought into a sharp
focus by triple rhymes: *отчаянья – одичания – молчания*

('despair' – 'isolation' – 'silence'). Most of them contain the possible elements of metaphor. They augment the semantic level of the text and demonstrate that Brodsky is capable of estranging himself to such an extent that the tragedy is conveyed only through his rhymes.

And so the themes death–silence, man–thing, word–thing enter and take firm footing in Brodsky's poetry. The de-animation of man and reification of language is closely connected with the situation of exile, not only in the political or even physical sense, but, principally, in the existential sense. To a certain extent, this theme is neutralized by the theme of Christ:

> Бей в барабан о своём доверии
> к ножницам, в коих судьба материи
> скрыта. *Только размер потери и*
> *делает смертного равным Богу.*

Beat the drum about your faith / in scissors in which the fate of matter / is concealed. *Only the degree of loss / makes the mortal equal to God.*

Such profound thinking about the idea of loss emerges in the poem in a highly unexpected and unobtrusive manner. Here Brodsky plays one of his favourite tricks: in formulating Christian ideas in the modern Russian language which had forgotten how they sound or how they are written, Brodsky achieves his object almost *en passant*, in subordinate clauses.

The greatest compensation for all the losses of 1972 was the meeting with W. H. Auden. Brodsky has talked about it in interviews,[79] and in two essays dedicated to Auden and his work. They met on 6 June in Auden's Austrian home in Kirchstetten. 'Wystan fussed about him like a mother hen,' writes Auden's biographer, 'an unusually kindly and understanding mother hen.'[80] They spent three weeks together in Austria, then Auden arranged the invitation for Brodsky to take part in the International Festival of Poetry in London. 'During those weeks in Austria', recalls Brodsky,

he looked after my affairs with the diligence of a good mother hen. To begin with, telegrams and other mail inexplicably began to arrive for me 'c/o W. H. Auden'. Then he wrote to the Academy of American Poets requesting that they provide me with some financial support. This was how I got my first American money – $1,000 to be precise – and it lasted me all the way to my first pay-day at the University of Michigan. (*L.* 377)

Before Brodsky left for America, he and Auden gave a recital together in the Queen Elizabeth Hall, then Auden took him to Oxford. He also wrote an introduction to the collection of Brodsky's poems for the Penguin edition. Relying on English translation alone, Auden did not fail to recognize a poet of the first order, saying that Brodsky 'has an extraordinary capacity to envision material objects as sacramental signs, messengers from the unseen'.[81]

They met once more, in the same place – Queen Elizabeth Hall – three months before Auden's death. Brodsky's first poem in English, 'Elegy', was dedicated to Auden.[82] Later, their meetings were commemorated in Russian in the poem 'York' (1976).

The same year, 1972, Brodsky met Robert Lowell. He offered his help by reading Brodsky's poems in English while Brodsky recited them in Russian during the International Festival of Poetry. Then he invited Brodsky to Kent: 'I was somehow perplexed – my English wasn't good enough.'[83] In 1975, they met again in the Five Colleges in Massachusetts, and Brodsky was again invited to Lowell's place in Brooklyn. 'By that time my English was somewhat better and I went. The time we spent was in many ways the best time I can recall having here in the States. We talked about this and that, and finally we settled on Dante . . . He knew Dante inside out, I think, in an absolutely obsessive way.'[84] Brodsky maintains that he felt more comfortable with Lowell than with Auden. He wrote his 'Elegy: For Robert Lowell' (1977) in English to please the poet's shadow.

For the next nine years Brodsky held the post of poet-in-residence with professorial status at the University of Michigan. He also lectured on comparative literature, English and Russian poetry, and Classical Studies in other American universities. In 1981, he moved to Massachusetts to the Five Colleges and took a permanent job as Professor of Literature at Mount Holyoke. He lectures with erudition and enthusiasm: 'When he talks about Mandelstam, or Tsvetaeva,' said one of his students,

they aren't dead poets set on paper. You really feel that a living dialogue is going on. And not just with the Russians – Homer and Dante are in the room too. It's almost eerie. I never had an American teacher who talked about Shakespeare as though he was some friend or a colleague who had just stepped out of the room for a minute.[85]

Brodsky's work since 1972 is an impressive achievement in Russian poetry and in poetry at large. It has been recognized by many. In 1978, he received the degree of Doctor of Letters *honoris causa* from Yale University. Next year, he won the Feltrinelli Prize for Poetry and the Mondello Literary Prize. He became a member of the Bavarian Academy of Fine Art and the American Academy of Art and Sciences.[86] As Czesław Miłosz put it: 'the strong presence of Joseph Brodsky has needed less than a decade to establish itself in world poetry'.[87] His poems have been translated into every European language, but have been banned in his country until recently. However, those who have left the Soviet Union during the 1980s testify:

In Russia Brodsky's works already have an enviable fate and the number of his admirers is enormous. Not to know Brodsky and to admit that you don't know him is somehow indecent, like not knowing all the names of the soviet cosmonauts or, if the worst comes to the worst, Zinovyev's philosophical novels. Anyone who wants can get hold of Brodsky's poetry.[88]

Brodsky's well-earned fame dispels the legend that 'a Russian writer cannot live without his motherland'.[89] Moreover, he has cured Russians of a chronic Russian illness – an inferiority complex towards Europe, the ailment of which Peter the Great tried to cure the nation by barbaric means.[90] Not having suffered from this ailment, Brodsky survives in any of the American provinces: 'I don't have a sense of provincialism; the moment I see a cigarette machine and a library I cease to feel in a province. And also the telephone doesn't ring here as if it were just invented.'[91]

Brodsky travels widely both in America and throughout Europe to give readings of his work and as a tourist. During his first eighteen months in the USA, he gave about sixty poetry readings.[92] After his very first semester at Ann Arbor, using his first salary, he headed to Venice to spend Christmas 1972 there. Since then, he has visited Italy almost every year, health permitting. Italy attracts Brodsky by its history, culture, and, of course, its poetry. He spent four months with a magnifying glass in his hand scouring the dusty manuscripts of Horace, Virgil, and Ovid in Rome in 1981, as a stipendiary of the American Academy. In Brodsky's view, these poets prepared the ground for the spread of Christianity in the Roman Empire and at the same time 'preserved it, as far as was possible, from the narrow fanaticism of the proselytisers'.[93]

Brodsky visits England no less frequently. In 1979 and 1981 he took part in the International Festival of Poetry in Cambridge. In 1978 and 1985 he visited several British universities to give lectures and public readings. He dedicated to England a cycle of poems which was published in a limited edition of only sixty copies for his birthday.[94] As he has acknowledged himself on more than one occasion, Brodsky has a lasting love affair with the English language: 'English is the only interesting thing that is left in my life.'[95] However, he consciously restricts this enthusiasm for the English language to the sphere of prose, half-jokingly, half-seriously explaining this by the fact that he does not wish to 'compete with the people for whom English is the mother tongue', doesn't want to create for himself 'an extra reality', doesn't want 'to be penalized twice', and he is 'not after a good seat on the American Parnassus'.[96] Does this mean that his Russian language is under threat? Both yes and no. His beloved fatherland, as Brodsky puts it, constantly reminds him of its existence; if only with the help of the means of communication, it doesn't let itself be forgotten. But, in understanding literally his own metaphor – a poet is first and foremost the instrument of language and not vice versa – Brodsky acknowledges that life outside Russia means for him above all else the lack of opportunity to track the development of events, the development of everyday idiomatic usage from which the purely linguistic everyday reality is formed. To a certain extent, this fact makes him nervous.[97] 'Whatever Brodsky may fear,' writes Henry Gifford, 'he is still marvellously at home in the language. At the same time, he is putting exile to good use, by seeking out affinities and extensions.'[98] But Brodsky has succeeded in turning this linguistic isolation to his own advantage: 'It helps you to win a notion of yourself unimpeded. It's not pleasant, but it is a more clinical notion of yourself. The relationship with your own language becomes more private and intricate; it hovers on the verge of esoteric.'[99]

The collection of Brodsky's essays, *Less Than One*, which recently appeared in English (1986), is a continuation of his poetry and a commentary on it. It is also the intellectual autobiography of the poet. His prose possesses the same semantic density, contains the same system of tropes, and displays the same absolute mastery. It is not surprising that the book was greeted with a flood of laudatory reviews. David Bethea of *The New York Times Review* wrote: 'Nowhere else in the now almost seventy-year history of this national literature in exile have we seen quite such a conjurer's act: Mr Brodsky bends down and lifts himself and his entire ailing tradition into the air.'[100] Bethea has in mind Brodsky's essays on non-Russian poets: 'the spiritual extremist' Cavafy, the poet of *amaro stile nuovo* Montale, 'the most humble poet of the English language' W. H. Auden, and, finally, 'the metaphysical realist' Walcott. These essays share a common theme with the essays on Russian poets, namely, the supremacy of language. They also have something else in common: they are all about Brodsky himself and his poetry, because he is writing either about those poets he is attracted to, like Cavafy, Montale, and Walcott; or those he admires – Akhmatova, Mandelstam, and Auden – or even adores, like Marina Tsvetaeva, with whom he 'decided not to compete'.[101] That is why Brodsky's prose is important for understanding his poetry and his personality. Brodsky tirelessly reminds us that we must look at every poet for a display of the unity of ethics and aesthetics, for craftsmanship and humility. For him, poetry is 'an instrument of self-betterment', 'a form of sentimental education' as well as 'the highest form of existence of language'. And a poet is an embodiment of language.[102]

And so, neither in 1972 nor later did the 'beheading' of the poet take place. Left alone with his language, Brodsky enters into a relationship with it of absolute dependence and obedience. As if continuing Auden's idea that time will forgive all those who write well, Brodsky declares: 'For a writer only one form of patriotism exists: his attitude towards language. The measure of a writer's patriotism is how he writes in the language of the people among whom he lives. Bad literature, for example, is a form of treason.'[103] He is inclined to ascribe all his own services to Russian poetry to the quality of the language itself. He goes so far as to make the risky declaration that 'the finest and most precious thing that Russia possesses is language . . . The holiest thing we have is, perhaps, not our icons, not even our history – it is our language.'[104]

If this idea is even only half-true, then Brodsky's contribution to Russian literature can hardly be overestimated. His enormous erudition and sensitivity towards language as well as his talent help him to transfer the Russian language, by means of its very own resources, to the centre of world culture. 'The force that drives him to do it' is the same as was behind Dostoevsky's writing, 'the omnivorousness of his language which eventually comes to a point where it cannot be satisfied with God, man, reality, guilt, death, infinity, salvation, air, earth, water, fire, money; and then it takes on itself' (*L.* 163).

In many of Brodsky's poems and essays language becomes the subject of philosophical meditation. It is either delineated as an omnipotent and timeless force, which does not obey any laws but its own, or described in terms of physical objects. No less frequently it is personified. In fact, in the six volumes of his poetry that have appeared over the last twenty-three years, language, in all the aspects of its existence, is endowed with equality of rights with man, or, in equal measure, is deprived of those rights. *A Part of Speech* is the very symbolic title of his fourth collection of verse:

> Жизнь, которой,
> как дареной вещи, не смотрят в пасть,
> обнажает зубы при каждой встрече.
> От всего человека вам остаётся часть
> речи. Часть речи вообще. Часть речи.   (*Ч.* 95)

Life, which / like a given thing, no one looks in the mouth, / bares its teeth at each encounter. / What remains of a man is a part / of speech. Just a part of speech as such. A part of speech.

Language turned out to be the firm ground for the poet's groundlessness, while the technique of *pars pro toto* as a metonymical depiction of man has become a vehicle for his spiritual and poetic expansion. If a man is no longer a whole oneness, then indeed 'one is perhaps less than one' (*L.* 17).

Despite all the changes in Brodsky's style since his exile, the original components of his poetry are preserved and developed. The clarity of his vision, the density of his focus, and the analytical power are very much intact. The keen observation of a naturalist, and the refined intellectualization of a philosopher, are the trademarks of his idiostyle. Echoes, references, direct quotations from his great predecessors fulfil in his poetry the function sometimes of a stereoscope, sometimes of a telescope. As often as not, it is through them that one regards the present which distances itself in time. The poet unlocks, as it were, artistic time, so that even the future imitates now the past, now the present. Through the same devices Brodsky enters into a relationship with world culture.

2

Longing for world culture

This notion of a world culture is distinctly Russian. Because of
its location (neither East nor West) and its imperfect history,
Russia has always suffered from a sense of cultural inferiority,
at least toward the West.[1]

In defence of culture

'There, there . . .'. They grin. *'Liberté, Egalité, Fraternité . . .'*.
Why does nobody add Culture?[2]

The word 'culture', which entered the lexicon of European
languages in the second half of the eighteenth century, still does not
have a simple definition; 'nothing was more indeterminate than this
word', wrote Herder.[3] A hundred years later, A. L. Lowell echoed
him from the other side of the Atlantic: 'Nothing in the world is
more elusive.'[4] Meanwhile, hundreds of definitions of culture have
arisen.[5] Many of them incorporate in the concept of culture
national customs, moral laws, art, the whole complex of human
knowledge and the material level of a society's development.

In the twentieth century, the concept of culture has not escaped
the universal problem of inflation. We have seen the appearance of
such terms as the counter-culture, sub-culture, folk culture, mass
culture, and many others. Is this not the reason, then, that Brodsky
thinks that there has arisen an urgent necessity to come to the
defence of culture? In his recent collection of articles, the words
'culture' and 'civilization' are encountered, on average, every ten
pages, and if we count the running title of the essay on Mandelstam,
'The Child of Civilization', every eight. We should not be surprised
that in the English translation of his article 'Puteshestvie v
Stambul', ('Flight to Byzantium'), the word 'civilization' is twice
translated as 'culture'.[6] They are synonyms for Brodsky: 'Civilization is the sum total of different cultures animated by a common
spiritual numerator, and its main vehicle – speaking both meta-

phorically and literally – is translation' (*L.* 139). Clearly, he is drawn towards the phenomenological approach to culture, believing, as he does, in the universal contents of culture which balance on the 'axial *terminus a quo*' – language itself. Recognizing the multifaceted nature of culture, Brodsky distinguishes within it a system of ethical, aesthetic, and spiritual values which are deeply embedded in our Judaeo–Graeco-Roman civilization. Each generation must uncover these values for itself, assimilate them and pass them on to future generations, like a relay baton. This position may seem axiomatic, even banal. To what danger is culture subject in our age of progress and reason, given that it has lived through at least two 'cultural revolutions' – the Russian and the Chinese? Why does he try to catch the tail of that 'dinosaur called civilization' which, according to Brodsky himself, has ceased to exist?

For all Brodsky's preoccupation with the state of 'world culture', the roots of this anxiety are undoubtedly very Russian. Perhaps this may also explain why Brodsky gives preference to the moral self-perfection of man and not the social amelioration of his condition, to the acquisition of knowledge and not its application to the goals of technological progress; in brief, to the spiritual spheres of culture as opposed to the material aspects.

To understand and evaluate all Brodsky's endeavours in his defence of culture one more brief and final excursus into the recent history of Russian culture is essential. It has become a common-place to talk of the tragedy of Russian culture, of its degeneration after the Revolution. Brodsky, unlike many others, has taken a completely novel angle on what has happened. In his opinion, the principal victim of the social Utopia has been the Russian language:

This country, with its magnificently inflected language capable of expressing the subtlest nuances of the human psyche, with an incredible ethical sensitivity (a good result of its otherwise tragic history), had all the makings of a cultural, spiritual paradise, a real vessel of civilization. Instead, it became a drab hell, with a shabby materialistic dogma and pathetic consumerist gropings. (*L.* 26)

Ideological propaganda has gradually supplanted the thousands of concepts which stand behind words, creating its own version of the future and producing a kind of linguistic inflation which, like a disease, has penetrated all levels of language, including the language of literature. We may consider the very fact of the rejection of the language of the state as the fundamental reason for the banning of the most loyal of the countless literary '-isms' from the start of the century, namely Futurism. Even Mayakovsky, the first poet of the Revolution, could not save Futurism. The state castrated him by canonizing works which are far from being his greatest. It is indeed Mayakovsky, whose greatest ambition was to become the first-ever poet of the masses, who will have to appear before the Last Judgement of the word and answer for this unprecedented inflation of poetic speech. It was he who allowed form as well as content to come under the purview of the Party.

As Vladimir Veidle put it, metaphor deceived the Russian avant-garde. Those artists who supported the Revolution, 'imagined that the Revolution and "revolution in art" were one and the same. The Revolution punished them for this.'[7] When the 'terrible war on the Russian Parnassus' was over, all those who had taken part were defeated. A new '-ism' was triumphant: socialist realism. 'The truth is that every "ism" operates on a mass scale that mocks national identity' (*L*. 82). Socialist realism was and is not an exception: 'the democratic principle', writes Brodsky in his essay on Russian literature, 'so welcome in nearly all spheres of human endeavour has no application in at least two of them: in art and in science. In these two spheres, the application of the democratic principle results in equating masterpiece with garbage and discovery with ignorance' (*L*. 302). And this is the principal reason why the cultural revolution in the USSR finished off Russian culture.

If the state of a nation's language acts as an indicator of its spiritual and emotional health, then this proposition is most clearly demonstrated in the novels of Andrei Platonov. Brodsky was one of the first fully to appreciate his novels, writing in his foreword to the parallel-text edition of *The Foundation Pit* (1973): 'Platonov speaks of a nation which in a sense has become the victim of its own language; or, to put it more accurately, he tells a story about this very language, which turns out to be capable of generating a fictitious world, and then falls into grammatical dependence on it.'[8] Mandelstam also divided all people into friends and enemies of the word. He advocated showing compassion for the state which rejected the word, warning at the same time that 'there is nothing hungrier than the contemporary state, and a hungry state is more terrifying than a hungry man'.[9] Before others he realized that in the 'century of pancomprehensibility' a culture is 'marked for death, and a new barbarism, terrifying yet perhaps potentially creative, is waiting at the gate'.[10]

However, these potential creative possibilities were destined not to be manifested for some time. With the banning of Dostoevsky and Berdyaev, the Futurists and the Acmeists, the level of philosophical thought and stylistic norms rapidly approximated the cultural standards of the Leader, who did not even have a proper command of the language of the nation that he ruled for more than a quarter of a century. Soon mediocrity became the norm. Several decades more of 'liberalization' of the country would be required before it returned to the cultural level of the Silver Age.[11] Even in 1988, the Soviet reader does not have access to the complete works of Khlebnikov, Mandelstam, or Tsvetaeva, does not know the religious philosophy of Berdyaev and Shestov, and has a distorted picture of Solzhenitsyn's and Brodsky's work. This has been, and remains, a conscious disparagement of the personality of the Russian reader, his spiritual and creative potential. In his essay on Tsvetaeva, Brodsky writes in connection with this:

Theoretically, the dignity of a nation degraded politically cannot be seriously wounded by obliterating its cultural heritage. Russia, however, in contrast to nations blessed with a legislative tradition, elective institutions, and so forth, is in a position to understand herself only through literature, and to retard the literary process by disposing of or treating as nonexistent the works of even a minor author is tantamount to a genetic crime against the future of the nation. (*L.* 193)

In Brodsky's work we can easily detect several areas in which he defends culture. Apart from those already mentioned – the linguistic and aesthetic, which will be illustrated throughout the present work by detailed analyses of his poetry – we should also highlight the ethical and religious aspects of culture. All these levels are closely interwoven and one differentiates them only conventionally, for the sake of analysis. We find this conception of the paths of the defence of culture confirmed by Brodsky himself: 'There is no love without memory, no memory without culture, no culture without love. Therefore every poem is a fact of culture as well as an act of love and a flash of memory – and, I would add, of faith.'[12] This was written in 1974. Since then, Brodsky has bound even more tightly the knots between ethics and aesthetics, between culture and religion. In essays from his already much-quoted collection, *Less Than One*, Brodsky discusses the problems of culture, spirituality, and the lack of it in our epoch, thereby formulating the basic premisses of his aesthetics. Not infrequently, his prose provides a commentary to his poetry. His essays on other poets, whether Russian (Mandelstam, Tsvetaeva, Akhmatova) or Western European (Montale, Auden), provide a glimpse through the doors of his own 'creative laboratory'. The poem 'A Halt in the Wilderness', which will be analysed below, reveals that Brodsky shares T. S. Eliot's view that 'The first important assertion is that no culture has appeared or developed except together with a religion: according to the point of view of the observer, the culture will appear to be the product of the religion, or the religion the product of the culture.'[13]

The ever-deepening division between religion and culture that began in Europe during the Renaissance and Reformation has been brought in Russia to the complete replacement of the former by the latter. Following the physical destruction of priests, believers, and places of worship during the period 1917–43, literature has taken on the role of the spiritual centre for society. The survivors Pasternak and Akhmatova became Christians towards the end of their days. They watched painfully as the cultural and ethical forms of everyday life to which they were accustomed disappeared. Nadezhda Mandelstam observes that the word 'conscience' disappeared from common usage even in the 1930s: 'it was not used in newspapers, books or schools because its function was now being fulfilled by, at first, "class feeling", and later by "usefulness for the state"'.[14]

Brodsky does not share the 'doctrine' of the religious Renaissance which is now so popular both among émigrés and in Russia itself. The rebirth of religious feeling amongst Russians is more connected with the growth of nationalism, which is coming to replace the atrophied forms of Marxism–Leninism, than with any development of a genuinely Christian consciousness. A belief in God is becoming a fashion, especially among the intelligentsia:

This is such a, how shall I put it, banal religiosity where there is an element which is, if not sectarian, then certainly pharisaical, whereby a man is almost proud of the fact that he believes in God. Of course, this is the psychology of the neophyte who has only just converted, who has only just discovered something for himself.[15]

In the broad mass of the Soviet population, as before, atheism is widespread. For the 275 millions of Russia's population there are only two theological academies and three seminaries. Religious literature appears in small runs and is not available to ordinary believers. The working churches and monasteries are harshly

controlled. Charitable work is forbidden under Soviet law, as is any
religious propaganda. Within the Church, the priests' sermons are
of low quality. The inflation of language over the last seventy years
in a state which has actively suppressed religion has affected even
those who 'have the right' to speak 'God's Word' aloud.[16]
    The painful realization that the rapid disappearance of Chris-
tianity in Russia threatens its culture was expressed by Brodsky in a
poem of 1966 which gave the title to his second collection, 'A Halt
in the Wilderness'. It is a poem in blank verse of irregular strophic
form, written in traditional iambic pentameters, but with many
deviations from the metre, and discursive in manner. Its subject is
the destruction of the Greek church in Leningrad in the early 1960s.
On the site of the destroyed temple there was erected the four-
thousand seat October Concert Hall, in the faceless style of
contemporary architecture:

> Теперь так мало греков в Ленинграде,
> что мы сломали Греческую церковь,
> дабы построить на свободном месте
> концертный зал. В такой архитектуре
> есть что-то безнадежное. А впрочем,
> концертный зал на тыщу с лишним мест
> не так уж безнадёжен: это – храм,
> и храм искусства. Кто же виноват,
> что мастерство вокальное даёт
> сбор больший, чем знамена веры?   (*O.* 166–8)

Now there are so few Greeks in Leningrad / that we have knocked
down the Greek Church / in order to build, on the vacant lot, / a
concert hall. In such architecture / there is something hopeless.
However, / a concert hall with a thousand and more seats / isn't that
lacking in hope: it is a temple, / and a temple of the arts. But who is to
blame / that the vocal arts are / bigger box-office than the outward
signs of faith?

    In the first, sixteen-line strophe only one line is in the 'pure' iambic
pentameter: 'концертныц зал на тыщу с лишним мест' ('a
concert hall with a thousand and more seats'). By its deliberate
conversational style, this phrase, with its semantics of substitution
for the real temple, seems to cancel out the classical prosody
contained within it, thereby reducing it to the banal:

> Жаль только, что теперь издалека
> мы будем видеть не нормальный купол,
> а безобразно плоскую черту.

It is a pity though, that now from afar / we will see not the usual cupola, / but an ugly plane line.

The last three lines contain two pyrrhic feet each. Perhaps these hiatuses in the metre reflect the lapses in taste of contemporary architecture. Since *образ* means both an 'image' and an 'icon', *безобразно* can be interpreted as being 'without an image or icon' as well as 'ugly':

> Но что до безобразия пропорций,
> то человек зависит не от них,
> а чаще от пропорций безобразья.

But as far as the ugliness of proportions goes / man does not depend on them / but more often on the proportions of ugliness.

The entire stanza is saturated with metrical and syntactic irregularities: of the six syntactic units which comprise it, three finish in mid-line. This disharmony between metre and grammar conveys something more than a purely aesthetic conflict. The fractured lines, like the destroyed temple itself, intensify the level of prosody. The basic theme of the poem – the indissoluble link and interdependence of ethics and aesthetics, of religion and culture – has also been written about by T. S. Eliot: 'I do not believe that the culture of Europe could survive the complete disappearance of the Christian Faith ... if Christianity goes, the whole of our culture goes.'[17] The replacement of God's temple by a 'temple' of art is insufficient, an impoverishment. The defective qualities of this replacement are accentuated by the almost complete absence of tropes in the first stanza, which, in its turn, can be interpreted in two ways: both as the stylistic simplicity of classical forms, and as the poverty of imagination of contemporary builders. The solitary simile is deliberately prosaic: 'But who is to blame that the vocal arts are bigger box-office than the outward signs of faith?' This essentially grammatical, rather than image-based, simile refers to the unstoppable disappearance of spiritual values in our 'hopelessly materialistic world' (*C.* 54).

The second strophe is a little shorter (fourteen lines) and tells of the process of the destruction of the temple, to which the poet was a witness:

> Прекрасно помню, как её ломали.
> Была весна, и я как раз тогда
> ходил в одно татарское семейство,

неподалёку жившее. Смотрел
в окно и видел Греческую церковь.
Всё началось с татарских разговоров;
а после в разговор вмешались звуки,
сливавшиеся с речью поначалу,
но вскоре – заглушившие её.

I remember perfectly how they demolished it. / It was spring and just then I / was visiting a Tartar family / who lived not far away. I looked / out of the window and saw the Greek Church. / It all began with Tartar talks, / but later on the sounds intervened / which, at first, blended with speech / but soon drowned it.

These Tartar conversations in a Tartar family command attention because of the tautology, and demand a reading other than the literal one. The reference sends us back to those difficult moments in the history of ancient Russia when the recently Christianized nation was subjected to mortal danger during the two and a half centuries of the Tartar yoke (1243–1480). Russia never fully recovered from the threat that Christianity might be destroyed. Everything begins with these Tartar sounds that muffled Russian speech. We are now witnesses to the end of this process. The reader is free to guess or speculate as to its culmination:

В церковный садик въехал экскаватор
с подвешенной к стреле чугунной гирей.
И стены стали тихо поддаваться.
Смешно не поддаваться, если ты
стена, а пред тобою – разрушитель.

Into the small church garden there entered an excavator / with a cast iron weight hanging from a boom / and the walls began, calmly, to give way. / It would be ridiculous if you were a wall and you didn't give way / while in front of you was a destroyer.

One modest trope – the personification of the church wall and its destroyer, the excavator with its cast-iron weight – conveys the tragedy of the end with deliberate sparseness. The repeated verb 'to give way' only emphasizes its inevitability. Then the poet, as if apprehensive lest we understand this personification of the two objects – the wall and the machine – as lending them 'equality of rights', hastens to dispel this illusory impression at the opening of the following stanza:

К тому же, экскаватор мог считать
её предметом неодушевлённым

и, до известной степени, подобным
себе. А в неодушевлённом мире
не принято давать друг другу сдачи.
Потом – туда согнали самосвалы,
бульдозеры . . .

What is more, the excavator could count on / the wall being
inanimate, / and to a certain extent like / itself. And in an inanimate
world / it is not customary to pay each other back. / Next there gather
together dumper trucks, / bulldozers . . .

The tropes that have only just been created are immediately
'liquidated'. On the one hand, 'the excavator could count', and 'in
an inanimate world it is not customary to pay each other back', are
metaphors of attribution to things of the human qualities of thought
and social intercourse. But on the other hand, the 'negatively'
coloured comparison of the wall with the excavator complicates the
internal relationships of the classical opposition 'thing–man–
Spirit'. The Spirit may be embodied not only in man, but in a thing
as well, but not in *any* thing. The church wall is permeated with
age-old spiritual energy, emanating both from man and from God.
But the excavator is a product of the soulless age of 'reason and
progress'. The twice-repeated polysyllabic word, *неодушев-
лённый* ('inanimate'), breaks the rhythm of the metre, arrests the
reader's attention, forcing him to ponder on a world in which 'it is
not customary to pay each other back', as the poet himself had
done, regarding the world 'through the prism of the church':

И как-то в поздний час
сидел я на развалинах абсиды.
В провалах алтаря зияла ночь.
И я – сквозь эти дыры в алтаре –
смотрел на убегавшие трамваи,
на вереницу тусклых фонарей.
И то, чего вообще не встретишь в церкви,
теперь я видел через призму церкви.

And one day at a late hour / I was sitting amidst the ruins of the apse.
/ In the gaps of the sanctuary yawned the night. / And I – through
those holes in the sanctuary – / watched the fleeing tramcars, / on
string of dim streetlights, / and [all] that which generally you don't
encounter in church, / I now saw through the prism of the church.

The metaphorical impoverishment of the preceding stanzas is
immediately compensated for by several metaphors of comparison

comprised of the same grammatical structure: 'In the gaps of the sanctuary', by analogy with the clichéd metaphor 'gaps in the memory', or with the literal expression 'gaps in the earth'; 'holes in the sanctuary', these gaps and open spaces which have appeared in the destroyed church wall, call to mind the holes in the parishioners' clothes and shoes. We have every reason to consider the last metaphor, 'through the prism of the church', to be a central one in Brodsky's work. He concludes his essay on Akhmatova with the following words: 'She was, essentially, a poet of human ties: cherished, strained, severed. She showed these evolutions first through the prism of the individual heart, then through the prism of history, such as it was. This is about as much as one gets in the way of optics anyway' (*L.* 52). Elsewhere, in talking of Mandelstam's collection, *Tristia*, Brodsky recognizes that the 'whole enterprise was being viewed through a somewhat Greek prism' (*L.* 128). And if we pursue our search for other prisms through which the poet or writer perceives the world, it is not difficult to unearth the principal ones – culture and civilization:

By itself reality isn't worth a damn. It's perception that promotes reality to meaning. And there is a hierarchy among perceptions (and, correspondingly, among meanings), with the ones acquired through the most refined and sensitive prisms sitting at the top. Refinement and sensitivity are imparted to such a prism by the only source of their supply: by culture, by civilization, whose main tool is language. (*L.* 152–3)

In the present poem, 'the prism of the church' undoubtedly provides Brodsky with 'the density of his focus' (*L.* 124). But what does he see through the gaps and holes in the sanctuary of the ruined church? However strange it may seem, it is the future and not the past:

> Когда-нибудь, когда не станет нас,
> точнее – после нас, на нашем месте
> возникнет тоже что-нибудь такое,
> чему любой, кто знал нас, ужаснётся.
> Но знавших нас не будет слишком много.
> Вот так, по старой памяти, собаки
> на прежнем месте задирают лапу.
> Ограда снесена давным давно,
> но им, должно быть, грезится ограда.
> Их грёзы перечёркивают явь.
> А может быть земля хранит тот запах:
> асфальту не осилить запах псины.

И что им этот безобразный дом!
Для них тут садик, говорят вам – садик.
А то, что очевидно для людей,
собакам совершенно безразлично.

Some day, when we are no more, / or rather – after us, in our place, / something similar will also arise / which to those who ever knew us, will be terrifying. / But those who knew us will not be too numerous. / Look, there by force of habit, the dogs / cock their hind legs on the old spot. / The fence was taken down long long ago / but they probably dream of the fence. / Their day-dreams cancel out reality. / But maybe the earth preserves that smell, / asphalt can't overpower the smell of dog. / And what's that ugly building to them! / For them there is a little garden – they're telling you – there's a garden. / And what is obvious to people / for dogs is quite indifferent.

The motif of knowledge, memory, and fidelity is introduced. The poet here speaks about knowledge of one's own history, remembrance of the 'ancient stones',[18] fidelity to culture. In conditions of the continuing destruction of the monuments of antiquity and the repeated rewriting of history, man loses his 'historical' memory. Only dogs remember the place where the Greek church once stood:

Вот это и зовут: "собачья верность".
И если довелось мне говорить
всерьёз об эстафете поколений,
то верю только в эту эстафету.
Вернее, в тех, кто ощущает запах.

This is what they call 'a dog's fidelity'. / And if I happened to talk / seriously about the relay race of the generations, / then I only believe in that relay race. / Or rather in those who have a sense of smell.

As in the preceding strophe, the poet cultivates the device of repetition of key words: знал ('knew'), знавших ('those who knew'); верность ('fidelity'), верю ('I believe'); which return us to the знамена веры ('outward signs of faith'), just as память ('memory') returns us to помню ('I remember') from the second strophe. Безобразный дом ('ugly building') is a paraphrase for the concert hall and recalls both безобразие пропорций ('ugliness of proportions') and пропорций безобразья ('proportions of ugliness'). The thrice-repeated запах ('smell'), which asphalt can't overpower because the earth itself preserves it, breaks away from its concrete sense of запах псины ('smell of dog') and is abstracted, in the запах which ends the stanza, as man's hypersensitivity to the values of the past. The technique of repetition (18 per cent of the poem's significant lexis is repeated from two to four times) imbues the poem with an exhortatory intonation. The penultimate strophe is especially characteristic of this tendency and contains explicit maxims:

> Так *мало* нынче в Ленинграде *греков*,
> да и вообще – вне *Греции* – их *мало*.
> По крайней мере, *мало* для того,
> чтоб *сохранить сооруженья веры*.
> А *верить* в то, что мы *сооружаем*
> от *них* никто не требует. Одно,
> должно быть, дело нацию *крестить*,
> а *крест* нести – уже совсем другое.
> У *них* одна обязанность была.
> *Они* её исполнить не сумели.
> Непаханное поле заросло.
> "Ты, сеятель, *храни свою соху*,
> А мы решим, когда нам колоситься".
> *Они свою соху не сохранили.*

There are so few Greeks in Leningrad nowadays, / and generally – outside of Greece there are very few. / At least, few for the purpose / of preserving the buildings of the faith. / But to believe in what we build / no one demands of them. It is one thing, / perhaps, to baptize a nation / – but to bear the cross – that's something completely different. / They had one duty only. / They were incapable of fulfilling it. / The unploughed field is overgrown with weeds. / 'Sower preserve your plough, / and we will decide when we are ready to reap.' / They did not preserve their plough.

The device of collocation of the concrete and abstract allows us to read the thrice-repeated complaint that 'there are so few Greeks' outside Greece as: there remain few propagators of the faith or guardians of it. The Greeks should have fulfilled the far-from-easy task of the ploughman, and not only that of the sower: according to the customs of Palestine the ploughing was done *after* the sowing. 'The unploughed field is overgrown with weeds' serves as a metaphor of substitution not only for ancient Russia, Christianized and then abandoned by the Greeks, but also for the whole contemporary world which has become overgrown with weeds. In the contemporary world, Christianity has lost its universal power which used to have the capability of subordinating all aspects of civilization to itself. It is no longer even capable of helping mankind

solve the problems of hunger, poverty, and work. It is precisely in
this context that the questions in the last stanza take on a profound
significance – questions that the reader himself is called upon to find
answers for. They are full of post-Christian tragic pathos and are
motivated by the artistic task of the entire poem:

> Сегодня ночью я смотрю в окно
> и думаю о том, куда зашли мы?
> И от чего мы больше далеки:
> от православья или эллинизма?
> К чему близки мы? *Что там, впереди?*
> Не ждёт ли нас теперь другая эра?
> И если так, то в чём наш общий долг?
> И что должны мы принести ей в жертву?

Tonight I gaze out of the window / and think, where have we got to? /
And which is further from us: / Orthodoxy or Hellenism? / What are
we close to? *What's there, up ahead?* / Doesn't a new age await us? /
And if that's so, then what is our common duty? / And what should
we sacrifice to it?

If, in the preceding stanza, the lyric 'I' was squeezed out by the
accusatory 'they', now in the last stanza it merges with the 'we'
which bears the responsibility. We all have the duty, without
deceiving ourselves, without flattering ourselves with the achievements of science, to give an honest evaluation of our age. In this
sense, the reference to Blok is highly significant, as he had asked
exactly the same question of himself on the border of a new era,
when he asked: 'What's up ahead?' in his revolutionary poem, 'The
Twelve'. And his answer surprised everyone: 'Ahead – is Jesus
Christ.' Less than half a century was needed for another Russian
poet to be bereft of Blok's certainty that, 'untouched by the bullet',
up ahead is Jesus Christ. It should be noted in passing, however,
that even Blok's contemporaries had lost his certainty. Vasily
Rozanov asked why Christianity had lost its central place in world
culture. Why had it turned out to be so limited that it was no longer
capable of answering

the most agonising questions of the intellect, the most legitimate demands
of life: and civilization is not so much hostile towards it, but rather has been
given the unexpected opportunity, the almost involuntary requirement to
regard it almost with sadness, with pity, as if it were a child, or, if you like,
an old man in his second childhood, who is no longer able to give advice, to
turn his children into adults, or even to understand properly their misfortunes, their needs . . .[19]

Those who write about Christianity today also talk of a profound crisis which not only Eastern, but also Western, Christianity is undergoing. In an epoch of 'neo-European civilization', laments Yevgeny Barabanov, 'neither science, nor philosophy, sociology or politics, nor art seems to need either the idea of a personal God, or religious beliefs'.[20]

But does the Church need politics, sociology, philosophy, and art? Does it even know them well? Brodsky has even accused Jesus himself of having small knowledge of the poets of his time:

The sad thing about Jesus Christ is that he never read the Latin poets. In theory, he should have known the language, since he lived in what was at that time the Roman Empire. So he had a chance. On the other hand, Pontius Pilate never read much poetry either. Had he done so, and had he read, in particular, Virgil's Eclogues (which were published a good seventy years before the events in Jerusalem), he'd surely have paid closer attention to the story Jesus was telling. Pilate might have recognized in the man brought before him somebody whose arrival was prophesied, as some scholars think, by Virgil in the Fourth Eclogue of his *Bucolics*. At any rate, the knowledge of this poem could have compounded Pilate's doubts enough to spare the man. Alternatively, Jesus, had he known the poem, could have built a better case for himself.[21]

Why does Brodsky ascribe to poetry such power and such responsibility? It comes from a profound conviction that the poet is merely an instrument of the language that is given to us all by someone who is greater than us, for the giver is always greater than his gift: 'What dictates a poem is the language, and this is the voice of the language, which we know under the nicknames of Muse or Inspiration' (*L.* 124–5). In a certain sense, the priest and the poet serve the same thing – God's Word. The only difference, possibly, is that the poet is harder on himself than the priest: he frankly confesses that:

Every writing career starts as a personal quest for sainthood, for self-betterment. Sooner or later, and as a rule quite soon, a man discovers that his pen accomplishes a lot more than his soul. This discovery very often creates an unbearable schism within an individual and is, in part, responsible for the demonic reputation literature enjoys in certain witless quarters. (*L.* 161)

The achievement of the pen, which metonymically represents language, is, of course, poetry. Has there perhaps fallen to its lot a kind of role of reconciliation between Christianity and culture? The poet never forgets that the Bible is the corner-stone of our civilization. For centuries it directed and corrected our culture. But a reciprocal dependence must also exist of religion *on* culture, in particular, on the concrete sphere of culture we are discussing here, namely poetry. Brodsky believes that 'poetry provides for a greater sense of infinity than any creed is capable of'.[22] That's why he regrets that Christianity was 'dismissive or ignorant of art that precedes' it. In his view, 'Christianity could have been a lot more triumphant, and less blood-stained, had it absorbed at the beginning the likes of Hesiod and Virgil'.[23] Does not some of this also apply to our age? Brodsky insists that 'At certain periods of history it is only poetry that is capable of dealing with reality by condensing it into something graspable, something that otherwise couldn't be retained by the mind' (*L*. 52). Poetry itself is treated by him as 'the closest possible interplay between ethics and aesthetics' (*L*. 99). The defence of the ethical aspect of culture is also conducted by Brodsky in unconventional ways. Alienated from the collective self-consciousness of the masses that is propagated over one sixth of the earth's land mass, he, naturally, lays the greatest stress on the spiritual autonomy of every individual and on self-perfection: 'I do not believe in political movements, I believe in personal movements, that movement of the soul when a man who looks at himself is so ashamed that he tries to make some sort of change - within himself, not on the outside.'[24] Any social or political movement removes the sense of personal responsibility for what has been done, instils in the individual a spurious confidence in protection, and thereby inflicts on man irremediable psychological and moral damage: 'Today, every new sociopolitical set-up, be it a democracy or an authoritarian regime, is a further departure from the spirit of individualism toward the stampede of the masses. The idea of one's existential uniqueness gets replaced by that of one's anonymity' (*L*. 115). Brodsky proposes that we re-examine traditional conceptions of good and evil. In our time, the poet asserts, evil is not only a moral, but also a physical and geographical category. Evil, according to him, 'always goes for big numbers, for confident granite, for ideological purity, for drilled armies and balance sheets' (*L*. 385). He has also suggested: 'subject your notion of good to the closest possible scrutiny' (*L*. 384). In the age of the 'triumph of vulgarity', of mass production, 'in the era of overpopulation, evil (as well as good) becomes as mediocre as its subjects' (*L*. 116). He proposes highly unorthodox methods of defence against evil: 'extreme individualism, originality of thinking, whimsicality, even – if you will – eccentricity. That is, something that can't be feigned, faked, imitated' (*L.* 385). These, at first sight, not entirely Christian qualities are dictated by humanity's experience of evil in the twentieth century, for which no parallels are to be found in the whole history of Christianity. Russia's experience, in particular, teaches us that we must seek a new mood of resistance. Nonviolent, or passive, resistance to evil is no longer capable of triumph: 'six decades of turning the other cheek transformed the face of the nation into one big bruise, so that the state today, weary of its violence, simply spits at that face' (*L.* 391). Cloaked in the same old ideas of equality, fraternity, and social justice, contemporary evil is sometimes indistinguishable from good in its old understanding. It is possible that Christ's teaching needs a new reading today: 'it seems to me, the twentieth century has exhausted the possibilities for salvation and come into conflict with the New Testament'.[25] Brodsky goes as far as stating that, in our age, after the absurd, 'Christ is not enough, Freud is not enough, Marx is not enough, nor is existentialism or Buddha. All of these are only means of justifying the holocaust, not of averting it. To avert it, mankind has nothing except the Ten Commandments, like it or not.'[26] And literature. Brodsky firmly believes in the ethical nature of literature. He declared that 'man is what he reads and poets even more so' (*L.* 58). He himself, beyond question, belongs to that category of people he calls *homo culturus* and who, in his opinion, 'help made it possible to survive in a world without consolation and without justification'.[27]

And here we must speak of yet one more aspect of world culture, which it is customary nowadays to call the intertextual. I have in mind the use of the texts of world culture by another poet in his own poetry. Russian poetry has always been full of references, resonances, and quotations from Western literature. We may evaluate this phenomenon as the inferiority complex of the Russian intelligentsia *vis-à-vis* the West, as an ineradicable necessity to prove to oneself and the world that Russia *is* a part of European culture: 'Out of this inferiority grew the ideal of a certain cultural unity "out there" and a subsequent intellectual voracity toward anything coming from that direction. This is, in a way, a Russian version of Hellenicism' (*L.* 130). It is possible to relate to this fact of 'dependence' on world culture entirely positively, as Likhachev does, for example, in claiming that 'the more "dependent" a culture is, the more independent it is'.[28] In his view, Russian culture has been lucky. As it was younger than its neighbouring cultures (European, Scandinavian, Byzantine), Russian culture was able 'to borrow much from them, yet remain itself'.[29] But there is also a deeper sense to the intertextual links of the poet. Each word, many images and motifs have their own cultural heritage:

No one absorbs the past as thoroughly as a poet, if only out of fear of inventing the already invented. (This is why, by the way, a poet is often regarded as being 'ahead of his time', which keeps itself busy rehashing clichés.) So no matter what a poet may plan to say, at the moment of speech he always knows that he inherits the subject. (L. 38)

The degree to which this entire heritage is realized depends on the cultural baggage of both the poet and his readers. In referring his readers to the texts of other authors, the poet, on the one hand, expresses his respect for them, but on the other, he reminds us that literature preserves the memory of man's spiritual experience. The 'maintenance of cultural continuity' is only one of the many functions of the poet's intertextual links. 'The other's word' in Brodsky, as Kreps has correctly observed, 'fulfils a variety of stylistic functions and cannot be reduced to any single dominating role – on each occasion we must speak of it separately.'[30] Kreps points to a multitude of examples of concealed quotation in Brodsky's poetry, from Dante, Shakespeare, Goethe, as well as from the Russian poets. Brodsky's encyclopaedic knowledge in the sphere of world culture does sometimes make his poetry too bookish and obscure for the average reader. His poetry demands the deciphering of historical, biblical, and mythological associations, the knowledge of what Mandelstam called in regard to Dante, 'the keyboard of references'.[31] It is Brodsky's conscious decision to keep up our cultural heritage as a living, active force in the contemporary world: 'I try to show ... how the classical heritage and the Judaeo-Christian ethic work in terms of poetry, because this is what we have to build on. It's a question of how a poet handles words and worlds.'[32] Culture, history, and myth also provide him with the depth of his focus. This quality, Brodsky argues, is essential if modern literature is to survive under totalitarian pressure. The only way to succeed, he suggests, is to 'develop density in direct proportion to the magnitude of that pressure' (L. 107). The density often emerges from the spiritual autonomy of the poet and his original thinking. He is capable of packing the most profound ideas about modern man into a single verse or a single image. Increasingly, his poetry acquires an extremely succinct nature and Brodsky is aware of this: 'A writer, however, is a democrat by definition, and the poet always hopes for some parallelism between the processes taking place in his own work and those in the consciousness of the reader. But the further a poet goes in his development, the greater – unintentionally – his demands are on an audience, and the narrower that audience' (L. 200). Democrat or aristocrat, Brodsky never takes a single step to meet his reader half-way, never simplifies his thoughts, for he respects him as an equal and always rewards the reader's endeavours.

The 'longing for world culture' has engendered in Brodsky's poetry the sort of qualities which enable him to resist at least two alien forces: topicality and vulgarity. On the former, Czesław Miłosz has warned the modern poets about the seductiveness of the burning topics of the day:

The modern age threatens him [a poet] with its noise of theories, intellectual fads, slogans appealing to his emotions, and novelties changing into clichés. By allowing himself to treat that noise too seriously, a poet risks forgetting that he is part of a tradition that lasted for thousands of years. If he forgets this tradition he is all the more likely to try to seduce his readers, offering them a false and distorted image of the present. A poet also risks being lured into serving the men who wield power. In resisting that temptation he will be helped by perceiving how miserable are their minds and how short-lived their schemes. They deserve their fate, which, after they have briefly thrashed about, is silence. So to use poetry to attack them is to do them too much honor.[33]

Brodsky understood this very early. According to Kheifets, even as a young man Brodsky declared: 'Why write about Soviet power, why should we? An insignificant moment in world history. Poetry must concern itself with more profound phenomena.'[34] Whether they be a mythological paradigm of love or a mythologization of time, these matters are older than any political system, and hence more important. Brodsky would also have agreed with Miłosz that 'a poet, before he is ready to confront ultimate questions, must observe a certain code. He should be God-fearing, love his country and his native tongue, rely upon his conscience, avoid alliances with evil, and be attached to tradition.'[35]

Brodsky's poetry, indeed, has immense breadth of cultural

resonances: Greek mythology ('Aeneas and Dido', 1967;' Odysseus to Telemachus', 1972); Old and New Testament ('Isaac and Abraham', 1963; 'Nunc Dimittis', 1972); and the classical world of Latin poets ('The Winter Eclogue', 1980). He has brought 'the nervous intellectual brio'[36] of seventeenth-century English metaphysical poets into a Russian context. Apart from Donne, Sidney Monas has noticed 'the occasional manner of Herbert and Vaughan'.[37] The presence of Samuel Beckett, T. S. Eliot, and W. H. Auden will be traced later. Beckett has had a very specific impact on Brodsky's poetics and *Weltanschauung*. This has not escaped the attention of scholars: 'He is increasingly concerned with culturological problems, haunted by a Beckett-like awareness of being overcome by wintry desolation against which human speech must be pitted as a token of survival.'[38]

Brodsky's Russian roots are fed by eighteenth-century poetry, primarily by Kantemir and Derzhavin. It would be more accurate to say that he has laid his hands upon the entire Russian cultural heritage, appropriated whatever interested him, and assimilated it into his style. In laying his road through the *taiga* of cultural possibilities, Brodsky, at first sight, has taken far from what is best, for which he is occasionally accused by the Russian reader: the bad taste of the 'sensual and the sensational' of Derzhavin; the unnecessary humility of the unlucky Baratynsky; and Pushkin's frivolity. The latter plays a prominent part in Brodsky's aesthetics, despite provocative remarks of the type: Baratynsky is no less a poet than Pushkin. This shocks Russian readers and admirers of Brodsky. In reality, for Brodsky Pushkin is just as much an ideal as he has been, and remains, for all Russian poets, without exception. The difference is that, unlike some of them, Brodsky has yet to succumb to the temptation of lapsing into Pushkinian simplicity, or of attempting Pushkin's clarity at any cost.

He has managed to comprehend the achievements and losses of the poetic schools from the early twentieth century. As Kreps has observed: 'in speaking of the influence of Russian poets, you are more certain whom to exclude than whom to include'.[39]

It is in the amalgamation of Russian and European cultures that Brodsky's service to Russian poetry is particularly hard to overestimate. He is widening the idiom and creating a new linguistic space for Russian poetry.

A modern descendant of Classicism

> In my opinion a regular metre and exact rhymes shaping an
> uncomfortable thought are far more functional than any form
> of free verse.[40]

Brodsky acknowledged his debt to Classicism in the middle of the
1960s, firstly by imitating the style of Kantemir (*O.* 130–1), then by
admitting: 'I am infected by routine classicism' (*O.* 142). Those
who took this declaration literally retorted categorically to the
poet: 'The one thing to which he bears no resemblance is classicism,
in the ranks of which the author numbers himself.'[41] That is not
quite fair. If we begin with Brodsky's central themes – time, faith,
language – which are classically supra-individual, the unshakeable
desire of the poet to get to the logical essence of things and
phenomena bears witness to the search for some kind of common
denominator. This, in turn, leads on to a cold rationalization of all
being. This quality was also characteristic of Classicism. And if we
do find in Brodsky's work stylistic traits from the Baroque, Romanticism ('To the aesthetics of a bygone century / my anapaests
correlating', (*C.* 21), and from Realism, it is none the less almost
impossible to fasten his poetic suit on all the buttons of past or
present '-isms'. Thus, the objective narrative tone which Brodsky
has created in transferring the English tendency to understatement
into the Russian language, with its inclination for dramatization,
does not mesh with Romanticism. Brodsky's lyric hero, who is
often shunted to the periphery, is not allowed to express sympathy
or emotional interest in what is happening. On the other hand,
even in Brodsky's most 'Classicist' works, we do not find a strict
correspondence between theme, genre, lexicon, and metre, that is,
all those components from which the harmony of Classicism is
formed. The nature of harmony in Brodsky's work is completely
different. It derives from a balance of opposites, whether they be
everyday reality and history, slang and archaisms, or the genre of a
sonnet, packed with the idiocies of émigré life. Brodsky has a clear
weakness for what is forbidden in classical poetics, namely, contrasting effects. In this he finds a source for the tension and energy
of his poetic tapestry. But all the same, for all his modernism,
Brodsky is the most traditional of contemporary Russian poets.
Czesław Miłosz has expressed a similar view: 'In syllables, feet,

rhyme, stanzas Brodsky follows a tradition, but not slavishly. The very nature of the Russian language seems to have determined a peculiar brand of modernism in our century: innovation within strict metrical patterns.'[42] Even such a characteristic feature of Classicism as relying on the 'classics' of ancient literature (which is where the name comes from) is functionally altered. He takes classical works not as models to be imitated, but uses them as a mask. Thus in the poem of 1967 'To Licomedes on Skyros', the myth of Theseus serves as a mask 'for the real situation of the lyric "I"', as has already been noted by Kees Verheul.[43] In 'Aeneas and Dido' (1969), a poem finely analysed by the same critic, Brodsky, following Akhmatova's example, employs a classical mask to describe relations between 'him' and 'her'. In other poems, classical motifs, classical characters, details of classical situations fulfil various poetic functions: *ostraneniye* ('making strange'), dramatization, composition:

In some cases the classical paraphernalia have a merely 'decorative' function, helping to establish a particular neo-classical quality. But when it really belongs to the essential aspects of the poetic structure, the classical background has a direct bearing on the presentation of the theme; it may be used either to give it a certain universality or put it in a special historical perspective.[44]

Such are Brodsky's poems 'Anno Domini' (1968) and 'Post aetatem nostram' (1970), about which more will be said in connection with the theme of 'Empire' and one of his central themes, 'after the end'. In both cases, the poet deviates from the concrete historical and national circumstances and lends the situation universality. The tracing of Brodsky's deviations from the tradition is the first task for the researcher, as it is precisely these deviations that his idiostyle consists of. A systematic analysis of these deviations allows us to discern at least two factors which push the poet towards a modernization of the tradition: the modern Russian language and the poetic system which he inherited.

In the history of the life of any language there comes a point when there is need of a poet who is capable of fixing the given state of the language in perfect poetic forms. In the past, this role has been played by such poets as Petrarch in Italy, Goethe in Germany, and Pushkin in Russia. The anonymous Soviet author of the article 'Pushkin and Brodsky' noted a decade ago a series of parallels in the fate and destiny of the two poets. Those who were indignant at such a blasphemous comparison overlooked the actual objective basis for such a parallel: 'the poetry of Pushkin (and of Brodsky) is, first and foremost, self-consciousness of the language – the colloquial, that is the personal language – and of the man (who appears as a mythical persona, surrounded by a polyvalent myth-in-life)'.[45] The foundations for comparing Brodsky with Pushkin are historical, and are not based on personality; they are functional, not emotional. It is by reason of Russia's 'imperfect history', also by Fate, and certainly because of Brodsky's phenomenal sensitivity towards language, that he has been assigned Pushkin's role of immortalizing the modern Russian language – with all the changes that have taken place since the Revolution – in the most stunning poetic forms, while permeating his poems with age-old human problems. It is precisely all that has happened to Brodsky that gives him the moral right (if a poet needs such a right), and the spiritual confidence to talk of what poets of all ages have talked about. Like Pushkin, he has succeeded in expressing man's fundamental drama in a very modern way by juxtaposing low and high, temporal and eternal, *byt* ('everyday life') and history. Like Pushkin, he is 'accused' of 'lexical promiscuity'.[46] He does, indeed, write 'in the language of his epoch', assimilating all the sub-systems of modern Russia: archaisms, dialects, prosaisms, expletives, foreign words, and ideological clichés.

According to Brodsky, 'a writer, willingly or unwillingly . . . simply serves the language: he is its instrument or rather a kind of accomplice of its development'.[47] Brodsky's observations on language are invaluable (and they have not as yet been fully evaluated) for an understanding of his poetics and his outlook. Whether he speaks of Platonov, Tsvetaeva, or Mandelstam, or of his contemporaries, he highlights language as the essence of what they are, what they are up to, and what has happened to them.

It is only natural that we should endeavour 'to master the language of the poet'.[48] But there is a more specific reason for concentrating on the poet's language. We will thereby be in a better position to resolve the problem of individual style *versus* tradition (which will, in turn, establish the poet's literary genesis), if we can find some objective factors which delimit the potentially arbitrary taste of a poet in the formation and development of his style. If such factors do exist, they are identified by the poet himself: they are the living native language and the poetic system he has inherited. The former demands of him an embodiment in the most perfect poetic form, since poetry is not only 'the best words in the best order';[49] 'for language it is the highest form of existence' (*L*. 186), while 'the poet is the one who masters language' (*L*. 127). The latter (the poetic system inherited by the poet) implies the need either to carry through its inherent potentialities or to renew it. 'Every author', writes Brodsky, 'expands upon – even by means of repudiating – the postulates, the idiom, the aesthetics of his predecessors' (*L*. 194). At the same time, poetic systems arise, stabilize, and function in constant interaction with the living language.

A third factor – the poet's view of the world – similarly depends on language:

I see it with my naked eye that what I am concerned with, to be more precise, what I put on paper, is to a large extent prompted by language rather than by my attitude to reality and that kind of thing. In this sense it may be said that being determines consciousness – not my being but the being of language itself.[50]

Such a degree of dependence on language was earlier typical perhaps of only two Russian poets – Khlebnikov and Tsvetaeva. Indeed, Brodsky's poetics show a greater stylistic affinity with them than with Mandelstam and Akhmatova. Like Khlebnikov, Brodsky makes language 'the principal hero'[51] of his poetry and the dominant force of his *Weltanschauung*. Like Tsvetaeva, he uses language to estrange himself from reality, from the text, 'from the self, from the thoughts of the self' (*L*. 219). It is significant that all three of them, despite their ultra-modernism, have a direct link with tradition.

To what extent is Brodsky's poetic style predetermined by certain evolutionary resources of existing poetic systems? Contrary to the common assumption, Brodsky can hardly be called the last Acmeist. By his own admission, 'Akhmatova has summed up the whole of Russian classical poetry'.[52] Although her influence had a profound psychological and personal effect, it did not dominate his style. Futurism, on the contrary, has never found its consummation, partially due to Khlebnikov's early death (1921), then Pasternak's and Mayakovsky's abandonment of it; but primarily because, in Pasternak's view, the Futurists halted mid-way, on 'the most promising ascent', and many wide-ranging notions, such as estrangement, remained largely untapped.[53] Losev has explained certain common features of Brodsky's and Mayakovsky's style – in particular, the mingling of high and low – by their common generic genesis (the eighteenth-century ode) and by the fact that their poetry is designed to be declaimed.[54] If we also take into account that their stylistic kinship is not limited to the features outlined above, but also extends to such characteristics as a penchant for compound rhymes, enjambement, inversion, the introduction to poetry of all the diversities of colloquial speech, then another explanation becomes necessary. It is especially important to discover it, because there are far more divergences between them than there are similarities:

A stranger to vain self-assertion, always standing alone, serving no-one, an outcast and an exile – Brodsky, according to all the indicators of his life and work, is more distinct from than close to Mayakovsky. Culture and revolution, the past and the future, the individual and the state, in the end simply good and evil – all these crucial universal concepts receive opposite treatments in the system of Brodsky and Mayakovsky.[55]

Karabchievsky sees the basis for similarities between the two poets in their creative method, in their means of perceiving the world and in its re-creation. Brodsky himself has spoken of his means of perceiving the world, regarding the very nature of the Russian language as the basis for this. In later chapters devoted to an investigation of Brodsky's tropes, we will have more to say in detail about his re-creation of the world, or, to be more precise, about his transformation of the real world into a poetic world. Karabchievsky has a somewhat narrow conception of Brodsky's creative method, limiting his discussion of it to the internal logic of the image, which is allegedly replaced in Brodsky's work by the 'external logic of the syntax'.[56] If we take into consideration the fact, noted by many investigators of the poetics of Futurism, that its inner possibilities for evolution were not exhausted,[57] then one is not at all compelled to regard Brodsky as a continuer of the work of Mayakovsky (in that he continues Khlebnikov's poetics to the same extent), or of that of Tsvetaeva, whose style affiliates her to the Futurists. She, incidentally, is also close to him in her perception of the world: 'My views of the world and history were thrust upon me by Tsvetaeva', Brodsky admits.[58] It is noteworthy that estrangement in particular – and Pasternak reproached the Futurists for not using this device sufficiently – was to the highest degree characteristic of Tsvetaeva's style and world-view. According to Brodsky's observations, estrangement in Tsvetaeva is 'at the same time both the method and the subject of the poem' (*L.* 221). In due course we will analyse the system of the imposition of the device of estrangement on the piercing lyricism of Brodsky himself. The poet's psychological portrait is more interesting when we discern that beneath the mask of deliberate iciness are concealed pain and orphanhood, that the supra-personal themes are almost always accompanied by the profoundly personal motif of undying love, either for a woman who has remained behind in Russia, or for abandoned Russia herself. In Brodsky's work, the device of estrangement, on the one hand, is summoned to support the quasi-classical objectivity of love, whereas on the other, it betrays the poet's emotional agitation. Rationalism proves to be powerless when confronted with the intense lyricism which keeps slipping from the poet's control. At the end of the second millennium of Christianity, we are not infrequently placed in the sort of situation to which we are not able to react adequately. Evil's inventiveness makes a mockery of any customary attempt to describe it. Encountering its multifarious manifestations, the poet more and more frequently recognizes that his ability is inferior to his experience.[59] Irony, sarcasm, cynicism, and indifference come into play. The cultural paradigm is at the poet's disposal. The contemporary world and personal experience, viewed through the prism of history, acquire the perspective of myth, and help us to find a feeling of distance from the overflowing present, to enclose it not only in cultural paradigms, but in classical forms as well. These last seem to discipline despair, ameliorate pain. This explains the poet's ascription of certain ethical qualities to classical verse: 'Apart from her metaphors, Russian poetry has set an example of moral purity and firmness, which to no small degree has been reflected in the preservation of so-called classical forms without any damage to content' (L. 142–3). Consequently, Brodsky insists on the retention of the structural elements of the verse in translation to another language, finding for this the highest justification by the spirit: 'It should be remembered that verse's metres in themselves are kinds of spiritual magnitudes for which nothing can be substituted. They cannot be replaced even by each other, let alone by free verse. Differences in metres are differences in breath and in heart-beat. Differences in rhyming pattern are those of brain functions' (L. 141).

Brodsky's own versification has been the object of detailed analysis by G. S. Smith and Barry P. Scherr.[60] Both note the poet's increasing tendency to reject certain customary requirements of

Russian versification. In his analysis of Brodsky's poem of 1982, 'Kellomiaki', Smith notes the occasional absence of the obligatory stressed syllable in the final ictus of the line, the irregular metrical length of the anacrusis, the extreme degree of degrammatization in rhyme, which is linked with the technique of the rhyme scheme. Smith concludes that 'Brodsky has created a rhythmic lexicon which deforms "normal" (that is, not metrically organized) speech far less than occurs elsewhere when more common rhymes are used in Russian poetry.'[61] Scherr, in investigating Brodsky's strophic forms, demonstrates his various deviations from the poetic norm he inherited. In twenty-five of Brodsky's sonnets, Scherr failed to find two with the same rhyme scheme. The originality of his hetero-strophics is accompanied, as a rule, by innovation in other structu-ral elements of the line. More and more often he gives preference to various types of *dol'nik*, which allows him significantly to lengthen his line. This striving to come as close as possible to prose, to colloquial speech, also leaves its traces on the structure of Brodsky's metaphors, which sometimes encompass several gram-matical sentences. Thanks to the fact that the contemporary Russian language allows a wide range of deviations from the norm, especially the weakening of syntactic dependence, Brodsky includes in his poetry instances of parataxis and inversion:

> И, глаза закатывая к потолку,
> я не слово о номер забыл говорю полку,
> но кайсацкое имя язык во рту
> шевелит в ночи, как ярлык в Орду.   (Ч. 79)

Rolling my eyes towards the ceiling, / I utter not the lay of – I've forgotten the number – (Igor's) Campaign, / but the tongue in my mouth / keeps stirring a Kaisak name in the night as a password to the Horde.

The second line is, in fact, a combination of these phenomena, which is complicated by the ambiguity of *slovo* in the sense of 'a word' and as the title of the twelfth-century masterpiece, *Slovo o polku Igoreve* ('Lay of Igor's Campaign'); *polk* in modern Russian means 'a regiment', hence its forgotten number.

It is precisely on the level of syntax, of this 'circulatory system of poetry'[62] which can so easily be struck by sclerosis, that Brodsky's innovations are especially significant. He uses ellipses, short nomi-native phrases alternating with cumbersome periods, which occupy an entire stanza. He makes ample use equally of the opportunities afforded by the subordinate clause, reflecting the reconstructions which have occurred in Russian in the system of compound constructions. And here he is the disciple not only of Tsvetaeva, but also of Dostoevsky, of whose syntax Brodsky has written in connection with the nature of the Russian language:

As intricacies go, this language, where nouns frequently find themselves sitting smugly at the very end of the sentence, whose main power lies not in the statement but in its subordinate clause, is extremely accommodating. This is not your analytical language of 'either/or' – this is the language of 'although'. Like a banknote into change, every stated idea instantly mushrooms in this language into its opposite, and there is nothing its syntax loves to couch more than doubt and self-depreciation. (*L.* 160)

Again and again, Brodsky places in direct interdependence the nature of a language and the spirit of a nation, a grammatical system and the national mentality, or more accurately, he seeks out such a dependence. And if you should happen to compliment Brodsky for a particularly successful phrase, image, choice of words, he will reply: 'There is no particular merit of mine here: all of this is in the Russian language itself.'

The systematic shattering of the classical norms extends to genres as well: narrative poems, elegies, sonnets. If the sonnets of the youthful Brodsky are nothing but copies of the traditional form, then any one of his 'Twenty Sonnets to Mary Stuart' (1974) is torn asunder from within. In tracing Brodsky's classical connections in formal terms, we uncover a paradox of sorts: the attempt to preserve the classical framework of the verse and the no less intense effort to go beyond this framework.

By way of example of Brodsky's 'classical' poetry, we may analyse his poem 'Nunc Dimittis' (1972). A great degree of stylistic unification is immediately obvious. This applies to the clearly worked-out rhythmic and phonetic organization of the poem, to the precise rhymes, and the system of tropes. The poem affects the style of the Gospel. The simple and elegant lexicon passes itself off as a direct quotation from the Gospel According to Luke:[63]

> А было поведано старцу сему
> о том, что увидит он смертную тьму
> не прежде, чем Сына увидит Господня.   (Ч. 20)

And it was revealed unto the sage / that he should not see the darkness of death / until he saw the Lord's Son.

Свершилось. И старец промолвил: "Сегодня,
реченное некогда слово храня,
Ты с миром, Господь, отпускаешь меня,
затем что глаза мои видели это
дитя: он – твоё продолженье и света
источник для идолов чтящих племён,
и слава Израиля в нём". – Симеон
умолкнул. Их всех тишина обступила.
Лишь эхо тех слов, задевая стропила,
кружилось какое-то время спустя
над их головами, слегка шелестя
под сводами храма, как некая птица,
что в силах взлететь, но не в силах спуститься.   (Ч. 21)

It came to pass. And the sage said, 'Today, // keeping your word,
spoken long since, / Thou lettest me depart in peace, lord, / for mine
eyes have beheld this / Child – Thy successor and a source of // light
unto those tribes which worship idols / and the glory of Israel is in
him.' Simeon / fell silent. Silence enclosed them all. / Only the echo
of those words, brushing against the rafters // circled for some time
afterwards / above their heads, gently rustling / beneath the arches of
the temple, like some bird, / strong enough to fly off, but not strong
enough to descend.

The smooth syntactic periods recall the impeccable metre of
Akhmatova's 'Rachel' and 'Lot's Wife', as well as Pasternak's
poem 'Christmas Star'. The amphibrachic tetrameter with its
rhyme scheme *aaBB* creates a classical framework, beyond which
the poet occasionally glances. In almost every one of the eighteen
stanzas, we come across breaks in the syntactic unit caused by the
end of a line. In the first stanza, *внесла* ('carried in') / *дитя*
('child'); *из числа* ('of those few') / *людей* ('people'); in the
second, *из рук* ('out of the hands') / *Марии* ('of Mary'); *вокруг*
('around') / *младенца* ('the child'), and so on. Even more noticeable are the enjambements which occupy the ends of stanzas 5 and
6 – *сегодня* ('today'), / *реченное некогда слово* ('the word
that was once spoken'); 6 and 7 – *и света* ('and of light') /
источник ('source'); 10 and 11 – *которым* ('which') / *терзаема
плоть его будет* ('his flesh will be torn'); 12 and 13 – *и в теле*
('and in the body') / *для двух этих женщин* ('for these two
women'); 14 and 15 – *а Бога* ('and God') / *пророчица славить
уже начала* ('the prophetess has already begun to glorify'). Such a
number of enjambements disturbs the rhythmical harmony of the
classical metre, but it also creates dazzling balance and tension. The

semantic function of these enjambements is to emphasize the pain of severance, the separation of the infant Christ from God, of Simeon from those who remain alive, the disputes among people:

И старец сказал, повернувшись к Марии:
"В лежащем сейчас на раменах твоих
паденье одних, возвышенье других,
предмет пререканий и повод к раздорам.
И тем же оружьем, Мария, которым
терзаема плоть его будет, твоя
душа будет ранена. Рана сия
даст видеть тебе, что сокрыто глубоко
в сердцах человеков, как некое око."

And the sage said, turning to Maria, // 'In him who lies now upon your shoulders / is the fall of some, the rise of others, / the objects of arguments, and a cause of discord. // And with those same weapons, Mary, with which / his flesh will be torn, your / soul shall be pierced. This wound / will reveal unto you, like unto an eye, / what is deep in the hearts of men.'

The fissure which runs through the closest semantic units, *это* ('this') / *дитя* ('child'); *твоя* ('your') / *душа* ('soul'), is compensated for by the paired rhymes which form new semantic units, emphasizing the central thoughts of the poem: *Анна* ('Anna') – *постоянно* ('constantly'), *Господня* ('Lord's') – *сегодня* ('today'), *храня* ('preserving') – *меня* ('me'), *глубоко* ('profoundly') – *око* ('eye'). These are a kind of rhyme-metaphor. This has been noticed by Irene Steckler who called them 'philosophical puns': '*Anna-postoyanno* functions as a philosophical pun. In this one rhyme Brodsky has compressed the biblical references to the prophetess Anna's essential attributes – her constancy, dedication, and faithfulness.'[64] Whereas the rhyme *Gospodnia–segodnia*, in Steckler's view, has several meanings: 'this is the day when the Son of God is presented to God; this is the day when God's promise to Simeon is fulfilled; this is the day when God's promise to mankind of a Redeemer is also fulfilled'.[65]

The free syntax which slips beyond the framework of the standard metre is also compensated for by the harmony of the vowels. For example, in the fourth stanza the dream of the infant Christ is accompanied by a repetition of a stressed 'o' in all four rhymes: *лучом* ('ray') – *ни о чём* ('about nothing') – *сонно* ('sleepily') – *Симеона* ('Simeon'). And in the thirteenth stanza

Simeon goes to his death accompanied by this same plaintive sound: *колонн* ('columns') – *он* ('he') – *пустому* ('empty') – *проёму* ('aperture'). If in the fourth stanza the sound 'o' symbolizes oblivion that *still* pertains (the dream of a child), then in the thirteenth it is oblivion (Simeon's death) that has *already* happened. In both instances, the assonances are orientated towards the name of Simeon, which is emphasized phonetically and lexically by the opening words of the lines of the sixteenth stanza:

> *Он* шёл умирать. И не в уличный гул
> *он*, дверь отворивши руками, шагнул,
> *но* в глухонемые владения смерти.
> *Он* шёл по пространству, лишённому тверли,
>
> *он* слышал, что время утратило звук.

He walked off to die. And not into the roar of the streets/ did he walk, flinging wide the door with his arms, / but into the deaf-mute domain of death. / He walked through a space which lacks solidity. // He heard that time had lost its sound.

The rhymes on stressed 'u', *гул* ('roar') – *шагнул* ('walk') are supported by assonances within the line: *умирать* ('to die'), *уличный* ('of the streets'), *руками* ('arms'), *глухонемые* ('deaf-mute'), *по пространству* ('through a space'), *лишённому* ('lacks'), and signal the erasure of boundaries (which are always fragile in Brodsky) between life and death. This tendency is also illustrated by the phonetic-lexical inversion: *он* ('he') – *но* ('but') in the initial position. However, assonances orientated to the name Anna dominate: the poem contains eighty-nine stressed 'a' sounds, as opposed to twenty-one stressed on 'u'. The open rhymes on the 'a' sound accompany the voice of the prophetess and the presence of Mary: *внесла* ('carried in') – *из числа* ('out of the number'), *рама* ('framework') – *храма* ('temple'), *началá* ('began') – *чела* ('brow'), *упрямо* ('stubbornly') – *храма* ('temple'). Simeon's path to the light is also illuminated by this very same sound. The sounds 'o' and 'a' are repeated in different variants and with varying frequency in all stanzas, at times squeezing out all other vocalic elements. The last stanza sees the entrance of the sound 'u', which bears the din of the street and the noise of time: it never leaves the poem.

> И образ младенца с сияньем вокруг
> пушистого темени смертной тропою
> душа Симеона несла пред собою,

как некий светильник, в ту чёрную тьму,
в которой дотоле ещё никому
дорогу себе озарять не случалось.
        Светильник светил, и тропа расширялась.

And the image of the infant with its radiance / of downy hair
Simeon's soul carried before it / along the deathward path // like
some lantern, in that pitch black / into which, till then no one had
self-illuminated gone. / The lantern shone and the path widened.

Amongst the consonantal elements, distributional figures are
formed by the liquids *p* and *л*, which represent simultaneously the
tragedy of death and love: the meeting between Simeon and Christ
before death symbolizes the bridge between the Old and the New
Testaments. As Brodsky explained: 'the image of Christ lights up
what has hitherto been hidden in darkness, in non-being'.[66]

In this poem Brodsky uses tropes extremely economically. There
are a few metaphors and almost all of them fulfil the traditional
function of spiritualization: *silence encompassed them all*; *your soul
will be pierced*; *this wound will let you see*. Even a metaphor-copula
does not draw attention to itself, as it is a paraphrase from the
Gospel: *He is your continuation and the source of light*. The similes
are more interesting. Amongst these we find a preponderance of
grammatical constructions with the conjunction *как* ('as' / 'like'). In
the first, man is compared with inanimate objects: *and three people
stood around the infant, like a fragile frame, on that morning, lost in
the gloom of the temple*. The temple itself is likened to nature: *The
temple enclosed them like a frozen forest. From the stares of the
people, and from the eye of the heavens the tops of the trees hid
Mary, the prophetess, the sage, by being able to hug the ground that
morning*. The comparison between Simeon's speech and the
strange bird that can fly up but is unable to descend is reminiscent of
the central image from 'Elegy for John Donne' of the bird-soul and
bird-word. In the essay on Tsvetaeva, language is likened to a bird:
'it is language's striving upward – or sideways – to that beginning
where the Word was' (*L.* 186). In these three comparisons the
whole world is encompassed: things, nature, man and Spirit (God's
temple and God's word). The other similes merely lend precision to
the separate sides of this square: *Silence was no less strange than
speech*. It is usually the case in Brodsky that silence is associated
with the 'deaf-mute domain of death'. Simeon's death is unusual in
that it is the first Christian death. The speech of Simeon, who has

fallen silent forever, will become the popular canticle, Nunc
Dimittis: 'The uniqueness of Simeon's "Nunc Dimittis"', states
Brodsky, 'lies in the fact that what one man says at a shattering
moment of his life becomes universal, becomes a prayer on the lips
of all men.'[67]

In the accepted traditions, the lexicon and rhetorical figures are
restrained. The Gospel text needs neither decoration nor a particular semantic reconstruction. The range of epithets is severely
limited: 'a chance ray', 'a fatal path'. They are not especially
striking and are almost tautological: 'black darkness', 'mortal
darkness', 'the deaf-mute domain of death'. Others belong to the
semantic field of indefiniteness, imprecision: 'unsteady frame', 'to
the dimly whitening opening of the door', 'through a space which
lacks solidity'. The thrice-repeated indefinite pronoun, некий ('a
certain bird', 'a certain eye', 'a certain lamp'), thickens the atmosphere of the miracle of the meeting. In this way, all the elements of
the poem are strictly controlled to preserve the maximum proximity to the text of Luke's Gospel. This is especially noteworthy
inasmuch as, in most of his other poems, Brodsky does not succeed
in hiding his technique beneath a veil of artlessness. Or else he
doesn't try to. Like Mandelstam, he has 'discovered a way to be a
"classic" while at the same time approaching very closely to
Futurist principles'.[68] His over-bookishness is compensated for by
the surplus of his democratic vocabulary. In allowing the banality of
everyday existence into his poetry, Brodsky neutralizes it by his
technical virtuosity. 'A democratisation of the poetic language',
writes D. S., 'as a rule, accompanied by aristocratic form.'[69]

The disharmony and its neutralization are also realized on the
level of content: youth and age, birth and death are reconciled in
the poem. 'Meeting' is both a beginning and an end. 'What is
central in the poem', Brodsky explains, 'is the relation between the
old man and the baby, between the end and the beginning of life'.[70]

The elimination or softening of contradictions, as will be further
demonstrated, is a characteristic feature of Brodsky's poetics. We
have here yet another parallel between his aesthetics and Pushkin's, whose harmony, according to Yury Mann, is shot through
with disharmony: 'Pushkin was able to broaden the horizon of his
sympathies to take in all that exists . . . disharmony exists for him as
none other than a part of the whole.'[71]

The philosophical consciousness of the poet suggests to him the idea of reconciliation. For Brodsky, in the poem analysed above, it is the synthesis of the Old and New Testaments. In his interpretation of culture and art, this is a synthesis of Classicism and Modernism.

Pushkin did not arrest the swings of the pendulum, according to Mann; he did not project identity. But he spoke of his own times with the sort of pitiless truth that is accessible only to the great. Equally, one cannot refuse Brodsky the claim to pitiless sincerity. As Losev has put it: 'the more often he [Brodsky] tests himself, his Muse and his God, the more living is his connection with faith'.[72]

It is significant that in one of Brodsky's early poems, 'Zofya' (1962), the central image is the pendulum:

Ты маятник, душа твоя чиста,
ты маятник от яслей до креста,

ты маятник от света и во мрак,

Ты маятник, как маятник я сам,
ты маятник по дням и по часам.

You are a pendulum, your soul is pure.
You are a pendulum from cradle to grave,
... you are a pendulum in light and in dark.
... you are a pendulum, as I am myself,
You are a pendulum by day and by hour ...

The insistent repetition of the lexicon, the grammatically identical metaphor and simile constructions, seem to imitate the movement of the very pendulum, this metonymic representative of time. The comparison of the poet himself with the monotonous function of the pendulum points to his eternal role of balancing antinomies, competing with time itself. The antinomies of being cannot be eradicated, they are primordial and eternal.

Elegies to the admired dead: John Donne, T. S. Eliot, W. H. Auden

All I hope for while writing in his tongue is that I won't lower his level of mental operation, his plane of regard. This is as much as one can do for a better man: to continue in his vein; this, I think, is what civilizations are all about.[73]

From all Brodsky's elegies, only three will be examined in this section: 'Great Elegy to John Donne'; 'Verses on the Death of

T. S. Eliot'; and 'York: To the Memory of Auden'. We cannot
trace the evolution of the genre as profoundly as it deserves here,
from its origins in the eighth century BC. Instead, we will concen-
trate on the elements of intertextuality that link Brodsky's elegies
with the aesthetics and poetics of Donne, Eliot, and Auden.

Although all of these elegies were written on the occasion of the
death of a poet, they are thematically much broader than the
tradition of this genre allows. Originating in the Greek word
elegeia, from *elegos* ('lament'), this genre was defined even in
Greek literature not merely in terms of theme, but form as well: the
hexameter was accompanied by a line of pentameter. Latin poets
defined the elegy by means of the metre, which had been consoli-
dated for it, and by its subject – the amorous complaint. In the
sixteenth century, Tasso and Ariosto wrote elegies that were
contained within a specific rhyme scheme which they borrowed
from Dante (iambic tercets rhyming *aba bcb . . . xyx y*). Boccaccio
and Petrarch often used *terza rima*. The French elegy of the
sixteenth century, copied from the Italian, was written in alexan-
drines, with a caesura after the third foot and alternating masculine
and feminine rhymes. In England, elegies appeared in the sixteenth
century, and thanks to Donne's 'A Funeral Elegy' (*An Anatomy of
the World*, 1611), the genre became associated with the dirge.
However, in his twenty elegies Donne renewed the genre, bringing
it as close as possible to the love lyric accompanied by philosophical
meditations. Formally, his elegies (except for the tenth) are constructed on the principle of the dystich, which is varied within the
boundaries of one and the same metre, and accords with the
rhythm of thought rather than with the measure. In conjunction
with his 'tortured syntax', Donne achieved a refined plasticity in his
elegies. In the eighteenth century, in the age of Classicism, the
elegy was demoted to the most modest of places by the other
genres. Greater precision in structural organization was required of
it, and more frequent reference to the canon, albeit metonymically,
by including names from antiquity. On the other hand, Romanticism saw the flourishing of the elegy: it proved the most suitable
genre to explore the human soul. In Russian poetry the best
examples were written by Zhukovsky, Batiushkov, Pushkin, and
Baratynsky. The common themes of these elegies were dissatis-
faction with life, complaints against solitude, the infidelity of a
mistress, grief over hopes destroyed.

In his early elegies, Brodsky is closest to Baratynsky. From him
he borrowed a meditative style and the ability to counterbalance
the emotional state of the soul with reason. In rejecting the elegy's
usual complaints and mannerisms, Brodsky develops it into the
genre of elegy-meditation. Philosophical questions concerning the
meaning of life are interwoven with religious metaphysics, the
teleology of language, and historico-cultural problems. Gradually
he removes personal lyricism to the periphery. The degree to which
philosophical speculation grows and the emotional field is nar-
rowed – that is, a change in the *dominanta* – may be traced in the
elegies considered below. Self-reflexion gives way to analysis of the
very phenomenon of language and poetry. Alienation is transferred into the sphere of the most inalienable categories of the 'I';
intimacy is replaced by abstraction. All this leads to an erosion of
the traditional markers of the elegy.

'The Great Elegy to John Donne' (1963) was written before
Brodsky seriously set about the task of translating the English
metaphysicals.[74] And it is significant that in the 'Great Elegy',
though written in iambic pentameters, with alternating masculine
and feminine rhymes, Brodsky forces the Russian language to
surpass itself. He succeeds in accommodating as many as nine or
ten monosyllabic and bisyllabic words in one line. According to
Yury Ivask's calculations, 75 per cent of all the lines in the 'Elegy'
retain all five stresses;[75] that is, pyrrhics, which are so typical of this
metre, are avoided. This is how the 'Elegy' begins:

> Джон Донн уснул, уснуло всё вокруг.
> Уснули стены, пол, постель, картины,
> уснули стол, ковры, засовы, крюк,
> весь гардероб, буфет, свеча, гардины.   (*C.* 130)

John Donne fell asleep, sleep reigned all around. / Walls, floor, bed,
pictures fell sleep, / table, carpets, bolts, hook – all fell asleep, / the
whole wardrobe, sideboard, candle, curtains.

The complete absence of polysyllabic adjectives and the domination by substantives makes the poem dense, approximating
Donne's 'strong line'. Moreover, in Ivask's view, 'the abundance of
spondees [two consecutive stresses] in Brodsky's "Elegy" brings
the Russian close to the English'.[76] Brodsky has dared to use the
verb *спать* ('to sleep') about a hundred times, as well as deri-
vations from the same root: *уснул* ('fell asleep') and *сон*

('sleep'), alternating their literal and transferred senses.[77] He has thereby made this routine verbal metaphor the compositional framework of the entire elegy. Moving upwards in ever-increasing circles, in imitation of a bird's flight or the ascent of the soul, Brodsky, in a single spreading metaphor, encompasses concrete things, natural phenomena, abstract concepts, creativity and the Spirit, in the form of a multiplicity of subjects from Donne's poetic world. Simultaneously, he rehearses in a schematic form both the major turning-points of Donne's personal life and the evolution of his poetics. From the dissipation of the passions and daring wit to the asceticism of the preacher, from the concrete multiplicity of the material world to complex metaphysical abstractions – this is the range encompassed by the sweeping cycles of Donne's life and creative work.

According to the author's commentary, the composition of the 'Elegy' was suggested by biographical facts from Donne's life: 'The position of a poet in St Paul's with its rotunda, in England – an island – gave me a terrific sense of a kind of circular expansion.'[78] It is significant that the device of the repetition of such key words as 'man', 'world', 'life', 'sun', and, especially, 'soul' is very noticeable in Donne's 'Of the Progress of the Soul'. We see the idea of the circle there too:

> She, who by making full perfection grow,
> Pieces a circle, and still keeps it so.

The starting-point of the first circle is to be found in Donne's home, the centre of his intimate, carnal world:

> Повсюду ночь: в углах, в глазах, в белье,
> среди бумаг, в столе, в готовой речи,
> в её словах, в дровах, в щипцах, в угле
> остывшего камина, в каждой вещи.

Everywhere night: in corners, in eyes, in the linen, / amidst papers, in the desk, in the ready speech, / in its words, in the firewood, in the gables, in the ingle / of the cold fireplace, in every thing.

This circle widens gradually and naturally. Glancing out of the window we see the sleeping snow, 'the white slope of a neighbour's roof. Its ridge is like a tablecloth. And the whole district is asleep.' As we go outside we enter a sleeping world of arches, railings, flower beds. 'Nowhere can be heard a whisper, a rustle, a knock.

Only the snow crunches. Everything sleeps. Dawn is far off.'
Despite a continuing description of the earthly world, to take in the
sleeping prisons and castles, it becomes necessary to become like a
bird and rise up above the poet's city. 'Mice, people sleep. London
sleeps soundly. A sailing ship sleeps in port. Water and snow
beneath its hull whistle in sleep, merging in the distance with the
sleeping sky.' As we proceed, we rise to a height from which we can
take in the whole sleeping island, enveloped in a single sleep:

> Уснуло всё. Спят реки, горы, лес.
> Спят звери, птицы, мёртвый мир, живое.
> Лишь белый снег летит с ночных небес.

Everything has fallen asleep. Rivers, mountains, forest sleep. /
Beasts, birds, the dead world and the living sleep. / Only white snow
flies from the night skies.

This refrain acquires the piercing tone of a dirge when we come to
the description of the sleeping heavens. This is the third circle,
which the bird may not enter:

> Спят ангелы. Тревожный мир забыт
> во сне святыми – к их стыду святому.
>
> Господь уснул. Земля сейчас чужда.
> Глаза не видят, слух не внемлет боле.

The angels sleep. The troubled world is forgotten / in dreams by the
saints – to their holy shame. // The Lord has fallen asleep. The Earth
is now alien. / Eyes do not see, ears no longer hear.

The traditional verbal metaphor of personification, 'sleeps', slips
imperceptibly into a metaphor of substitution: sleep = death.

> Все крепко спят: святые, дьявол, Бог.
> Их слуги злые. Их друзья. Их дети.
> *И только снег шуршит во тьме дорог.*
> И больше звуков нет на целом свете.

All sleep soundly: the saints, the devil, God. / Their evil servants.
Their friends, their children, / *And only the snow rustles in the
darkness of the road.* / And there are no other sounds in the entire
world.

The snow weaves a white shroud of death, which is simultaneously
something new between the soul and the sleeping body. The
appearance of the poet's soul in the 'Elegy' is presented in

semi-detective terms. Into this 'deaf-mute domain' of sleep =
death, on a fine, piercing note, bursts someone's voice, lamenting
the death of a poet-priest:

> Но, чу! Ты слышишь – там в холодной тьме,
> там *кто-то* плачет, *кто-то* шепчет в страхе.
> Там *кто-то* предоставлен всей зиме.
> И плачет он. Там *кто-то* есть во мраке.

But, hark! You hear – there in the cold darkness, / there, someone is
crying, someone is whispering in terror. / There, someone has been
left alone to face winter's all. / And he is crying. There is someone
there, in the darkness.

These are not the cherubim of St Paul's, nor Paul himself, nor the
Archangel Gabriel, nor even the Lord himself. The lamenter gives
the answer himself:

> "Нет, это я, твоя душа, Джон Донн.
> Здесь я одна скорблю в небесной выси
> о том, что создала своим трудом
> *тяжёлые, как цепи, чувства, мысли.*
> Ты с *этим грузом* мог вершить полёт
> среди страстей, среди грехов, и выше.
> Ты птицей был и видел свой народ.

No, it is I, your soul, John Donne. / Here I alone grieve, upon
heaven's heights, / because I created by my own effort, / *feelings,
thoughts, heavy, as chains.* / You, *with that burden*, could continue
the flight / midst passions, midst sins, and go higher. / You were a
bird and saw your own nations.

This third centre of the metaphysical circle of the poet's world
completes the classical triad, 'thing–man–Spirit'. However,
Brodsky complicates the usual scheme of the world by introducing
the poetic word into this scheme. As early as the first refrain at the
beginning of the 'Elegy', lines, rhymes, and images from Donne's
poetry appear alongside things:

> Джон Донн уснул. Уснули, спят *стихи.*
> Все образы, все рифмы. Сильных, слабых
> найти нельзя. Порок, тоска, *грехи,*
> равно *тихи,* лежат в своих силлабах.

John Donne has fallen asleep. They have fallen asleep, they sleep,
his verses. / All the images, all the rhymes. Strong, weak, /

impossible to tell. Vice, anguish, sins / are equally quiet, they lie in their syllabaries.

From the concrete material world of the first part of the 'elegy' – which had nurtured the 'poetry-sins' of Donne – and set off by the internal rhyme *тихи* ('quiet'), we switch to a new circle, an intermediate one, linked simultaneously with both the material and spiritual worlds; a circle of creativity, animated by predicative metaphors and comparisons with man:

> *И каждый стих с другим,* как близкий брат,
> хоть шепчет другу друг: *чуть-чуть подвинься.*
> Но каждый так далёк от райских врат,
> так *беден,* густ, так *чист,* что в них – единство.

And every verse with the other, like the close brother, / *whisper to each other: move a little.* / But each [of them] is so far from heaven's gates, / so *poor,* so dense, so *pure* – that in them is a unity.

The idea of 'unity' ('in them is a unity') is further developed by abolishing contradictions, by means of encompassing, still with the same metaphor of sleep, not only objects but abstract categories as well: fame, misfortune, vice – good and evil intertwined. This device of unifying heterogeneous things and concepts by a chain of subjects and objects for one predicate was also a characteristic of the poetics of the metaphysicals. What is new, and uncharacteristic of Donne but highly typical for Brodsky, is the new type of transformation of the sense in the tropes: from things, to man, to his creative and spiritual sphere. Thus, the modest metaphor of substitution, *with this burden,* which may be elucidated by a comparison between Donne's thoughts and feelings and heavy chains, reifies them. The same function is fulfilled by the genitive metaphors, *Covered with the ice of oblivion, the rivers of words sleep, straining in the fear of the thickets,* in which memory, poetry and feelings are reified. But in this 'Elegy' such metaphors are rare; for the moment they merely hint at the incompleteness of the classical triad 'thing–man–Spirit'. The fourth element, 'word', will be introduced by Brodsky only later on, and will expand the triangle into a square. Appearing in the 'Elegy' in the form of self-description, the 'word' as yet does not represent all of language, but only poetry:

> Все строки спят. Спит ямбов строгий свод.
> Хореи спят, как стражи, слева, справа.

И спит виденье в них летейских вод.
И крепко спит за ним другое – слава.

All lines sleep. An austere arch of iambs sleeps. / The trochees sleep like guards, to the left, to the right. / And within them sleeps the vision of the waters of Lethe. / And beyond them soundly sleeps another vision – fame.

The poetic word, subjected simultaneously to a transformation in two directions (it is endowed with human qualities, *whisper*, and the qualities of things, *arch of iambs*, *river of words*), acquires unique qualities, being identified with the poet:

Ты видел все моря, весь дальний край.
И Ад ты зрел – в себе, а после – в яви.
Ты видел также явно светлый Рай
в печальнейшей – из всех страстей – оправе.
Ты видел: жизнь, она как остров твой.
И с Океаном этим ты встречался:
со всех сторон лишь тьма, лишь тьма и вой.
Ты Бога облетел и вспять помчался.

You saw the seven seas, the furthest-flung of lands. / And Hell you gazed upon, in yourself, and later – in reality. / You also saw radiant Paradise / in the most melancholy setting, that of all the Passions. / You saw life: she is like your island. / And you encountered that Ocean: / on all sides just darkness, just darkness and howling. / You flew round God and hastened back.

The Donne-like, daring, *you flew round God* is motivated precisely by the *all-seeing eye of words* (a metaphor from one of Brodsky's later poems). Only the poetic word is capable of simultaneously encompassing both Heaven and Hell, being a non-being (substituted for by the metaphor of the ocean) in the vain attempt to reconcile them.

We should also note that in the 'Elegy' there are no colours other than black and white, except for the *grey crowd of empty nesting boxes*, a metaphor for the philistines who have surrounded the poet from time immemorial. This contrast between black and white is repeated no less insistently than the lullaby to the world that has gone to sleep in honour of the death of the poet. However, if white is designated directly, or given in adjectival synonyms as a property of people and things – *the white slope of the roof*, *the chalk bank*, *white snow*, *the grey head of St Paul;* – then black is exclusively represented by substitutions: *night, darkness, gloom, murk*. We are given the impression that, while God and the poet-priest slept, the world was submerged in primordial darkness. And this is why the attempted reconciliation of the eternal antinomies of darkness and light, life and death, faith and lack of faith falls to the lot of the poetic word. On the other hand, however, the illusory nature of abolishing these fundamental oppositions is expressed in the question which has no answer:

> Ведь если можно с кем-то жизнь делить,
> то кто же с нами нашу смерть разделит?

It may indeed be possible to share our life with someone, / but who will share our death with us?

Apart from the references to Donne's poetry that we have noted, the 'Elegy' also contains self-references. For example, the image of bird-soul first appeared in a poem of 1961:

> Скажи, душа, как выглядела жизнь,
> как выглядела с птичьего полёта?   (*C.* 62)

Tell me soul, how life looks, / how does it look from a bird's point of view?

The motif, *the snow of non-being*, from the same youthful poem is verified in the 'Elegy', while the verbal metaphor *to sew* goes back to the *poema* of 1961, "Шествие" ('The Procession'): *And to sew one's life to a new life*. In the 'Elegy' other metaphors grew out of this one: 'needle', 'white shroud', 'cloth', 'tailor', 'kaftan'. Snow fulfils the role of the needle: *flies into the darkness, not melting / sewing here our parting, the snow, / and back and forth the needle, the needle flies*. The white shroud under which Donne lies is sewn by snow and sleep. The cloth which covers the space *between the soul and the sleeping body*, unites, in this way, the age-long antinomies of being: life and death, the heavens and earth, light and darkness, *sewing the night to dawn*. In this metaphor of *cloth*, we are entitled to see the poet's attempt to reconcile oppositions. However, the last lines of the 'Elegy' reveal how well Brodsky understands that such a reconciliation is unstable and temporary:

> Дыра в сей ткани. Всяк, кто хочет, рвёт.
> Со всех концов. Уйдёт. Вернётся снова.
> Ещё рывок! И только небосвод
> во мраке иногда берёт иглу портного.

Спи, спи, Джон Донн. Усни, себя не мучь.
Кафтан дыряв, дыряв. Висит уныло.
Того гляди и выглянет из туч
Звезда, что столько лет твой мир хранила.

There is a hole in this fabric. Everyone who wants to can rip it. /
From every edge. He'd be gone. He'd return. / Another jerk! And
only heaven's vault / in the gloom sometimes takes up the tailor's
needle. / Sleep, sleep, John Donne. Go to sleep, don't torment yourself. / The robe is full of holes, full of holes. It hangs despondently.
/ It looks as if the star that so many years guarded / your world
will appear out of the clouds.

It is significant that Donne himself saw his soul as suffering, but in
'The Progress of the Soul' he depicted it more in the style of
medieval superstitions than in the spirit of the Christian myth
concerning the soul, as Brodsky has done.

Under the 'Verses on the Death of T. S. Eliot' stands a precise
date: 12 January 1965. T. S. Eliot died on 4 January 1965. At this
time, Brodsky was in exile in Norinskaya and found out about the
poet's death from friends who wrote to him, sent him books, and
even occasionally visited him. Amongst these books was an anthology of English poetry, including Auden's elegy, 'In Memory of
W. B. Yeats' (1939). From the author's commentary below, it
becomes clear why 'Verses on the Death of T. S. Eliot' are oriented
not only to Eliot's texts, but to Auden's elegy as well:

I was young then and therefore particularly keen on elegies as a genre . . .
So I read them perhaps more avidly than anything else, and I frequently
thought that the most interesting feature of the genre was the authors'
unwitting attempts at self-portrayal with which nearly every poem 'in
memoriam' is strewn – or soiled. Understandable though this tendency is,
it often turns such a poem into the author's rumination on the subject of
death, from which we learn more about him than about the deceased. The
Auden poem had none of this; what's more, I soon realized that even its
structure was designed to pay tribute to the dead poet, imitating in reverse
order the great Irishman's own modes of stylistic development, all the way
down to his earliest: the tetrameters of the poem's third – last – part.
(*L*. 361–2)

Brodsky's own elegy, therefore, is consciously constructed on
the model of Auden's, although, of course, with certain deviations.
The first part consists of five uniform eight-line stanzas written in
iambic pentameter with the rhyme scheme *AAAbBBBb*. In the

second half, the metre is preserved and transferred to sonnet form, now rhyming *AbbAAbbAccDDee*. As in the Auden original, the metre changes in the third part into trochaic tetrameter with paired masculine rhymes, *aabb*. The metrical form that Brodsky borrowed from Auden is reinforced by substantive references: time, the poet, poetry, language – the principal themes of both elegies. However, in interpreting these central themes of Brodsky's, we will note differences from Auden as well as similarities.

The difference can be detected in the very first stanza and is expressed in another type of semantic transformation in the tropes:

> Он умер в январе, в начале года.
> Под фонарём стоял мороз у входа.
> Не успевала показать природа
> ему своих красот кордебалет.
> От снега стёкла становились уже.
> Под фонарём стоял глашатай стужи.
> На перекрёстках замерзали лужи.
> И дверь он запер *на цепочку лет*.   (*O.* 139)

He died in January, at the beginning of the year. / Beneath the street lamp frost stood at the entrance. / Nature did not manage to show / him the beauties of her corps-de-ballet. / The panes grew narrower with snow. / Beneath the street lamp stood the herald of severe frost. / At the crossroads the puddles had frozen over. / And he had shut the door *on the chain of years*.

The similarity lies in the fact that the metaphor *cold/death* is personified by both poets: see, for example, Auden's 'in the dead of winter', 'snow disfigured the public statues', 'the mercury sank in the mouth of the dying day'. In both writers, death is metonymically associated with time: days, months, years, summers. As opposed to Auden, Brodsky simultaneously animates and reifies time, as can be seen from the genitive metaphor *on the chain of years*. Most likely, this metaphor harks back to Khlebnikov's 'And a vicious dog on the chain of days'.[79] In his poetry, too, the abolition of boundaries between the physical and metaphysical worlds is highly characteristic. In the context of Brodsky's elegy, this metaphor is motivated by the fact of the death of the poet: he died and shut the door of his life on the chain of years. In the new world, time, even if it has not stopped, has not been petrified, it is no doubt measured differently from amongst the living: 'The tolling bell / Measures time not our time'; there 'The future futureless' and 'time is never ending' (*Four Quartets*: 'The Dry Salvages', I).

Time, the theme that dominates the elegy, is one of the central themes for Eliot, who was capable of hearing 'the murmuring shell of time' ('The Dry Salvages', III) in any language. It is significant that in his *Four Quartets* the theme of time is conveyed by images of the river, the sea, the ocean. Brodsky continues this association between time and water:

> Уже не Бог, а только время, *Время*
> зовёт его. И молодое *племя*
> огромных волн его движенья *бремя*
> на самый край цветущей бахромы
> легко возносит и, простившись, бьётся.
> о край земли. В избытке сил смеётся.
> *И январём его залив вдаётся*
> *в ту сушу дней, где остаёмся мы.*

Now it is not God, but only time; Time / calls to him. And the young brood / of huge waves raises with ease the burden of its [time's] motion / at the very margin of the flowering fringe / and saying farewell, beats on against the edge of earth. Exuberant in strength, it laughs. / And *his gulf as January strikes / the dry land of days where we remain.*

The comparison of January, the month of Eliot's death, with the gulf resonates with Eliot's metaphors from 'The Dry Salvages' (I): 'The river is within us, the sea is all about us; The sea is the land's edge also'. In this simile, as in the metaphor *the dry land of days*, time is once more reified. One may reasonably assume that the later identification of time and water, of which Brodsky talks with Volkov, is also inspired by Eliot:

The change of year, the change of time, time emerges from the water . . . it's pure metaphysics. This *idée fixe* – regarding time and water – started even when I was in the Crimea. It was there that I understood a few things for the first time. I remember, I was celebrating New Year in Gurzuf with the Tomashevskys. And towards midnight – that is, 11.45, I went outside. I looked at the sea, at the *gulf*. From the *gulf* towards the land a cloud was moving. What's more, I was standing on a slope, so it seemed to me that the cloud was getting lower, and I could see it very well. It was moving – like those Biblical clouds with God or someone or other inside. I remember the sensation that this cloud was a mist which had risen from the sea, and had rolled up into a ball. Or rather, a dishevelled ball. And at midnight precisely it touched dry land.[80]

In his essay on Leningrad, when talking about the Neva, which cuts through the city for twelve miles, and its canals and the Gulf of Finland – that is, about the water in which the city is reflected – Brodsky notes: 'The inexhaustible, maddening multiplication of all these pilasters, colonnades, porticoes hints at the nature of narcissism, hints at the possibility that at least in the inanimate world water may be regarded as a condensed form of time' (*L.* 77).

The departures from Eliot in the interpretation of the theme of time are marked by the fact that the two poets place different emphases on the two parallel, and no less important, themes of faith and language. Brodsky only introduces by implication in the first part of the fourth stanza the theme of faith which is absolutely central for Eliot:

> Католик, он дожил до *Рождества*.
> Но, словно море в шумный час прилива,
> за волнолом плеснувши, справедливо
> назад вбирает волны – торопливо
> от своего ушёл он *торжества*.

A Catholic, he lived on until Christmas. / But like the sea during the noisy hour of rising tide, / splashing the sea-wall, justly / draws its waves down and away – hastily / he left [the scene of] his triumph.

'Christmas' (*Рождество́*), which rhymes with 'triumph' (*торжество́*) transfers the religious theme into the sphere of creativity, while in the lexico-semantic context of the stanza, the theme of faith is absorbed by images of water-time, as is explicitly expressed by the opening of the following stanza: 'No longer God, but only time, Time calls him.' The mythologization of time is signalled not only by the insistent repetition of the lexeme 'time', but also by the use of the capital letter. Its omnipotence is underscored by the identification of time with death. The extent to which these two are identified gradually increases in Brodsky's work until, in 1969, he says: 'Time is created by death' (*K.* 59):

> Без злых гримас, без помышленья злого,
> из всех щедрот Большого *Каталога*
> смерть выбирает не красоты *слога*,
> а неизменно самого *певца*.
> Ей не нужны поля и перелески,
> моря во всём великолепном блеске.
> Она щедра, на небольшом отрезке
> себе позволив накоплять *сердца*.

With no malicious grimaces, no malicious thought / from all the
bounty of the Great Catalogue /death selects not the beauty of style /
but, infallibly, the singer himself. / She has no use for fields and
copses, / the sea with all its splendid shimmer. / She is generous in a
small segment / indulging herself piling up hearts.

The opposition 'time–poetry' is counterposed to this parallel 'time–
death'. As early as the second stanza, poetry is compared with time
directly by means of the nymph and Narcissus:

> Наследство дней не упрекнёт в банкротстве
> семейство Муз. При всём своём сиротстве,
> поэзия основана на сходстве
> бегущих вдаль однообразных *дней.*
> Плеснув в зрачке и растворившись в *лимфе,*
> она сродни лишь эолийской *нимфе,*
> как друг Нарцисс. Но в календарной *рифме*
> она другим наверняка *видней.*

The legacy of days will not reproach / the family of Muses with
bankruptcy. For all its orphaned state / poetry is grounded upon the
similarity / of the monotonous days which run on into the distance. /
Splashing the pupil [of the eye], dissolving into lymph she is akin
only to an Aeolian nymph, / like friend Narcissus. But with her
calendar rhyme / she is certainly more visible to others.

The metonymical representative of poetry, 'rhyme', is comple-
mentary to the semantically loaded rhymes: *в лимфе – нимфе –
рифме* ('into lymph' – 'nymph' – 'rhyme'), and is given the epithet
календарная ('calendar'). (In the poem 'Letter in a Bottle', 1965,
we find a direct indication of the temporal nature of rhyme: 'What a
paired rhyme will give us, then to it / we give back under the guise of
days', *O.* 155) By these associations, poetry has ascribed to it the
capability of resisting time. Time itself is also shifted into a rhyming
position, both in this as well as other stanzas: *года* ('year') – *у
входа* ('by the entrance'); *лет* ('years') – *кордебалет* ('corps-de-
ballet'); *дней* ('days') – *видней* ('more visible'); *Время* ('Time') –
племя ('tribe') – *бремя* ('burden'); *прочь* ('away') – *ночь*
('night'). This equation of poetry – and via it, all language – with
omnipotent time may be traced throughout all of Brodsky's works.
In the context of our present poem, we should refer to Auden's
elegy, especially to a section omitted from some editions:

> *Time* that is intolerant
> Of the brave and innocent,

> And indifferent in a week
> To a beautiful physique,
> *Worships language and forgives*
> *Everyone by whom it lives.*

Brodsky recalls what an impact these lines of Auden's had on him in 1965:

the train of thought that statement set in motion in me is still trundling to this day. For 'worship' is an attitude of the lesser toward the greater. If time worships language, it means that language is greater, or older, than time, which is, in its turn, older and greater than space. That was how I was taught, and indeed felt that way. (*L.* 363)

If we may paraphrase Tsvetaeva, we should say: for poets read poets in this way.[81]

A third opposition, 'time–memory', is closely linked to the first two, 'time–language' and 'time–poetry'. In the second part of the elegy on Eliot's death he is lamented by 'two bereaved figures', 'two maidens – but one cannot say that they are maidens: not passion, but pain determines gender'. The lyric note, perceptibly intensified in the second part, stumbles over this highly unexpected definition of gender. The no less strange comparison of the two mourning figures with our first parents also hints at the age of the poetry: 'One is like Adam – in profile. But the hair style is – Eve's.' At this very juncture, grief streams through the feminine rhymes: *где вы* ('where are you'), – *напевы* ('refrains') – *девы* ('maidens') – *Евы* ('Eve's'). The last stanzas of the second part remove the mourners' masks:

> Склоняя лица сонные свои,
> Америка, где он родился, и,
> и Англия, где умер он, унылы,
> стоят по сторонам его могилы.
> И туч плывут по небу корабли.
> Но каждая могила – край земли.

Bending their somnolent faces, / America, where he was born, and, / England, where he died, downcast / they stand by the sides of his grave. / And ships of clouds sail through the sky. / But every grave is the edge of the earth.

The metaphor-copula, *every grave is the edge of the earth*, which draws to a close the second part, once more articulates the theme of death and leads it on to a supra-individual level.

Just as death is associated with time which spares no one, so in opposition to them we find faith, love, memory, poetry, and language. Feeding each other, they comprise a no less powerful force, a force which is able to withstand time. In the last, third – and most melodic – part of the elegy, these themes pass through all the structural elements of the verse:

> Будет помнить лес и дол.
> Будет помнить сам Эол.
> Будет помнить каждый злак,
> как хотел Гораций Флакк.

Wood and vale will remember. / Aeolus himself will remember. / Every ear of corn will remember / as Horatius Flaccus wished.

In the rhyme *злак* ('ear of corn') – *Флакк* ('Flaccus'), we may note the metonymical allusion to Horace's celebrated poem *Exegi monumentum*, which initiated this genre. And, in a rhyme from the third stanza of the first part, *певца* ('singer'), – *сердца* ('heart'), we hear resonances with Pushkin's 'Prophet': 'And going round seas and lands, / Burn the hearts of people with your word'. The rhymes *слова* ('words') – *жива* ('alive'), – *Каталога* ('Catalogue') – *слога* ('syllable'), are imbued with the same semantics of the immortality of the poetic word. The theme of the poet who lives on in the memory of generations is explicit in Auden's elegy:

> The words of a dead man
> Are modified in the guts of the living,

and the text of Eliot's *Four Quartets*:

> That the past experience revived in the meaning
> Is not the experience of one life only
> But of many generations – not forgetting
> Something that is probably quite ineffable.

The extent to which the opposition between time and language is eliminated varies between the three poets. Auden, in acknowledging the precedence of language over time, removed from the third part of his elegy the three stanzas which so shook Brodsky, but left the phrase: 'poetry makes nothing happen', which is a further assertion of Auden's view on poetry expressed in 'New Year Letter' (1940):

> No words men write can stop the war
> Or measure up to the relief
> Of its immeasurable grief.

For T. S. Eliot, 'the past and future are conquered, and reconciled' only in the Incarnation. In 'Ash Wednesday' he makes a clear distinction between a word and the Word:

> If the lost word is lost, if the spent word is spent
> If the unheard, unspoken
> Word is unspoken, unheard;
> Still is the unspoken word, the Word unheard,
> The Word without a word, the Word within
> The world and for the world;
> And the light shone in darkness and
> Against the Word the unstilled world still whirled
> About the centre of the silent Word.

For Brodsky, as we will see, the primacy of language is unquestionable. Brodsky's first 'Elegy to W. H. Auden' (1974) is greatly inferior to his two essays about the poet, as well as to his second elegy written three years later. However, this modest poem deserves our attention, if only because it was written in English. Brodsky himself provides us with an interesting explanation as to why he switched from Russian to English:

When a writer resorts to a language other than his mother tongue, he does so either out of necessity, like Conrad, or because of burning ambition, like Nabokov, or for the sake of greater estrangement, like Beckett. Belonging to a different league ... I ... set out to write (essays, translations, occasionally a poem) in English for a reason that had very little to do with the above. My sole purpose then, as it is now, was to find myself in close proximity to the man, whom I considered the greatest mind of the twentieth century: Wystan Hugh Auden ... writing in English was the very best way to get near him, to work on his terms, to be judged, if not by his code of conscience, then by whatever it is in the English language that made his code of conscience possible ... My desire to write in English had nothing to do with any sense of confidence, contentment, or comfort; it was simply a desire to please a shadow. (L. 357–8)

We should look at the poem in the light of this confession:

> The tree is dark, the tree is tall,
> to gaze at it isn't fun.
> Among the fruits of this fall
> your death is the most grievous one.
>
> The land is bare. Firm for steps,
> it yields to a shovel's clink.
> Among next April's stems
> your *cross* will be the most unshaken *thing*.

Seedless it will possess its dew,
humiliating grass.
Poetry without you
equals only us.

The words are retreating to the stage
of lexicons, of the Muse.
The sky looks like an empty page
which you did not use.

The tree is dark, the tree is tall,
pleasing its Maker's scheme.
The thing I wish to talk
of least of all is Him.

Crossing horizons objects shrink;
it's hard to realize
there is someone for whom *the thing*
gains its previous size.

Coming upon this 'Elegy' in a collection edited by Stephen Spender, *W. H. Auden: A Tribute*,[82] I was surprised not to find the name of a translator under it. And so, in all simplicity, I asked Brodsky who had translated his 'Elegy to Auden' só badly. This was, perhaps, the only time I've ever seen Brodsky confused, upset, and impotent: 'So badly! Why did I give permission for it to be included in the collection ... and so I've ruined the whole book.'[83]

Having re-read and re-read this elegy, I now see that I was not quite fair in giving it such an entirely negative evaluation. In this elegy there is a lack of the characteristic features of his poetics, its dense metaphoricity, semantic breaks, dislocated syntax, which he was able to transfer to his 'Elegy: For Robert Lowell' (1977), also written in English, though it, too, is far from perfect. In the English 'Elegy to Auden' there is no lack of interest. The neutralization of the poet's death through poetry is realized not only explicitly, but also implicitly, by means of the rhymes. In rhyming 'dew' with 'you, he includes the dead poet in the association 'water–time'. While the rhyme 'grass – us' includes the poet, who remains among the living, in the majority, *ipso facto* it introduces a small note of Russian self-effacement. The rhymes form the poem, like a frame, they supply the idea of the poem 'with a sense of inevitability' (*L.* 305). The unsuccessful opening to the elegy, which is repeated in the fifth stanza, is significantly improved thanks to the daring rhyme 'scheme – Him'. The rhymes of the last stanza lend words the qualities of things, as does the metaphor *The stage of lexicon*. The whole importance of this type of sense transfer in the tropes will be elucidated in the following chapters. For the moment, it is important to note that this type of semantic transformation is so characteristic of Brodsky that it is retained even when he is not using his native language. Not only language, but faith too is subjected to the process of reification. A sign of semantic equivalence is placed between 'cross' and 'the thing', between 'Him' and 'scheme'. 'The thing' calls to mind the rather gloomy poem by Theodore Roethke with this title, which he wrote while staying at Auden's house in Forio, Ischia. As opposed to this, however, Brodsky's 'thing' does not vanish but, on the contrary, returns to its former magnitude, by identifying itself with the poet's immortality.

Brodsky's second elegy to Auden, 'York', also opens with landscape, possibly inspired by his visit to York in the summer of 1976 in the company of Véronique Schiltz, and Diana and Alan Myers, to whom the whole cycle 'In England' is dedicated. Brodsky clearly orientates himself towards the Auden texts, in which landscape is used for a meditation on death, love, and poetry:

> Бабочки северной Англии пляшут над лебедою
> под кирпичной стеной *мёртвой фабрики*. За средою
> наступает четверг, и т.д. Небо пышет жаром,
> и поля выгорают. *Города отдают лежалым*
> *полосатым сукном*, георгины страдают жаждой.
> И твой голос – "Я знал трёх великих поэтов. Каждый
> был большой сукин сын" – раздаётся в моих ушах
> с неожиданной чёткостью. Я замедляю шаг   (*У.* 78)

The butterflies of Northern England dance above the goose-foot, / beneath the brick wall of a dead factory. After Wednesday / comes Thursday etc., etc. The sky blazes with heat / and the fields become parched. The towns smell of musty, / striped broadcloth, dahlias suffer from thirst. / And your voice, 'I knew three great poets. Each one of them / was a prize son of a bitch', resounds in my ears / with unexpected clarity. I slacken pace //.

The last section of the stanza is reproduced and explained in Brodsky's essay, 'To Please a Shadow': '... even though you may end up echoing Auden's own: "I have known three great poets, each one a prize son of a bitch." I: "Who?" He: "Yeats, Frost, Bert

Brecht." (Now about Brecht he was wrong: Brecht wasn't a great poet)' (*L.* 374).

The voice of the poet against the background of the dead landscape sounds just as unexpected as the voice of Donne's soul in the sleeping universe. The difference between the 'Great Elegy to John Donne' and the elegy which is modestly named after Auden's birthplace lies in the latter's deliberate prosaic quality. The choice of a non-classical metre (free *dol'nik* with six feminine rhymes and a pair of masculine ones that conclude each of the seven stanzas) corresponds to the non-elegiac lexicon: the written abbreviation 'etc., etc.' is no less shocking than the phrase 'son of a bitch'. The syntax, like the blood from a damaged heart-valve, courses beyond the boundaries of the poetic line, and even the stanza. Enjambements, which were introduced to the elegy by the Romantics, are here loaded with poetic and semantic functions. If one were to write out any of the seven stanzas in prose form, then even the native speaker would be hard pressed to pick out the line-ends, even given the presence of rhymes:

и готов оглянуться. Скоро четыре года, как ты умер в австрийской гостинице. Под стрелой перехода ни души: черепичные кровли, асфальт, извёстка, тополя. Честер тоже умер – тебе известно это лучше, чем мне. Как костяшки на пыльных счетах, воробьи восседают на проводах. Ничто так не превращает знакомый подъезд в толчею колонн, как любовь к человеку; особенно, если он . . .

 and am on the point of glancing round. It will soon be four years since you died in an Austrian hotel. At the pedestrian crossing there's not a soul in sight: tiled roofs, asphalt, stucco, poplars. Chester also died – you know that better than I do. Like beads on a dusty counting frame the sparrows sit in state on the wires. There is nothing that so transforms a familiar portico into a scrum of columns. as love for a man; especially if he . . .

'is dead' – is the opening of the third stanza. This enjambement is motivated by one of the themes of the elegy, the theme of death. Death is a break, a parting from people, 'the edge of the earth'. This idea of the end, of a rupture, is expressed, firstly, implicitly, by the repeated: 'You died', 'Chester also died' (a reference to Auden's lover, Chester Kallman), 'He is dead'; and, secondly, by the interstrophic enjambements: 'I slacken pace / and am on the point of looking round', 'especially if he / is dead'. Thirdly, the elegy's landscape is emphatically lifeless: dead factories, the fields bleached by the sun, sleeping or abandoned towns, 'at the pedestrian crossing there's not a soul in sight', in the entrances to the houses 'a scrum of columns', instead of people. Even the birds do not sing: the sparrows are like 'beads on a dusty counting frame', while the call of the starling dissolves into the air even before he takes off. The only living creatures in the poem are the dancing butterflies. But their activity is illusory. Butterflies in Brodsky's poetry, like moths, settle in the most marginal sphere of being, symbolizing the crumbling barriers between life and death:

> Танец белых капустниц похож на корабль в бурю.
> Человек приносит с собою тупик в любую
> точку света; и согнутое колено
> размножает тупым углом перспективу плена,
> как журавлиный клин, когда он берёт
> курс на Юг. Как всё движущееся вперёд.

The dance of the cabbage-whites resembles a ship in a storm. / A man brings with him his own dead-end no matter what / spot of the globe he is on; and a bent knee, / with its obtuse angle, multiplies the perspective of captivity, / like a wedge of cranes when they set / course for the South. Like everything that moves forward. //

In this stanza we can easily pick out a number of stylistic features that are close to Auden, in particular, the same technique for constructing the poetic line. Its unity – rhythmic, melodic, grammatical – is broken either by long words, or repetitions, or the syntax. Thus, in the third and in the last stanzas, the end of the period disrupts abruptly the melody of the lines. The semantics of the phrase, 'A man brings with him his own dead-end no matter what spot of the globe he is on', is illuminated by an intonational dead-end. Heterogeneous lexicon, following the model of Auden and the English metaphysicals, is introduced. Apart from the abbreviations and curses already mentioned, the scientific terminology 'angle', 'perspective', 'vertical', is cheek by jowl with the bookish-bureaucratic 'set course for the South', 'subtracting the greater from the lesser', 'on general foundations'. This lexicon, alien to an elegy, is used to achieve, if not 'blinding precision', then, at the least, an extremely dry tone, qualities which Brodsky so values in Auden. The range of epithets is deliberately meagre and equally departs from the traditional lexicon of an elegy. The rhymes are grammatically disparate and phonetically inexact:

жаром ('heat') – *лежалым* ('stale'), – *извёстка* ('lime'), – *известно* ('known'), *смысле* ('sense') – *если* ('if'), *скалюсь* ('grimace') – *палец* ('finger'). These inexact rhymes add their own measure of neutrality to a lyricism which is strictly controlled in any case. This is further facilitated by the compound-complex rhymes which by their very nature are anti-lyrical: *счетах* ('counting frame') – *ничто так* ('nothing so'), *колонн* ('column') – *если он* ('if he'), *руки и* ('arm and') – *другие* ('others'), *в Риме* ('in Rome') – *Время* ('Time'). As in Auden's poetry, the enjambements, apart from their semantic role, also fulfil the function of the formation of new rhymes, as well as having a compositional function: they throw bridges from one stanza to another. Thus, the difficult problem of the stanza opening is resolved by means of carry-over. Both poets dare to rupture the tightest semantic units by line and stanza, leaving at the end of the line a preposition or conjunction:

> Пустота, поглощая солнечный свет на общих
> основаниях с боярышником, увеличивается наощупь
> в направлении вытянутой *руки, и*
> мир сливается в длинную улицу, на которой живут другие.
> В этом смысле *он – Англия. Англия* в этом смысле
> до сих пор *Империя* и в состоянии – *если*
> верить музыке, булькающей водой –
> править морями. Впрочем – любой средой.

The emptiness, absorbing the sunlight, on the same / basis as the hawthorns [do], grows tentatively / in the direction of the out-stretched arm and / the world merges into a long street on which others live. / In this sense, *he is England. England*, in this sense, / is still an *Empire* and still capable – *if* / you believe the music gurgling like water – / of ruling the waves. Or any other medium, for that matter. //

The line-ends, 'arm and', 'capable – if' correspond structurally to Auden's line-ends in 'In Praise of Limestone': 'To death as a fact, no doubt we are right. But if'; 'Having nothing to hide. Dear, I know nothing of'. In both instances, such a line-end gives the effect of an exclamation, unexpressed by both grammar and semantics.

The identification of Auden with England reflects both Brodsky's personal perception of him and the objective equation of the poet with his nation, as he polishes and preserves its language. In

Brodsky's view, one of the reasons for Auden's move to America was his desire to master all the idioms of English:

what Auden had in mind from the very outset of his poetic career was the sense that the language in which he wrote was transatlantic or, better still, imperial: not in a sense of the British Raj but in the sense that it is the language that made an empire. For empires are held together by neither political nor military forces but by languages. Take Rome, for instance, or better still, Hellenic Greece, which began to disintegrate immediately after Alexander the Great's own demise ... What held them for centuries, after their political centres collapsed, were *Magna lingua Grecae* and Latin. Empires are, first and foremost, cultural entities; and it's language that does the job, not legions. (*L.* 309)

Therefore, Auden, who personified English culture, also personified both England and the Empire.

Я в последнее время немного сбиваюсь: скалюсь
отраженью в стекле витрины; покамест палец
набирает свой номер, рука опускает трубку.
Стоит закрыть глаза, как я вижу пустую шлюпку,
замершую на воде посредине бухты.
Выходя наружу из телефонной будки,
слышу голос скворца, в крике его – испуг.
Но раньше, чем он взлетает, звук

растворяется в воздухе. Чьей беспредметной сини
и сродни эта жизнь, где вещи видней в пустыне,
ибо в ней тебя нет. И вакуум постепенно
заполняет местный ландшафт. Как сухая пена,
овцы покоятся на темнозелёных волнах
йоркширского вереска. Кордебалет проворных
бабочек, повинуясь невидимому смычку,
мельтишит над заросшей канавой, не давая зрачку
ни на чём задержаться. И вертикальный стебель

Recently, I've been a bit run down. I grimace / at my reflection in the glass of the shop window; while my finger / dials my own number my hand lets the receiver fall. / I have only to close my eyes and I see an empty boat, / frozen, in the middle of the bay. / Coming out of the telephone kiosk / I can hear the voice of a starling, in his cry alarm. / But before he flies off the sound // is dissolving in the air. Whose object-free blue / is akin to this life, where things are more visible in the desert – because you're not there. And the vacuum gradually / fills up the local landscape. Like dry foam / the sheep lie upon the dark-green waves / of Yorkshire heather. The corps-de-ballet of sprightly / butterflies, obeying an unseen bow, / tediously flits above

an overgrown ditch, not giving the pupil // anything to linger on. And
the vertical stalk . . .
The emptiness increases, thickens from stanza to stanza, not only
filling the local landscape, but even absorbing the sun's rays. But a
complete eclipse does not take place, the emptiness and vacuum
reduce to a minimum all activity, all actions: hence the minimum of
verbs in the poem. Substantives predominate: they are two-and-a-
half times more common than verbs and three-and-a-half times
more common than adjectives. In using any particular part of
speech in verse, Brodsky follows the rule he adopted from Yevgeny
Rein in the 1960s: 'in a poem, you should try to reduce the number
of adjectives to a minimum. So that if somebody covered your poem
with a magic cloth that removes adjectives, the page will still be
black enough because of nouns, adverbs, and verbs. When that
cloth is little, your best friends are nouns' (L. 314–15). In this
elegy, the substantives convey the concreteness and dryness of the
style. Counterposed to the materiality of earthly being is the
'object-free blue', a metaphor of substitution for air, a word for
which, in Brodsky's view, it is harder to find an epithet than for fire
or water.[84] Water imagery is given an unexpected twist in the fifth
and sixth stanzas: to 'music, gurgling water' is counterposed the
'dry foam of sheep'; the seas which wash the British Empire narrow
to a mere bay. The 'empty boat' hints at Charon's ferry, which has
already taken Auden to Hades and is now frozen in the middle of
the bay awaiting the next passenger, who may be the writer of the
elegy to the dead poet. The sixth line is full of premonition of his
own death, a motif that appeared in Brodsky's work soon after his
expulsion from Russia, and which is clearly expressed in the poem
'1972': 'We're not yet talking of a shroud. But already they who will
carry you out are coming in the door' (Ч. 24). The 'I' which appears
twice in the elegy has not escaped the general, somnambulistic
state: 'I slacken my pace . . . I've been a bit run down, I grimace . . .
My hand lets the receiver fall.' The telephone, which was once a
reliable means of communication with the world, becomes more
and more useless: as the years go by, there's only oneself to ring.
This theme of a break in communication, behind which alienation
amidst people hides, implicitly permeates another, also 'English',
poem, 'The Thames at Chelsea' (1974):

> Город Лондон прекрасен. Если не ввысь, то вширь
> он раскинулся вниз по реке как нельзя безбрежней.

> И когда в нём спишь, *номера телефонов прежней*
> *и текущей жизни, слившись, дают цифирь*
> *астрономической масти.* И палец, вращая диск
> зимней луны, обретает бесцветный писк
> "занято"; и этот звук во много
> раз неизбежней, чем голос Бога.   (Ч. 48)

London Town is beautiful. If not upwards, then crossways / it
spreads itself down to the river as far as possible boundless. / And
when you sleep in it *the phone numbers of your past / and present life*
blend to produce a figure of astronomical proportions. And your
finger turning the dial / of the winter moon finds the colourless peep /
'engaged' and that sound is far / more inevitable than the voice of
God. //

'The finger turning the dial of the winter moon' and the finger which
dials one's own number belong to the same hand stretched out
towards the living world across space and time. The figures in both
poems are merely metonymical representations of time, which
express the whole irreconcilability of two opposing masses, man
and time: the motif of the last stanza:

> И вертикальный стебель
> иван-чая длинней уходящей на Север
> древней Римской дороги, всеми забытой *в Риме.*
> *Вычитая из меньшего большее, из человека – Время,*
> *получаешь в остатке слова, выделяющиеся на белом*
> фоне отчётливей, чем удаётся *телом*
> это сделать при жизни, даже сказав *"лови"*!
>
> *Что источник любви превращает в объект любви.*

And the vertical stalk / of the willow-herb is longer than the
northbound / ancient Roman road, forgotten by all at Rome. /
Taking the greater from the lesser – subtracting Time from man / –
what you've got left over are words, which stand out / more distinct
on a white background than the body / is capable of while it's alive,
even when it says 'catch me!' // Thus the source of love is transformed into the object of love.

The last line, which is set apart both graphically and syntactically,
expresses the main idea of the whole poem. The concept of 'source'
in Brodsky's poetry incorporates the Kierkegaardian triad, 'ethics–
aesthetics–religion'. In the poem 'Nunc Dimittis' which we analysed
earlier (pp. 66–71), and which concerns the infant Christ, the
following is said: 'He is your continuation and of light / the source

for the idols of worshipping tribes'. In his commentary on this poem for his American translator, George L. Kline, Brodsky referred to Robert Frost's 'West-Running Brook':

> The brook runs down in sending up our life.
> The sun runs down in sending up the brook.
> And there is something sending up the sun.
> It is this backward motion towards the source.

Brodsky comments:

by using words in such a way that they suddenly take on a quite different meaning, become semantically greater than they are. For example, when Robert Frost in 'West-Running Brook' speaks about the source of the brook, you suddenly realize that the word 'source' means much more than the word 'source'. It means even more than the word 'God'; it is an absolutely transcendental word.[85]

In the context of the elegy, by the word 'source' we must understand poetry, for only poetry, in Brodsky's definition, incorporates within itself ethics, aesthetics, and faith. The object of love (the poet – in this instance, Auden) is metonymically represented by the words of his poetry set out on the white ground of the paper. In this very stanza, we witness a virtuoso expression of the opposition 'time–poetry' and 'time–man'. In rhyming *Время* ('time') with *в Риме* ('Rome'), Brodsky succeeds in uniting the ontological aspect of time with the historical and religious. The moment when the Roman Empire accepted Christianity and spread it throughout Europe was a genuine seizure of power over time by the idea of eternal life. In such an interpretation, the rhyme *в Риме* ('in Rome') – *Время* ('Time') becomes a rhyme-metaphor and turns the following two rhymes into metaphors as well: *на белом* ('on a white') – *телом* ('the body'), and *лови!* ('catch me!') – *любви* ('of love'). The comparison of the stalk of willow-herb with an ancient Roman road heading north, though forgotten by everyone in Rome, hints at the direction Christianity took, and, alongside it, civilization: 'Unlike the Ice Age, civilizations, of whatever sort, move from south to north, as if to fill up the vacuum created by the retreating glacier ... As for latitudes, it's only nomads who move along them, and usually from east to west' (*L.* 430). Only birds head south, if only to imitate the shape of a cross in the 'object-free blue'. This idea of the cross, which is deeply submerged in the elegy and which is expressed so naively and openly in the first elegy to

Auden as 'the unshaken thing', is rendered here by the strokes and directions of being itself. Time, which flows horizontally ('After Wednesday comes Thursday etc., etc.'), is intersected on the vertical, from south to north, by the movement of Christianity and civilization. This cruciform shape is repeated by the life of man, who repeats the evolution of civilization and who intersects time. This vivid sense of the cross-movement is expressed in various ways: beginning with the pedestrian crossing and the direction of the hand stretched out to the world, which merges into a long street, everything seems to imitate the movement of time. The columns in the entrance to the house of the dead poet are vertical, the plants and trees (poplars, hawthorns, heather, willow-herb) stretch upwards, finally, of course, the human body in life. The configuration of the cross is also repeated by the words of any Christian civilization, which are written horizontally by vertically disposed letters.

Time, which has been neutralized by Rome, suffers yet another defeat in the game of *lapta*,[86] in the rhyme *лови!* ('catch me!') – *любви* ('of love'). Situated in a poem addressed to Auden, this rhyme is dragged into a competitive game with his rhyme 'Diaghilev – have – love' from the poem 'September 1, 1939'. In his lecture on the poem Brodsky comments on the difficulties faced by a contemporary poet writing in any European language, in the search for an original, semantically charged rhyme for the word 'love'. Brodsky argued that Auden found such a rhyme in the lines quoted below:[87]

> What mad Nijinsky wrote
> About Diaghilev
> Is true of the normal heart;
> For the error bred in the bone
> Of each woman and each man
> Craves what it cannot have,
> Not universal love
> But to be loved alone.

In his essay on the poem, Brodsky says: 'He comes up with the unthinkable: with a new rhyme for love.' After explaining why it is so important that Auden placed 'Diaghilev' first and 'love' afterwards, Brodsky stressed that:

to rhyme 'Diaghilev' with 'love' straight would mean to equate them . . . By interjecting 'have' Auden scores a terrific hit. For now the rhyme scheme itself becomes a statement: 'Diaghilev–have–love' or rather 'Diaghilev cannot have love'. And 'Diaghilev', mind you, stands here for art. So the net result is that 'Diaghilev' gets equated with 'love', but only via being equated with 'have', and 'having', as we know, is opposite to 'loving', which is, as we remember, Nijinsky, which is 'giving'. (*L.* 346)

It is interesting that such an interpretation of the semantics of Auden's rhyme not only stems from Brodsky's own ethics of love, but also resonates with another of Auden's rhymes from 'In Praise of Limestone' (1948), 'Dear, I know *nothing of* Either, but when I try to imagine a faultless *love*.' 'A faultless love' does not exist among mortals. Brodsky has no doubts that such a poetic technique 'simply shows you to what extent a writer is the tool of his language and how his ethical notions are the sharper, the keener his ear is' (*L.* 347).

This attempt to accommodate ethics, aesthetics, and faith in poetry stems from the triad of Kierkegaard, to whom both poets have paid the tribute of enthusiasm. Brodsky was overjoyed 'to learn one day about his [Auden's] devotion to the Kierkegaardian triad, which for many of us was the key to the human species' (*L.* 377). We can find other common sources and common interests of all three poets we have been discussing. Thus, their borrowings from various epochs and cultures are dictated by their concern to preserve a cultural heritage in an age of increasing vulgarity. 'Keeping an eye on civilization' (*L.* 364) became for them second nature. In the sphere of poetry itself, their common roots go back to the poetry of the English baroque. Typical for all three is an encyclopaedic range of references and a heterogeneity of material, be it Sanskrit in the case of Eliot, psychoanalytical jargon (Auden), or Soviet slang (Brodsky). Bookishness, rationalism, sensitivity of mind, philosophizing lead them not infrequently to a cultivation of asymmetry and disproportion. All these qualities can be found in abundance in the metaphysicals.

It is revealing that almost all the features of Auden's style that Brodsky has isolated are characteristic of his own work. He has dubbed Auden 'a master of understatement', 'a self-disgusted moralist', and 'the most humble poet of the English language'. He has praised Auden's 'capacity for objective, dispassionate discourse', his 'dryness of tone', and 'detached posture', that is for those qualities which are, to the highest degree, intrinsic to his own style. Certain of these qualities have already been illustrated; we

will speak in more detail of the others in due course. For the
moment, we may adduce examples of how their fear of sentimentality pushes them towards understatement, self-irony, and the
shifting of emotions to subordinate and parenthetic clauses:

> Having nothing to hide. Dear, I know nothing of
> Either, but when I try to imagine a faultless love
>   Or the life to come, what I hear is the murmur
> Of underground streams, what I see is a limestone landscape.

In Brodsky, we may find examples of deliberate self-effacement in
any poem: 'here I am ending my days, losing / hair, teeth, verbs,
suffixes' (Ч. 26); 'For him on whose shoulders lies the burden / of
darkness, heat and – need it be said – grief' (Ч. 106). This sort of
roundabout conceit in preference to direct speech has something in
common with the use of quotations and allusions to the poets of
foreign traditions as a mask for personal experience and inner
feelings. Eliot's search for objective correlatives of emotion was
carried further by each of them, albeit in a different way. The
reconstruction of Brodsky's intertextual links with English poetry
would be the theme of a special piece of research. These links are
much more multifaceted than the schemas outlined here, and are
by no means entirely unobscure. Even when they go back to a
common source, they are re-worked differently, as they are subject
to different thematic demands and a different linguistic frame of
mind. And for all the many similarities, the differences are no less
fundamental. I do not have in mind, however, such extra-poetic
factors as Brodsky's profound indifference to the teaching of the
two great thinkers who dominate our age and who subjugated
Auden at various times and to varying degrees – Marx and Freud.
In his own turn, Auden was not caught by an *idée fixe* – the search
for a poetic mythology of time or the creation of a teleology of
language – to the extent that is characteristic for Brodsky. What I
do have in mind is the (in principle) different means of transforming the real world into the poetic. Their common a-logical image-
building and use of paradoxes mask a different technique of
constructing the image, a different grammatical structure of the
metaphor and its semantics. Believing in the unity of the material
and spiritual worlds, both Eliot and Auden are inclined to ascribe
qualities of the latter to the former, and very rarely do we find in
their poetry the reverse process which is so characteristic of
Brodsky. Auden explains this more-than-traditional method of

constructing tropes by a feeling of moral responsibility towards the material world. While constructing 'a secondary world', that is, a work of art, 'physical impossibility and magical means were forbidden'.[88] Brodsky, following Auden's technique, 'drives the apparatus of common sense to further extremes, takes the argument further, almost to the absurd'.[89] The erosion of the boundaries between physical data and the products of mental activity will be traced in Brodsky's poetics in an analysis of his metaphors. This tendency was inherited from Khlebnikov, whose poetics are characterized by the abolition of all boundaries: grammatical, lexical, and semantic. However, the aim of equating 'logos with life',[90] the Spirit with matter, is somewhat different from that of Khlebnikov.

3

The mask of metaphor

The modern art of the mask is the art of creating a scale against which things can be measured.[1]

A web of metaphors

For a poet, any faith, any system is an act of choice of metaphors, that is language.[2]

In Brodsky's opinion, in modern literature it is no longer possible 'to speak of life in an open text'.[3] He sees Cavafy's empire, Frost's irony, and Wilbur's formal perfection as a mask to conceal what has really been said. Brodsky has created his own metaphorical empire, has exhibited a startling irony and astonishing variety of metaphors which constitute a great part of his technical achievement. Brodsky's metaphors, like metaphors of any poet, can be viewed as a mask for his personality, for his ideas, even for his faith. According to Pasternak, the individuality and uniqueness of the poet's metaphors express his personality:

Metaphors are the natural consequence of man's brief lifespan and the enormity of the tasks which he ponders so long. Given this disjunction, man is forced to look at things with an eagle's sharp eye and to explain himself through these instantaneous, immediately graspable flashes of light. This is what poetry is. Metaphors are the shorthand of a great personality, the stenography of its spirit.[4]

Since metaphor pertains to the linguistic, the compositional, the psychological, and the conceptual orders alike, a systematic examination of the metaphors used by a poet allows us to describe the peculiarity of his poetic style as well as to understand his poetic universe. Bearing in mind that metaphor, like any other formal element of verse, exists within the sphere, and against the background, of tradition, a systematic study of any aspect of metaphor will enable us to resolve the problem formulated by Mandelstam: 'A critic may decline to answer the question as to what the poet intended to say, but he is obliged to answer the question: where the poet came from.'[5] In order to trace the poetic tradition that Brodsky develops, and to estimate the extent of his departure from it, his metaphors have been compared with those of ten other Russian poets.[6]

An examination of a large number of poetic metaphors clearly shows the inadequacies of many modern theories of metaphor. Based merely on a few simple metaphors or a few poems, these theories cannot be applied to more complex or more extensive material. In fact, the actual material of poetry refutes every theory of metaphor of which I am aware. This holds true for the most widespread and traditional theories of metaphor, such as comparison and substitution, as well as for the theory of interaction;[7] and also for more contemporary theories of metaphor, such as double metonymy,[8] or double synechdoche.[9] Amongst the numerous studies of metaphor I have, as yet, been unable to discover a single work dedicated to an analysis of *all* the metaphors of a single author. This perhaps has something to do with the problem of finding a mechanism to isolate the metaphor from its context. It is generally held that 'there can be no routine method for (1) detecting metaphors when they appear ... or (2) unpacking the metaphor once it is known'.[10] However, one effective method of detecting metaphors is grammar-based, as Brooke-Rose has demonstrated;[11] while to 'unpack' the metaphor and reach the conceptual level requires a description of the transformation of meaning that occurs in metaphors of different grammatical structures, and their classification according to semantic type.

As this chapter will argue that Brodsky's metaphors are not necessarily based on the principle of similarity, two more semantic types of metaphors need to be added to the traditional metaphors of comparison and substitution: metaphors of attribution[12] and metaphors of identification. The following working definition of metaphor may be suggested: *metaphor represents a specific transformation of meaning, based either on an actual similarity or supposed analogy of two described objects. It may, moreover, arise from the arbitrary attribution of the qualities of one object to another or from the assumed identity between the objects.*

This chapter is primarily an attempt to reconstruct Brodsky's poetic world. By describing and analysing each of the four proposed semantic types of metaphor, we can identify a unifying principle of organization which runs through the entire metaphoric system of his poetry. A formal analysis of some of his poems will be given to demonstrate how metaphor works in relation to the other distinguishing features of Brodsky's poetics. Moreover, it has to be recognized that selection of metaphor is governed not only by the theme of the poem; it is also dependent on metre, genre, rhyme, stylistic environment, and, finally, on the correspondence and intermingling of metaphor with other tropes and figures of speech, such as, in particular, metonymy, irony, and simile. By concentrating our attention on the systematic study of one trope, i.e. metaphor, we shall be able to comprehend its internal system of relations and functioning in the context of the poet's complete work, thereby penetrating a miasma of associations in our search for a model for Brodsky's poetic world. Such an approach allows us to ask whether poetic language is able to create its own reality by means of metaphoric transferences, and what types of interrelation exist between the poetic world and the real world. As a result, a better understanding of how reality is perceived by means of metaphor can be gained. And, perhaps, 'the scandal of metaphor'[13] will be unravelled.

There is one more reason for concentrating on a study of metaphor. Brodsky himself clearly defines the path along which a metaphor travels as a vector of the entire poem's development:

There are two elements which constitute a metaphor: the object of description (the 'tenor' as I. A. Richards called it), and the object to which the first is imagistically, or simply grammatically, allied (the 'vehicle'). The implication which the second part usually contains provides the writer with the possibility of virtually endless developments. This is the way a poem works. (*L.* 56)

Metaphors of substitution

In metaphors of substitution the described object (phenomenon) is not named, but is substituted for in its entirety. Many critics, like Brooke-Rose, call these metaphors 'pure metaphors' or 'simple replacement'; others, after Aristotle, term them 'enigmatic metaphors'; while some include them under the class of periphrasis.[14] Although the very nature of synonymic substitution (replacement of one word by another) as a device appears to link periphrasis to metaphors of substitution, it must be agreed, as Grigoryev comments, that 'the principle of periphrasis lies at the basis of any metaphor'.[15] The fact that metaphors of substitution tend to involve an image distinguishes them from periphrases.

This type of metaphor is by no means the most popular among poets, as some students of metaphor would like us to believe. Culler gives a clear account of this confused state of affairs: 'the notion of replacement, on which the whole typology of figures depends, seems to fall away as irrelevant when tropes not based on replacement are placed in the same taxonomic categories. Metonymy, synedoche, and metaphor are defined by the rhetorical approach in terms of replacement, but then tropes not involving replacement are brought under these three headings.'[16]

Metaphors of substitution, in Brooke-Rose's opinion, depend greatly on the context, since they are formed on the principle of a 'hidden comparison':

> Ты видел: жизнь, она как остров твой.
> И с *Океаном этим* ты встречался:
> со всех сторон лишь тьма, лишь тьма и вой.   (*C.* 134)

You have seen life, she is like your island, / and you have encountered *this Ocean:* / on all sides, only darkness, only darkness and howling.

Only from the context of 'The Great Elegy to John Donne' can we guess that *this Ocean* stands for time-honoured eternity. In Goethe's *Faust*, for example, *Ocean* is identified with Spirit.

Brooke-Rose enumerated the purely grammatical means by which the significance of substitution is disambiguated. Among the processes discussed is the use of articles. Because of the absence of articles in Russian, demonstrative and possessive pronouns take on the function of explaining the specificity of these metaphors:

> Дыра *в сей ткани*. Всяк, кто хочет, рвёт.
> Со всех концов. Уйдёт. Вернётся снова.
> Ещё рывок! И только небосвод
> во мраке иногда берёт иглу портного.   (*C.* 136)

There is a hole in *this fabric*. Everyone who wants to can rip it. / At every edge. He'd be gone. He'd return. / Another jerk! And only heaven's vault / in the gloom sometimes takes up the tailor's needle.

This fabric, here, is a metaphor of substitution for life as well as for the unity of body and soul. Moreover, the context of the elegy can clarify this metaphor to a greater extent than a demonstrative pronoun can. In all probability, the limited capacity of anaphoric pronouns to express the specificity of metaphors of substitution explains their infrequent usage by Brodsky (in all, only 2 per cent).

Metaphors of substitution that involve an adjective, on the other hand, have a much greater capacity to detach themselves from the described object, while at the same time pointing to their connection: 'крылатый полёт *серебристой жужжащей пули*, / уносящей жизни на Юг в июле' (*Ч.* 85) ('the winged flight of *the humming silver bullet*, / carrying off lives to the South in July'). Here *the humming silver bullet* stands for an aeroplane; elsewhere, *mechanical elephant* (*Ч.* 97) stands for a Soviet tank in Afghanistan, and *stone nest* (*Ч.* 113) represents Florence. Similar metaphors of substitution that lack an additional adjective would be difficult to interpret. Sometimes, the adjectives have been formed from the nouns which are substituted by the metaphor: *brick backbone* – walls of a brick house (*K.* 66); *stone needle* – an obelisk (*Ч.* 138). Metaphors of substitution incorporating an adjective make up 55 per cent of all Brodsky's metaphors of this type. The following tendency can be observed: the more the distance between the metaphor and the depicted object increases, the greater the degree of grammatical and contextual support required for the metaphoric formation. The position of the attributive may be occupied by a participial phrase:

> Тебе, когда мой голос отзвучит
> настолько, что ни отклика, ни эха,
> а в памяти – улыбку заключит
> *затянутая воздухом прореха*,   (*H.* 45)

For you, when my voice ceases to resound, / that there is no reply, no echo – *a slit stitched with air* / will preserve a smile in memory.

This *slit stitched with air* is a metaphor of substitution for a mouth, as another genitive link metaphor from the same year (1964) demonstrates:

> Бормочет предо мной вода,
> и тянется мороз в *прореху рта*.   (*H.* 53)

Water mumbles in front of me / and the frost lingers in *the slit of my mouth*.

The ability of metaphors of substitution to transform meaning clearly increases when they are expressed by a genitive syntagma: *a crowd of zeroes* (*K.* 75) – eternity; *a charge of classical case-shot* (*Ч.* 51) – a sonnet. Not all of them are constructed according to the principle of comparison; some of them are built on the principle of attribution: *the face of a plate* (*Ч.* 108) – a clock; while other metaphors are based on the principle of identification:

> Право, чем гуще *россыпь*
> *чёрного на листе,*
> тем безразличней особь
> к прошлому, к пустоте
> в будущем.   (*H.* 111)

It's true, the thicker *the deposit* / *of black on the page*, / the more indifferent the individual is / to the past, to the emptiness / in the future.

In genitive syntagmas, as in the attributive, one component of the metaphor, frequently the second one in the genitive case, contains the key to interpretation: *the fox of darkness* (*У.* 59); *the herald of severe frost* (*O.* 139). Both components of the genitive metaphor may have an epithet, either logical or metaphorical, which serves to simplify their intelligibility considerably: *the black and white flower of the twentieth century* (*C.* 36) stands for nuclear explosions.

However, the meaning of several genitive metaphors of substitution is only elucidated with the aid of a context which is larger than that of a single poem:

> В нашей твёрдости толка
> больше нету. *В чести*
> *одарённость осколка,*
> жизнь сосуда вести.   (*O.* 95)

In our firmness there is no longer / any sense. *In honour of the talented splinter* / to lead the life of the vessel.

A synonym for this *talented splinter* can be found in the twelfth of the 'Roman Elegies':

> Я был в Риме. Был залит светом. Так,
> как только может мечтать *обломок*!

I was in Rome. I was flooded with light. The way / only *a fragment* can dream of!

The reduction of the lyrical 'I' in these metaphors to a non-human condition, to a piece of an object, corresponds to an identical metaphor in a poem by Baratynsky:

Предрассудок! он *обломок*
Древней правды. Храм упал;
А руин его потомок
Языка не разгадал.

Prejudice! It's *a fragment / of ancient truth.* The temple has fallen; /
posterity did not decipher / the language of its ruins.

It has been noted that many of Brodsky's metaphors either
attribute human qualities to the inanimate world (a traditional
function of metaphor), or they attribute inanimate properties to the
animate world (*oveshchestvliayut*). These two opposite functions
include the abstraction of concrete things by attributing the
capacity for logical thought to things, and the concretization of
abstract concepts. It may be that these functions form the basic
principle for the organization of all semantic types of Brodsky's
metaphors, 'enabling semantic classes to polarise and combine in
higher classes'.[17]

For the purpose of uncovering such a single organizational
principle for the metaphors of the substitutional type, it is advisable
to compare them with their closest relative – metaphors in apposition. In the appositional structure, the nominal function of the
metaphor is weakened, insofar as the parallel usage of direct and
implied appellation is laid bare. This allows the poet not only to
compare but also to place in opposition and even to identify the
most distantly related phenomena of reality without risking obscu-
rity as to the metaphor's meaning: *пыль – этот загар эпох*
(Ч. 39) (*dust – that sunburn of epochs*); *телефонный номер –
порванная ячейка / опустевшего навода* (У. 74) ('*a telephone
number – the torn cell of the emptied sweep-net*').

Since the poet himself is a part of his poetic world, it is
worthwhile to consider the figurative means by which the lyrical 'I'
is constituted. In metaphors of substitution, we find the following:
contemporary Orpheus (C. 207); *a new Gogol* (O. 171); *a singer
not out of his mind, not fallen silent* (O. 114); *an unknown Hephaes-
tus* (C. 233); *a new Dante* (Ч. 9). Such tropes that establish an
equivalence between the 'I' and major historical figures always
carry an ironical nuance which is significantly increased in appositional metaphors: *Я – один из глухих, облысевших,
угрюмых послов / второсортной державы* (К. 58: *I am one of
the deaf, bold, gloomy ambassadors / of a second-rate power*). The
irony is deepened when it is revealed that not only the 'great power'

to which the poet belongs, but also the era in which he is condemned to live, is second-rate:

> *Гражданин второсортной эпохи*, гордо
> признаю я *товаром второго сорта*
> *свои лучшие мысли* и дням грядущим
> я дарю их как опыт борьбы с удушьем.   (*K.* 107)

A citizen of a second-rate epoch with pride / I recognize *my best thoughts as second-rate merchandise* / and I give them to the days to come / as an account of the struggle with suffocation.

This conception of the double mediocrity of country and epoch is present from his earliest poems:

> Прости *меня – поэта, человека –*
> о, кроткий Бог убожества всего,
> как *грешного* или как *сына века*,
> всего верней – как *пасынка его*.   (*C.* 22)

Forgive me – as a poet, as a man, / O meek God of misery, / as *a sinner* and as *son of my time* / or more precisely *a stepson of the era*.

The substitution of the clichéd metaphor, *son of the era*, by *stepson of the era* (*C.* 22), echoes Mandelstam (1. 99). Several years later, Brodsky replaced the synonymical phrase *son of the fatherland* by *stepson of the Empire*, adding the epithet *wild* to the word *power*:

> *Я, пасынок державы дикой*
> с разбитой мордой,
> другой, не менее великой,
> *приёмыш гордый*, –   (*У.* 93)

I am a stepson of a wild power / with a bruised face, / now *I am a proud adopted son* / *of another no lesser power*.

Brodsky justifies this not particularly original form of relation to his native empire in the context of his exile. He deliberately selects pejorative metaphors to stand for his own personality, as if wishing to anticipate the criticism of sarcastic readers and the literary functionaries of the Empire:

> *я, прячущий во рту*
> *развалины почище Парфенона,*
> *шпион, лазутчик, пятая колонна*
> *Гнилой цивилизации* – в быту
> *профессор красноречья* –   (*Ч.* 28)

I, who hide in my mouth / ruins comparable with the Parthenon, / a spy, a scout, fifth columnist / of a rotten civilization – in everyday life / a professor of rhetoric.

The humiliation of the lyrical 'I' in these metaphors should not, however, lead us to the conclusion that Brodsky, when referring to himself as *a singer of nonsense, superfluous thoughts and broken lines* (*У.* 112), is unaware of his own value. As Losev has already commented: 'completely serious and profound comparisons of his personal fate to the fate of Dante and even Christ are characteristic of his poetry'. And he correctly observes that these comparisons contain no trace of delusions of grandeur: 'the serious and almost pious attitude of the poet to another Joseph Brodsky expresses his conception of the poet's mission as a votary of the Muse and performer of God's Will whose fate is unravelled in the form of the Christian mystery or Dante's tragedy of the Titans.'[18]

The poet's consciousness of his own personality is no less important than his conceptualization of the world. Indeed, Potebnia considered these two processes to be inextricably linked.[19] Poets have always used metaphors as a mask for their 'I', whether this is the romantic 'egotistical sublime' or *le Narcisse exhaussé* of the Symbolists or, finally, the *pluralis majestas* of the Futurists dreaming of their merging with a class (Mayakovsky) or with the entire universe (Khlebnikov).

Brodsky's attitude to his own work is no less ambivalent than his self-image. On the one hand, we find a complete alienation from the written poem:

> Теперь отбой
> и невдомёк,
> зачем так много *чёрного на белом?*
> Гортань исходит грифелем и мелом,
> и в ней – комок.   (*К.* 67)

Now retreat / and ignorance / why so much *black on white?* / The larynx grows weak from slate and chalk / and there's a lump in it.

Thus, *black on white* stands for the poem's manuscript, as if black letters on white sheets of paper bore no relation to the Muse and language itself. The throat is filled not with song and music, but with slate and chalk. A similar reification (*oveshchestvleniye*) of inspiration and talent appears earlier:

сумма страданий даёт абсурд;
пусть же абсурд обладает телом!
И   да маячит его сосуд
чем-то чёрным на чём-то белом.   (*К.* 33)

the sum total of suffering gives the absurd. / This absurd possesses the body. / Let its vessel loom / *with something black on something white.*

But, on the other hand, a sorrowful and grateful attitude of the poet towards his gift may be observed:

И *нежности приют*
и *грусти вестник,*
нарушивший уют,
любви ровестник –
с пушинкой над губой
стихотворенье –
пусть радует собой
хотя бы зренье.   (*Н.* 42)

And *the refuge of tenderness* / and *the herald of sadness*, / which has disturbed comfort, / *the same age as love* – / *with down on the lip* / *a poem* / – may it rejoice in itself / if only the eye.

In both cases, metaphors of substitution for poetry, for the process of creation, and for the poet as creator are far removed from traditional poetic phraseology, although the divine essence of creativity is not held in any doubt. Instead of Pushkinian periphrases (such as *son of the bold Muses; one of Phoebus' darlings; favourite of the Muses and Graces; spoilt child of the gods*) Brodsky presents us with the twentieth-century attitude to a poet: *stepson of a wild Empire; an absolute nobody; a man in a cape; a spy and informer.* Instead of the Castalian spring, Brodsky introduces the humble metonymy, *Castalian dampness* (*K.* 61); instead of the usual classical model expressed by 'lyre' metaphors, Brodsky speaks of a *barbed-wire lyre* and *borzoi-script, thicker than treacle* (*Ч.* 88).

Finally, Brodsky's appositional metaphors create a relation of identity between the lyrical 'I' and a poem:

Навряд ли, я,
бормочущий комок
слов, чуждых цвету,
вообразить бы эту
политру смог.   (*Ч.* 33)

I doubt that *I*, / *a mumbling clod* / *of words* alien to colour, / would be able to dream up / that palette.

Here the genitive metaphor *clod of words* appears in apposition to the 'I', thereby seeming to reduce both the 'I' and his language to a non-human state, while the attributive metaphor, *mumbling*, simultaneously raises the *clod of words* to the semantic level of a living creature. The poet's identification of himself with language in metaphors reflects the degree of his dependence on language. Brodsky constantly emphasizes that language is not the poet's tool; on the contrary. Talking about Walcott's poetry, Brodsky explained his own metaphors:

Walcott identifies himself with that 'disembodied vowel' of the language which both parts of his equation share. The wisdom of this choice is, again, not so much his own as the wisdom of his language – better still, the wisdom of its letter: of *black on white*. He is simply a pen that is aware of its movement, and it is this self-awareness that forces his lines into their graphic eloquence. (*L.* 168–9)

It was Khlebnikov who was the first Russian poet to proclaim an identity between the poet and language: '*Я слова бурного разбойник* (III. 365) (*I am a brigand of the stormy word*); and between language and reality: *мешки слов* (*bags of words*); *азбуки столетий* (*the alphabet of centuries*); *росчерки пера морей* (*the flourishes of the pen of the seas*). As a poet-linguist, Khlebnikov created a 'grandiose linguistic Utopia',[20] termed an 'imaginary philology' by Grigoryev.[21]

While interpretation of Brodsky's metaphors of all semantic types is in progress, it is none the less important to realize that language implies not only the poet and poetry; it also stands for Russia:

там толпа говорит, осаждая трамвайный угол,
на языке человека, который убыл.   (Ч. 113)

there the crowd talks, besieging the tram corner, / on the tongue of a man, who has departed

Or for the Russian people (see his early poem 'Verbs'). In one of his interviews, Brodsky has said: 'for everything that I have in my soul I am obliged to Russia and to its people. And – this is the main thing – obliged to its language.'[22] Language also stands for people in general:

От всего человека вам остаётся часть
речи. Часть речи вообще. Часть речи.   (*Ч.* 95)

Of the whole person you have left a part / of speech. Just a part of
speech as such. A part of speech.

Or it can stand for God himself. It is precisely the presence of the
latter that distinguishes Brodsky's Christian consciousness from the
heathen world-view of Khlebnikov.

It can be seen from even a limited quantity of metaphors of
substitution and apposition how various categories of meaning are
gathered into a complex of several semantic fields, either by
repetition of the metaphor or its variant, or by repetition of one
component of the metaphor. Thus, the metaphoric epithet
проволочный (*barbed-wire*) provides a link between the *barbed-
wire lyre* (the lyre of the imprisoned poet), *barbed-wire Ravenna*
(*Ч.* 112) (the town of Dante's exile), and the *barbed-wire cosmos*
(*O.* 98), which may represent a place of universal exile.

It is possible, therefore, to isolate constantly repeated metaphoric transformations of reality and identify the principles of these
transformations. This permits more adequate analysis of the conceptual functions that these metaphors perform. We cannot fail to
notice that Brodsky often concretizes abstract categories of our
everyday experience: *cloth, fabric, thread, needle,* and *sewn up*
represent human existence in 'The Great Elegy to John Donne'; a
fast-moving train in the poem 'Isaac and Abraham' stands for time:
Бесшумный поезд мчится сквозь поля (*C.* 153) (*The
noiseless train rushes through the fields*). And later, another variant
of this metaphor appears: *an insane locomotive* (*H.* 107). Indeed,
all man-made means for the representation of time turn out to be
fruitful material for the creation of yet more metaphors on the
theme of time – one of the most central themes in Brodsky's poetry.
Ordinary watches, thus, give rise to a number of associations, such
as *circle, plate,* and *dish*:

Дух-исцелитель
Я из *бездонных мозеровских блюд*
так нахлебался *варева минут*
и *римских литер,*   (*K.* 64)

Spirit-Healer! / I from the *bottomless Moser's dishes* / stuffed myself
with the *soup of minutes / and Roman script.*

It is significant that in these three metaphors of substitution for time, one includes a Latin name for 'letter' which takes us to the opposition 'time-language'. These metaphors for time frequently include an epithet with the prefix *без* ('without'): '*безумный локомотив*' ('insane locomotive'), '*бесшумный поезд*' ('noiseless train'), '*бездонных мозеровских блюд*' ('bottomless Moser's dishes'), which serve to intensify our awareness of the endlessness of time. This is just one of many means, however, by which the reader is confronted with this theme:

> Никто меня, я думаю, не ждёт
> ни здесь, ни *за пределами тарелки,*
> *заполненной цифирью.*   (*O.* 200)

No one, I think, waits for me / either here, or *beyond the boundaries of a plate / full of figures*

This metaphor will give birth to the one from 'The Thames in Chelsea': *цифирь / астрономической масти* (*Ч.* 48) (*a figure of / astronomical colour*). By using the word *масть* ('colour of the hair of an animal'), Brodsky creates an image of an unknown species, a brutal beast of exile, or, more likely, a monster of time.

The realization of the conceptualization of time in Brodsky's metaphors is intimately connected with the themes of life and death. This link is forged with particular clarity by the image of scissors cutting through emptiness. The genesis of the metaphor *scissors* goes back to the early poems: 'A Guest' (*whistling of scissors*) and 'A Gardener in a Quilted Jacket' (*O.* 103) (*beak-like scissors*). It reappears in the poem '1972' in a religious context that subdues its ominous image:

> Бей в барабан о своём *доверии*
> *к ножницам, в коих судьба материи*
> *скрыта.* Только размер потери и
> делает смертного равным Богу.   (*Ч.* 27)

Beat the drum about your *trust / in scissors, in which the fate of matter / is hidden.* Only the size of the loss / makes a mortal equal to God.

In 'Twenty Sonnets to Mary Stuart' we again come across the *clanking of scissors, a sensation of sudden chilliness* (*Ч.* 56), and in 'Lullaby of Cape Cod', it is juxtaposed with a semantic chain of metaphors for life: *kaftan, thread, needle.*

In order to understand the way in which metaphor allows

Brodsky to re-examine a series of philosophical and religious problems, we must have a closer look at the remaining semantic types of this trope.

Similarity in disparity

This is a comment of language ... a semantic reply to the meaningless and abundant reality.[23]

Metaphors of comparison are the most widespread and traditional type of metaphor. They can be expressed by a wide range of grammatical structures and can combine any type of lexis: *бисер слов* (*У.* 68: *a necklace of words*); *распускается день* (*С.* 92: *day unfolds*); *Время – волна, а Пространство – кит* (*О.* 151: *Time is a wave, but Space, a whale*).

When one component of a metaphor expresses an abstract concept, the other component, as a rule, makes the abstraction concrete, giving rise to a visual similarity: *несчастия по следу посылая* (*С.* 207: *putting misfortune on the trail*, like a dog); *сшить своею плотью, сшить разлуку* (*С.* 135: *to sew up with my flesh, to sew up separation*, like a torn garment). But by no means all metaphors of comparison may be adequately translated into simile: *памятник лжи* (*С.* 46: *a monument to lies*); *язычком небытия* (*С.* 218: *with a tongue of non-existence*).

By frequent comparisons of human life – its emotional and intellectual aspects – with the world of things, Brodsky tends to render emotions and abstract concepts in concrete forms: *на стену будущего* (*У.* 77: *on the wall of the future*); *фонарь печали* (*С.* 52: *the street lamp of sorrow*).

In his search for hidden correspondences between the material and spiritual worlds, Brodsky tends to reify the latter: *клинопись мыслей* (*У.* 15: *the cuneiform of thoughts*); *В больших амфитеатрах одиночеств* (*С.* 68: *In the vast amphitheatres of loneliness*). External similarities are often ignored as irrelevant when seeking the inner essence of two described phenomena: *сучки календаря и циферблата* (*Н.* 43: *the twigs of a calendar and clock-face*); *пыль безумия* (*Ч.* 88: *the dust of madness*); *на край / памяти* (*Ч.* 103: *on the edge of / memory*).

The most frequently used grammatical structure for such metaphors is the genitive syntagma. This appears in Brodsky's metaphors of comparison three times more frequently than an attributive, and five times more frequently than the noun-predicative syntagma. It is surpassed in frequency only by verbal metaphors. But, unlike the verbal syntagma, the genitive case can perform a multiplicity of functions. It is this fact, in Levin's view,[24] that explains why genitive syntagmas are so widely used in Russian poetry. The genitive syntagma provides a grammatical structure for all metaphorical transformations – substitution, comparison, attribution, and identification. Despite this seemingly obvious versatility in the genitive's grammatical and semantic role, analysis of this form of the Russian metaphor has tended to regard semantic purpose as belonging exclusively to the comparative function.[25]

A comparative analysis of the genitive metaphors of four poets (Baratynsky, Khlebnikov, Akhmatova, and Brodsky), gives conclusive evidence on the frequency of their usage. In Baratynsky's work they are forty-six times more frequent than the metaphor-copula; in Khlebnikov's, they appear four times more than his record quantity of copula metaphors. In Akhmatova's case, it is possible to give a more·exact percentage for the number of genitive metaphors as against four other grammatical types: 4.5 per cent metaphor copula; 4 per cent metaphors with an instrumental predicative; 24 per cent genitive metaphors; and 70.5 per cent verbal metaphors.

The first, rather obvious, feature to note is the large number of 'poetical' metaphors amongst the genitive metaphors of Baratynsky and Akhmatova, which shows how well established this grammatical construction is: *storms of the world; heat of the heart; flame of desire;* (Baratynsky); *waves of* [horses'] *manes*; *heat of love*; *black wing of death* (Akhmatova). Although less frequent, similar poetic clichés can be found in Khlebnikov's work: *dreams of existence*; *blow of fate*; *a cloud of arrows*. A few can also be found in Brodsky's work: *burden of the sky*; *threads of rain*; *tongue of the candle*.

Each poet renews this poetic phraseology in his / her own way. Baratynsky, for example, replaces the cliché of everyday language *дорога жизни* (*the road of life*), with the phrase *прогоны жизни* (*cattle tracks of life*). Khlebnikov, too, often replaces one element of a clichéd genitive metaphor with a new component: in place of *язык без костей* (*a tongue without bones*), he gives us the fresh metaphor *день без костей. Смена властей* (*day without bones. A change of powers*). Brodsky prefers to add an attribute to one component of the metaphor, which is a well-established device for the renewal of poetic phraseology in the genitive structure: *от прозы дней суровой* (Ч. 73: *from the rigorous prose of days*, Brodsky); compare *в молитве тоскующей скрипки* (*in the prayer of the sorrowful violin*, Akhmatova); *язвительных стихов какой-то злобный жар* (*malicious heatedness of bitter poems*, Baratynsky). The metaphorical epithet may also create a double metaphor: *Гость белой нищеты* (С. 121: *a guest of white poverty*); *в гирлянде каменных подруг* (Ч.52): *in a garland of stone friends*, Brodsky).

Far more than any other poet, Khlebnikov tends to develop his genitive metaphors by means of a second genitive, complicating the construction by inversion: *на шествия судеб пяты* (*on the heel of Fate's procession*); *на рубежах судьбы межи* (*on the margin of Fate's boundaries*). We even find him introducing a triple genitive: *я застёгиваю перчатку столетий запонкой переменного знака* (*I fasten the glove of centuries with the cuff-link of the sign's alteration*). Brodsky uses this device infrequently: *превращенье бумаги в козла / отпущенья обид* (К. 73: *the transformation of paper into a scapegoat of injuries*).

Khlebnikov's distinctive creation of metaphors on phonetic principles is not characteristic of Brodsky's poetics. Despite this, he has a greater affinity with Khlebnikov than with any other poet as far as the transformation of meaning in genitive metaphors is concerned. The de-animation of the living world and the reciprocal concretization of abstract concepts is not characteristic of Akhmatova's and Baratynsky's poetry, whereas Brodsky and Khlebnikov 'materialize' everything: *с вязанкой жалоб и невзгод* (*with a bundle of complaints and misfortunes*, Khlebnikov); *перед изгородью дней* (К. 114: *before the garden fence of days*); *от лакомого куска / памяти* (Ч. 95: *from a sweet morsel / of memory*); *края местоимений* (Н. 139: *the edges of pronouns*, Brodsky).

They both depersonify man: *люди мы иль копья рока Все в одной и той руке* (*whether human or spears of destiny we are all in one and the same hand*, Khlebnikov); *в мягкой глине возлюбленных* (У. 58: *in the soft clay of our loved ones*, Brodsky). Khlebnikov's most favoured metaphorical epithets are *stony, glass, iron*. We regularly come across such metaphors as *stone girls*; *stone book*; *stone brain*; *the stone of equally great words*; *the old man of the glass sheepskin*; *a cast-iron glance*. There are many more such

metaphors of human, linguistic, and spiritual petrification in
Khlebnikov's poetry which are motivated by one of his major
themes – the theme of time. This proposition is supported if we
consider different grammatical types of metaphors, in which time is
directly associated with stone: *Я времушком-камушком игрывало*
(II. 271: *I used to play with a little time-stone*); *Где каменья
временьем, Где время каменьем* (II. 275: *Where stone like time,
Where time like stone*); *Где камни – время* (III. 62: *Where stone is
time); Идёмте, идёмте в веков каменоломню!* (III. 87: *Let's go,
let's go to the age-quarry!*).

The *vision of time in stone* (v. 104) was also characteristic of
Mandelstam. However, Khlebnikov's *white temples of time* (III. 95)
were moulded from heterogeneous material – glass, iron, steel, and
bronze. For Khlebnikov, *saws of time* sliced through everything:
Пилы времени трупы людей перепилили (III. 282: *The saws
of time sawed through people's corpses*). Everything – spiritual,
creative, and conceptual forces – serves as *a pen in the hands of time*
(III. 312). His hundreds of metaphors of reification are motivated
by the world-view of the poet; to be more precise, by his concept of
number and his desire to compute the course of history.

We have already come across some of Brodsky's 'stony' metaphors: *in a garland of stone friends*; *a stone nest*; *a stone needle*; *a
stone handkerchief*. He has also included numbers in his poetry.
The significance of their semantic and conceptual implications will
be seen later. Although the variety of analogical modes keeps
developing in Brodsky's poetry, it is none the less possible to
discover a single principle of organization in his metaphors of
comparison. This principle is, as in Khlebnikov, *oveshchestvleniye*
– reification of human emotion, of humanity itself, its rational
capabilities and its language:

> ... и при слове "грядущее" *из русского языка*
> *выбегают мыши* и всей оравой
> отгрызают от *лакомого куска*
> *памяти*, что твой сыр дырявой.   (Ч. 95)

and at the word 'future' *from Russian language* / *mice scurry out* and
with all their crowd / gnaw away at the sweet morsel / of memory,
which is as holey as Swiss cheese.

The metaphor *дырявая память* (*holey memory*), commonly
encountered in everyday language, is here renewed by its com-

parison with Emmenthaler cheese and by the genitive metaphor
assigning to a concrete quality an abstract concept by analogy with
a piece of cheese, 'a piece of memory'.

The interaction of metaphors of comparison with similes would
appear to be a characteristic quality of metaphors of this semantic
type rather than being a feature of a poet's idiostyle. The tendency
of such various poets as Mayakovsky, Khlebnikov, Pasternak, and
Tsvetaeva to attach similes to metaphors of comparison seems to be
caused by their striving towards the fusion of unrelated concepts.
Instances of this are only rarely encountered in Akhmatova's
poetry: *На позорном подмостье беды, Как под тронным
стою балдахином* (III. 73: *On the shameful scaffold of woe, I
stand as if under a regal canopy*). Although I have not analysed
Mandelstam's genitive metaphors, similes appear frequently in
connection with his metaphor-copula: *Язык булыжника мне
голубя понятней, Здесь камни – голуби, дома, как
голубятни* (I. 109: *The language of cobblestones is clearer to me
than the language of doves*; / *here, stones are doves and the houses,
dovecotes*). All these poets' works are characterized by a large
quantity of metaphorical comparisons; Brodsky is no exception:

> Это сковывало разговоры; *смех
> громко скрипел, оставляя следы, как снег,*
> опушавший изморосью, *точно хвою, края
> местоимений и превращавший "я"*
> в кристалл, отливавший твёрдою бирюзой,
> но таявший после твоей слезой.   (*H.* 139)

This fettered conversation, *laughter / squeaked loudly, leaving its
traces, like snow,* / covered with sleet, like pine-needles, *the edges / of
pronouns and transforming 'I' / into crystal,* shot through with hard
turquoise, / but melted after by your tear.

Laughter is compared with snow, which freezes both laughter and
speech (*edges of pronouns*) and transforms the 'I' into crystal: the
'I' here is simultaneously a part of speech (pronoun) and a person.
Moreover, the reification of the 'I' is produced in the rhyme-
metaphor *края / я* (*edges / I*); *бирюзой / слезой* (*turquoise / tear*).
The latter may be found in an early poem, 'Pesenka' ('A Song'), as
a metaphor in apposition: *А у меня – слеза, / жидкая бирюза, /
просыхает под утро* (*H.* 8: *But I have – a tear, / liquid turquoise,
/ dries up near morning*).

A brief analysis of Brodsky's poem, 'The Renunciation of the

Sorrowful List' (1967; *O*. 87–8), will serve to demonstrate how metaphors and similes complement one another, causing transference of sense by various means:

> Отказом от скорбного перечня – жест
> большой широты в крохоборе! –
> *сжимая пространство до образа мест,*
> *где я пресмыкался от боли,*
> *как спившийся кравец* в предсмертном бреду,
> *заплатой* на барское платье
> *с изнанки твоих горизонтов* кладу
> на движимость эту заклятье!

The renunciation of the sorrowful list is a gesture / of a great breadth in a pedant! / *Compressing all space into an image of those places* / where *I crawled with pain,* / *like a drunkard tailor* in a pre-death delirium / *sews a patch* on a grand dress / I cast my curse on your chattels / *from your horizons turned inside out.*

Here, the genitive metaphor, *from the seamy side of your horizons,* is inspired and motivated by two similes: *like a drunkard tailor* (*кравец* – dialect for 'tailor, fitter') and the instrumental comparison *заплатой* (*patch*). These carefully selected similes amplify the ambiguity of the metaphor. The somnolent, alcoholic tailor is able to sew his patch on to the horizon; the horizon itself, in the plural, can mean either the line at which earth and sky coincide or a circle of interests and ideas: *your horizons.* As for the addressee, the latter is clearly so different from the poet that this may have been the reason for the pair's separation. A not very original verbal metaphor, *I crawled with pain* – a reference to the poet's recently ended exile – is supported by a series of alliterations: отказом, скорбного, жест, большой, широты, сжимая, образа, мест, пресмыкаясь, спившийся etc. In fact, every other word in this stanza contains one or two sibilants: s, z, zh, sh.

The second stanza presents interest, because of the treatment of the solitary, uninteresting metaphor *ложе любви* (*couch of love*):

> Проулки, предместья, задворки – любой
> твой адрес – пустырь, палисадник, –
> что избрано будет для жизни тобой,
> давно, *как трагедии задник,*
> настолько я обжил, что где бы *любви*
> своей не воздвигла ты *ложе,*
> всё будет *не краше, чем храм на крови,*
> и *общим бесплодием схоже.*

Lanes, suburbs, backyards – whatever / your address – wasteland, front garden – / whatever will be chosen for your life, / long ago I've known it so well / *like the backdrop of a tragedy* / wherever you happen to make your *couch of love* / *nothing will be better than the Temple on the Blood* / nor more alike in its common barrenness.

This clichéd poetical metaphor *couch of love*, has been treated with such a high degree of inversion that its second element appears in a rhymed pair no less banal than the metaphor itself: *любви* / *крови* ('love' / 'blood'). Indeed, there would be no need to devote any attention to this unoriginal metaphor and trivial rhyme if they had not occurred in the work of a poet who has given an hour-long lecture on a single rhyme of Auden's upon the same theme: *Diaghilev* / *have* / *love*. In consequence, the poet's choice of these banal devices is not a sign of poor technique, but is rather a conscious decision to indicate the banality of any amorous situation. Significantly, the weakness of the metaphor is not compensated for; on the contrary, this is emphasized by a series of similes with negative emotional colouring: *like the backdrop of a tragedy, nothing will be better than the Temple on the Blood.*

> Прими ж мой процент, разменяв *чистоган*
> *разлуки на брачных голубок!*
> За лучшие дни поднимаю стакан,
> *как пьёт инвалид за обрубок.*
> *На разницу в жизни свернув костыли,*
> будь с ней до конца солидарной:
> *не мягче на сплетне себе постели,*
> чем мне – на листве календарной.

Take my percentage, exchanging *the cash* / *of separation for the wedding doves!* / To better days I raise my glass / *like the amputee drinks to his stump.* / *Having cast away your crutches to life's disparity* / express your solidarity with life: / *make your bed on gossip no more comfortable* / *than mine – on the leaves of a calendar.*

Here, the first two metaphors are distinguished by differing degrees of novelty and unoriginality: *чистоган разлуки* (*cash of separation*); *брачных голубок* (*wedding doves*). The first metaphor is notable not only for its bold combination of concept of separation with ready cash, but also for its position in the stanza, where the enjambement interrupts its syntactic coherence and thereby strengthens the alienation it implies. The second metaphor is deliberately hackneyed and ironic. The next one, *на разницу в жизни свернув костыли* (*Having cast away your crutches to life's disparity*), cannot be comprehended without reference to the preceding comparison with an invalid. The final simile, however, is not expressed by a comparative figure of speech, but by a complete comparative sentence, which permits the inclusion of two comparative metaphors: *make your bed on gossip*[26] and *than mine – on leaves of a calendar*. These metaphors can be seen to refine and renew the dead metaphor, *couch of love*, with the qualification that the addressee's *couch of love* represents gossip, while the poet's stands for time – *the calendar's leaves*.

> И мёртвым я буду существенней *для*
> тебя, чем холмы и озёра:
> не большую правду скрывает *земля*,
> чем та, что открыта для взора!
> В тылу твоём *каждый растоптанный злак*
> *воспрянет, как петел лядащий.*
> И будут круги расширяться, *как зрак*,
> вдогонку тебе, уходящей.

And dead I'll mean more to / you than hills and lakes: / no greater truth earth hides / than that which opens to the eyes! / In your rear *every trampled ear of corn / will start up, like a wretched cockerel,* / and circles will expand like pupils, / in pursuit of you, departing.

This entire stanza is a development by comparison of the metaphor, *the leaves of a calendar*, which established the themes of time, death, and immortality. The metaphor appears to be forced into a rhyming position. The boldness of the first rhyme, *для* – *земля* ('for / earth') can perhaps only be measured by death itself, because of the audacious enjambement which represents, we must conclude, the fact that the earth takes everything and everybody into itself, including a rejected lover as well as a part of speech, and a preposition cast out to the end of the line. *The trampled ear of corn* and the fading image of the beloved (the bookish, obsolete *зрак*), which leaves behind it ripples on the water, as if from a stone, has clearly created another metaphorical rhyme, *злак* – *зрак*, in conjunction with the archaism, *лядащий* – *уходящий* ('wretched' / 'departing'), which now emphasizes not banality, but the age-old timeless features of the situation.

> *Глушёною рыбой* всплывая со дна,
> кочуя, *как призрак – по требам,*
> *как тело*, истлевшее прежде рядна,

так тень моя, взапуски с небом,
посвюду начнёт возвещать обо мне
тебе, *как заправский мессия*,
и корчится будет на каждой стене
в том *доме, чья крыша – Россия.*

Like a stunned fish surfacing from the bottom, / wandering, *like a phantom at rites*, / *like a body* that has rotted before its shroud, / *my shadow, emulating heavens*, / will everywhere proclaim to you about me, / *as a true Messiah*, / and will writhe on every wall / in the house *whose roof is – Russia.*

The repetitive structure created by similes with the conjunction *как* ('like', 'as') shows that similes are far more suited than metaphors to participate in the rhythmical-compositional structure of a stanza. By establishing syntactical and semantic parallelism, the similes draw the poem towards its highest lyrical point, which is crowned by two metaphors: the copula metaphor, *в том доме, чья крыша – Россия* (*in the house whose roof is – Russia*), and the rhyme-metaphor *Messiah / Russia*. This crowning metaphor lifts the whole poem from a personal level on to a national one, with just a hint of immortality, since a rhyme-metaphor does not merely compare, but provides some kind of equivalence.

James Deese recognized that

because the metaphor is one of the richest results of the interaction between the structure of the human mind and its perceived world, it can illuminate far more than the specific information it is consciously designed to reveal. It can provide a key to the interpretation of a whole work, or even a whole era or culture, as, I suspect, students of literature have known for some time.[27]

Inasmuch as a metaphor may depict human existence in more than one dimension, it is undoubtedly one of the main ways of creating a poetic world. A systematic analysis of the various aspects of metaphor allows us to describe the semantic centres or semantic fields of an artistic work with greater reliability than is the case with a traditional thematic approach. On this count, we have the very definite views of the poet:

The inferiority of analysis starts with the very notion of theme, be it a theme of time, love, or death. Poetry is, first of all, an art of references, allusions, linguistic and figurative parallels. There is an immense gulf between *Homo sapiens* and *Homo scribens*, because for the writer the notion of theme appears as a result of combining the above techniques and devices, if it appears at all. Writing is literally an existential process; it uses thinking for its own ends, it consumes notions, themes, and the like, not vice versa. What dictates a poem is the language, and this is the voice of the language, which we know under the nicknames of Muse or Inspiration. (*L.* 124–5)

In studying the grammar and semantics of a poet's metaphors, we sense the extent to which his world-view, personality and idiostyle are intertwined. Language itself plays far from the least important role in this. The fact that certain semantic transformations are firmly attached to the corresponding grammatical structures places substantial restrictions on the poet's choice of metaphors.

Ars est celare artem

A poet hides as much as he reveals.[28]

The nature of analogies in metaphors of attribution differs to an extent from the principles of likeness and resemblances on which metaphors of substitution and comparison are built. It is less conditioned by the subject-matter and seems more arbitrary. The dominant principle of this semantic type is the transference of human characteristics to the entire, non-human world: nature, things, and abstract concepts.

So far, in our analysis of the two preceding types of metaphor, we isolated the function of reification of the animate and abstract as a specific function of Brodsky's metaphorical system as a whole. In metaphors of attribution, this function is counterbalanced by the function of animation of a world deprived of consciousness and creative activity.

When we come to an examination of metaphors of attribution, we immediately encounter the problem of validation, or, rather, of having sufficient grounds to isolate them as an independent semantic type. The fact of the matter is that there exists a widespread tendency either to separate them as an independent trope – personification – or to subsume them under metonymy.

In observing nature man ascribes to it the attributes and actions of his own views, *not on the basis of similarity* or *through metaphor*, but on the basis of his innate striving to come close to the object of observation and cognition, by the characteristic feature of human reason itself to lay the imprint of its activity on everything it touches. Language expresses this activity of the reason very simply, namely: things are called not what they really are, but what they seem.[29]

The problem is complicated by the fact that the associations in metaphors of modern poetry go beyond the framework of 'apparent impressions'; they are summoned to create new impressions about the object, contrary to what seems and *a fortiori* to the obvious.

> *Негашёная известь зимних пространств, свой корм*
> *подбирая* с пустынных пригородных платформ,
> *оставляла на них* под тяжестию хвойных лап
> *настоящее в чёрном пальто, чей драп,*
> более прочный, нежели шевиот,
> *предохранял там от будущего и от*
> *прошлого* лучше, чем дымным стеклом буфет.   (*H.* 140)

The quicklime of winter expanses, its fodder / gathering from deserted suburban platforms, / *left on them* under the weight of coniferous paws / *the present in a black overcoat*, the worsted of which / is more durable *than tweed*, / *protected there from the future and from / the past* better than the buffet by its smoked glass.

The quicklime of winter expanses is a metaphor of substitution for snow, which is personified by verbal metaphors of attribution: *gathering*, *left*, and *protected*. Time, which is rendered metonymically – present, past, future – is also personified by being dressed in a black overcoat. The pure metonymy – the smoked glass of the buffet – replaces what this buffet contains, namely the alcohol which allows time to be forgotten and, *ipso facto*, allows 'protection' against it. Wintering in this *lost in the dunes . . . small veneered town* (*H.* 137), and buried by snow, one feels cut off from the world and from time: *Winter puts life in brackets* (*O.* 114).

The conceptualization of time by means of metaphors of attribution complements the complex picture of artistic time in Brodsky's poetry. Grammar presents to the poet the broadest opportunities. Virtually any part of speech can endow the described object with qualities which are alien to it. Naturally, of course, there are limits to this as well. Thus, the adjective, as one of the most ancient means for personifying the forces of nature and gods, exhausted its poetic possibilities earlier than other parts of speech. Moreover, as we know, the number of adjectives in any language is limited, and their constant use in the role of metaphoric epithet has converted them with time into poetic phraseology. In Russian poetry, as early as Tiutchev, we see the introduction under the influence of German poetry of compound epithets, designed to renew poeticism: *moth falsely carefree*; *the earth sadly becoming an orphan*; *a dream prophetically unclear*. This device has become the common property of Russian poetry. We find compound attributes in Pasternak and in Akhmatova. Brodsky does not use this device at all. It is revealing that, in the first period, when the percentage of adjectival metaphors is fairly high (58 per cent), many of them are repetitive: над утлой мглой (*C.* 21: *above fragile gloom*); утлый дым (*C.* 21: *fragile smoke*); утлые птицы (*C.* 36: *fragile birds*); утлая нежность (*C.* 51: *fragile tenderness*). Certain adjectives are repetitive even in his second period, when the percentage of adjectival metaphors falls to 45 per cent:[30] *naked thing* (*Ч.* 27); *naked briar* (*K.* 71); *naked grasshopper* (*У.* 16); *naked columns* (*У.* 22); *pale wind* (*C.* 77); *pale river* (*C.* 110); *pale flame* (*K.* 95). Instances of poetic phraseology can be found: роковая черта (*Ч.* 52) (*fateful line*); слепая сила (*Ч.* 66) (*blind force*). In the third period, which has only 34 per cent, Brodsky discovers vivid and unexpected adjectives: ухмылки изумрудные гостей ('Zofya': *the emerald smirks of the guests*); белое многоточье (*У.* 82: *white printer's dots*); слепое, агатовое великолепье / непроницаемого стекла (*у.* 83: *the blind agate splendour of the impenetrable glass*). But their semantics change as well: man is endowed with the qualities of things.

More and more frequently, the adjectives give way to other parts of speech, especially the adverb and participle. The latter, which is, of course, formed from the verb, possesses all the formal qualities of adjectives, and presents great opportunities for characterizing the object being described from an unexpected point of view: глаз, засорённый горизонтом, плачет (*Ч.* 23: *the eye, obstructed by the horizon, weeps*); для глаза, / вооружённого слезой (*K.* 75: *for the eye, / armed with a tear*); присохшим плачем (*Ч.* 67: *congealed weeping*). In participial metaphors, we find particularly clear evidence of Brodsky's departure from tradition – in them we see the de-animation of man more often than the personification of things: с затвердевающим под орех мозгом (*Ч.* 102: *with the brain hardening like a nut*); затвердевшие седины (*Ч.* 52: *hardened grey hair*). Such a metonymic depiction of man in metaphors was characteristic of the poetics of Futurism.

As Smirnov observes, the Futurists obliterated the distinction between the part and the whole, 'by bringing to the picture of the world the characteristics of particular homogeneity'.[31] In Brodsky's poetic world, the function of the neutralization of part–whole is completely different. Here, we are not simply witnessing the metonymic depiction of human beings; we are also seeing the metaphoric transformation of parts of the body on to the plane of objects, thereby achieving the alienation of the most inalienable human activity: thoughts, consciousness, memory, speech and creativity: *молчанье горла, мозга* (*C*. 138) (*silence of throat, of brain*); *оттиском ... уст* (*Ч*. 80: *off-print of lips*); *гортани великую сушь* (*У*. 63: *larynx's great dryness*).

The same must also be said of the next similarity between Brodsky's poetics and that of the Futurists which is manifested in the sphere of attributive metaphors. Like the Futurists, he endowed 'the sign with the quality of a thing'.[32] Words, parts of speech, sounds are simultaneously objectified and personified: *Как быстро разбухает голова / словами, пожирающими вещи* (*O*. 205: *How quickly the head swells / with words that devour things*);

> сказуемое, ведомое подлежащим,
> уходит в прошедшее время, жертвуя настоящим,
> от грамматики новой на сердце пряча
> окончание шёпота, крика, плача. (*H*. 106)

the predicate, led by the subject / departs for time past, sacrificing the present, / hiding the ending of a whisper, cry, lament / from a new grammar for the heart.

The conceptual load of such metaphors will receive more attention in the next chapter.

Visual associations are certainly not always the basis for Brodsky's attributive metaphors. In theme we can also trace a logical basis for metaphorical transfer: *прямоугольный сухой мороз* (*rectangular dry frost*) receives its first definition because it penetrates into the house through rectangular windows. *In a garland of stone friends*, a metaphor of substitution for the monuments to the kings in the Luxembourg Gardens, is motivated by the material from which they are made. It is important to note that relative adjectives are most suitable for such fusion of two tropes: *metallic gill*; *metallic dew*; *stone grass*; *bronze stream*.

The next, and perhaps most widely used, means of attribution is the verb. In the two poets I have compared on the basis of four types of metaphors, Akhmatova and Brodsky, verbal metaphors clearly dominate over all others. In Akhmatova, they comprise 70 per cent, compared with 22 per cent genitive, 4 per cent copula, and 4 per cent instrumental predicatives. In Brodsky, verbal metaphors comprise 75 per cent. According to Brooke-Rose's data, Chaucer, Spenser, Shakespeare, Donne, Pope, Hopkins, Yeats, and Thomas used verbal metaphors much more frequently than nominal. It is revealing that in all of them, Brooke-Rose singles out their most traditional function – personification – as the main one: they humanize things far more often than they change them into things.[33]

Being one of the most ancient means for personification, verbal metaphors are bound to include a large number of general poetic metaphors. The spirit, gods, the heavens, diabolical forces, are all-powerful and capable of any act. Such eternal themes as the soul, death, love, the Muse, time, and so on have incorporated the inertia of poeticisms. It is hardly surprising, therefore, that neither Akhmatova nor Brodsky is free of poetic phraseology: *silence floats*; *sadness swirls*; *a cry flies*; *anguish lies down* (Brodsky). Both poets renew hackneyed metaphors by the choice of an unexpected predicate or subject: *The Muse went deaf and blind*; *While doom wailed at the doors*; *Disasters are bored without us*; *While glory dragged itself here for the morning*; *Such nights were crawling towards me* (Akhmatova). In all these metaphors, the lofty semantics of the subject is deliberately lowered by the selection of a prosaic verb. This device for control over a potentially dramatic situation is highly characteristic of Brodsky's poetics: *Здесь время врёт, а рядом Вечность бьёт* (*С.* 198) (*Here time tells lies, while next door Eternity beats*); *Пусть Время взяток на берёт – / Пространство, друг, сребролюбиво!* (*К.* 57) (*Though Time takes no bribes – Space, my friend, is fond of money!*); *Покуда Время / не поглупеет, как Пространство* (*У.* 95: *Until Time gets as stupid as Space*).

Unlike Akhmatova, Brodsky commonly attaches to a single verb several subjects or objects from various semantic fields: *Here I will end my days, losing hair, teeth, verbs, suffixes* (*Ч.* 26); *The future always fills the earth with grain, voices – with cordiality, fills the hours with their hither and thither* (*У.* 65). As in the genitive and attributive metaphors analysed above, it was not possible to discover either structural or functional similarities in the verbal metaphors of Akhmatova and Brodsky. Thus, Brodsky almost never has recourse in his verbal metaphors to the oxymorons which are quite common in Akhmatova: *silence crashes*; *silence responds*; *horror comforted*; *snowstorm warmed*; *where waterfalls remain silent*. Brodsky's verbal metaphors do not fall into traditional semantic orders, like Akhmatova's, with slightly transformed poetic models. For example, a large group of her verbal metaphors are linked by images of fire, flame, dawn: *the shadow of smile dawned*; *love caught fire*; *alarm catches fire*; *we set fire to . . . golden, magnificent days*. This order is counterposed by a series of verbal metaphors with the semantics of extinguishing, cooling down, smouldering: *the sky gets cold*; *amorous drowsiness gets cold*; *where the flaming letters are reduced to ashes*; *memory has been extinguished*; *reason has been extinguished*; *my unprecedented gift has been extinguished*. The majority of these metaphors belong to the semantic type of comparison and are mentioned here purely for the sake of a system of analysis.

To conclude my description of verbal metaphors, it should be added that their specificity is manifest not on the grammatical level, but on the level of semantic combinations. Such a fundamental feature of this part of speech as transitivity/intransitivity is not used by the poets – at least, not to the extent which would form a perceptible tendency. A specialized syntactic position of the verb, such as the imperative with address, also does not facilitate an intensification of the expressive possibilities of verbal metaphors. The heterogeneous semantics of the objects, and not the form of the verb *сумей . . . вернуться* ('manage . . . to return'), creates an unrepeatably authorial metaphor in the early poem by Brodsky, 'The Pskov Register':

> Сумей же по полям,
> по стрелкам, вёрстам,
> по занятым рублям
> (почти по звёздам!)
> по формам без души
> со всем искусством
> Колумба (о, спеши!)
> вернуться к чувствам. (*H.* 41)

Manage then over the fields, / over the arrows, the versts, / over the borrowed roubles / (almost over the stars!) / over the forms without soul / with all Columbus' art / (O, hurry!) / to return to the feelings.

In his verbal metaphors, Brodsky follows Khlebnikov, realizing the principle of metamorphosis of each and everything:

> *Солнце*, войдя в зенит,
> луч кладя на паркет, *себя*
> *этим деревянит.* (*У.* 20)

(*The sun*, reaching its zenith, / laying a ray on the parquet, / *thereby turns itself to wood.*)

> Духота. Светофор мигает, *глаз превращая в средство*
> *передвижения по комнате к тумбочке с виски.* Сердце
> замирает на время, но всё-таки бьётся: *кровь,*
> *поблуждав по артериям, возвращается к перекрёстку.*
> Тело похоже на свёрнутую в рулон трёхвёрстку,
> и на севере поднимают бровь. (*Ч.* 99)

It's stifling. The traffic-lights wink, *turning the eye into a means / of moving around the room to a night-table with a whisky.* The heart / dies for a time, but beats all the same: *the blood, / having wandered through the arteries, returns to the cross-roads.* / The body is like a rolled-up map, / and in the north they raise a brow.

Once more, man is depicted metonymically: the eye, the heart, the blood, the arteries, the eyebrow. Each part of the body is estranged by means of verbal metaphors. the heart, although mentioned, is also replaced in a metaphor of comparison, *the cross-roads*. The body is compared to a rolled-up map.

Like Khlebnikov, Brodsky systematically objectifies man in order to develop the theme of the 'ice age is coming', the theme of time and alienation. More will be said about these themes later. In emphasizing the function of reification in any semantic type of metaphor, it is important to remember that a 'thingist' conception of man is not peculiar to Brodsky. The pathos of the individual, the spiritual, constitutes the distinguishing feature of his model of the personality. And nature and abstract concepts are abundantly endowed with these features: *печаль моя с цветами в стороне* (*С.* 164: *my sadness with flowers on the side*); *и рядом детство плачет на углу* (*С.* 118: *and close by childhood cries on the corner*); *и зима простыню на верёвке считала своим бельём* (*Н.* 139: *and winter thought the sheet on the line its linen*); *Шиповник каждую весну / пытается припомнить точно / свой прежний вид* (*К.* 71: *The sweetbriar every spring / tries to remember exactly / its former appearance*).

Nature is even given speech: *Горизонт на бурге* / *не проронит о бегстве ни слова* (*H.* 44: *The horizon on the hill will not say a single word about flight*);

> Что ветру говорят кусты,
> листом бедны?
> Их речи, видимо, просты,
> но нам темны.
> Перекрывая лязг ведра,
> скрипящий стул – "Сегодня ты сильней. Вчера
> ты меньше дул."
>
> (*H.* 14)

What do the bushes, poor in leaf, / say to the wind? / Their utterances, obviously, are simple, / but obscure to us. / Exceeding the clank of the bucket, / the squeaking chair / – 'Today you are stronger. Yesterday / you blew less.'

In all types of Brodsky's metaphors, there is created a kind of mirror reflection of the constant characteristics of all aspects of human existence: the dead world of things and nature is personified, while man himself, his mental and emotional qualities, are made inanimated in the redefinition of this opposition, 'living–thing', consists the specificity of Brodsky's metaphorical system. To exclude from our analysis the metaphors of attribution on the basis that they correspond to personification would mean a distortion of the picture of the author's poetic world.

A form of identity of two versions

> Any thought driven to its logical conclusion turns out to be a nightmare.[34]

Metaphors of identification are distinguished by a constant grammatical structure. They are expressed exclusively by a predicative noun, according to the formula *A is B*:

> *Воздух, в сущности, есть плато,*
> *пат, вечный шах, тщета,*
> *ничья, классическое ничто,*
> *гегелевская мечта.*
>
> (*У.* 22)

Air in essence *is a plateau,* / *a stale-mate, an eternal check-mate, a vanity,* / *a draw, a classical nothing,* / *a Hegelian dream.*

In this semantic type of metaphor, the depicted object is named (it is usually the subject of the sentence) and directly identified with another object which is also present as the nominal predicate of the sentence: *Воздух – вещь языка* (*У.* 64: *Air is a thing of language*). Two cases are possible in Russian for the nominal predicative metaphor: the nominative case or the instrumental; the choice depends principally on the link-verb and its tense. The instrumental is not favoured by Brodsky. Only 13 per cent of all his nominal predicative metaphors are expressed by this case. In Akhmatova's work, 45 per cent of the nominal metaphors are in the instrumental case and 54 per cent in the nominative. However, in her poetry metaphors of identification are four times less common than in Brodsky. The model and semantic differences between the two cases are particularly marked when they are in proximity to each other:

> *Время есть холод. Всякое тело*, рано
> или поздно, становится пищею *телескопа*:
> остывает с годами, удаляется от светила.   (*У.* 119)

Time is cold. Every body, sooner / or later, *becomes food for a telescope*: / grows cold with the years, moves away from the *luminary*.

The second metaphor, *every body becomes food for a telescope*, does not express complete identity. It is less dogmatic by comparison with the first metaphor, *time is cold*. We could not translate this metaphor into the past or future. It is marked, to use Vinogradov's expression, by 'aloofness from the momentary'. It is interesting that Vinogradov denies the instrumental case any part in the formation of metaphors: 'the instrumental predicative,' he states, 'even when it consists of a link verb and a name ascribed to the subject figuratively, metaphorically, cannot be taken as a metaphor, but only as a metaphorical application'.[35] Following Vinigradov, many of those who have studied the Russian metaphor call instrumental predicative metaphors 'metamorfoza'.[36]

Metaphors of identification have a paramount place among other types for number of reasons: (1) Grammatically they are more independent than verbal, adjectival, or genitive link metaphors, incorporating as they do both subject and predicate, and often being coterminous with the sentence: *Любовь есть предисловие к разлуке* (*О.* 211: *Love is the foreword to parting*). (2) The choice of 'pure' copulas – *есть* ('is'), *суть* ('in essence'), or those such as *это, это есть* ('this is'), *это то же* ('this is the same as') – which contain a nuance of conditionality – points to various degrees of identification. (3) There are additional sentences of cause and effect which explain the reason for identification and which signal the degree of deformation of similarity, upon which metaphors of comparison are constructed:

> *Север – честная вещь. Ибо* одно и то же
> он твердит вам всю жизнь – шёпотом, в полный голос
> в затянувшейся жизни – разными голосами.   (*У.* 122)

The north is an honest thing. For one and the same thing / it repeats to you all life long – in a whisper, at the top of its voice, / in one's prolonged life – in various voices.

(4) Repetition of the conjunction 'and'; the combination of a link-verb and the conjunction *и есть* ('and there is') and paraphrases such as 'in essence', or 'as a matter of fact', may emphasize a relation of identification: *Пространство – вещь. / Время же, в сущности, мысль о вещи* (*Ч.* 106: *Space is a thing. Time, though, in essence, is a thought about a thing.*)

At the lexical level, the distinction between Brodsky's metaphors of identification and comparison is created by their tendency to form various combinations of 'abstract/concrete' oppositions. Metaphors of comparison which are expressed by the same grammatical structure usually appeal to the senses and often contain an image, a concrete object: *Дерево за окном – пасмурная свеча* (*К.* 83: *The tree behind the window is an overcast candle*); *Но смерть – это зеркало, что не лжёт* (*О.* 152: *But death is a mirror, which does not lie*). Metaphors of identification, on the other hand, are based on logic, rather than visual, similarities between the described objects or phenomena. They can equally well include two abstract concepts: *Silence is the future of the days* (*О.* 206); *Time is cold* (*Н.* 119); *Life is a form of time* (*Ч.* 106). Dealing primarily with ideas, metaphors of identification include such speculative categories as *a form, a method, a cause, a mechanism, a guarantee, consequence*; *Грядущее есть форма тьмы* (*К.* 76: *The future is a form of darkness*); *Постоянство такого родства – основной механизм Рождества* (*Ч.* 5: *The constancy of such kinships is the basic mechanism of Christmas*). These metaphors are metaphors of statement, not suggestion. They usually have an authoritative, at times even categorical, tone:

Сама
вещь, как правило, пыль
не тщится перебороть,
не напрягает бровь.
Ибо пыль – это плоть
времени; плоть и кровь.   (*K.* 110)

The thing itself, as a rule, does / not endeavour to overcome the dust, / does not furrow its brow. / *For dust is the flesh* / *of time; flesh and blood.*

This assertiveness of tone is accentuated by means of repetition or by particles (*only, none the less, just*), and by the intonation:[37]

и, если бы *душа* имела профиль,
ты б увидал,
что и *она*
всего лишь слепок с горестного дара.   (*K.* 61)

And, if *the soul* had a profile, / you would see, / that *even it* / *is only a copy of a grievous gift.*

This grammatical structure allows Brodsky to create metaphors with aphoristic succinctness and poignant paradoxicality. An extensive use of such metaphors, however, may not suit all tastes, or, indeed, every poetic system. Thus, in English poetry, according to Brooke-Rose, there have been only three poets who have used them extensively: 'It is surprising how little the copula is exploited for metaphor in English poetry. With the notable exception of Donne, Shakespeare and Spenser are the boldest and the most varied; others on the whole use it more rarely, more dully, or more cautiously.'[38]

Among the Russian poets I have examined eleven, two of them Symbolists – Bal'mont and Blok. As one may easily guess, these metaphors of statement are the least suited to Symbolist aesthetics. I have found about sixty metaphor–copulae in Blok and slightly over 150 in Bal'mont. I have traced about sixty metaphors with nominative predicate in Derzhavin and only nine in Baratynsky. In the case of Brodsky's great predecessors, I have found fifty metaphor–copulae in Mandelstam and the same number in Akhmatova, in Pasternak 85; in Mayakovsky 350, in Tsvetaeva 500, and in Khlebnikov 550; all this compared with Brodsky's 350.

These data can help to establish the poet's genesis. Sergei Bobrov was correct in claiming that 'if we possessed statistical data about the work of different poets, we would have no difficulty in identifying their respective precursors'.[39] Still, it is also important to understand what constitutes a poet's originality. Thus, neither Mayakovsky's nor Tsvetaeva's metaphor–copulae are discursive, as is the case with most of Khlebnikov's and Brodsky's metaphors.

The commanding presence of personal pronouns in the copulae metaphors of the Symbolists is their characteristic feature. Of Bal'mont's metaphor–copulae, 41 per cent include personal pronouns. Mayakovsky's copulae metaphors also tend to relate to the 'self', the 'I': *Я – бесценных слов мот и транжир* (I. 56: *I am a squanderer and spendthrift of priceless words*); *Вот – я весь боль и ушиб* (I. 106: *Here it is – I am all pain and injury*). Of all Mayakovsky's metaphors with a nominal predicate, 9.5 per cent are directed to the self. Smirnov has made an interesting observation concerning Mayakovsky's 'I': 'Mayakovsky's lyrical subject, mainly presented as a central bodily configuration absorbing a world body, is either a centre of "metaphorical expansion" or a "metaphorical attraction".'[40] When Mayakovsky 'scrambles out of the lyrical hole', as he puts it, and substitutes 'we' for 'I', he proceeds irresistibly to inflate his metaphors: *Мы – зодчие земель, планеты декораторы, мы – чудотворцы* (II. 240: *We are the architects of lands, the decorators of the planet, we are miracle-workers*). Mayakovsky used precisely this type of metaphor in the service of ideological propaganda: 'Communism is the youth of the world . . .' (VII. 174); 'GPU is the fist of our dictatorship' (VIII. 231).

In Tsvetaeva, the presence of lyrical 'I' in metaphors with a nominal predicate is also very pronounced: 12.5 per cent of all her copula metaphors are directed to the self: *Я – страница твоему перу* (II. 226: *I am a sheet of paper for your pen*); *Я – бренная пена морская* (II. 286: *I am a perishable sea-foam*). Like Mayakovsky's, Tsvetaeva's copula metaphors tend to be emotive although her metaphors are susceptible to more varied semantic transformation than Mayakovsky's. She uses them more frequently and with more skill than any other Russian poet. Such poems as 'Your Name is a Bird in my Hand' (I. 227); 'White Guard! Gordian Knot' (II. 74); 'All the Splendour of Trumpets is just the Murmur of the Grass Compared to you' (II. 98); 'I am a Sheet of Paper for Your Pen' (II. 226), are constructed entirely on the pattern *A is B*; or *A is B of C*. It is only Tsvetaeva's metaphor–copulae which consist exclusively of compound words fusing together different parts of speech and different concepts:

> Ночлег-человек,
> Навек-человек!
> Простор-человек,
> Ниотколь-человек,
> Сквозь-пол-человек
> Прошёл человек.   (II. 162)

Night-rest-man, Forever-man! Full-range-man, From-nowhere-man, Through-the-floor-man, Passed-by-man.

Mayakovsky and Khlebnikov use compound words, too, but not in this type of metaphor.

In Brodsky, only 2.3 per cent of all the metaphors of this type have an 'I' as the subject, including such discursive instances as: *Я – круг в сеченьи* (*O*. 184: *I am a circle in the section*); "*Я – только ножка циркуля. Они – / опора неподвижная снаружи*" (*O*. 196: '*I am only a compass leg. They are the motionless support from the outside*').

Unlike any of these three poets, Brodsky never builds his metaphors on purely phonetic principles, although his metaphors may be accompanied by alliteration. But one never finds anything like Mayakovsky's *Наш бог бег* (II. 7: *Our God is speed*); or Khlebnikov's *Пение пыли из пены* (III. 12: *singing of dust of foam*). The repeated phoneme /p/ is associatively linked with semantic keywords in the poem 'Perun': *Perun*, *pena* ('foam'), *pyl'* ('dust'), *peshchera* ('cave'), *peniye* ('singing'). Khlebnikov was convinced that 'words which begin with the same consonants travel in the same direction, like a swarm of falling stars'.[41] His 'initial method' enables him to merge in metaphors the remotest objects and concepts.

A description and comparison of any given type of metaphor used by poets helps to prove their stylistic affinity or divergence, as the case may be. With all the poets, the simple pattern *A is B* exceeds all others in quantity. It can, however, be varied by an epithet or a subordinate clause. This pattern is at times made more complex by a chain of metaphors – a device found in all, including Akhmatova and Mandelstam, although they never link together more than three metaphors, and more often only two: *Я – голос*

ваш, жар вашего дыханья, / *Я – отраженье вашего лица*
(Akhmatova, II. 137: *I am your voice, the heat of your breath, I am
the reflection of your face*).

With Khlebnikov and Brodsky, the pattern *A is B and C of D and
E of F* is not at all uncommon: *E – это чисел ручей, два и дым
чисел* (Khlebnikov, III. 76: *E is the stream of numbers, the two and
smoke of numbers*); *Небосвод –* / *хор согласных и гласных
молекул,* / *в простонечии – душ* (*У.* 64: *The firmament* / *is the
choir of the molecule of consonants and vowels,* / *in common
parlance, of souls*). Tsvetaeva and Brodsky alike extend the chain
of metaphors to a strophe and even over a whole poem. In their
poetry one observes the frequent tendency to split metaphors into
parts and to extrapolate the parts into independent sentences by
means of punctuation, which does not change their grammatical
structure:

> *Местность*, где я нахожусь, *есть пик*
> *как бы горы.* Дальше – воздух, Хронос.
> Сохрани эту речь, *ибо рай – тупик.*
> *Мыс, вдающийся в море. Конус.*
> *Нос железного корабля.*
> Но не крикнуть "Земля"   (Ч. 108)

The place where I am *is the peak* / *as it were of the mountain.* Further
on is the air, Chronos. / Preserve this speech, *for heaven is a
cul-de-sac.* / *A cape, falling into the sea. A cone.* / *The prow of an iron
ship.* / But one can't shout 'Land'!

In both cases, such a practice can be explained by the poet's
attempt to characterize the described object simultaneously from
different angles, to bring out the essential, as it were the definitive,
features. A typical way of creating dual and triple metaphors is the
use of a genitive-link syntagma in the subject or predicate of the
metaphor. This is a practice followed by all poets. Khlebnikov,
Tsvetaeva, and Brodsky often use a double genitive; even a triple
genitive link is not rare: *Мы торговки чёрных небесных
очей,* / *Моты золота осени листьев* (Khlebnikov, III. 257: *We
are the traders of black heavenly eyes,* / *the squanderers of the gold of
the leaves of autumn*). They also use other cases instead of the
genitive: *потому что смерть – это всегда вторая* / *Флоренция
с архитектурой Рая* (Ч. 111: *because death is always a second* /
Florence with the architecture of Paradise).

The intention of penetrating to the very essence of the object

described by means of metaphor leads to a rich variety of grammatical patterns (*A is B of C or D of E; A is B is C of D and E of F*),
or an inverted pattern (*B of C is A; C is A of B*):

> Жизнь есть товар на вынос:
> торса, пениса, лба.
> И географии примесь
> к времени есть судьба.   (*Н.* 110)

Life is goods to take away: / of the torso, the penis, the brow. / And
the admixture of geography / to time is fate.

Metaphors which are introduced by the predicative particle *это*
('is' or 'this is'), create a different pattern, not of the familiar kind:
Море, мадам, это чья-то речь (*O.* 155: *The sea, madam, is
somebody's speech*), but those denoting a generalization or part of
a reasoning process:

> Воздух, пламень, вода, фавны, наяды, львы,
> взятые из природы или из головы, –
> всё, что придумал Бог и продолжать устал
> мозг, превращено в камень или металл.
> *Это – конец вещей, это – в конце пути*
> *зеркало, чтоб войти.*   (*Ч.* 39)

Air, flame, water, fauns, naiads, lions, / taken from nature or from
the head, – / everything that God invented and which the brain was
too tired to continue, / it has been turned into stone or metal. / *This is
the end of things. This is the mirror at the end of the journey so that
one may enter.*

We do not encounter such metaphors among Tsvetaeva's and
Mayakovsky's metaphor–copulae. Equally, no such metaphors are
to be found in the early Brodsky. They appear with his growing
tendency towards a logical, rationalistic manner of poetic thinking.
They incorporate general statements, deductions, and depend to a
greater extent on the context than the other variants of metaphors
with a nominative predicate:

> Вглядитесь в пространство!
> в его одинаковое убранство
> поблизости и вдалеке! в упрямство,
> с каким, независимо от размера,
> зелень и голубая сфера
> сохраняет колер. *Это – почти что вера,*
>
> *род фанатизма!*   (*У.* 126)

Look into space! / into its identical attire / near and far! into the stubborness / with which, irrespective of the size, / the green and the blue sphere / preserve colour. *This is almost like faith, // a kind of fanaticism!*

The only related cases to be found in Akhmatova and Pasternak are a variation on the pattern *A is B of C*, for in both cases *это* replaces the subject – verse – which is stated in the title. I have in mind Akhmatova's poem, 'About Poetry' (Akhmatova, I. 225), and Pasternak's 'The Definition of Poetry' (I. 22). Khlebnikov, again, is closer to Brodsky in this respect:

> Это не люди, не боги, не жизни,
> Ведь в треугольниках – сумрак души.
> Это над людом в сумрачной тризне
> Теней и углов Пифагора ковши!   (II. 244)

This is not people, not gods, not lives. / Surely in triangles is the darkness of a soul. / *This is above the people in a gloomy mourning / the ladles of shadows and the angles of Pythagoras!*

Any description of the grammatical variations in those metaphors with a nominative predicative would be incomplete without mentioning the so-called negative metaphors and metaphors including inversion. The latter are notably rare in all the poets under consideration. It is also notable because inversion – at times of a rather ponderous type – is a peculiarity of Derzhavin's, Khlebnikov's, Mayakovsky's, and Brodsky's syntax.

Brodsky's negative metaphors reproduce all the above-mentioned grammatical patterns: *A is not B but C*; *A is not B of C*; *A is not B of C but D of E*; *A is not B and not C but D of E*.

> Данная песня не вопль отчаяния.
> Это – следствие одичания.
> Это – точней – первый крик молчания,   (Ч. 27)

This song is not a wail of despair, / It is the consequence of becoming wild. / It is, more precisely, the first cry of silence.

The combination of negation with opposition enables him to reinvigorate stale metaphors, even clichés, to mix the sublime with the ridiculous, to bring together notions derived from remote semantic fields and to elicit a concealed irony:

> Жужжанье мухи,
> увязшей в липучке – не голос муки,

но попытка автопортрета в звуке
"ж".   (У. 126)

The buzzing of a fly, / stuck on fly-paper is not the voice of anguish, /
but the attempt at a self-portrait in the sound / 'zh'.

Tsvetaeva's negative metaphors are rather distinctive. They
almost always contain an opposition: *Два зарева! – нет, зеркала! /
Нет, два недуга! / Два серафических жерла, / Два чёрных
круга / Обугленных – из льда зеркал* (II. III: *Two glows! No,
mirrors! No, two ailments! Two seraphic muzzles, / Two black
circles / charred – from the ice of mirrors*). Many metaphors of
negation in Mayakovsky may be taken literally, precisely because
they do not include an opposition. Derzhavin, Baratynsky, and
Pasternak have hardly any negative metaphors. Other poets use
them only sporadically. Khlebnikov has very few negative metaphors, and they are similar to Tsvetaeva's pattern: *A is not B but C.*
In Brodsky, they are found throughout his work and with particular
regularity in the second period.

If the poet's outlook may be said to affect the structure of his
metaphors, then, for Brodsky, this metaphorical type serves to
create multiple points of view. In his own words, 'the multiplicity of
meanings assumes a corresponding number of attempts to discover
the meaning'.[42] The copula structure can easily incorporate several
metaphors:

> *Наши оттиски*! в смятых сырых простынях –
>   этих рыхлых извилинах общего мозга! –
> в мягкой глине возлюбленных, в детях без нас.
>   *Либо – просто синяк
>   на скуле мирозданья от взгляда подростка,
>   от попытки на глаз
> расстоянье прикинуть от той ли литовской корчмы
>   до лица, мрогооко смотрящего мимо,*   (У. 58)

Our imprints! In the crumpled damp sheets – / of these crumbly
curves of the common brain! – / in the soft clay of the loved ones, in
the children in our absence. / *Or is it simply a bruise / on the
cheek-bone of the universe from the glance of a youth, / from the
attempt by eye / to estimate the distance from that Lithuanian inn / to
the face, many-eyedly looking sideways.*

Strictly speaking, the beginning of this metaphor is to be found
some lines above: *Наша письменность, Томас!* ... *Прочный*

*чернильный союз, / кружева, вензеля, / помесь литеры
римской с кириллицей: цели со средством, / ... Наши
оттиски!... (Our written languages, Thomas! ... A solid, inky
union, lace, a monogram, the mixture of Roman script with Cyrillic:
the ends with the means ... Our imprints!...).*

The grammatical type delineated here enables the poet with a
paradoxical turn of mind both to reach the extremes of semantic
alienation and yet to bring together disparate ideas. Lodge con-
tends that the distance between the signified and the signifier is
more characteristic of poetic style than the choice of metaphors:
'The greater the distance (existentially, conceptually, affectively)
between the tenor (which is part of the context) and the vehicle of
metaphor, the more powerful will be the semantic effect of metaphor, but the greater also will be the disturbance to the relationships of contiguity between items in the discourse and therefore to
realistic illusion.'[43]

The change of distance can be seen by examining Brodsky's
metaphors for *life*, used at different periods but homogeneous in
their grammatical structure:

> И вся-то жизнь – биенье сердца,
> и говор фраз, да плеск вины,
> и ночь над лодочкою секса
> по слабой речке тишины.   (*C.* 51)

And all of life then is the beating of the heart, / and the murmur of
phrases, and the splash of guilt / and night above the boat of sex /
along the weak river of silence.

Here we have a combination of metonymy (*the beating of the heart,
the murmur of phrases*) and metaphors of comparison (*the splash of
guilt*; *the boat of sex*; *the river of silence*). Life does not appear as
alienated, bracketed by means of rationalistic metaphors, although
abstract notions such as guilt and silence are materialized. But not
more than five years later, in the philosophical poem 'Gorbunov
and Gorchakov' (1965–8), Brodsky set life between inverted
commas, as it were:

> "Жизнь – только разговор перед лицом
> молчанья". "Пререкания движений".
> "Речь сумерек с расплывшимся концом."
> "И стены – воплощенье возражений."   (*O.* 206)

'Life is only a conversation in the face / of silence'. 'The argument of movement.' / 'The speech of dusk with an indistinct end.' / 'And the walls are the embodiment of objections.'

Here, *silence* is a metaphor of substitution for death, as can be seen from a whole series of metaphors of identification to be found a few lines above:

> Молчанье – это будущее дней,
> катящихся навстречу нашей речи,
>
> . . .
>
> Молчанье – это будущее слов,
> уже пожравших гласными всю вещность,
>
> . . .
>
> Молчанье – настоящее для тех,
> кто жил до нас.   (*O.* 206)

Silence is the future of the days, / that roll to meet our speech, . . .
Silence is the future of the words, / whose vowels have already devoured the stuff of things, . . .
Silence is the present for those, / who lived before us.

This multilayered metaphorical construction is sustained by antinomic ideas, which are central to Brodsky's poetic world: silence–speech; death–life; spirit–matter; present–future (time).

Losev has observed correctly that Brodsky matured early as a person, and has basically changed little.[44] However, he has progressed by tirelessly taking the next logical step in interpreting some fundamental existential situations. In 1975, his metaphorical definition of life is even more abstract:

> Жизнь – форма времени. Карп и лещь –
> сгустки его. И товар похлеще –
> сгустки. Включая волну и твердь
> суши. Включая смерть.   (*Ч.* 106)

Life is a form of time. The carp and bream / are its clots. And goods a little bit more substantial / are clots. Including the wave and the firmness / of dry land. Including death.

Here not only human life (*goods a little bit more substantial* – a metaphor of substitution for man) but also the life of the planet (i.e. the metonymy, *the waves and the firmness of dry land*) and death itself are included within the orbit of the poet's observation. It seems, moreover, that these observations are conducted from the point of view of time: 'there is no further way to go', as Brodsky stated in the same poem, 'elsewhere there is only a series of stars. And they are burning away' (*Ч*. 104).

He always practises in verse what he theorizes about in prose. In 1976, he wrote on the importance for a poet of having a sense of distance: 'The ability to distance is a unique thing in general, but in the case of the poet ... it also indicates the scale on which his consciousness is working. In the case of the poet, distancing is not "one more boundary," it is a going beyond the boundary.'[45] Brodsky's drive to think things to their limit results in a relatively large number of 'metaphor – definitions': *Пространство – вещь. / Время же, в сущности, мысль о вещи* (*Ч*. 106: *Space is a thing. Whereas Time is, in essence, the thought of a thing*); *Жизнь – сумма мелких движений* (*У*. 124: *Life is a sum of small movements*).

To use Coleridge's expression, Brodsky does not operate under the 'despotism of the eye',[46] but under that of reason. And this is reflected in the structure and semantics of his tropes. In depicting abstract notions by abstractions, he is compelled to create dual, triple, and multiple metaphors, and provide explanations in subordinate or parenthetic clauses. It seems at times that he has set out to prove that some existentialist philosophers were not daring enough. 'It is always easy to be logical', wrote Camus, 'it is almost impossible to be logical to the bitter end.'[47] By trying to be logical to the bitter end, Brodsky often arrives at a paradoxical conclusion:

> Поскольку боль – не нарушенье правил:
> *страданье есть*
> *способность тел,*
> *и человек есть испытатель боли.*
> Но то ли свой ему неведом, то ли
> её предел.   (*K*. 63)

Inasmuch as pain is not the breaking of the rules / *suffering is* / *the capability of bodies, / and man is the endurer of pain. / But whether his own limit is unknown to him, or / its limit.*

The simplicity and extreme nature of these metaphors is quite remarkable. The very paradoxical nature of these metaphors permits some of them to be turned into semantic palindromes: *Space is a thing* (*Ч*. 106); *Thing is a space, beyond which there is no thing* (*K*. 111). The very grammatical structure of metaphors of identification is well suited to Brodsky's paradoxical frame of mind.

Now, perhaps, the reasons for the division of metaphor–copulae into two independent semantic types have become clearer. They arose from the observation that analogies are drawn between profound, essential features and the qualities of the depicted objects in the majority of Brodsky's metaphors of this grammatical structure (*A is B*). Analogies based on external similarities of colour and texture, for example, are less frequent. They can be seen as two different types of perception of the world: imaginative and concrete (metaphors of comparison); and conceptual and abstract (metaphors of identification). The latter are unpacked by means of logical inference rather than by visual recognition.

'Metaphor', according to Shilbers, 'may be regarded as a structure forcing us to see reality in a certain way, just as does the subject–predicate category'.[48] This is particularly relevant as regards metaphors of identification which correspond to a subject–predicate relation. By postulating equality between the most essential characteristics of subject and predicate, these metaphors seem to be more fundamentally related to the nature of truth than other semantic types. To the greatest possible extent, they appear to fulfil the function of establishing the identity of a described object, as well as having the structure of a scientific definition. 'Equivalence is not lifeless identity,' argues Lotman, 'that is why it implies dissimilarity. Similar levels organize dissimilar ones by establishing relations of similarity'.[49] The mode of comprehension of this similarity in metaphors of identification is logical, speculative, and independent of the poetic image. Definition of an abstract concept by another abstraction compels Brodsky to seek assistance by introducing other tropes, in particular, metonymy: *Человек – только автор / сжатого кулака* (*H.* 110: *Man is only the author of a clenched fist*); *Любовь есть предисловие к разлуке* (*O.* 211: *Love is the foreword to parting*); *Грядущее есть форма тьмы* (*K.* 76: *The future is a form of darkness*); *Молчанье есть грядущее любви* (*O.* 206: *Silence is the future of love*).

'Metonymical' metaphors can be found in Mandelstam's and Khlebnikov's poetry. In Khlebnikov's metaphors, all combinatory restrictions are lifted: everything possesses reason, consequently, everything is mortal:

> Я верю: разум мировой
> Земного много шире мозга
> И через невод человека и камней
> Единою течёт рекой,   (I. 302)

I believe the world reason / much wider than earthly brain / And
through the net of man and stones / it flows like a single river.

In Brodsky, an amalgamation of two tropes is sustained by the
metonymic principle of cohesion of ideas in the poem:

> *Одиночество учит сути вещей, ибо суть их то же*
> *одиночество. Кожа спины* благодарна *коже*
> *спинки кресла* за чувство прохлады.   (Ч. 101)

*Solitude teaches the essence of things, for their essence is the same /
solitude. The skin of the back* is grateful to *the leather / of the
chair-back* for the feeling of coolness.

The repetition of such words as *solitude, skin, back*, creates an
illusion of analogy. In actual fact, these and the following metaphors are what Genette calls 'diegetic' metaphors,[50] in which the
'selection of the vehicle is dictated by the proximity of a detail that
happens to be present in the narrative context'.[51]

Etkind, in his analysis of the conflict between 'syntax and
rhythm', has already noticed the ironic relation between Brodsky's
prosaic speech and the fabric of his verse, and he emphasized
Brodsky's affinity with Tsvetaeva in this respect.[52] What is at issue
here is the relation between the metaphorical nature of lyrical verse
and the metonymic principle of prose. The further Brodsky moves
from himself – towards the metonymic pole of language – the
greater the need there is for compensation, whether by strict metre
and precise rhymes or by way of saturating his verse with metaphors. The energy of the verse slackens as the density of metaphors
diminishes, as, for example, in such narrative poems as 'Homage to
Yalta' or 'The New Jules Verne'.

In Brodsky's early period there is no more than one metaphor
every four lines, in his second period there is one metaphor every
three lines, and in his third period, one metaphor every two lines.
This statistic proves that metaphor, being a linguistic store-house
for spiritual wealth, successfully resists the poet's attempt to free
his poetry of any tropes.[53]

4

Words devouring things

Whether we like it or not, we are here to learn not just what
time does to man but what language does to time.[1]

Thing – Veshch

One of the basic principles of art is the scrutiny of phenomena
with the naked eye, out of context and without inter-
mediaries.[2]

From his earliest poems (including the love poetry), material things
and objects proliferate in Brodsky's poetry with frightening insist-
ence. The poems often derive their dramatic character from the
sheer activity of things, depicted tropologically: *Глядят шкафы
на хлюпающий сад, / от страха створки мысленно сужают*
(*C.* 229: 'The cupboards look on to the squelching garden, / their
leaves mentally narrow in fear'). Innumerable verbal metaphors
make things the major active characters in the poem. Objects are
able to observe people: *Только дверной проём / знает: двое,
войдя сюда, / вышли назад втроём* (*H.* 96: *Only the doorway /
knows: two people, coming in here / went back out as a threesome*).
From the standpoint of *любой предмет / – свидетель жизни*
(*H.* 41: *every object / is a witness of life*), things take part in every
sphere of human activity. They are given many of the essential
features of man's personality, appearance, and consciousness.
Metaphors of attribution play a leading role in animating the world
of things: *висит гнездо над крыльцом / с искажённым лицом*
(*H.* 50: *A nest hangs over the porch / with a twisted face*); *железо
крыш на выцветших домах / волнуется, готовясь к
снегопадам* (*C.* 182: *The iron of the roofs on faded houses / is
agitated, anticipating a snowfall*).
  A whole gamut of gradations is opened up in the way in which
things imitate the various aspects of human existence, beginning

with the banal *the chair's profile* and the ability to remember and understand: *Города знают правду о памяти, об огромности лестниц в так наз. | разорённом гнезде, о победах прямой над отрезком* (Ч. 18: *The cities know the truth about memory, about the immensity of stairways in so-called | pillaged nests, about the victories of the linear over the section*), and going on to 'the Paradise of the object': *where the thing is sharp, that's where the Paradise of the object is found* (Ч. 108).

On the other hand, we have seen that, in Brodsky, man is de-animated both as a whole and in part: *Бился льдинкой в стакане мой мозг* (H. 9: *my brain was rattling like an ice-cube in a glass*); *Мозг в суповой кости тает* (Ч. 105: *The brain melts in soup's bones*). The most inalienable qualities of man are de-animated in metaphors and similes: *И крутится сознание, как лопасть | вокруг своей негнущейся оси* (O. 143: *And consciousness twists like a blade, | around its unbending axis*); *Плевать на состоянье мозга: | вещь, вышедшая из повиновенья, | как то мгновенье* (Ч. 169: *To hell with the state of the brain, | a thing, which has quitted obedience, | like that moment*). 'That moment' is a reference to Goethe's *Faust:* 'Verweile doch, du bist so schön'. The brain, consciousness, feelings, and instincts are either directly called 'a thing', or are identified with things, in particular, for example, with continents: *Africa of the brain, its Europe, Asia of the brain* (Ч. 107).

Both nature and the animal world are de-animated no less systematically: *у щуки уже сейчас | чешуя цвета консервной банки, | цвета вилки в руке* (H. 132: *the pike already has | a scale in the colour of a jar of preserves, | the colour of a fork in the hand*). The future, as it were, casts a shadow on the present, objectifying all that lives, turning fish into preserves, and man into 'molluscs of the future', for:

> *мы только части*
> *крупного целого, из коего вьётся нить*
> *к нам, как шнур телефона, от диназавра*
> *оставляя простой позвоночник; но позвонить*
> *по нему больше некуда, кроме как в послезавтра,*   (H. 133)

We are only part | of a great whole, out of which thread spirals | towards us like a telephone cable, from the dinosaur | remains just the backbone but you wouldn't be able to get a line out | to anywhere, except to the day after tomorrow.

By rhyming *диназавра* ('dinosaur') with *послезавтра* ('day after tomorrow'), the poet hints at our common future which will de-animate everything: man, the life of the planet, and death itself: *смерть – это всегда вторая / Флоренция с архитектурой Рая* (Ч. 111: *death is always a second / Florence with the architecture of Paradise*). In Brodsky's poetry, life and death are depicted as 'a form / of identity between two variants' (*K.* 22) of existence, 'where timber is transferred into trees and back again into timber' (Ч. 60).

In this way, Brodsky's tropes subject everything to reification: from vodka – *they took into the street the main thing* (Ч. 56) – to a beloved woman:

> Ты, гитарообразная вещь со спутанной паутиной
> струн, продолжающая коричневеть в гостиной,
> белеть а ля Казимир на выстиранном просторе,
> темнеть – особенно вечером – в коридоре   (*H.* 131)

You, a guitar-shaped thing with entangled spider's web / strings which goes on being brown in the sitting-room, / being white *à la Kazimir* against the laundered expanse, / being dark – especially in the evening – in the corridor.

It is worth noting that almost the same semantics of reification are used to describe a meeting with the same woman in a poem of 1962, 'I embraced these shoulders and glanced' (*C.* 96): 'диван в углу сверкал коричневою кожей' ('the brown leather of the sofa glistened'), 'темнела печка' ('the stove was dark'), 'в раме запылённой застыл пейзаж' ('the landscape froze in a dusty frame'). In the 1978 poem, the guitar-shaped thing is reduced to the white 'nothing' by means of a metonymical reference to Kazimir Malevich's celebrated painting, 'A White Square on White Ground' (1918; New York, Museum of Modern Art), and by the metaphor of substitution for bedsheet, *на выстиранном просторе* ('against the laundered expanse').

What does this world of things signify? 'Nothing', replies Limonov, for whom Brodsky's poetry is reminiscent of a 'catalogue of objects':

Things are his weakness. Almost all his poems are written using one and the same method: a motionless philosophising author surveys a panorama of things around himself. Let's say that it's as if Brodsky wakes up in a room in a Venice hotel and with sad dutifulness (there's nothing to be done, they are there), enumerates for us the things he finds in his room . . . Then, (almost the only moment in the poem) the poet moves across to the window and communicates to us what he sees outside: ships, boats, launches . . .[3]

There is, however, every reason to think that a more interesting explanation can be found for Brodsky's 'weakness for things' than the 'immobility' of a poet who has, in fact, travelled all over the two contemporary Empires as well as over a large part of the Roman and Byzantine Empires.

Two other Russian poets, Losev and Kublanovsky, have detected organic links with Acmeism in Brodsky's *veshchnost'*. Thus, Losev speaks of the 'acmeist quality' of Brodsky's work,[4] while Kublanovsky comments on his 'acmeist intentness and gravity'.[5] Attention to detail, 'the focusedness on the object' as opposed to 'abstract existence', was, undoubtedly, the distinguishing feature of Acmeist poetics. Mandelstam urged us 'to love the existence of the thing more than the thing itself'.[6] Shklovsky, in his review of Akhmatova's *Anno Domini MCMXXI*, wrote: 'The thirst for concreteness, the struggle for the existence of things, for things "with a small letter", for things, and not concepts – this is the pathos of contemporary poetry.'[7]

Against this it may be said that such poetic qualities are achieved to no less an extent in Tsvetaeva's poetry with its 'verblessness' and in Khlebnikov's work at the price of the nouns' dominance. There are 550 copula metaphors and more than 2,000 genitive metaphors in the latter's poetry. The corresponding figures in Akhmatova are about 50 and just over 200. The semantic function of Brodsky's 'thingness' argues against its direct lineage from Acmeist poetics. Objects in his poetry rarely serve to reflect the psychological condition of the lyrical persona; instead, they live their own lives, which are 'not ours to understand'. The poet, in turn, strives to understand this mode of existence. Using the metaphor as both telescope and stereoscope, Brodsky perceives objects from *their* point of view:

> Знающий цену себе квадрат,
> видя вещей разброд,
> не оплакивает утрат;
> ровно наоборот:
> празднует прямоту угла,
> жёлтую рвань газет,

> мусор, будучи догола,
> до обоев раздет.   (*Н.* 96)

The square knowing its own value, / seeing the dispersal of things, / does not weep over the loss; / quite the reverse: / celebrates the rightness of the angle, / the yellow tatters of newspapers, / the rubbish, being undressed, / stripped down to the wallpaper, left naked.

The point of observation is stated explicitly in several poems: *С точки зрения воздуха*, край земли / всюду (*Ч.* 90: *From the air's point of view*, the earth's edge / is everywhere);

> я сменил империю. Этот шаг
> продиктован был тем, что несло горелым
> с четырёх сторон – хоть живот крести;
> *с точки зренья ворон, с пяти.*   (*Ч.* 100)

I've changed Empires. This step / was dictated by the fact that the smell of burning came / from all four quarters (time for crossing oneself), *from the crow's-eye view, from five.*

The crow's-eye view, i.e. only an increasing of the distance of view. This innate feeling of distance is increased with the years up to *the point of view of time* (*H.* 140).

It is precisely *the point of view of time* (the most remote conceivable) that permits the poet to attribute the properties of man's entire intellectual and spiritual experience to the inanimate world and, thereby, to create a new layer of meaning. From the point of view of time, objects may manifest themselves as representatives of eternity. The rhyming of these two concepts: *вещность* / *вечность* ('thingness' / 'eternity'), therefore, is clearly not arbitrary:

> Молчанье – это будущее слов,
> уже пожравших гласными всю *вещность*,
> страшащуюся собственных углов;
> волна, перекрывающая *вечность*.   (*О.* 206)

Silence – is the future of words, / whose vowels have already devoured the essence of thingness, / which is afraid of its own corners; / it is a wave which floods eternity.

In this same poem, 'Gorbunov and Gorchakov', *вечность* ('eternity') rhymes with *конечность* ('finiteness'), *бесчелове-*

чность ('inhumanity'), *бесконечность* ('infinity'). Things also have their limit: they, like man himself, *run into Time*.

> Ибо созданное прочно,
> продукт труда
> *есть пища вора и прообраз Рая,*
> *верней – добыча времени:* теряя
> (пусть навсегда)
>
> что-либо, ты
> не смей кричать о преданной надежде:
> *то Времени, невидимые прежде,*
> *в вещах черты*
> *вдруг проступают,* и теснится грудь   (*K.* 64–5)

what is created well, / a product of labour, / *is food for a thief, a prototype of Paradise, / or rather – the spoils of Time:* losing / (let it be for ever) // something / do not dare to scream about betrayed hopes: / *the previously invisible features of Time / in things / suddenly appear,* and the chest is oppressed.

This appears to suggest a solution to the enigma of *veshchnost'*. Things for Brodsky are only a 'pretext for penetrating other spheres'. Things participate in the development of one of the central themes in Brodsky's poetry – the theme of time. Losev has perceived an analogous conceptual role for Brodsky's material objects in connection with Chekhov's poetics:

The activity of things is here purely grammatical, that is, imaginary. Things only *seem* to act. Things which are immortal by comparison with mortal man, do live, but their life is illusory, the life of phantoms. And this frightens man . . . he is frightened by his own proximity to this phantasmal world, to the world of illusory life, to the transformation into a thing, into Hamlet's 'patch a wall t'expel the winter's flaw'. The eternal, that is, the illusory life of things, is only a background which contrastingly highlights the central theme of the poem – the march of time.[8]

We can find supportive evidence for such an interpretation of thingness in a number of poems. In '1972', briefly discussed in the first chapter, the motif of growing old in exile is transformed into the theme of silence, that is, into the theme of death and time:

> Вот оно – то, о чём я глаголаю:
> *о превращении тела в голую*
> *вещь!* Ни горé не гляжу, ни долу я,
> но в пустоту – чем её ни высветли.
> Это и к лучшему. *Чувство ужаса*

вещи не свойственно. Так что лужица
подле вещи не обнаружится,
даже если вещица при смерти.   (Ч. 27)

There it is – what I'm talking about: / *about the transformation of the*
body into a naked / *thing!* I'm not looking on high, or below, / but
into emptiness – whatever may illuminate it. / Still, it's for the best. *A*
feeling of horror / *is not the quality that things possess. So little*
puddles / *won't be found beneath a thing* / *even if a thing is facing*
death.

In his attempt to avoid clichés, Brodsky lapses into paradox, or
else into tautology: man should not fear the conversion of his body
into a thing because a feeling of fear is not a quality that things
possess, and it does not wet itself (a paraphrase of 'little puddles
won't be found beneath a thing') from terror.

The opposition *people* / *things* is either highlighted or eliminated
in Brodsky's poetry. On the level of the semantics of the metaphors, each component of the opposition is endowed with features
of the other, whereas in metaphors of identification, they are
directly placed on the same footing with each other. On the conceptual level, that is, from the point of view of time, there is, in effect,
no difference between them. Time converts man into thing 'so as to
end a Cycladean thing with its featureless face' (*H.* 109).

As if persuading himself to come to terms with this inevitability,
the poet strives to comprehend the world of things and to come to
love things:

За что нас любят? За богатство, за
глаза и за избыток мощи.
А я люблю безжизненные вещи
за кружевные очертанья их.

Одушевлённый мир не мой кумир.   (*H.* 59)

What are we loved for? For our riches, for / our eyes and for an
excess of strength. / *But I love lifeless things* / *for their lace-like*
outlines. // *The animate world is not my idol.*

A hymn to things is sung in a masterpiece from 1971, 'Nature
Morte' (*K.* 108–12), which has received remarkable analyses from
both Etkind[9] and Losev[10] from different points of view. In this
poem, the reader encounters the provocative declaration from the
poet: 'I do not like people.' One of the reasons for this lack of love

is their unwillingness to accept death; they cling to life like dead man's fingers on the hull of a sunken ship.

> Вещи приятней. В них
> нет ни зла, ни добра
> внешне. А если вник
> в них – и внутри нутра.
>
> Внутри у предметов – пыль.
> Прах.   (*K*. 109)

Things are pleasanter, there's in them / neither evil nor good / on the outside. And if you probe / into them – inside, there's no core. / Within objects – there is dust, / ashes.

Dust in Brodsky's poetry is a metaphor of substitution for time, for which we can easily find parallels in the cultural memory, most notably in the Bible itself and in Shakespeare. With time in Brodsky's work both things and people are reduced to dust or covered with dust: '*Dust settles on the table, / and you can't wipe it off*' (*H*. 115); '*There the mirrors / accumulated the dust till nightfall, / settling like the ashes of Herculaneum on / its inhabitants*' (*Ч*. 23). In 'Nature Morte', dust is directly identified with time: *пыль – это плоть / времени; плоть и кровь* (*dust is a flesh of time; flesh and blood*).

The picture of death, ashes, and dust is drawn with extremely spare means:

> Дерево. Тень. Земля
> под деревом для корней.
> Корявые вензеля.
> Глина. Гряда камней.
>
> Корни. Их переплёт.
> Камень, чей личный груз
> освобождает от
> данной системы уз.   (*K*. 111)

Tree. Shadow. Earth / beneath the tree for the roots. / Twisted monograms. / Clay. A ridge of rocks. // Roots. They interweave. / A stone whose individual weight / frees from / the knots of the given system.

The short nominative sentences break the rhythm (three-stress *dol'nik* with alternating masculine rhymes). The discourse keeps being interrupted, just as death itself interrupts life. The rhymes break all, even the closest, semantic links, as if imitating time: throwing a preposition to the end of the line, rhyming it with an intentionally lengthy word (*переплёт* / *от* ('interweave' / 'from'), is tantamount to repeating the act of death itself, in that removing the preposition from an inalienable noun is the same as separating body and soul. The conflict of metre and syntax expresses the essence of the conflict of human existence. 'Death, it would seem, cannot be described', wrote Piatigorsky. 'It cannot be described by force of the rather trivial circumstance that you have to be alive to describe it, while, if you are still alive, it's impossible to describe your own death.'[11]

The ninth part of 'Nature Morte' opens with the simplest and most terrifying description of death in Russian poetry, a description which is reminiscent of Beckett:

> Вещь. Коричневый цвет
> вещи. Чей контур стёрт.
> Сумерки. Больше нет
> ничего. Натюрморт.   (*K.* 112)

A thing. The brown colour of / a thing. Whose outline is effaced. / Twilight. Nothing / more. Nature morte.

As regards the colour of the thing, we find an elucidation in Brodsky's 'Fifth Eclogue': *The colour of a thing is indeed the mask of infinity* (*Ч.* 125). As Professor Etkind has perceptively remarked, this 'poem is replete with the internalised horror of death, faced with dissolution, non-being, inevitability and the further one goes the deeper grows the paradox of the unity of the business-like rational forms of speech and the rhythmic pattern of the poetry'.[12] If we take into account the fact that Brodsky was seriously ill while writing this poem (he even thought he was dying),[13] a dichotomy of 'man–thing' is out of the question. And everyone who accused the poet of lack of love for people, of a weakness for things, has read him too literally.[14]

Any one-level opposition, be it people–things, or life–death, speech–silence, would contradict the very nature of poetry, whose essence is to engender new meanings which are not equivalent to the meanings which comprise the verbal structures. This applies not only to the tropes, but also to the rhymes, the rhythm, the syntax, and the entire lexis of the poem. Each poem is a kind of microcosm of the poetic world as a whole, with a multiplicity of meanings and their unity. In Brodsky's case, all the structural elements of the poem to a greater or lesser extent express his interest in modifications and contradictions in his attempts to take into account all possible points of view, including the most unlikely and unacceptable ones.

'Nature Morte' once more demonstrates all the above. The unexpected turn of thought in the tenth and final part suggests a religious solution to the problem:

> Мать говорит Христу:
> – Ты мой сын или мой
> Бог? Ты прибит к кресту.
> Как я пойду домой?
>
> Как ступлю на порог,
> не поняв, не решив:
> ты мой сын или Бог?
> То есть, мёртв или жив? –
>
> Он говорит в ответ:
> – Мёртвый или живой,
> разницы, жено, нет.
> Сын или Бог, я твой.   (*K.* 112)

His mother says to Christ: / 'Are you my son or my / God? You are nailed to the cross. / How am I to go home? // How can I cross the threshold, / not comprehending, not able to resolve / whether you are my son or my God? / That is, are you dead or alive?' // He says in answer: / 'Dead or alive, / the difference, woman, is nil. / Son or God, I am yours.'

It would seem that the very fact of God's appearance in the dead world of things is a symbol of overcoming death. The murk of the brown things, like the gloom of the pre-Christian temple in the poem 'Nunc Dimittis', is suddenly lit up by 'a light from nowhere'. Thus, the end of the poem is an answer to the world of things, an elimination of the opposition inherent in the title: that is, death-in-life is neutralized by life-in-death.

In concluding his analysis of the poem, Losev writes:

The poem has two apparent endings. The first is the conclusion of the author's elaboration of the people/objects theme for which Brodsky uses Pavese's line: 'Death will come and it / will have your eyes'. Death, alias the realm of objects, triumphs. *Homo homini res est: человек человеку вещь.* But the final conclusion (part x) proposes a different kind of interhuman relationship, a mystical communion that supersedes the life/death dilemma.[15]

Losev observes with some subtlety how, at the expense of the peculiarities of Russian grammar, which demands the omission of the verb 'est'' which serves simultaneously as the copula 'is' and the signifying 'I exist', Brodsky removes the opposition life/death.

Close scrutiny of the structure of the last three stanzas, and especially of the semantics of the rhymes, reveals that they once more repeat the whole problem: *Христос – к кресту* ('Christ' – 'to the cross'); *не решив – жив* ('not able to resolve' – 'alive'); *ответ – нет* ('answer' – 'nil'). The last rhyme is the most unexpected; it reveals the poet's doubts more than any direct declaration. What does it mean? Is there no answer in general to this insoluble question? Or is there merely no answer from the poet, and each of his readers must seek an answer for himself? If it is the latter, then another parallel with Chekhov suggests itself, in addition to those which Losev designated: the writer should not confuse a solution to the problem with a correct formulation of the problem. Only the latter is required of him. The poet is not obliged to offer answers to the eternal questions of existence. We should be thankful if he has managed to stir and disturb us by the unexpected way in which he poses these questions.

The picture of the world of things grows even more complex if we take into account the fact that, apart from the themes of death and time, things play an active part in the development of the theme of alienation, which is also one of the central themes of Brodsky's poetry. When things begin to lose their profiles as a dual result of the *winter of things* and memory's leakiness, we see time *in pure form* (Ч. 109), i.e. we no longer participate in it, and the images of *nothing* and *nowhere* appear: *A winter evening with wine in nowhere* (Ч. 80); *From nowhere with love* (Ч. 77). These negative adverbs and pronouns stand for time: А то возникали чайки из снежной мглы, / как *замусоленные ничьей рукой углы* / *белого, как пустая бумага, дня* (Н. 137: 'Or else seagulls arose from the snow darkness / like *corners well-thumbed by no one's hand* / *of the white, like blank paper, day*'); for non-existence: *you [the butterfly] are better than nothing*; and for exile. Sometimes all three merge, as in 'Lagoon':

> И входит в свой номер на борт по трапу
> постоялец, несущий в кармане граппу,

совершенный никто, человек в плаще,
потерявший память, отчизну, сына,   (Ч. 40)

And there enters his cabin by ship's ladder / the guest, carrying
grappa in his pocket, / *an absolute nobody, a man in a raincoat,* / *who*
has lost his memory, his homeland and son.

This poem was written after Brodsky's first visit to Venice,
during his first Christmas outside Russia: hence the spatial opposition between the unnamed native city, which is also built on water
and is reflected in the water, and the city which is sinking in the
Adriatic. There is a parallel treatment of two different perceptions
of time: the pagan and the Christian. Water, *as a condensed form of*
time, mythologizes time itself:

створку моллюска пустив ко дну,
пряча лицо, но спиной пленяя,
Время выходит из волн, меняя
стрелку на башне – её одну.   (Ч. 41)

letting the shell of the mollusc go to the bottom, / *concealing the face*
but captivating by its back / *Time emerges from the waves changing* /
the clock hand on the tower – just one clock hand.

In the context of all-powerful time, the images *nowhere* and *nobody*
acquire a multipurpose load, encapsulating the themes of exile,
time, and alienation:

Ночь на Сан Марко. Прохожий с мятым
лицом, сравнимым во тьме со снятым
      с безымянного пальца кольцом, грызя
ноготь, смотрит, объят покоем,
в то "никуда", задержаться в коем
      мысли можно, зрачку – нельзя.

Там, за нигде, за его пределом
– чёрным, бесцветным, возможно, белым –
      есть какая-то вещь, предмет.
Может быть, тело. В эпоху тренья
скорость света есть скорость зренья;
      даже тогда, когда света нет.   (Ч. 42–3)

Night on St Mark's. The passer-by with creased / face, in the
darkness like a ring taken / from the fourth finger, biting / a nail,
serene, looks towards / *that 'nowhere' where it's* / *possible for thought*
but not the eye to dwell. // *There, beyond nowhere, beyond its*
boundary / *black, colourless, possibly white –* / *there is a thing, an*

object. / *Maybe a body.* In the epoch of friction / the speed of light is the speed of sight, / even when there is no light.

Thing, object, and, perhaps, a body 'without the features of a face' are directly associated with *nowhere.* The ground for the white nowhere, as in the Malevich painting mentioned earlier, is also suggested by the semantics of the rhymes. In rhyming *за пределом / белом* ('beyond its boundary' / 'white'), Brodsky refers the reader to the semantics of the rhymes of the poem 'Песчаные холмы' ('Sand Dunes'): *тел / предел* ('bodies' / 'boundaries'), *о теле / пределе* (*H.* 105: 'concerning the body' / 'losses'). This rhyme is again repeated in the poem 'Kellomiaki': 'как бы кладя *предел* / покушеньям судьбы на *беззащитность тел*' (*H.* 142: 'as if putting *an end* / to Fate's attempts upon *the defencelessness of bodies*'). In the elegy to Auden, 'York', this rhyme changes the pairing: *белом / телом* ('white' / 'body'), while in 'Venetian Strophes', *белей* ('white') rhymes with *нулей* ('zeroes'). As a result of this small excursus we go out into the semantic field *за белым – телом – предел – нулей* ('beyond the white – body – end/limit – of zeroes'). This boundary/limit/end is zero/nowhere/nothing, or infinity, which can be penetrated only by thought, and not by the eye, not even light: *В одушевлённом теле / свет узнаёт о своём пределе* (*In the animated body / light finds out about its own limit, У.* 126).

How then are we to understand the last metaphor of identification, *In the epoch of friction / the speed of light is the speed of sight*? The *epoch of friction* is not only a periphrasis for the epoch of Newtonian physics, but also a metaphor for our age, the age of alienation:

> Масса, / увы, не кратное от деленья
> энергии *на скорость зренья*
> *в квадрате, но ощущенье тренья*
> *о себе подобных.*   (*У.* 125–6)

Mass, / alas, is not the result of energy / divided *by speed of sight / in a square, but the feeling of friction / against those who are similar.*

The metaphor *speed of sight* replaces the poetic vision of the world which distinguishes the poet from the masses. We can observe the genesis of this metaphor in the poem 'Speech about Spilled Milk' (1967):

Но скорость внутреннего прогресса
больше, чем скорость мира.
это – основа любой известной
изоляции. Дружба с бездной
представляет сугубо местный
интерес в наши дни.   (*K*. 11)

But the speed of internal progress is / greater than the speed of the
world. / And this is the ground of any known / isolation. A friendship
with the abyss / is only a local / interest nowadays.

The difference between physical speed and metaphysical 'speed
of internal progress' creates the personality. 'Speed of sight' is the
essence of the poet's gift. His ability to see further, faster, and more
fastidiously than the rest of us has something to do with his ability to
create metaphors. This essential quality of the poet produces the
gulf not only between *Homo sapiens* and *Homo scribens*, but also
between the poet and the rest of *Homo scribens*. Only the former
has the tendency to move 'over the horizon, beyond the boundary'
(*У*. 155).

Man–thing–number

the reduction of man to things, to a hieroglyph, to numbers.
This is a vector into nothingness.[16]

Brodsky's poetic vision of the world and of man in this world forces
him to think and to talk ideas to their logical conclusion. Once
discovered, semantic units entail new couplings of ideas. Thus, the
de-animation of man *in toto* and in part is constantly being verified:
от лица остаётся всего лишь профиль (*K*. 103: *of the face there*
only remains the profile); *от тебя оставались лишь губы, как*
от того кота (*H*. 138: *of you remained only the lips, like that from*
that cat). Taking the next 'step to the side of his own body', he sees
the body 'with a stone face' (*H*. 37), 'in a garland of stone friends'
(*Ч*. 52), 'among stone mushrooms' (*Ч*. 70), and 'stone fish'
(*K*. 92). Being inexorable and ineluctable, time converts everything into 'future molluscs'. In his futile attempts to overcome time,
man, in reality, has imitated its actions, erecting himself bronze and
stone statues, marble busts, turning himself into a thing:

В результате – бюст
как символ независимости мозга

от жизни тела. Собственного и
имперского.   (У. 135)

As a result – a bust / as a symbol of the independence of the mind /
from the life of the body. His own and / the Emperor's.

This is all that time has left of the once all-powerful Roman
Emperor:

Голова,
отрубленная скульптором при жизни,
есть, в сущности, пророчество о власти.
Всё то, что ниже подбородка, – Рим: (У. 135)

The head / severed by the sculptor while alive, / is, in essence, a
prophecy of power. / All that is beneath the chin is Rome.

The capaciousness of Brodsky's metaphors, their psychological
precision, allows him to leapfrog over what seems to stand to
reason, over everything that the reader can establish for himself.
What is left of Tiberius's Rome is equal to that: 'what is left, as a
rule, of any great faith, is only holy relics'.

It would seem that all the 'i's' are dotted, there is nowhere
further to go. But for Brodsky, this is precisely where everything
begins. Taking into account the fact that even a thing has its limits,
and that they, too, like man, 'lose [their] profile', Brodsky abstracts
from them, reduces them to the level of a sign, whether that be
ancient cuneiform, hieroglyphs, a letter, or a number. In fact, he
consciously or unconsciously rehearses the evolution of literature;
he imitates not so much time as language. Churches are compared
with cuneiform, *колокольная клинопись* ('bell cuneiform'), as
is light, *клинопись лунных пятен* ('the cuneiform of moon
spots'). Man and the animal kingdom are reminiscent of hieroglyphs (cf. the poem 'The Letters of the Ming Dynasty'), or letters:
Сад густ, как тесно набранное "Ж" (Ч. 61: *the garden is dense
like a tightly set "ZH"*); or a figure: *в прихожей вас обступают
две старые цифры "8"* (Ч. 112: *in the sitting-room you are
surrounded by two old "8"s*). This comparison of two old women
with the figure 8 is not so much visual as logical: an old person
enters eternity, which is mathematically depicted by an upended
sign ∞.

In taking the idea of time, the idea of nothingness, to the
absolute, Brodsky follows Khlebnikov into the sphere of pure,
non-corporeal abstractions, the sphere of numbers.

Вспять оглянувшийся: тень, затмив
профиль, чьё ремесло –
затвердевать, уточняет миф,
повторяя число

членов. Их – *переход от слов
к цифрам* не удивит.
Глаз переводит, моргнув, *число в
несовершенный вид.*

Воздух, в котором ни встать, ни сесть,
ни, тем более, лечь,
воспринимает 4, 6,
8 лучше, чем речь.   (*У.* 20)[17]

Backwards glancing: shadow darkening / the profile, whose trade is /
to harden, clarifies myth, / repeats the number // of limbs. *Their
transformation from words / to numbers* is unsurprising. / The eye
translates, blinking, *a number into / the imperfective aspect.* // The
air, in which you can't stand or sit / or, what's more, lie down /
perceives 4, 6, / 8 better than speech.

This is the second part of the poem 'Midday in the Room' (1978),
which consists of sixteen parts of three stanzas each. It is written in
quatrains with alternating three- and two-ictus *dol'nik* lines with
all-masculine clausulae according to the scheme *abab*. These harsh
masculine rhymes afford great interest, not only in terms of their
poetic novelty, but also because of their semantics. On the one
hand, they illustrate the semantic immateriality of numbers, the
principal 'heroes' of this poem, in rhyming semantically 'empty'
words (prepositions, conjunctions, particles) with each other: *из /
и с* ('out of' / 'and with'), *и т.д. / где* ('etc.' / 'where'). On the
other hand, by replacing one of the elements of the rhyme by a
number, the author places the word on the same footing as a sign:
сесть / 6 ('sit' / 6), *в сто / то* ('into a hundred' / 'that'). This leads
on to the next logical step, when insignificant words are rhymed
with significant ones; and the sense of the latter is reduced to the
absurd: *дотемна / на* ('till darkness' / 'on'); *мрак / как* ('darkness' /
'how'); *как во / ничего* ('as into' / 'nothing'); *раз / глаз* ('once' /
'eye').

A word which is rhymed with a number is detached from its
referent and is transformed into a pure sign. Here Brodsky practises what Khlebnikov theorized about in connection with the
correlations between words and numbers. In Khlebnikov's view,

even Pythagoras and Amenophis IV 'foresaw the victory of the number over the word, as a device of thinking' (*V*. 446–7). Khlebnikov preferred numbers on the grounds that 'in the verbal thinking the basic condition of measurement is absent – the constancy of the unit to be measured'. (*V*. 446–7) Brodsky also asserts that: 'В цифрах есть нечто, чего в словах, / даже крикнув их, нет' ('In figures there is something which in words / does not exist, even shouting them').

However, having placed the word on the same footing as a sign – *слов / число в* ('of the words' / 'number into') – Brodsky is obliged to compensate for the 'impoverished' semantics of the sign with all the lexical and formal elements of the poem. Thus, the intermediate stage of the transition from man to sign – the thing – is hinted at by the reference to the myth of Lot's wife and expressed first and foremost in the rhyme system: *овал / сковал* ('oval' / 'forged'), *скул / стул* ('cheek-bones' / 'chair'), *торс / мороз* ('torso' / 'frost'), *рельеф / замерев* ('relief' / 'died down'), *календарь / вдаль* ('calendar' / 'into the distance'). To load the rhymes with the semantics and ideology of the poem to such a degree is possible only by using other structural elements of the poem, in particular by creating a conflict between the syntax and rhythm of the poem. The asymmetrical rhythmical segmentation, the abrupt halts in the mid-line, the rupture of syntactic units by line-ends, are greatly intensified. 'Midday in the Room' contains, perhaps, the largest percentage of enjambements, on average once in each of the forty-eight stanzas. The poetic line disrupts any semantic and grammatical unit: preposition and substantive: 'то есть из / небытия' ('that is from / non being-'); 'и с / лёгкостью мотылька' ('and with / the lightness of a moth'); conjunction and the dependent subordinate clause: 'возвращается в воздух, где / твёрдого не найти' ('returning into air, where / firmness is not to be found'); subject and predicate, predicate and object: 'Зеркала / коптили там дотемна / пыль' ('Mirrors / smoked there to blackness / the dust'); two objects, connected by a possessive genitive: 'Так отчаянно по лицу / памяти пятерней скребя' ('Thus desperately over the face of / memory scratching with the five fingers'); and even the elements of a compound predicate: 'Всё, что я говорю, могло / быть сказано до меня' ('All that I am saying could have / been said before me').

Thus, on the level of grammar, metre, and rhymes Brodsky

emphasizes the absurdity of both being and non-being. Before we can 'fill in the holes in beings' we have to see them. Arming himself with the strongest magnifying glass – the linguistic one – Brodsky keeps raising this glass to the eyes of the reader and invites him to take off his rose-coloured spectacles:

В будущем цифры рассеют мрак,
Цифры на умира.
Только меняют порядок, как
телефонные *номера.*

Сонм их, вечным пером привит
к речи, расширит рот,
удлинит собой алфавит;
либо наоборот.

Что будет выглядеть, как мечтой
взысканная земля
с синей, режущей глаз чертой –
горизонтом нуля.   (*У.* 25)

In the future numbers will disperse the gloom. / *Numbers don't die.* / They only change order like / telephone *numbers.* // By the eternal pen their throng is grafted / on to speech, widens the mouth, / extends the alphabet; / or the reverse. // This will resemble an earth / punished by a dream, / with blue line blinding the eye – / *a horizon zero.*

Running through the entire poem, the rupture in the fabric of the verse seems to imitate life itself. 'To live is terrible in general. Have you noticed how all this ends?' Brodsky asks half in jest, half in earnest.[18] But the immortality of numbers, if you read between the lines of the poem, is as illusory as the immortality of things. The grammar gives away their mortality: the semantics of the negative verb 'don't die' is neutralized by the daring and unexpected severance of the verb-ending, *не умира.* Behind this poetic *tour de force*, conceivably, lies the desire not to repeat Mandelstam's rhyme from the famous poem 'I Returned to my City' (1930):

Петербург, я ещё не хочу *умирать:*
У тебя телефонов моих *номера.*

Petersburg! I do not want to die yet: / You have my telephone numbers.

The immortality of numbers is also illusory by virtue of the appearance of the metaphor *a horizon zero* at the end of the stanza.

Like things, figures, once included in a metaphor, become the essence of something else. Amongst the numerical metaphors, zero is a synonym for death: *нуль открывает перечень утратам* (*Ч. 9: Zero opens the list of losses*); for time: *И вечер делит сутки пополам, / как ножницы восьмёрку на нули* (*Н. 31*): *and evening divides the twenty-four hour day, as the scissors divide the figure eight into zeroes*); for exile: *сумма мелких слагаемых при перемене мест неузнаваемее нуля* (*Ч. 90: the sum of small items at the change of places is small, more recognizable than zero*); finally, for the underlying absurdity of existence: *и зараза бессмысленности со слова / перекидывается на цифры; особенноно на ноли* (*У. 88: and the infection of meaningless-ness is transferred from words on to figures, especially the zeroes*).

The comparison of figures with the alphabet, that is, with language, also has more than one meaning: do figures lengthen the alphabet, or the opposite? The metaphorical interweaving of words and numbers is encountered several times, not only in 'Midday in the Room', but in other poems as well:

> Навсегда – не слово, а вправду цифра,
> чьи нули, когда мы зарастём травою,
> перекроют эпоху и век с лихвою   (*О.* 174).

Forever – is not a word, but in truth a figure / whose zeroes, when grass grows above us / will stretch out beyond our epoch, our century.

Both word and number are raised to the metaphysical level in the poem 'Lullaby of Cape Cod' (1975):

> Есть крылатые львы, женогрудые сфинксы. Плюс
> ангелы в белом и нимфы моря.
> Для того, на чьи плечи ложится груз
> темноты, жары и – сказать ли – горя,
> они разбегающихся милей
> от брошенных *слов нулей*.   (*Ч.* 106).

There are winged lions and full-breasted sphinxes. Plus / angels in white and sea-nymphs. / For one on whose shoulders is placed burden of / darkness, of heat – should it be said – of grief, / they are more dear than the scampering / *zeroes* from the dropped *words*.

The comparison between words and zeroes is placed in the sort of inversion which demands a return to the normal syntax to under-stand it: 'они [крылатые львы, женогрудые сфинксы и

ангелы в белом] милей разбегающихся нулей от брош-
енных слов' ('They [the winged lions etc.] are more dear than
the zero scampering from words dropped [on paper]').

In this way, figures, just like things, develop the 'theme of
freezing', that is, of non-being. On the purely poetic plane, one
should regard the introduction of numbers as a widening and
renewal of poetic language. Khlebnikov apart, no one has introduced numbers into Russian poetry as systematically as Brodsky.
We find figures in his early poetry: 'вновь / второе января
пришлось на вторник' (*O.* 100: 'the second of January fell again
on a Tuesday'); 'и тридцать дней над морем, языкат, / грозил
пожаром Турции закат' (*O.* 100: 'and for thirty days the tongue-
like sunset over the sea threatened Turkey'). However, in this kind
of use of numbers and dates there is something of the Acmeist
passion for precision of detail. When Brodsky begins to introduce
terms from mathematics and physics alongside these figures, he
comes close to Khlebnikov's poetics: 'Физики "вектор" изобрели.
/ Нечто бесплотное, как душа' (*O.* 148: 'Physicists invented the
vector. / Something fleshless, like soul'). More and more frequently,
Brodsky begins to describe both everyday reality and being itself in
terms of multiplication, addition, and subtraction: 'Помножив
краткость бытия' (*O.* 103: 'Having multiplied the brevity of
existence'); 'А мне оставь, как разность этих сумм, / победу
над молчаньем и удушьем' (*O.* 185: 'Leave me as the difference
of these sums / the victory over silence and suffocation'). He even
supplies as an epigraph to the poem 'Over East River' a quotation
from an old arithmetic primer: 'Вычитание из двух есть
последнее действо русской арифметики' ('Subtraction from two
is the final operation of Russian arithmetic').[19] However, this rule,
which everybody observed in their childhood, does not stop our
poet from attempting to break it:

> Вычитая из меньшего большее, из человека – Время,
> получаешь в остатке слова, выделяющиеся на белом
> фоне отчётливее, чем удаётся телом
> это сделать при жизни, даже сказав "лови!"   (*У.* 79)

Taking the greater from the lesser – subtracting Time from man – /
what you have left over are words, which stand out more distinctly
on a white background / than the body is capable of / while it's alive,
even when it says 'catch me'!

It is noteworthy that the sporadic attempts to incorporate numbers into poetry that have been made by other poets – the Futurists as well as contemporary ones – have been perceived as the incorporation of extraneous material. Poetry rejects them not only because they are abstract, but also because they lack personality. The union between them and the *matière du vers* in Khlebnikov and Brodsky has been achieved on the level of their *Weltanschauung*. Khlebnikov's use of numbers is justified by his theory of the universe, his striving to 'discover the laws of time', his conviction that 'the severe columns of time' in the universe itself were made with the 'moulding of numbers'.[20] Khlebnikov animates numbers, by including them in metaphors of all semantic types. His identification of man with number is motivated by his view that 'every man has his number'.[21] Khlebnikov's own number is abstract in the highest degree: 'Мой отвлечённый строгий рассудок / Есть корень из Нет единицы' (v. 93: 'My abstract, precise mind / is the square of not one'). The negative particle *Нет* ('not') allows us to ascribe this highly original metaphor to identification between the poet's reason and the mathematical sign $\sqrt{-1}$. This sign is elucidated in Khlebnikov's prose: 'Coming to love signs like $\sqrt{-1}$, which have rejected the past, we acquire freedom from things' (v. 321). He identifies not only himself with numbers but the entire universe: 'And stars are numbers, And freedoms are numbers, And deaths are numbers, And rights are numbers.'[22]

In 'The Boards of Fate', Khlebnikov writes: 'if all is one, then there remain in the world only numbers, as numbers are nothing other than the relationship between the unitary, between the identical, that by which the unitary may differ' (v. 512). 'Having thrown a net of numbers over the world', Khlebnikov could not but 'scientificize' his poetry. He introduced into his poetry an abundance of mathematical signs, scientific terms, syntactic constructions on the model of scientific discourse. Brodsky is his direct descendant in this 'scientificization' of the poetic language. It is worth remarking that in the works of both poets numbers occasionally lose their abstract quality, as if they were no longer able to resist the image-making poetry:

> Теперь, когда мне попадается цифра девять
> с вопросительной шейкой (чаще всего, под утро)
> или (заполночь) двойка, я вспоминаю лебедь,   (*У.* 179)

Now, when I meet number nine, / with its neck like a question mark (most often towards morning) / or (after midnight) a two, I'm reminded of a swan.

Khlebnikov's numbers are also endowed with qualities of people and animals:

Я всматриваюсь в вас, о числа,
И вы мне видитесь одетыми в звери, в их шкурах,
Рукой опирающимися на вырванные дубы.
Вы даруете – единство между змееобразным движением
Хребта вселенной и пляской коромысла,
Вы позволяете понимать века, как быстрого хохота зубы.
Мои сейчас вещеобразно разверзлися зеницы.
Узнать, *что будет Я, когда делимое его – единица.*   (II. 98)

I stare at you numbers, / and I see you dressed as animals, in their skin, / leaning by your hand against uprooted oaks. / You grant – the unity of the snaky movement / of the universe's spine and the dance of the yoke, / you allow to understand the centuries as a row of flashing teeth. / Now my eyes open wide, like a clairvoyant's, / to find out *what I will be, when its dividend is – one.*

To the last question, Brodsky seems to have an answer, using it as a title for his prose: 'one is perhaps less than "one"' (*L.* 17). In this poem by Khlebnikov, all is tied in one metaphoric knot: numbers, animals, trees, mountains, and man.

As in Khlebnikov, Brodsky's numbers sometimes retain their traditional symbolism. Thus, the number eight almost always serves as a sign for infinity, as has been noted more than once. Every time, however, this number is included in a concrete system of imagery: *insane counting, noiseless train*, are associated with the figure eight in the poem 'Isaac and Abraham'; two old émigrées living out their days in Dante's Florence are substituted by *two old figure 8s* in the poem 'December in Florence'; in the poem 'East Finchley', a figure eight is included in the hackneyed image of a rose:

Посредине абсурда, ужаса, скуки жизни
стоят за стеклом цветы, как вывернутые наизнанку
мелкие вещи – *с розой, подобной знаку*
бесконечности из-за пучка восьмёрок,   (*У.* 77)

In the midst of absurdity, horror, life's tedium, / beyond the windows stand the flowers, like trifling things / turned inside out – *a rose, symbol* / *of infinity with its clustered eights.*

In a seminar analysis of Zbigniew Herbert's poetry, Brodsky noted that in our day and age the inclusion of a rose in poetry signifies something awful, because roses no longer have any relationship with reality.[23] In the same poem 'December in Florence', numbers are present not only implicitly but are also concealed beneath the poem's compositional structure. Dedicated as it is to Dante's favourite number – nine – it consists of nine stanzas, each of nine lines.

In other poems, figures are used on a purely phonetic basis: 'Муха бьётся в стекле, жужжа, / как 80 или – 100' (*У.* 21: 'A fly beats against the glass, buzzing / like 80 or – 100'). On the other hand, this onomatopoeic device is generously endowed with the semantics of the brevity and fragility of existence in the poem 'The Fly'.

Things, figures, words, transformed by the tropes, are antinomically linked: not one of the elements of opposition is capable of resolving the problems of being in isolation. This striving to re-examine commonly held notions of the world forces the poet continually to change his angle of vision, to look from a reverse direction. Hence the very strange metaphoric definitions: *Одиночество есть человек в квадрате* (*У.* 158: *Loneliness is a man squared*); *жизнь – синоним / небытия и нарушенья правил* (*У.* 168: *life is a synonym of non-existence and a breaking of the rules*); *это – клинопись мыслей: любая из них – тупик* (*У.* 15: *This is the cuneiform of thoughts: any of them is a cul-de-sac*). The problem of the metaphysical cul-de-sac which so occupies Brodsky finds expression in Khlebnikov in a paradoxical metaphor of identification with a mathematical sign: *Тупик – это путь с отрицательным множителем* (v. 38: *A cul-de-sac is a path with a negative multiplier*). One cannot help noting a resemblance to it in Brodsky's work: *зоркость этих времён – это зоркость к вещам тупика* (*К.* 60: 'The vigilance of these times is / the vigilance of the things of a cul-de-sac').

These quasi-scientific definitions can in no way be called over-precise. They are contradictory, at times irreconcilable, or else mutually exclusive. These are diverse attempts to unearth the key to the doors of being, which remain firmly shut. Forging the keys first from metal, then from stone, trying various combinations for the safe of meanings, Brodsky moves 'forwards, over the horizon, beyond the boundary'. Thereby he reveals a highly Russian mental-

ity, which has been noted by many Western commentators on
intellectual Russia:

This yearning for absolutes was one source of that notorious consistency
which, as Berlin pointed out, was the most striking characteristic of
Russian thinkers – their habit of taking ideas and concepts to their most
extreme, even absurd, conclusions: to stop before the extreme con-
sequences of one's reasoning was seen as a sign of moral cowardice,
insufficient commitment to the truth.[24]

In changing his angle of vision, intensifying the density of focus,
Brodsky carries on from where Dostoevsky, Berdiaev, and Shestov
left off. He begins where others put a full stop, from the *fin de
partie*, after the end. He is also akin to these predecessors in that he
is not afraid to admit aloud: '*Вот и ещё одна / комбинация цифр /
не отворила дверцу*' ('1983': '*Here is one more / combination of
numbers / that hasn't opened the door*').

Man–word–Spirit

In my case, if I were to begin to create some form of theology,
I think it would be a theology of language. In this sense, the
word is really something sacred for me.[25]

The repetitive frequency of analogies between things, man, and
language (with individual words, letters, typographical marks, and
grammatical categories) is such that these analogies can and ought
to serve as a key element in our interpretation of Brodsky's poetic
world. It is easiest to start with his similes. Because of their lack of
metaphorical ambiguity, similes express the author's perception of
the world more directly than his metaphors. Consequently, any
improved accuracy in recognizing parallelism of meaning and
lexical-thematic relatedness of metaphor and simile will increase
the reliability of our understanding of the metaphor's burden of
conceptual content.

Comparison of the world with language can be found throughout
Brodsky's poetry: *на площадях, как "прощай", широких, / в
улицах узких, как звук "люблю"* (Ч. 42: *On squares broad as the
word 'farewell', / in streets narrow like 'I love'*; *и улица вдалеке
сужается в букву "у", / как лицо к подбородку* (Ч. 92: *and the
distant street narrows into the letter 'y', / like a face falling on to its
chin*).

People, too, are reduced to a letter as life is to a phrase: *Полицейский на перекрёстке / машет руками, как буква "ж", ни вниз, ни / вверх* (Ч. 113: *The policeman on the crossing / waves his arms like the letter 'zh', no higher, no / lower*); *вся жизнь, как нетвёрдая честная фраза* (У. 57: *all life is like an unstable, honest phrase*); *Как тридцать третья буква, / я пячусь всю жизнь вперёд.* (Н. 111: *Like the thirty-third letter, / all my life, I am advancing backwards*). The thirty-third letter of the Russian alphabet is the last letter 'Я', which also means 'I' and looks like a man moving from right to left, while Russian writing moves in the opposite direction. Therefore, this image hints at Brodsky's position in relation to Russian letters. I would also like to think that this simile sheds light on several essential features of Brodsky's poetics as regards his use of metaphor and metonymy, metre and syntax, lyricism and anti-lyricism, to name but a few. A similarly significant comparison is that of the poet with a letter 'г': *"Как ты жил в эти годы?" – "Как буква "г" в "ого"* (Ч. 47: *'How did you live in these years?' – 'Like the letter g in ogo'*). The letter 'g' in the Russian interjection 'ogo' is, of course, pronounced like the sound [ɦ], as in 'Bog' ('God'), which is not represented by a separate letter in the Russian language. Similarly, Brodsky, as a poet, did not exist in official Soviet literature until he was awarded the Nobel Prize for Literature in 1987.

Many of his 'linguistic' similes and metaphors are motivated, on the one hand, by his 'theology of language', and on the other, by the fate of the poet in exile:

> *Можно сказать уверенно:*
> *здесь и скончаю я дни, теряя*
> *волосы, зубы, глаголы, суффиксы,*   (Ч. 26)

It can be said with certainty, / here I will end my days, losing / my hair, my teeth, my verbs and suffixes.

Severed from his linguistic milieu, Brodsky seems to survive thanks to language alone, as many of his metaphors demonstrate: *where I, worse than a mouse, / gnawed the breviary of the native vocabulary* (K. 61); *you will not let me find / a shelter in this tower, / in the Babylonian great-granddaughter, the tower of words, / continually unfinished* (K. 64). Once again, in an analysis of the analogy between the world and language, the parallels between Brodsky's and Khlebnikov's poetry are striking:

Ты поворачиваешь страницы книги той,
Чей почерк – росчерки пера морей.
Чернилами служили люди,
Расстрел царя был знаком восклицанья.
Победа войск служила запятой,
А толпы – многоточия.   (v. 26)

You are turning the pages of that book / whose handwriting is the strokes of the sea's pen. / People served as ink, / the shooting of the Tsar was an exclamation mark. / The armies' victory served as a comma. / And the masses were dots.

'Graphic' images of this type are often encountered in Brodsky: *И те же фонари горят над нами, / как восклицательные знаки ночи* (С. 68: *And the same street lamps burn above us, / like the exclamation marks of night*); *всё виснет на крюках своих вопросов* (К. 63: *everything hangs on the hooks of its questions*); *фонари обрываются, как белое многоточье* (У. 82: *the street lamps stop suddenly, like white dots*); *Супротив друг друга стояли, топча росу, / точно длинные строчки ещё не закрытой книги, / армии, занятые игрой* (Ч. 100: *the armies on manoeuvres / stood opposite one another, trampling the dew / like the long lines of a book about to close*).

Fascinating as it may be to unearth lexical repetitions of tropes and figures of speech from the texts of the two poets, it is even more important to understand the significance of such semantic and thematic similarities. Khlebnikov, in making language the protagonist of his poetry, hoped, with the help of poetry, to penetrate the secret of nature, things, and the Spirit. He equally attempted to find in the word the 'roots of the world' and to re-establish, with the aid of morphological formations – that is, his multitudinous neologisms – a mythic consciousness. Brodsky also mythologizes language to a significant degree, albeit with other aims:

The poet's spiritual temperament inclined to catastrophe [writes Mandelstam]. Cult and culture offered a hidden, protected source of energy, a uniform and expedient motion: 'the love which moves the sun and all the luminaries'. Poetic culture arises from the attempt to avert catastrophe, to make it dependent on the central sun of the system as a whole, be it love, of which Dante spoke, or music, at which Blok ultimately arrived.[26]

In Brodsky, such a self-protective mechanism is the cult of the word. And this cult is created exclusively by means of the word itself, first and foremost by means of metaphor. Language in all its aspects undergoes the same semantic transformations as those performed upon man and things. Man is often substituted by or compared with parts of speech and letters of the alphabet: *И лицо в потёмках, словами наружу* (Ч. 112: *and a face in darkness, with words on the outside*). Language, like man's mental and spiritual phenomena, is sometimes presented in physical terms: *я, / бормочущий комок / слов* (Ч. 33: *I, / a mumbling clod / of words*); *и во рту от многих "ура" осадак* (У. 98: *and there's a nasty taste in the mouth from many 'hurrahs'*); *и чернеет, что твой Седов, "прощай"* (Ч. 78: *'Farewell' grows black like Sedov*). On the other hand, language, its words, sounds, and grammatical categories, becomes not only object-like, but also animated in metaphors of attribution, losing its signifying content in the process: *К какой зиме торопятся слова?* (С. 193: *towards which winter do the words hasten?*); *сбивается русский язык, / бормоча в протокол* (С. 233: *the Russian language contradicts itself, / muttering in the protecol*); *над улыбкой прошедшего времени* (Н. 28: *over the smile of the past tense*); *любви / звука к смыслу* (У. 62: *the love of a sound for meaning*).

In metaphors of identification, language is equated both with man and with things:

> "Но ежели взглянуть со стороны,
> то можно, в общем, сделать замечанье:
> *и слово – вещь.* Тогда мы спасены!"
> "Тогда и начинается молчанье."   (О. 205)

'But if you look from the side, / then you can, in general, make the remark: / *the word is also a thing.* Then we are saved!' 'And then silence begins.'

The virtuoso transformation of the word into a thing may be observed in the fifth canto of the poem 'Gorbunov and Gorchakov', entitled 'A song in the Third Person':

> "И он ему сказал". "И он ему
> сказал". "И он сказал". "И он ответил".
> "И он сказал". "И он". "И он во тьму
> воззрился и сказал". "Слова на ветер".   (О. 189)

'And he said to him.' 'And he / said to him.' 'And he said.' 'And he answered.' / 'And he said.' 'And he.' 'And he gazed into the darkness / and said.' 'Words on the wind.'

The multiple repetition of the verb 'to say' in the sixteen-line stanza deprives it of any meaning, while the poet deprives it of even its minimal natural context by gradually surrounding it with an alien semantic field:

"И молча на столе сказал стоит".

. . .

"Сказал – кольцо." "Сказал – ещё кольцо".
"И вот его сказал уткнулся в берег".
"И собственный сказал толкнул в лицо,
вернувшись вспять". (*O.* 189)

'And quietly, on the table, said stands.' . . . / 'Said, a ring.' 'Said, another ring.' / 'And now his said rammed the shore.' / And his own said elbowed the face, / turning back.'

The view of human life as fundamentally absurd is expressed with Beckett-like daring, by means of the transformation of a simple verb into the images of a ring, boat, ripple on the water, from a word that has been cast into it like a pebble; by means of the rhythm of a train:

"Сказал". "Сказал". "Сказал". "Сказал". "Сказал".
"Суть поезда". "Всё дальше, дальше рейсы".
"И вот уже сказал почти вокзал".
"Никто из них не хочет лечь на рельсы".
"И он сказал". "А он сказал в ответ". (*O.* 189)

'Said.' 'Said.' 'Said.' 'Said.' 'Said.' / 'The essence of a train.' 'Farther and farther it runs.' / 'And already said is almost a station.' / 'But none of them want to lie on the rails.' / 'And he said.' 'And he said in answer.'

And so on throughout the thirty lines until, finally, not only the verb 'said' but also its subject, the pronoun 'he', are directly identified with a thing:

"Сказал исчез". "Сказал пришёл к перрону".
"И он сказал". "Но раз *сказал – предмет,
то также относиться должно к он'у*". (*O.* 189)

'Said has vanished.' 'Said arrived at the platform.' 'And he said.' / 'But if *said is an object / the same must be said about he'm.*'

The opposition of word and thing is first emphasized, then eliminated in the poem by a whole series of metaphors. The profusion of things and their illusory immortality is completely dispelled by the omnipotence of the word:

> "*Вещь*, имя получившая, тотчас
> становится немедля *частью речи*".   (*O.* 204)

'*A thing*, having received a name, straight away / becomes *a part of speech*,'

If 'everything has its limit', then so do the things which are 'devoured by words'. 'The only word on earth which so far has not devoured the object' is eternity. But can even it defend us against words?' asked the insane interlocutor of his double, Gorbunov:

> "Едва ли". "Осеняющийся Крестным
> Знаменем спасётся". "Но не весь".
> "*В синониме не более воскреснем*".   (*O.* 205)

'Scarcely.' 'He who crosses himself with a sign of / the Cross saves himself.' 'But not completely.' 'We will be resurrected only in the synonym.'

In this poem we have a highly ambiguous relationship of identity between the word and the thing, which we may conventionally express as 'word-thing'. The named thing is immediately transformed into a word, that is, into a part of speech, and so one of the philosophizing interlocutors concludes logically: 'there are no objects, there are only words' (*O.* 147). On the other hand, the word itself, because of its frequent and senseless repetition, becomes petrified, like the ray of sun in 'Midday in the Room', like the verb 'said' in the mouth of a man whose 'lips sing in two voices' (*O.* 184). The relations of equalization between word and thing are differentiated from the identification between word and man, although man, just like things, is transformed into letters and punctuation marks:

> Человек превращается в шорох пера по бумаге, в кольца,
> петли, клинышки букв и, потому что скользко,
> в запятые и точки.   (*Ч.* 112)

Man is transformed into the rusle of pen on paper, into the rings, / the noose, the wedges of letters and, because it is slippery, into commas and full stops.

A part of speech survives both things and man: *От великих вещей остаются слова языка* (*Ч.* 109: *From great things, the words of language remain*).

These, and other metaphors of analogous semantics, implicitly
resonate with a poem by Derzhavin:

> Река времён в своём стремленьи
> Уносит все дела людей
> . . .
> *А если что и остаётся*
> *Чрез звуки лиры и трубы,*
> *То вечности жерлом пожрётся*
> *И общей не уйдёт судьбы.*

The river of time in its striving / Carries off all deeds of men . . . *And
if aught remains* / Through the sounds of lyre and trumpet, / Then *it
will be swallowed by the maw of eternity* / And the common lot
cannot be avoided.

In this poem, in Mandelstam's view, Derzhavin uttered the 'hidden
thought of the future' – the basis of relativity and relativism: 'and if
aught remains'.[27] Brodsky, in pursuit of an answer to the question
of what time does to man, arrives at the same conclusion: *от
всякой великой веры / остаются, как правило, только мощи*
(*O.* 173: *of any great faith, / as a rule, only holy relics remain*); *от
великой любви остаётся лишь равенства знак* (*У.* 18: *of great
love only an 'equals' sign remains*); *От всего человека вам
остаётся часть / речи. Часть речи вообще. Часть речи* (*Ч.* 95:
*What is left of a man is a part of / speech. A part of speech in general.
A part of speech*).

In these series of metaphors with an identical grammatical
structure Brodsky equates the material with the ideal, man with
both things and language, language with Spirit and time. Although
in all these metaphors we keep coming up against the constant
dualism of the humanization of inanimate matter and the de-
animation of man, it is precisely the introduction of the word into a
system of equalization between animate and inanimate that alters
the quality of identification 'word–man'. Language, in being
included in this dualism of life itself by way of all its aspects, reflects
the dualism of matter and spirit. It is precisely language which
indicates the way to synthesis of the spiritual and material:

> *Воздух – вещь языка.*
> *Небосвод –*
> *хор согласных и гласных молекул,*
> *в просторечии – душ.*   (*У.* 64)

*Air is a thing of language | the firmament is | a chorus of molecules of
consonants and vowels, | in the vernacular – of souls.*

The job of a writer, Brodsky insists, is to make 'his pen catch up
with his soul' (*L.* 161). His 'theology of language', or conceptualization of the word by metaphorical means, is practised from the very
beginning:

> И уходя, как уходят в чужую память,
> мерно ступая от слова к слову,
> всеми своими тремя временами
> глаголы однажды восходят на Голгофу.   (*С.* 72)

And going away, as they go into another's memory, / measuredly
stepping from word to word, / in all their three tenses / verbs are one
day ascending Golgotha.

Verbs as a part of speech frequently undergo all kinds of semantic
transformations in Brodsky's tropes: *Глаголы в длинной
очереди к "л"* (*У.* 174: *Verbs in a long queue for 'l'*), where the
letter 'l' represents all that remains of love.

Words, like man, are susceptible to alienation. This provides the
motivation for the transference of words into things, and explains
why man does not always succeed in identifying himself with
language: *Иногда голова с рукою | сливаются, не
станавясь строкою* (*Ч.* 94: *Sometimes the head fuses with the
hand without becoming a line*). Not only man but the language itself
has become a victim of the grandiose social Utopia of this century:

In general it should be noted that the first victim of talk about Utopia –
desired or already attained – is grammar; for language, unable to keep up
with thought, begins to gasp in the subjunctive mood and starts to gravitate
towards timeless categories and constructions; as a consequence of which
the ground starts to slip out from under even simple nouns, and an aura of
arbitrariness arises around them.[28]

And surely it is these temporal and social upheavals in Russian
history that explain certain semantic shifts in Brodsky's metaphors:
О как из существительных глаголет (*О.* 206: *O how it
verbalizes from substantives!*); *не жизнь передо мной – победа
слов* (*О.* 206: *Not life before me – the triumph of words*). In a world
where the complete triumph of words over life has taken place,
where *word moves against word* (*слово надвигается на слово*),
man becomes the victim of language:

Знаешь, все, кто далече,
по ком голосит тоска –
жертвы законов речи,
запятых, языка.   (*H.* 111)

You know, all who are out of reach, / to whom yearning cries out – /
are victims of the law of speech, / of commas, of language.

By introducing linguistic terminology into poetry, Brodsky is
doing two or three things at once. On the conceptual level, by
introducing the word as a fourth and equal member of the classical
triad 'Spirit–man–thing', he neutralizes the opposition within it.
Each of the elements in the equation is illuminated in a new light
and can be described anew. The relations between man and Spirit,
man and matter, acquire new dimensions. And the word, any part
of speech, imitates and substitutes for any of the elements of the
equation:

сказуемое, ведомое подлежащим,
уходит в прошедшее время, жертвуя настоящим,
от грамматики новой на сердце пряча
окончание шёпота, крика, плача.   (*H.* 106)

the predicate, led by the subject, / recedes into the past, sacrificing
the present, / from the new grammar, hiding in the heart / the
termination of whisper, shout, lamentation.

By its assocation with spirit, the word is capable of protecting man
not only from things, but even from time. It enables man to realize
that there is something in life greater than ourselves, which *warms
us, without warming itself* (*O.* 214). As the material means and goal
of poetry, the word becomes the bearer of the spiritual content of
human life. The poetic word is also capable of predicting the future
and travelling into it:

кириллица, грешным делом,
разбредаясь по прописи вкривь ли, вкось ли,
знает больше, чем та сивилла,
о грядущем. О том, как чернеть на белом,
покуда белое есть, и после.   (*У.* 123)

cyrillic, a sinful matter, / roaming over writing aslope and aslant, /
knows more than the Sybil / about the future. About how to be black
on white / as long as white remains, and after.

On the poetic level, the introduction of linguistic terminology
extends the boundaries of poetic language. As opposed to Khleb-

nikov, who was also extremely concerned with the renewal of poetic lexis, Brodsky issues poetic visas to all major sub-systems of language, with the exception of home-made ones, that is, neologisms. The formation of artificial words is alien to his poetics. In all else, the paths of the extension of the poetic language coincide in Brodsky and Khlebnikov. Both poets create their own idiostyle, which is free from accepted literary and aesthetic conventions.

Apart from the tropological use of punctuation marks of which we spoke earlier, inverted commas, full stops, hyphens etc. are present in Brodsky's poetry as such, as words in the language: *"Ну, о неограниченности душ / слыхал я что-то в молодости. Точка."* (*O*. 195: '*Well, as for the absoluteness of soul / I heard something about it in my youth. Full stop*'); *"увы" – мужская реплика. Кавычки.* (*O*. 202: '*alas' – is a masculine rejoinder. Inverted commas*); *"На свой аршин ты меряешь, тире'* (*O*. 212: '*you measure by your own yardstick, dash*'). This is not so much the Futurist device of 'laying bare the device' as a parody of it. At the same time, it is self-reflexive language, be it everyday or poetic language. This is confirmed by the introduction of poetic terminology into the poetry:

> Стук молотка
> вечным ритмом станет.
> Земля гипербол лежит под ними,
> как небо метафор плывёт над нами.   (*C*. 73)

The tap of the hammer / will become an eternal rhythm. / The land of hyperbole lies beneath them, / as the sky of metaphors floats over us.

Brodsky carries on a general tendency of twentieth-century literature, its tendency to become increasingly self-reflexive. More and more often, it is both the object and the analysis of that object. Brodsky's poetry, as we have seen, cites other poets no less than himself. And, by admitting the terminology of poetics, it analyses itself, as it were: *хотя бы эдак век свой удлинив / пульсирующим, тикающим ямбом* (*H*. 37: *(even like this prolonging his lifetime / with a pulsating, ticking iamb)*); *Но рифма, что на краешке строки, / взбирается к предшественнице выше* (*H*. 37: *But rhyme, which is on the edge of the line, / clambers up to the one that has gone before*). This process of the aesthetic conceptualization of poetry by poetry does not diminish over the years: *Что парная рифма нам даст, то ей / мы возвращаем под видом* дней (*O.* 155: *What a paired rhyme will give us, / we give back to it under the guise of days*); Всё – только пир согласных / на их ножках кривых (*O.* 111: *Everything is but a feast of consonants / on their bent little legs*). The perception and description of the world through the prism of language facilitates an increase in degree of estranged depiction: и при слове "грядущее" из русского языка / выбегают мыши (*Ч.* 95: *and at the word 'future' from the Russian language / the mice scurry out*); Голос / представляет собою борьбу глагола с / ненаставшим временем (*У.* 75: *Voice / represents the struggle of the verb with / non-present tense*).

The future of the poet, and so too his present, is his interconnection with the language. The cycle 'A Part of Speech' expresses the psychological and linguistic situation of the poet in exile. It is a dialogue with his own psyche, an attempt to penetrate his own consciousness. Equally, it represents a word about the word, a dialogue with other writers. The technical virtuosity of the entire cycle illustrates Brodsky's conviction that 'poetry seems to be the only weapon able to beat language using language's own means' (*L.* 56). It also neutralizes a profound existential lack of well-being. For if this poet is able to display such linguistic wit and poetic virtuosity, in no matter what despair he finds himself, then there is hope.

In Brodsky's 'linguistic' tropes, two extreme views of language coalesce: 'language is only language' and 'language is all'.[29] Море, мадам, это чья-то речь (*O.* 155: *The sea, madam, is someone's speech*); Сиротство / звука, Томас, есть речь (*У.* 63: *Orphanhood / of a sound, Thomas, is speech!*). In talking of the *all-seeing eye of words*, Brodsky has in mind not ubiquitous universal reason, but the hypostasis of God in the word. He believes that language is something mystical, of immense significance. We do not utilize even one-tenth of what exists in language. We come into language; we have not created it. Every generation discovers language for itself. He who has given us language is greater than the receiver.[30] Brodsky recalls his youthful impressions of Herodotus's *History*, where it is said of the Scythians that 'they exist in a state of constant surprise at their own language', and he thinks that little has changed since then. 'That's why I think that language, which is given to us, is such that we are in the position of children who received a gift. A gift, as a rule, is always less than the Giver and this indicates the nature of language.'[31]

His metaphors also indicate the central place of language in Brodsky's world-view. The ontological unity of the word, the Spirit, and man is emphasized in the metaphors of identification. The word correlates with the world by means of direct and negative correlations, which may be depicted schematically as follows: *word = thing; word = man; word = Spirit; word = word.* The poet moves in the direction of identification of the whole diversity of the world with the word since the pull to a sufficiently firm linguistic basis is self-evident. He moves towards the idea of a synthesis of matter and spirit. And the language is the organizing force of this synthesis. Using metaphor as an equalizing force, Brodsky creates a system of equivalence in which equality of rights between the elements of the quadrant is forced. Not one of the right-hand elements of the equation can exist without the others. Using Viacheslav Ivanov's terminology, we may call this system *antinomische Identität*.[32]

In words, man *communicates with being* (*O.* 199) and with the Spirit. *And craving to be at one with God, as with the landscape* (*и жажда слиться с Богом, как с пейзажем. К.* 63) can only be achieved in language:

и в горячей
полости горла *холодным перлом*
перекатывается Гораций.
Я не воздвиг уходящей к тучам
каменной вещи для их острастки.
О своём – и о любом – грядущем
я узнал у буквы, у чёрной краски.   (*У.* 113)

And in the hot / cavity of the throat *like a cold pearl* / *Horace rolls over*. / I have not erected a departing for the clouds' / *stone thing* as a warning to them. / *Of my own – and of any – future* / *I've learned from the letter, from its black colour.*

The simile *the cold pearl*, the metonymy *Horace* (standing for his poetry); the metaphor of substitution *departing for the clouds' stone thing*, which implies Horace's poem *Exegi monumentum*, translated into Russian with personal variations by Derzhavin and Pushkin; the personification of a letter, as in *I've learned from the letter*; and the semantically charged rhymes *горячей / Гораций* ('hot' / 'Horace'), *к тучам / о грядущем* ('for the clouds' / 'of the future') – all serve to emphasize the all-powerfulness of the word.

Brodsky's letters and, in his view, the letters of any language, stand in eternal expectation of meaning, as Soviet citizens must stand in line for the rudimentary necessities of their existence. *The all-seeing eye of words* (K. 81) perceives and cognizes *with a greater reach than that of the body* and the physical eye, *moving forward, starts to send back all that it absorbs*(Y. 26). The pupil, the eye in Brodsky's poetry, substitutes metaphorically for poetic vision, the imagination of the poet, whence was born the metaphor of attribution, *the all-seeing eye of words*. It leads the poet to 'philosophical insights ... not so much through thesis and antithesis, as through language itself, from which all that is superfluous is banished'.[33] Brodsky has in mind poetic language – the highest form of existence of language (L. 186). 'A poet in his development, if he is a true poet', Brodsky has said, 'repeats the development of language; he begins with some sort of childish babble, then moves to maturity, and to greater maturity and, finally, to language itself.'[34]

In answer to my question, when did this idea first occur to him, that all can be reduced to language, that language is all-powerful, Brodsky said that he had the impression that he had always known this.[35] He modestly downgrades to a minimum his own achievements in poetry: 'I merely pass on what exists in the Russian language, there is no special merit of my own.'[36] The poet only catches the idioms which exist in language, scoops up rhymes which were always there. This is taken over from Mandelstam, who also thought that every new poetic image is only a recognition and repetition.[37]

An intellectual and poetic tour de force

> The more powerful an individual's thinking, the less comfort it affords its possessor in the event of some tragedy.[38]

The poetic world of Brodsky, designed as it is on a metaphorical model, has a tangible objective quality. This is achieved by various kinds of alienation of meaning in the trope. The classical triad 'Spirit–man–thing' is extended by the inclusion of language as a fourth and equal term. Language, as we have seen, is either subjected to personification or else is depicted as a thing. The poem 'Butterfly' can be viewed as an embodiment of Brodsky's four-dimensional perception of the world, which includes 'an embodiment of nothingness itself' (L. 12). During the discussion of this poem we will be able to see how the chain of equalization (thing = man = word = Spirit) allows the poet to reinterpret some of the most fundamental existential situations, as well as to create essentially new types of metaphors in Russian poetry.

'Butterfly' was written in 1972 and is one of the wittiest and most aphoristic of Brodsky's poems. A butterfly is only the starting-point for a prolonged meditation on the typical Russian obsession with God and man. The poem is a traditionally rhymed meditation with favourite metaphysical rhetorical characteristics: a butterfly is seen as a frail buffer between life and death.

The purely graphic scheme of line arrangement resembles the butterfly. Its slender form almost threatens to disappear while we are analysing it, as the butterfly has faded in the poet's cupped hand. This fleshless poem has a structure so tight as to make it impossible to unravel without the poem disintegrating. But the first impression is deceptive. Brodsky himself again and again provides us with the key to the poem: 'because a poem sits in the very middle of the page surrounded by the enormity of white margins, each word of it, each comma carries an enormous – i.e., proportionate to the abundance of unused space – burden of allusions and significances' (*L*. 316). The choice of a rare metre seems to convey the very fragility of the butterfly: the iambic trimeter of odd lines (1, 3, 5, 7, 9, 11) alternates with iambic dimeter (4, 8, 12) and pyrrhic (2, 6, 10). Accordingly, the rhyme scheme is the following: *aBBabCCbcDDc*. Every one of the fourteen stanzas has a regular structure of twelve lines. Only two other poems were written before by Brodsky in this stanza structure: 'One Crow . . .' (1964; O. 83) and 'Verses in April' (1969; *O*. 136).

The continuous symmetry and tension constitute both the framework and the content of the poem. Brodsky's exquisite modulations of tone, shifts of pace, syntactic displacements, reflect the butterfly's movements and suit the poet's own movements from one idea to another. But this does not mean his thoughts are not consistent. On the contrary, there are several themes that run through the poem: being and nothingness, light and darkness, and, above all, faceless and all-powerful time. It is almost as if he travels in a circle – ending where he began.

As Kreps has observed: 'Brodsky's "Butterfly" gives the impression of having flown out of English Metaphysical poetry where it had been a mere caterpillar. In its brevity of line, the type of rhyme and its overall intellectual tonality it is reminiscent of certain poems of Herbert, Vaughan and Marvell.'[39] A careful reading of this poem reveals other echoes. Thus, as opposed to the 'nice speculations of philosophy' of the English Metaphysical poets, Brodsky exhibits a Beckettian gloom and 'limitless negation'. There are Russian connections, too.

In stanza one, Brodsky comments on the short life-span of the butterfly by introducing the opposition 'alive–dead' and by eliminating it almost straight away:

> Сказать, что *ты мертва?*
> Но ты жила лишь сутки.
> Как много грусти в шутке
> Творца! едва
> могу произнести
> *"жила" – единство даты*
> *рожденья* и когда *ты*
> в моей горсти
> *рассыпалась,* меня
> смущает *вычесть*
> *одно из двух количеств*
> *в пределах дня.* (Ч. 32)

Say that *you're dead?* / *But you lived for just one day.* / [There's] so much sadness in the Creator's / jest! I can hardly / say / *'lived'*; *your date of* / *birth and* [the time] when *you* / *were disintegrating* / in my hands / *are one:* / it confuses my *subtraction of the one quantity from the second* / *within the confines of a day.*

The butterfly's brief existence is emphasized here in rhyme-metaphors: *мертва* / *едва* ('dead' / 'hardly'); *сутки* / *в шутке* ('one day' / 'a jest'); *вычесть* / *количеств* ('subtract' / 'quantity'); *даты* / *когда ты* ('date' / 'when you'). The mathematical terminology of the stanza allows for the depiction of the 'one date' of the birth and death of the butterfly not only as the Creator's jest, but also as the abstraction ± a day. 'One quantity from the second within the confines of a day' is equally difficult to subtract as 'time from man' (У. 79). This 'one date' forms the starting-point for the poet's meditation on the nature of time and relativity of its measurement by the various creatures which live in it. The syntactic and semantic ambiguity of these ordinary words, as well as the consistent enjambements (*в шутке* / *Творца; едва* / *могу; даты* / *рожденья; ты* / *рассыпалась; меня* / *смущает*), make one

read on without pausing all the way to the end to bring its shifting
surface to a point of rest.

The intangible quality of days is more directly stated in the
metaphor of identification at the beginning of the second stanza:

> Затем что *дни для нас –*
> *ничто. Всего лишь*
> *ничто.* Их не приколешь,
> и пищей глаз
> не сделаешь: они
> на фоне белом,
> не обладая телом,
> незримы. *Дни,*
> *они как ты*; верней,
> что может весить
> уменьшенный раз в десять
> один из дней?

Because *days are to us just / nothing. Simply / nothing.* You can't pin
them down, / and you can't make food for the eyes of them. / On the
white background, / they possess no body, / are invisible. *Days, / they
are like you*; or rather, / what can the weight / be of a single, /
tenfold-diminished, day?

The repetition of *nothingness* introduces a negative element to
man's existence in time. A comparison of days with the butterfly is
paradoxically given in a chain of negative metaphors. The lack of
colour, flesh, and weight is used as a basis for the similarity between
day and the butterfly. Here we come across a familiar rhyme,
белом / телом ('white' / 'body'), which was discussed at the
beginning of this chapter as a substitution for nothingness, or else a
reflection of another universe (stanzas IV and V).

> Я думаю, что ты –
> и то, и это:
> звезды, лица, предмета
> в тебе черты.

I think that you are / both, this and that: / in you there are traces / of
star, of face, of object.

Surely this perfect, fragile creature is not a fragment of the
imagination of the poet who is identified with *a mumbling clod of
words* (stanza III). The butterfly is a creation of someone greater
than a man:

Кто был тот ювелир,
что, бровь не хмуря,
нанёс в миниатюре
на них тот мир,
что сводит нас с ума,
берёт нас в клещи,
где ты, как мысль о вещи,
мы – вещь сама?

Who was that jeweller, / with brow serene, / who drew in miniature / on those wings that world, / which drives us mad, / and holds us in its pincers, *where you are like the thought about things; / we – the thing itself.*

The jeweller is a metaphor-substitution for God, whose power is emphasized by the everyday phrase *бровь не хмуря* ('brow serene'), suggesting that God had no difficulty in creating such detailed perfection. Compared with this sort of talent, man seems very insignificant. From the creation of the butterfly to the presence of God or a power superior to man that has created our universe, we are led to the unanswerable questions of our own existence. The bold metaphor of identification of man with a thing is the most startling, while the simile *you are like the thought about a thing* echoes the definition of time in 'Lullaby of Cape Cod': *Пространство – вещь. / Время же, в сущности, мысль о вещи* (Ч. 106: *Space is a thing. / Time is, in essence, the thought of a thing*). The origin of this idea can be found in the earlier poem 'The Candlestick' (1968): *поскольку заливает стеарин / не мысли о вещах, но сами вещи* (О. 118: *for the stearin floods / not the thoughts about things, but the things themselves*). The equation of man and a thing is extended by the introduction of speech. The answer to the question why the butterfly is given so brief an existence dies with it because it has not been given a voice:

Ты не ответишь мне
не по причине
застенчивости и не
со зла, и не
затем, что ты мертва.
Жива, мертва ли –
но каждой Божьей твари
как знак родства
дарован голос для
общенья, пенья:

продления мгновенья,
минуты, дня.

You will not answer me, / not because of / any shyness, and not / from malice, and not / because you are dead. / Living or dead though, / all God's creatures, / as a sign of kinship, / are given a voice, for / communication, for singing: / for stretching out a second, / a minute, a day.

In the last part of the stanza, Brodsky may be referring to Goethe's *Faust*, since elsewhere in his works is repeated (almost always ironically) Faust's plea: *Verweile doch, du bist so schön* ('Stay, moment! You are splendid'). In the poem 'Two Hours in an Empty Tank' (1965), a quotation from *Faust* appears:

От человека, аллес, ждать напрасно:
"остановись, мгновенье, ты прекрасно".
Меж нами дьявол бродит ежечасно
и поминутно этой фразы ждёт.   (*O.* 163)

From man, *alles*, one waits in vain: / 'Stay, moment, you are splendid.' / The devil wanders among us by the hour / and by the minute awaits this phrase.

In the poem 'A Winter Evening in Yalta' (1969), Brodsky returns to this thought: *Остановись, мгновенье! Ты не столь / прекрасно, сколько ты неповторимо* (*O.* 135: *Stay, moment! You are not so much / splendid as unrepeatable*). In the poem 'Fly' (1986), the poet's brain is compared with *a thing which has quitted obedience / like that moment* (вещь, вышедшая из повиновенья, / как то мгновенье, *У.* 169). In 'Butterfly', we find the first non-ironical context for the idea that not only is the devil capable of extending the moment, the minute, the day, but man is as well, by means of language. *To stretch a moment, a minute, a day*, means to gain a victory over man's greatest enemy, time. This can be done only by means of language (a voice, speech, words). The spoken or printed word can be passed down from one generation to the next, so that even after death great ideas will live on.

One could perhaps regard the butterfly's muteness as a curse, for when it dies it will be as if it never existed. But Brodsky cannot help creating one more paradox. It seems almost a blessing in disguise:

А ты – ты лишена
сего залога.
Но, рассуждая строго,

так лучше: на
кой ляд быть у небес
в долгу, в реестре.
Не сокрушайся ж, если
твой век, твой вес
достойны немоты:
звук – тоже бремя.
Бесплотнее, чем время,
беззвучней ты.

And you are lack / of this pledge. / Though strictly speaking, / it is better that way: / why in hell's name be in debt / to heaven, or be in their books? / Don't get upset though if / your life-span, your weight / merits muteness. / *Sound is also a burden.* / *You are less corporeal than time,* / *more silent.*

This stanza fulfils the paradox: language is used to deny language. It is significant that the idea that speech is a burden is given in the copula construction. A man as a conscious language-user has a responsibility to fight time, which creates meaninglessness and nothingness. Language is his only hope. Otherwise, time will devour him without trace. Everything in the poem works in this way: the butterfly is compared with days, nothingness, and time. If the butterfly is more speechless and more fleshless than time, we are entitled to ask whether the butterfly is dead or alive. Is it nearer to being or to nothingness? Perhaps the very fact that it is born and dies on the same day places the butterfly outside time. Hence, it knows no fear of death:

Не ощущая, не
дожив до страха,
ты вьёшься легче праха
над клумбой, вне
похожих на тюрьму
с её удушьем
минувшего с грядущим,

Not feeling, not / living long enough to know fear, / you spiral lighter than dust, / above the flower-bed, you / are outside the *seeming prison,* / *the suffocation,* / *of the past and future.*

Unlike the butterfly, we are trapped by our conception of time, between our past and future which resemble a prison. In this comparison, we can detect a reference in the subject-matter to Auden's poem 'In Memory of W. B. Yeats': 'In the prison of his

days / Teach the free man how to praise.' But it is even more
directed back to Brodsky's own texts. In the poem 'Gorbunov and
Gorchakov', the metaphor *победа над молчаньем и удушьем*
(*O.* 185: *victory over silence and suffocation*), also subsumes time.
And, in a poem written a year before 'Butterfly', *грядущее* ('the
future') and *удушье* ('suffocation') are linked by their position as
rhymes:

> Гражданин второсортной эпохи, гордо
> признаю я товаром второго сорта
> свои лучшие мысли и *дням грядущим*
> я дарю их как опыт борьбы с удушьем.   (*K.* 107)

A citizen of a second-rate epoch with pride / I recognized my best
thoughts as a second-rate merchandise / and I give them *to the days to
come* / *as an account of the struggle with suffocation*.

The attempt to come to grips with time, to find a reconciliatory
relationship with that very real abstraction within which we all live,
is one of the central themes of Brodsky's poetry. Time and death
are interwoven; in fact, according to Brodsky, *Time was created by
death* (*K.* 59). To conquer both we are given language. It can shape
great thoughts, it can preserve great ideas. This 'call for form' is
answered within the poem by the butterfly itself:

> когда летишь на луг,
> желая корму,
> *приобретает форму*
> *сам воздух вдруг.*

when you fly in the meadow / seeking food, / *of a sudden the very air* /
acquires form.

The butterfly, placed between being and nothingness, acquires
the features of both. By spinning around its pulsating wings, the
butterfly brings shape to air. This must be the purpose of the
butterfly's existence. The comparison with the poet's pen, ignorant
of its fate, cannot be overlooked:

> Так делает перо,
> скользя по глади
> расчерченной тетради,
> не зная про
> судьбу своей строки,
> где мудрость, ересь
> смешались, но доверясь

толчкам руки,
в чьих пальцах *бьётся речь
вполне немая,*
не пыль с цветка снимая,
но тяжесть с плеч.

That's what the pen does, / sliding along the smooth surface of / a lined exercise book, / not knowing / the fate of its own line / where wisdom and heresy / mingled, but trusting in / the impetus of the hand / in whose fingers *throbs speech / that is completely mute,* / not taking pollen from a flower, / but weight from the shoulders.

Речь вполне немая (*speech that is completely mute*), as Kreps has pointed out, stands for a poem that has just been written, but not yet read aloud.[40] Brodsky sees human creativity as a means of easing the burden of existence. He also sees it as a means of bringing shape to an emptiness. He believes in form as an expressive meaning, as a 'resistance to chaos'.[41] Hence, the demand for the tightly structured lyric and his use of traditional metre and rhymes. We need poetry and art to give sense to our existence, since:

не высказать ясней,
что в самом деле
мир создан был без цели,
а если с ней,
то *цель – не мы.*

It can't be made any plainer / that in reality / the world was created with no purpose, / or if there is a purpose in it – / *it is not us.*

This bold statement that the purpose of God's creation is not ourselves is even more startling than the metaphor *we are a thing.* This train of thought is quite hard to accept. We take it for granted that we are God's children and that the world was perhaps created specially for us. This idea is well expressed both by the English Metaphysical poets (e.g. Herbert's poem 'Man') and by some Russian poets (see Derzhavin's 'God'). Or this position is challenged by Mayakovsky and Tsvetaeva, as has been noted already by Kreps.[42] Brodsky relates to both groups. The existence of God is never questioned by him, but he does question 'the entire existential order' (*L.* 136). In Brodsky we encounter an almost joyful rejection of the generally accepted conception of the world and of man. Man can pin down a butterfly and can exalt his superiority over other creatures, but he has no power over the essence of life, over light and dark. He cannot pin down days and time because they are constant and he is not.

> Днуг-энтомолог,
> для света нет иголок
> и нет для тьмы.

Dear entomologist, / there are no pins, neither for the light / nor for the darkness.

In discussing the most important ontological problems of being, Brodsky is pitilessly truthful and logical, first and foremost towards himself:

> Есть люди, чей рассудок
> стрижёт лишай
> забвенья; но взгляни:
> тому виною
> лишь то, что за спиною
> у них не дни
> с постелью на двоих,
> не сны дремучи,
> не прошлое, – но *тучи*
> *сестёр твоих!*

There are people whose reason / is stripped by the ringworm / of oblivion; but look: / the blame lies / in the fact that behind / them there are no days / of shared beds, / no thickets of dreams, / no past – but only *the storm clouds / of your sisters*.

The metaphor *storm clouds of your sisters*, in the context of the poem, stands for non-existence, which is identified with the butter-fly in the last stanza:

> Ты лучше, чем Ничто.
> Верней: ты ближе
> и зримее. *Внутри же*
> *на все на сто*
> *ты родственна ему.*
> В твоём полёте
> оно достигло плоти;
> и потому
> ты в сутолке дневной
> достойна взгляда
> *как лёгкая преграда*
> *меж ним и мной.*

You're better than Nothingness. / Or to be more precise, you're
closer / and more visible. *But deep down, / you're a hundred per cent /
relative of it.* / In brief flight / it is fleshed out / and for that reason /
amidst the bustle of daily grind / you are worthy of my gaze, / *being a
frail barrier / between it and me.*

It is significant that a similar metaphor for nothingness can be
found in Khlebnikov's poetry:

Ведь нечто – тяжесть, сила, долг, работа, труд,
А *ничто* – пух, перья, нежность, дым,
Объёма ящик, полный пустоты,
То ящик бабочек и лени и любви.
И тучею крылатых ничего, нема и грустных ни
Откроется мешок молчанья.   (III. 146–7)

Something – gravity, strength, duty, work, labour. / but *nothingness* –
fluff, feather, tenderness, smoke, / a box of volume, full of emptiness,
/ *a box of butterflies*, laziness and love. / *The sack of silence opens /
with clouds of winged nothingness, of no and sad neither.*

It is almost as if Khlebnikov's butterflies and moths flew over into
Brodsky's poetry and settled on the edge of existence and
nothingness. In both poets the butterfly is merely an unsteady,
almost ethereal barrier between man and nothingness, between
speech and silence. In formulating definitions of the basic categories of being, both poets tend to go beyond the bounds of logic.
Losev feels that Brodsky often 'tests himself, his Muse and his
God'.[43] To this one should also add: and his reader. He draws our
mind away from the 'worship of the eternal and mediocre idol of
the average' and he deploys a wide variety of poetic means to do so.

His syntax, his carefully selected images, his choice of vocabulary, create an atmosphere of sincerity and intimacy. The syntax is
particularly interesting in this respect. He is maximally drawn to
conversational speech. Short, fragmentary sentences, which recall
the butterfly's movement, alternate with sentences which are
coterminous with an entire stanza:

Сказать, что вовсе нет
тебя? Но что же
в руке моей так схоже
с тобой? и цвет –
не плод небытия.
По чьей подсказке
и так кладутся краски?

Say that you don't exist / at all? But what is it / in my hand that so resembles you? And colour / is not the fruit of non-existence. / At whose prompting / was colour thus applied?

The syntax is not to be subordinated to the prosody, which forms a multiplicity of intonational shifts both within the line and at its end. Approximately one third of the 168 lines end with interrupted semantics. These carry-overs which fragment the lines form a conflict between the metre and the grammar, a conflict which expresses the very essence of the conflict between being and non-being. At the same time, we feel that a butterfly, locked into the strict metre of a cage, is making helpless attempts to escape by flying over the next line, almost in a circle. Hence the abundance of enjambements. Each stanza flows into the next one with the ease of a butterfly. The chains of enumerations and threads of questions also serve this end:

> Возможно, ты – пейзаж,
> и, взявши лупу,
> я обнаружу группу
> нимф, пляску, пляж.
> Светло ли там, как днём?
> иль там уныло,
> как ночью? и светило
> какое в нём
> взошло на небосклон?
> чьи в нём фигуры?
> Скажи, с какой натуры
> был сделан он?

Maybe you're a landscape, / and taking a magnifying glass / I will detect a group / of nymphs, a dance, a beach. / Is it bright there, like day? / or cheerless, / like night? What luminary / rose above its horizon? / Whose figures are they there? / Tell me from what model / was this made?

Kreps has conducted an analysis of the sound repetition in 'Butterfly', which reveals that words are placed in close proximity on phonetic principles: *u nikh ni dni 'ni – ni'; ono dostiglo ploti 'tilo – loti'; mezh nim i mnoi 'me – nim – imn'*. It should be noted that Brodsky's alliterations are never obtrusive: they are not an end in themselves, as with the Symbolists or Futurists, but they are present and can be picked out on careful reading, as, for example, in the fifth stanza quoted above: *pliaska* ('dance') – *pliazh* ('beach') '*plia – plia*'; *skazhi s kakoi natury* ('tell me from what model') '*ska – ska*'.

No less mastery is revealed in the poet's rhyme scheme. Assonance in the rhymes is rather more variable than identical: *natiurmort / prostior; ne khmuria / v miniatiure*. The assonances, as is also the case with the alliterations within the line, are sometimes intensified, sometimes abbreviated, which is achieved partially at the expense of their structure, with a preponderance of compound rhymes: *мертва ли / твари* ('living or' / 'creature'); *лишена / лучше на* ('lack of' / 'better in'); and partially by rhyming different parts of speech: *тюрьму / потому* ('prison' / 'because'); *ересь / доверясь* ('heresy' / 'trusting'); *дремучи / тучи* ('thickets' / 'storm clouds'). Brodsky uses both morphological and lexical rhymes: *ресницы / птицы* ('eyelashes' / 'birds'); *зрачок / сачок* ('pupil' / 'net'); *глади / тетради* ('smooth surface' / 'exercise book'). These rhymes are often loaded with the semantics of comparisons and metaphors. The associative role of the rhymes is reinforced by moving semantic key words to the rhyme position: *время / бремя* ('time' / 'burden'); *грядущим / удушьем* ('the days to come' / 'suffocation'); *белом / телом* ('white' / 'body'). It is most interesting to trace from this angle the semantic links which are forged with the word *день* ('day') with which the butterfly is identified. It is significant that it is placed in a rhyming position at least seven times: *меня / дня; они / дни; дней / верней; днём / в нём; даден / на день; для / дня; взгляни / не дни*. Four times out of the seven, *day* is rhymed with words which do not have independent meanings, that is, with prepositions and pronouns, as if thereby illustrating the poet's declaration: *Because days for us are / nothing. Only nothing.*

In this way, rhyme functions simultaneously on several levels of the organizational structure of the poem and, thereby, takes on an active part in the developing of the principal idea.

The concept of *nothingness* which dominates the poem opens and gives 'Butterfly' its crowning point. However, the poem embodies other seminal motifs of Brodsky's work: problems of life and death (man–thing); the aims of the universe (man–Spirit); and man's sojourn as a captive of time (man–language). Language, as in other poems, is isolated as the sole direct link with the Spirit, as the only weapon for victory over time.

Here Brodsky exhibits an amplitude that no other Russian poet among his contemporaries can claim. His range is such that he encompasses, it would seem, the incompatible: a Pushkinian lightness and elegance of style and thought with Beckett's way of looking at the world, which demands a dotting of all the 'i's' and then leaves only the dots. The emotional climate of the poem is also, *à la* Beckett, profoundly negative: *the world which drives us mad holds us in its pincers*. But it is precisely the Pushkinian playful lightness of the form which imbues the negative world-view with its own kind of optimism. This is the optimism of language itself, which is so rich that within it lies salvation. This is the victory of language over the profound pessimism of the poet. It is the gratitude of language for the faithful service to it. Possibly this is the most important quality which makes 'Butterfly' one of the most perfect of Brodsky's poems.

5

A song of disobedience

Because civilizations are finite, in the life of each of them comes a moment when centers cease to hold. What keeps them at such times from disintegration is not legions but languages. Such was the case with Rome, and before that, with Hellenic Greece.[1]

Poet versus *Empire*

And what kind of freedom can we speak of once we have experienced fear?[2]

Empire is one of Brodsky's principal conceptual metaphors. It runs through all his works, including a play in three acts, *Мрамор* (*Marbles*). Behind the mask of 'Empire', he hides not only the two actual empires, his natural motherland and his adopted country, but also his beloved Great Britain with its lost Empire, as well as an illusory Maximilian Empire, and, perhaps most important of all, the Universal Future Empire.

The associations with the two contemporary empires in which the poet has happened to live lie on the surface. He speaks directly about his forced change of empire in the poem 'Lullaby of Cape Cod'. His relationship with both empires is also frankly ironic. And their similarities are deliberately sketched within supranational parameters:

И здесь перо
рвётся поведать про

сходство. Ибо у вас в руках
то же перо, что и прежде. В рощах
те же растения. В облаках
тот же гудящий бомбардировщик,
летящий неведомо что бомбить.
И сильно хочется пить.   (Ч. 102)

And here the pen / longs to tell of // the resemblance. For in your hands / is the same pen as before. In the groves / the same plants. In

195

the clouds / the very same humming bomber / flying to bomb who
knows what. / And what you really need is a drink.

This stanza summarizes several aspects of the poet's relationship
with the world: the principal significance of poetry does not depend
on where the writer lives: 'for in your hands is the same pen as
before'; the principal problems of the world also do not change, for
the poet remains on the same sinful earth: 'in the groves the same
plants'; The militaristic essence of Empire is also constant,
wherever this empire might be: 'the very same humming bomber,
flying to bomb who knows what'. Finally, the change of empire
brings no change in the existential nature of being, for 'man brings
with him his own dead-end no matter what / spot of the globe he is
on' (У. 78); and 'in the hemisphere of heads dreams contain the
bad awakening / of the hemisphere of tails' (Ч. 103).

Scattered over different poems, the descriptions of the landscape, everyday life, and architecture of America do not in themselves create an image of Empire: 'A street. Some houses are /
better than others: more things in the shop-windows' (Ч. 92);
'From the patrol car, gleaming on the waste lot / Ray Charles
chords tinkle out' (Ч. 99). The paraphrases which Brodsky uses so
frequently instead of naming the USA directly are also quite
neutral: 'a country of dentists' (Ч. 28); 'one of the five continents
propped up by cowboys' (Ч. 77). Such an estranged description of
the country of exile is sometimes intensified, sometimes smoothed
over, at times coming to such diametrically opposed points as
'nowhere, from nowhere', and 'another, no less great [power]'
(У. 93). However, for all its greatness, this country remains
someone else's land: 'tear / running like a wide arrow down the
slanting cheek-bone / of a wooden house in someone else's land'
(Ч. 79). To Savitsky's question of 1983, 'What has America
become for you after all these years?', Brodsky answered: 'What it
always was, merely a continuation of space.'[3]

In relation to England, it is not difficult to isolate predominantly
cultural aspects of a once-great empire, first and foremost its
language, which many of its former colonies still speak and write.
There are more complex and ambivalent relations to the other
contemporary empire – the Soviet Union. They cannot be reduced
to a criticism of ideology and politics, although this aspect is
expressed quite explicitly in 'Verses on the Winter Campaign 1980':
'A new ice-age – the ice-age of slavery – / is creeping across the

globe'. An emotional involvement in the depiction of this empire complicates the picture. Apart from the presence of shame and pain for all the actions of his step-motherland, the neutrality of tone is disrupted not only by irony, but also by a love which the years have not extinguished. In spite of the realization that 'if a man may go back / to the scene of the crime, to the place / where he was humiliated, he cannot return' (*H*. 80), the idea of returning to the native land does not disappear with time. But if he wishes to flee from the empire in which the poet is now 'a proud foster-child' (*Y*. 93), then it is not so much to find 'a place to live', but 'a place to die'. It is in this particular context, it seems to me, that we should understand Brodsky's wish to return to the Soviet Union which so surprised Savitsky:

– Would you go back to the Soviet Union?
– With pleasure.
– That is, you mean, literally, if the chance cropped up, simply . . .
– Well, no, of course, it's not all as simple as if the chance should crop up. In the world we live in . . .
– In certain circumstances . . . ?
– In certain circumstances . . . What's more I would dictate these circumstances. I would return to Russia on one particular condition – if all I've written were published there, a collected works.[3]

The theme of Russia in Brodsky's poetry merits a more detailed investigation and, consequently, it is dealt with in the next section of the present chapter.

Apart from the contemporary empires, several ancient ones also figure in Brodsky's poetry: the Hellenic, the Roman, and the Byzantine. The Hellenic Empire is present only implicitly, through allusions to Kuzmin or Cavafy, for whom the 'nostalgic and elegiac Alexandrias', as Losev has noted, were 'forms of escapism'.[4] 'Near Alexandria', published at first under the title 'Washington',[5] has a purely symbolic relationship with the historical Alexandria as a new capital of a new empire. This is, in essence, yet another still-life of an imperial city during the 'dead season': *a stone syringe injects the heroines / in a cumulus muscle, crumbling as if in winter* (*Y*. 138). The first metaphor substitutes for an obelisk, rising up to a sky as empty 'as before prayer' (*Y*. 115); the second one substitutes for clouds. Once-great imperial conquerors sit solemnly on pedestals. Another metaphor of comparison of foliage with the green of dollar bills, *the rustle of eternally green money* (*Y*. 138), hints at the economic might of Empire. The de-animation of everything from man to nature creates the impression of a post-nuclear landscape: *The sunset, releasing a mouse from the crevice, / gnaws – each incisor is bared – / into the electric cheese of the suburbs* (*У.* 138–9).

It is precisely this idea of 'after the end' of civilization, of Christianity, of our era, that explains the frequent appearance of the Roman Empire in Brodsky's work as a symbol of the future. Brodsky's Rome is not Mandelstam's 'place of man in the universe', but rather Khlebnikov's 'place of the encounter between the poet and the state'. Rome first appears in this context in an unfinished poem of 1964–5, 'Ex Ponto: The Last Letter of Ovid to Rome'. Ovid, who ended his days in exile in the Crimea on the shores of the Black Sea, was an object of interest to Pushkin, who was exiled to the same place by the Emperor of the Third Rome. In exile in the years 1964–5 at the diametrically opposite end of the empire, near the White Sea but also 'on the edge of space', Brodsky identifies himself with the position of the poet in Empire:

> пишу я с моря. С моря корабли
> сюда стремятся после непогоды,
> чтоб подтвердить, что это край земли.
> Но в трюмах их я не ищу свободы.

I write from the sea. From the sea ships / hurry here after bad weather, / to confirm that this is the edge of the earth. / But I do not seek freedom in their holds.

Brodsky's Empire, as one of the themes of the cycle of poems entitled 'Post aetatem nostram' (1970), 'Lithuanian Divertissement' (1971), 'Letters to a Roman Friend' (1972), 'Mexican Divertimento' (1975), and 'Lullaby of Cape Cod' (1975), as well as of a series of later works, is first of all a metaphor for a system of government which is inimical to the human personality. By using the emblems of the Greek and Roman Empires – legionaries, hetaeras, marble statues, conspiracies against the Emperor, etc. – Brodsky identifies an imaginary empire of a future, post-Christian period in the history of mankind with the historical, pre-Christian Roman Empire, and closes a circle of civilization.

The cycle entitled 'Post aetatem nostram' begins with a sarcastic sentence about the complete victory of mediocrity in the Empire: 'The Empire is a country for fools' (*K.* 87). The next lines may be applied, without stretching the point, to the Soviet reality of the Stalin or Brezhnev regimes:

Движенье перекрыто по причине
приезда Императора. Толпа
теснит легионеров – песни, крики;
но паланкин закрыт. Объект любви
не хочет быть объектом любопытства.   (*K*. 87)

Traffic is suspended on account of / the Emperor's arrival. The mob /
crowds the legionaries – songs, cries; / but the palanquin is closed.
The object of love / does not wish to be the object of curiosity.

However, the inertia, somnolence, the collapse of morality, are all
more reminiscent of Brezhnev's times than Stalin's. Apathy had
reached such proportions in the Empire that a fly crawling across
the face of a Greek vagabond who had fallen asleep with his head
soaped evokes the 'peltasts of Xenophon in the Armenian snows' –
yet another parody of the once-great campaigns of a once-great
empire. Other signs of a polyglot Empire are also discernible: the
poverty of its citizens, the 'pillar of the state'; meagre food; poor
amusements; the numerous puddles alternating with numerous
statues of the Emperor; the gigantic stadium, whose builders fed
the lice for seventeen years in the *gulag*. And in the phrase 'the
well-known, / local kifared', who boldly demands that the
'Emperor be taken off [on the next line] the bronze money',
parodies Voznesensky's call, 'Take Lenin off the money!'[6]
On the other hand, the deliberate mingling of geographical
place-names, Greek and Latin names, the parallels with modernity, all serve the same goal of indicating that Empire is not a
geographical idea behind which some concrete country lurks, a
country we could locate on the map, but a concept. Consequently,
the empires are united by lexical repetitions, recurrent images,
common motifs, such as marble statues, slaves, dried-up fountains
with satyrs and nymphs, hetaeras, a howling mob in the stadium –
such is the typical landscape of Empire. The primitive, harsh level
of everyday life, the stagnation and poverty eat away at Empire
from within, like a cancer: 'Wherever you may wander, / everywhere cruelty and crass stupidity will exclaim: "Greetings, / here
we are."' (*Ч*. 71). The motif of 'dryness' as a reflection of the
aridity of the spiritual and intellectual life of the Empire dominates
in 'Post aetatem nostram': on the dry, hot stone; the dry post-
festival night; reason is dry; the court's judgements are also
distinguished by dryness.[7] This same motif can be heard, albeit less
insistently, in 'Lullaby of Cape Cod', where even speech becomes

dry (Ч. 109). In 'Roman Elegies', the motif of dryness is associated
with departure to the coldness of Time (Ч. 116).

The common semantics of many 'imperial' metaphors is no less
indicative, beginning with the metaphor of marble. The monumentality of marble expresses the monumentality of the Empire itself.
The crowning metaphor of marble is taken as the title of the play
Мрамор (1982), in which the prisoners in the Tower are allowed to
keep marble busts of their favourite classics. They direct the
barbarian Publius to a chiasmus: 'Marble because they're classics or
– uufffs – classics because they're marble?' (p. 214) Nature itself
seems to imitate the marble indestructibility of Empire, to which
the numerous metaphors of reification bear witness: *stone fish*
(*K*. 92); *drops of metallic dew* (*K*. 93); *jungle in a cast-iron variant*
(*K*. 93); *stone mushrooms* (Ч. 70); *stone nest* (Ч. 113); *stone stur-
geons* (У. 77). The oppressive presence of white stone instils
respect and fear in the citizens of Empire: 'The servants apathetic-
ally / stare straight ahead like sculptures' (*K*. 88). In the fictitious
empire of Maximilian ('Mexican Divertimento'), where 'a bullet is
a natural draught' (Ч. 62), and 'the skull in the bushes always has
three eyes' (Ч. 64), the gods petrify from horror and man becomes
numb 'with *dried-up weeping*' (Ч. 67).

The de-animation of man in his entirety or in part is characteristic
of all the poems under discussion. In the Lithuanian province of the
Empire, 'man / becomes . . . a detail of the local baroque' (*K*. 102),
and 'from the face there remains only the profile' (*K*. 103). The
world of substitutions and reifications in 'Lithuanian Divertissement' has been commented on by Thomas Venclova:

> The singer is replaced by his statue, a dictator by a detached house, dead
> Jews from the vanished ghetto are equated with snow. It is a soundless,
> purely visual world of non-existent communications, silent (but possibly
> tapped) phones. There is emphasis on the semantics of things closed off, of
> stagnation, narrowness, damage, suffocation. There is no movement – at
> best there is a senseless rush of things, accidental change of directions,
> crowds.[8]

Oppressive heat is the basic motif of the poem 'Lullaby of Cape
Cod'. From it the brain hardens and 'rattles, like an ice-cube
against the edge of the glass' (Ч. 101).

Having laid down their lives for Empire in the deserts of Africa,
the jungles of South America, or the mountains of Afghanistan, the
soldiers of Empire are immortalized in the marble of statues and

obelisks. The poet's attitude to this kind of immortality is expressed implicitly:

> Духота. Опирающийся на ружьё,
> Неизвестный Союзный Солдат делается ещё
> более неизвестным.   (*Ч.* 101)

It's stifling. Leaning on his gun, / the Unknown Union Soldier grows still / more unknown.

We see here a resonance with Zbigniew Herbert's poem 'The Rain', in which there is the image of a brother who has been turned into a monument to the Unknown Soldier and, consequently, is forgotten by everybody.

The splendour of Empire is overshadowed by the all-pervasive sense of the fear and defencelessness of its citizens: 'Звук собственных шагов вполне зловещ / и в то же время беззащитен' (*K.* 89: 'The sound of one's own steps is utterly ominous / and at the same time defenceless'). The moonlight over everything does nothing to lessen the atmosphere of frightening coldness and horror: 'In the uncertain light of the northern moon'; 'The labyrinth of deserted streets is flooded with moonlight'; 'But the moonlight road streams further'; 'The moon shone, as it always / shines in July' (*K.* 88–95). The insistent presence of the moon in 'Post aetatem nostram' emphasizes that the imperial world is situated on the other side of Christianity. It is an empire 'without a pantheon, without the pre-Christian, pre-Judaic idea of the cyclicity of time which makes sense of its existence'.[9]

It is as if time has stopped in the post-Christian Empire. This idea finds expression either in the grammar of the verbs, as in 'Lithuanian Divertissement', or in lexical repetitions, as in 'Post aetatem nostram', or by taking away the clocks and seasons from those confined in the Tower, which disappears into the clouds. These repetitions take in not only individual words, but whole sentences, which reappear in poem after poem: 'Fine acoustics! ... The acoustics are fine' (*K.* 90–1); 'A fine and destitute country'; 'the constitution is fine' (*Ч.* 71–2); 'The dance of the hot letters / of Coca-Cola' (*Ч.* 68); 'And above / all burn in the darkness, as at Belshazzar's feast, / the letters of Coca-Cola' (*Ч.* 101). This Biblical allusion to Belshazzar, the last Babylonian Emperor, is not made without a purpose. During a thronged feast, Belshazzar saw a hand in the heavens which wrote *mene tekel fares* – a prophecy about the collapse of his rule. On the very night, the troops of the Persian king Syrus invaded Babylon.

The repeated lexis has tinges of irony, hyperbole, and the absurd:

> Движенье есть, *движенье* происходит.
> *Мы всё-таки плывём.* И нас никто
> не обгоняет. Но, увы, как мало
> похоже это на былую скорость!
> И как тут не вздохнёшь о временах,
> когда всё шло довольно *гладко. Гладко.*   (*К.* 94)

There is *movement, movement* is taking place. / *We're floating all the same.* And no one is / outstripping us. But, alas, how little / like the former speed this is! / And how can you not sigh over times / when everything went quite *smoothly. Smoothly.*

In reality there cannot be any movement because the 'oarsmen strike their oars against dry land' (*K.* 94). Empire is at a dead-end. The idea of a dead-end is conveyed by one of the most persistent images in Brodsky's poetry – the image of a mirror. In the poem 'Torso' (1972), the semantics of the images is extremely loaded with the function of de-animation reflecting the dead-end of Empire, which is directly identified with a mirror:

> Если вдруг забредаешь в *каменную траву,*
> выглядящую *в мраморе* лучше, чем наяву,
> иль замечаешь фавна, предавшегося возне
> с нимфой, и оба *в бронзе* счастливее, чем во сне,
> можешь выпустить посох из натруженных рук:
> ты в Империи, друг.
>
> Воздух, пламень, вода, фавны, наяды, львы,
> взятые из природы или из головы, –
> *всё,* что придумал Бог и продолжать устал
> мозг, *превращено в камень или металл.*
> *это – конец вещей, это – в конце пути*
> *зеркало, чтоб войти.*   (*Ч.* 39)

If you suddenly wander *into stone grass* / which looks better *in marble* than in reality, / or you notice a faun which has got up to mischief / with a nymph, and both are happier *in bronze* than asleep, / you may let go your crook from your worn-out hands: / you're in the Empire, friend. // Air, fire, water, fauns, naiads, lions, / taken from nature or from the head, / – *everything* that God invented and brain grew too tired to continue / *is transmuted into stone or metal.* / *This is the end of things, it is – at the end of the road* / *a mirror in order to enter.*

A mirror or its substitutes – glass, smooth stone, running water, the shining chrome steel of the Tower – all throw back like a boomerang a reflection of the deadness and dead-end of an empire which has reached the end of space. Another conceptual metaphor of the dead-end is the Prison Tower, whose image first appeared in the seventh part of the cycle 'Post aetatem nostram':

Подсчитано когда-то, что обычно –
в сатрапиях, во время фараонов,
у мусульман, в эпоху христианства –
сидело иль бывало казнено
примерно шесть процентов населенья.
Поэтому ещё сто лет назад
дед нынешнего цезаря задумал
реформу правосудья. Отменив
безнравственный обычай смертной казни,
он с помощью особого закона
те шесть процентов сократил до двух,
обязанных сидеть в тюрьме, конечно,
пожизненно. Неважно, совершил ли
ты преступленье или невиновен;
закон, по сути дела, как налог.
Тогда-то и воздвигли эту башню.   (*K.* 91–2)

It was reckoned once that usually – / in satrapies, in the time of the pharaohs, / among Muslims, in the Christian era – / in prison or executed / were about six per cent of the population. / And so a hundred years ago / the present Caesar's grandfather thought up / a reform of the legal system. Abolishing / the immoral custom of the death penalty, / he, with the help of a particular law, / reduced those six per cent to two, / obliged to stay in prison, of course, / for life. No matter whether you had committed a crime or were innocent, / the law, in essence, is like tax. / It was then that they erected this Tower.

One cannot help noticing how the idea of the Prison Tower, which symbolizes the Empire, does not leave the poet. The iron spire of the Tower, which serves as a lightning-conductor, lighthouse, and pole for the state flag, soars high above the Empire, so that it is lost somewhere in the clouds. Its metaphorical double appears in a poem of 1982, 'Near Alexandria', as a 'stone syringe' (*У.* 11). The idea of the Tower forms the basis of *Мрамор* (*Marbles*), Brodsky's only extant play,[10] which he began while still in Leningrad but which was completed only in 1982. It is significant that in the play the idea of the Prison Tower is ascribed to the Roman Emperor

Tiberius (14–37 AD), during whose reign Christ was crucified.
There is a reference to this cruel act, which hastened the 'general
fate of things', in the poem 'The Bust of Tiberius', which was
written after the play:

> Вообще – *не есть ли*
> *жестокость только ускоренье общей*
> *судьбы вещей?* свободного паденья
> простого тела в вакууме?
> . . .
> Я тоже опрометью бежал всего
> со мной случившегося и превратился в остров
> с развалинами, с цаплями. И я
> чеканил профиль свой посредством лампы.
> Вручную. Что до сказанного мной,
> мной сказанное никому не нужно –
> и не впоследствии, но уже сейчас.
> *Не есть ли это тоже ускоренье*
> *истории?* успешная, увы,
> *попытка следствия опередить причину?*
> Плюс, тоже в полном вакууме –   (*У.* 136–7)

On the whole – *isn't cruelty just / an acceleration of the common
destiny of things?* of the free fall / of a simple body in a vacuum? . . . I,
too, ran headlong away from everything / that has happened to me
and became an island / with ruins, herons. I, too, / coined my own
profile with the aid of a lamp. / By hand. As for what I've said / my
words are not vital to anyone – / and not in time to come, but right
now. / *Isn't this too an acceleration / of history? An, alas, successful /
attempt of consequence to forestall the cause?* / Plus, also in total
vacuum –

The allusions to Donne ('I, too . . . became an island') and to
Horace's *Exegi monumentum* ('I, too, / coined my own profile') are
given in an ironic context. The parallel with history is expressed in
the play: 'with all that history, who gives a damn about the present.
Not to mention the future' (p. 209). We are also told that 'acceleration of free fall is nine-point eighty-one' (p. 222). At the same
time, the twice-repeated 'vacuum' refers us to the poem 'Gorbunov
and Gorchakov': '"There stands an enormous madhouse." / "Like
a vacuum within the world order"' (*O.* 204). The madhouse itself
serves as a metaphorical equivalent of the Tower.

As opposed to the 'poetic' empires, the Empire in the play is
depicted in 'its self-confident days', and not in a period of decline.

Hence the spatial and temporal perspectives are extremely extensive, although the action takes place (more precisely, nothing
happens) within cell number 1,750, which is situated on the top
floor of the Tower, so that the cell recalls the cockpit of a
space-ship. In the centre of the Tower is a Doric column, within
which is a lift which delivers to the inmates the most exotic dishes
and marble heads of the classics. The lift takes down the left-overs,
which are consumed by crocodiles who live at the foot of the
Tower. All modern conveniences are to be found in the cell: bath,
table, toilet, telephone, television. The telephone, however, only
works one way – out into the Empire. This recalls the lines from
Brodsky's poem, 'Conversation with a Celestial Being': 'all faith is
no more than a one-way / postal system' (*K*. 62).

The Empire which is depicted through the prism of the prison
conveys an atmosphere of complete self-sufficiency. It is almost
impossible, or rather, senseless, to escape from this prison, for the
Empire is everywhere. Clever Tullius, who escaped for a bet and
bought on the streets of Rome two kilos of millet for a canary which
sits in a cage in the cell, immediately returns to prison. The canary
also does not fly away to freedom when it is released. Just as the
Tower embodies the idea of miniaturization of the Empire, so, too,
the canary's cage is a miniature of the prison, a cage within a cage.
Losev sees in the prison yet another of Brodsky's conceptual
metaphors: 'The metaphor of the prison is telescopic: flesh is a
prison, the tower where the protagonists are is a prison; the empire
they inhabit is a prison; finally, human reason, limited from all sides
by the incomprehensible, is a prison.'[11]

Tullius, who is inclined to philosophizing, defines the prison as 'a
shortage of space compensated by surplus of time' (p. 208). The
Empire is a prison because it has occupied all space. Nothing is left
but time. And this is the real dead-end. In this dead-end, in
Tullius's view, even 'a window is a cell. Even when it's open.' So,
too, the door to the canary's cage. From all windows and doors the
view and exit are only to the Empire. The essence of Rome, as
Tullius understands it, is 'to take everything to its logical end – and
further' (p. 214). The next logical step is to merge with time,
thereby realizing the metaphor *the eternal city*. Tullius himself
dreams only of this, of merging with time. Does it follow from this
that a complete merger of the idea of the state with the personality
has occurred? After all, this idea has been, and remains, the ideal

of the poet's native empire, which dreams of creating the 'new man', who does not have and cannot have conflicting interests with the state system, which allegedly was invented for him and which is built on his bones. It is as if in *Marbles* Brodsky has finally fulfilled the 'social command', by reducing the ideal of the Communist Utopia to its logical conclusion, in beginning where the philosophers of Marxism–Leninism stopped. The real aesthete, Brodsky reproaches his fellow writer, the Czech Kundera, is capable of foreseeing foreign tanks crawling along the streets of his native city.[12] It is no accident that it is not the plebeian Publius, the rebel, who is unreconciled to his position, but rather the refined intellectual Tullius who is the incarnation of the ideal citizen of the Empire, calling himself a 'true Roman'. He views his incarceration in the Tower not only as a state 'tax', but also as a *sui generis* 'ideological purification'. He tells Publius, who dreams of becoming a Praetor, that he would not be accepted for this position because none of his family had ever been imprisoned in the Tower: 'Nobody was ever arrested in your family. That sort of person can't be employed by the government. One can get to be a Praetor, Senator Consul, only if one's ancestors did time in the Tower. Even at fourth remove. What good would an official be to Rome if one fine day ... Just think, what sort of a senator can you make if your prospect is in the Tower?' (p. 208).

Tullius's stoic acceptance of his position is justified by the fact that he understands better than Publius the lack of perspective of the Empire, in which Paradise on earth has been attained both in the physical sense (complete material well-being) and in the metaphysical, 'for Paradise is a place of impotence. For / it is one of those planets / where there is no perspective' (Ч. 108). This is why time has stopped in the Empire: 'for the clocks, so that comfort in Paradise / is not disturbed, do not strike' (Ч. 108). Hence, even the noiseless sand-glass is removed from cell number 1,750.

The idea of Paradise as a dead-end was expressed by Brodsky as early as 1973, in his Preface to Platonov's social-philosophical Utopia, *The Foundation Pit*:

The idea of Paradise is the logical end of human thought in the respect that it, thought, goes no further; for beyond Paradise there is nothing else, nothing else happens. And therefore one can say that Paradise is a dead-end; it is the last vision of space, the end of things, the summit of the mountain, the peak from which there is nowhere to step – except into Chronos, in connection with which the concept of eternal life arises. The same may be said of Hell.[13]

Two years later, this same idea was given a poetic formulation in one of the poems on the theme of Empire:

> Местность, где я нахожусь, *есть пик*
> *как бы горы.* Дальше – воздух, Хронос.
> Сохрани эту речь, ибо *рай – тупик.*
> *Мыс, вдающийся в море. Конус.*
> *Нос железного корабля.*
> Но не крикнуть "Земля!"   (Ч. 108)

The place where I am *is the peak / as it were of the mountain.* Further on is the air, Chronos. / Preserve this speech, for *heaven is a cul-de-sac.* / *A cape, falling into the sea. A cone.* / *The prow of an iron ship.* / But one can't shout "Land!'

In an even more compressed form, this idea is realized in a system of metaphors: if Paradise and Hell are a dead-end of human thought, and the Empire, which has constructed a self-sufficient and self-completed world, has embodied the idea of Paradise on earth, then its inhabitants live in a triple dead-end: of their own flesh, their own thoughts, and of the Empire; in short, 'in heavenly dwellings with the hell / of voices behind your back' (Ч. 67). The mirror is chosen as the metaphor of the dead-end as such. Hence the comparison of the human body with a mirror expresses the idea of an existential dead-end:

> Как хорошее зеркало, тело стоит во тьме:
> на его лице, у него в уме
> ничего, кроме ряби.   (Ч. 109)

Like a fine mirror, the body stands in darkness: / on its face, in its mind / nothing but speckles.

From all this we may discern a whole transformational series, interconnected by generalizations and abstractions: Paradise/Hell – dead-end – Empire – man – mirror – Chronos: *человек есть конец самого себя / и вдаётся во Время* (Ч. 109: *man is an end of himself / and flows into Time*). This is why Tullius, who looks at the world 'from the point of view of thought', regards his own life sentence in the Tower, at 'the edge of space', as 'an instrument for knowing Time', as a unique opportunity, while still alive, 'to find out what things are going to be like afterwards. And a Roman must not miss such an opportunity' (p. 243). Like the philosophizing 'knight of the idea' Dvanov from Platonov's *Chevengur*, Tullius has decided to 'live in death'. Going off into the 'curiosity of death', Dvanov acknowledged the bankruptcy of the idea of 'universal brotherhood', for which he had killed hundreds of brothers. In Tullius's Empire, all murders are behind him. But along with them has been destroyed the source which had warmed the veins of the cold marble of the classics and Time itself. The presence in the cell of the marble busts of the classics cannot fill the spiritual vacuum of the inmates. Tullius is sufficiently intelligent and educated to understand this true situation. It is not for nothing that he calls the busts 'the severed heads of civilization' (p. 203).

This also serves to explain why culture is no longer a danger to the Empire: it has been castrated. Christianity, once an inseparable part of culture, has now been severed from imperial civilization. The ideal of the cultural and physical perfection of the Empire is spiritually empty. This is a persistent motif of Brodsky's poetic ideology; it resonates as a warning of the universal catastrophe of the Spirit. The true poet, like the true aesthete, must foresee not only the Empire's tanks but also a variant of the future more terrible and more real than Orwell's Oceania or Zamyatin's One State.

Brodsky's Empire is an amalgam of Utopia and history. By magnifying the historical perspective in the direction of the past and future, Brodsky has painted a picture which is very different from that of Zamyatin or Orwell. In Losev's view, he has 'sensed the atmosphere of a hypothetical future much more accurately than the well-known anti-utopians who, frightened by the book-burning of Stalin, Hitler and Mao, projected it onto the future'.[14]

In an interview with Savitsky, Brodsky himself called the play a 'double anachronism'. Vail and Genis decipher this remark in their interesting article, 'From the World to Rome' as follows: 'the past and future are symmetrically aligned alongside of the author-commentator who inhabits the present'. They also see it as the application to modernity of the architectural ideas of the ancient world; finally, as a test of the durability of the ancient world-view.[15] One should add that the author is present in the play not only as a commentator, but also as the commentated – by means of his own texts, which are spoken by Tullius. The latter, who is well-read, knows poetry well and loves it. From time to time he peppers his speech with quotations from world poetry, most frequently from Brodsky himself. More simply than the author could, he comments on several premisses of the former's poetics and aesthetics, explains the provenance of the images. Thus, the idea of majority, it transpires, was inculcated in man by nature itself, which sends the reader scurrying to several of Brodsky's poems: '*Овацию листвы унять там вождь бессилен*' (*У*. 71: 'There the leader is powerless to repress the leaves' ovation'); '*листва их научит шуметь / голосом большинства*' (*У*. 151: 'The foliage will teach them to resound / with the voice of majority'); '*Не чета КПССу, / листья вечно в большинстве!*' ('*Лесная идиллия*') ('No match for the CPSU, / the leaves are eternally in the majority!', 'Woodland Idyll'). We find the solution to the image of the pendulum from the early poem 'Zofya' (1962). It turns out that this reflects the essence of art itself. The author's skill is objectively and impartially to balance two opposing points of view, a lesson Brodsky learned from Dostoevsky, and Dostoevsky from the classics: 'From classicism, he took the principle that before you come forth with your argument, however right or righteous you may feel, you have to list all the arguments of the opposite side' (*L*. 162). Inasmuch as 'God Himself did not separate the wheat from the chaff till the end' (*K*. 33), Dostoevsky demonstrated how good and evil coexist in man, showed the 'tug of war – between faith and the utilitarian approach to existence, about this *pendulum motion* of the individual psyche, between two abysses, good and evil'.[16]

It is precisely the principle of the pendulum which characterizes the entire structure of the play-dialogue, where 'there occurs a clash not only of temperaments, not only of cultures, but of world-views: the ancient and modern'.[17] Vail and Genis, who have offered a penetrating analysis of the play, have also noted several structural and thematic similarities between the play and the poem 'Gorbunov and Gorchakov', in particular, the bifurcation in the author's voice. It is conceivable that this very idea of bifurcation came to Brodsky from Pushkin's 'Mozart and Salieri', whose dialogue reflects two opposing points of view on the world, art, and man, and from whom a long series of oppositions has been derived: genius and villainy, harmony and elemental force, love and treachery, individual and state, good and evil, and so on.

The play's protagonists differ from Gorbunov and Gorchakov by virtue of the fact that they are not doubles, despite the identical hint at a unitary voice: 'I occasionally can no longer distinguish your voice from my own', Publius admits. In their relations there is no resemblance to the situation of Christ and Judas in the poem. In the latter, the reader is haunted by the impression that he is listening to a monologue in the form of a dialogue, the speech of a single man who suffers and who kills not only Gorbunov but also his own soul, being unable to bear the experience of prison and the state system with its psychiatric 'hospitals'. He beseeches Gorbunov to forgive him and that he should be heard by God. In the post-Christian world, Tullius has no one to address his prayer to. It would appear that his vocabulary no longer contains the expression 'forgive me'. The idea of God is replaced by the naked abstraction of 'time in its pure form', a kind of 'white on white', like a dream of Malevich. Here one should note *en passant* that the Empire is depicted almost exclusively in black and white tonalities: 'by the white door'; 'on the white soaped cheek'; 'the terrible black eyes'; 'the spire with its cross indifferently / is looking black'; 'the white-toothed colon-nade', and so on. The Greek vagabond escapes from the Empire with the help of twelve black cats, while Tullius arranges his flight from the Tower with the aid of the white marble classics.

Returning to the Tower and assimilated to Time, Tullius leaves the Empire. The idea of the harmony of the individual and the state has not passed the test. In the Empire of the beginning of our era, the Vice-Regent persuades himself: 'Why dash off somewhere from the palace – / we are not the judges of the Fatherland' (*O*. 90). In the Empire after our era Tullius dashes out of the palace-prison, albeit into white nothingness. And by his departure 'into dumb time' he condemns the Empire.

A masochistic joy

> I regard my situation as a loss of an absolutely classical variety, at the very least of the nineteenth or eighteenth century, if not simply antiquity.[18]

Brodsky's own exit from Empire took place even while he was still physically located within it. Neither the themes nor the style of his poetry were suitable for adornment of its granite splendour. As opposed to certain of his fellow writers, Brodsky declined to sing of the might of his native state, did not attempt to convey the 'rhythm of the epoch', asserting that the 'speed of inner progress / is greater than the speed of the world' (*K.* 11). The reciprocal non-acceptance of the poet and the state forms the basis of the conflict that lies on the surface.

The image of Russia in Brodsky's poetry is made more complicated by a whole complex of dramatic collisions, which are evoked on the one hand by the life situation of the poet, and, on the other, by the dualistic nature of the country of his birth. In this way, the official name of this multinational empire, the USSR, is constantly replaced in his poetry either by the metonymy, 'one sixth of the earth's surface': 'My brain was rattling in oblivion like the ice cube in a glass: / *over one sixth*' (*H.* 9); or else by the impersonal periphrasis 'a big country': 'Only a thought about oneself and about *the big country* / casts you in the night from wall to wall / like a cradle song' (*Ч.* 109). At the same time, the words *отечество* ('fatherland'), *отчизна* ('homeland'), entered the active lexicon of his very early poetry (*C.* 63, 84, 92, 102, 202). But even with Russia, who 'bore and nursed' him (*Ч.* 177) and gave him the greatest gift – the Russian language – the poet's relations are not straightforward. Given his understanding of religion as the spiritual source that has nurtured culture, Brodsky has always considered that Russia has the peculiar characteristic of exaggerating its religious mission ('if only the Lord had not puffed up / the value of my country', *C.* 199). For this, or for some other reasons – possibly purely aesthetic ones – the poet has remained a step-son, and not a son, of Russia. The situation has been both understood and accepted from his very early poetic ventures: 'pressing my cheek against an indifferent homeland' (*C.* 63). This is, in fact, a direct quotation from Mandelstam: 'And once more against an indifferent homeland / a reproach will soar up like a wild duck' (1. 13); Mandelstam also was not accepted by the new Empire.

Brodsky refrained from reproaches for at least a decade. Even though he endured three arrests, being beaten up by the militia, confinement in a madhouse, a humiliating trial, and ending up 'on the sidelines, overboard' (*O.* 159), in 'no man's land' (*O.* 158), on the edge of Empire, the poet refuses to condemn: 'no, Lord! my eyes are clouded / I will not turn into a judge' (*O.* 159). Returning from exile, Brodsky still refused both 'to respond in kind' (*K.* 14) and to 'look for the pearl in the compost heap' (*K.* 15). One cannot consider a single one of his poems written in the USSR as political or even civic. However, the position he adopted in exile: 'I'm slightly deaf. Oh God, I'm slightly blind' (*O*. 159), gradually begins to alter. Without allowing either the state or dissidents to use him, the poet, perhaps against his own wishes, gets drawn into political conflicts by the all-devouring ideology of the Empire. In this view, the whole poem 'Speech about Spilled Milk' (1967) is permeated by hopeless irony with a kind of 'anti-Soviet' declarations of the type: 'Slavery always engenders slavery. / Even with the help of revolutions' (*K*. 8); 'Usually the man who spits on God, / first spits on man' (*K*. 14). In the poem 'Letter to General Z' (1968), we see expression of the theme of the dead-end situation not only of government politics ('General! I'm afraid we've got into a dead-end'), but of existential situations as well ('For those who have experienced the great bluff / life leaves a scrap of paper').

The familiar atmosphere of stagnation, somnolence, and inertia is conveyed in the programmatic poem with the ironic title, 'The End of a Beautiful Epoch' (1969):

Ветер гонит листву. Старых лампочек тусклый накал
в этих грустных краях, чей *эпиграф – победа зеркал*,
при содействии луж порождает эффект изобилья.   (*K*. 58)

The wind chases the leaves. The dull glow of the old lamps / in these sad parts, whose epigraph is *the triumph of mirrors*, / with the help of puddles creates the effect of abundance.

The metaphor of the dead-end, *mirror*, is accompanied by new associations: the reflection of a self-enclosed world in the hundreds of puddles conveys its decay and narrowing to the point of complete loss of perspective, and to death from suffocation. In the last stanza, the theme of the dead-end is intensified and ends on a sad lyrical note:

Зоркость этих времён – это *зоркость к вещам тупика*.
Не по древу умом растекаться пристало пока,
но плевком по стене. И не князя будить – динозавра.
Для последней строки, эх, не вырвать у птицы пера.
Неповинной главе всех и дел-то, что ждать топора
да зелёного лавра.   (*K*. 60)

The vigilance of our time – is the *vigilance for the things of the dead-end.* / And it's not yet befitting to 'range in thought [like the nightingale] over the tree'[19] / but by spitting on the wall. And one should not wake the prince – but the dinosaur. / To pen the last line, ah, one can't tear a feather from the bird. / What is left for the innocent head – but to await the axe, / and the green laurel.

Indeed, not having waited for the laurel, in 1972 Brodsky, finding himself 'in an unfamiliar locality' (Ч. 26), wrote the poem '1972' in which, amidst irony, wit, sarcasm, and philosophical digressions we find the first serious reproach against Russia:

> Слушай, дружина, враги и братие!
> Всё, что творил я, творил не ради я
> славы в эпоху кино и радио,
> но ради речи родной, словесности.
> За каковое раченье-жречество
> (сказано ж доктору: сам пусть лечится)
> чаши лишившись в пиру Отечества,
> нынче стою в незнакомой местности. (Ч. 26)

Listen *druzhina*, enemies and brethren! / Everything I've created, I've created not for / fame in the age of movies and radio, / but for my native tongue, for literature. / For this kind of sacrificial zeal / (it is said, physician, heal thyself), / deprived of a cup at the feat of the Fatherland, / I now stand in an unfamiliar locality.

The theme of Russia not only does not disappear from the writing in exile, but appears in the most unexpected places, most often in the poems dedicated to other countries and cities. Thus, Venice reminds the poet of his native city by the sea, 'and also that power, / where arms stretch out like a pine forest / before a petty, but predatory demon / and saliva freezes in the mouth' (Ч. 41). The reference to demons reminds the reader not only of Dostoevsky's *Devils* but also of the less well-known satirical novel by Sologub, *The Petty Demon*. These allusions introduce the theme of evil, which contrasts powerfully with the penetrating lyrical note of profound love for 'that power' where these petty demons have triumphed.

The other Italian city of Florence hints at the reason for the exile not only of Dante, but of all poets: 'under the volcano / one cannot live, without showing a clenched fist; but / one cannot unclench it when one dies' (Ч. 111). The epigraph for 'December in Florence' is taken from Akhmatova: 'Leaving, he did not look back', which hints at Dante's refusal to return to the place where he was humiliated as well as at Brodsky's own fate:

> Есть города, в которые нет возврата.
> Солнце бьётся в их окна, как в гладкие зеркала. То

есть, в них не проникнешь ни за какое злато.
Там всегда протекает река под шестью мостами.
Там есть места, где припадал устами
тоже к устам и пером к листам. И
там рябит от аркад, колоннад, от чугунных пугал;
там толпа говорит, осаждая трамвайный угол,
на языке человека, который убыл. (Ч. 113)

There are cities to which there is no return. / The sun beats on their windows, as on smooth mirrors. That / is you can't get into them at any price. / There the river always flows under six bridges. / There there are places where my lips touched / lips and my pen touched the pages. And / there you're blinded by the arcades, colonnades, the wrought-iron scarecrows; / there the crowd speaks, as it besieges the corner of the tram, / the language of a man who has gone away.

This poem consists of nine stanzas, written in free *dol'nik*; each stanza consists of nine lines with three triple feminine rhymes – a variant of Dante's *terza rima*: *возврата – зеркала*. *То – злато* ('return' – 'mirrors'; 'That' – 'gold'); *мостами – устами – к листам. И* ('bridges' – 'lips' – 'to the pages. And'); *пугал – угол – убыл* ('scarecrows' – 'corner' – 'has gone'). These rhymes once more fulfil the function of tropes: the first and last triplets cultivate the semantics of the dead-end; indeed, the metaphor of the dead-end, *mirror*, is even placed in a rhyming position. In the last triplet, this theme is extended by the word *ugol* ('corners') and the rhyme with it, the verb *ubyl*, which manifests here both its meanings, 'has gone away' and 'has died', as Gifford has commented.[20] The ironic metaphor of substitution for the wrought-iron adornments of the city of Peter – 'wrought-iron scarecrows' – placed in a rhyming position with *ubyl*, simultaneously substitutes for the poet as well – the poet whose work is used by the Empire as a scarecrow for its citizens. The theme of exile is expressed by other formal resources as well, especially by daring enjambements: *To / есть, И / там* ('That / is', 'And / there'). The particle *to* ('that') and the conjunction *i* ('and') are mercilessly split asunder and, orphan-like, are cast out to the end of the line. Thereby, they seem to personify the absurdity of the poet's exile from his native city. And so an extremely simple and expressive poetic equivalent is found for the ideological and existential conflict.

The native city is almost always naturally ascribed to 'someone else's' landscape. It is virtually impossible not to notice how routinely it appears in Brodsky's more recent poems and how it would appear to serve as a bridge between the poet and Russia. Its image corresponds to those near and dear people who remain in the city, and it is almost always yoked to the theme of language – an idea which receives particularly economical expression in the rhymes *мостами – устами – к листам. И* ('bridges' – 'lips' – 'to the pages. And').

In 1985 Brodsky wrote the poem 'In Italy', which begins with an exposed note of orphanhood:

> И я когда-то жил в городе, где на домах росли
> статуи, где по улицам с криком "растли! растли!"
> бегал местный философ, тряся бородкой,
> и бесконечная набережная делала жизнь короткой.
>
> Теперь там садится солнце, кариатид слепя.
> Но тех, кто любили меня больше самих себя,
> больше нету в живых. Утратив контакт с объектом
> преследования, собаки принюхиваются к объедкам.   (*У.* 181)

And I once lived in a city where on the houses grew / statues, where through the streets, with a cry of 'corrupt! corrupt!' / a local philosopher ran, with his beard shaking, / and the endless embankment made life short. // Now the sun sets there, blinding the caryatids. / But those who loved me more than themselves / are no longer alive. Losing contact with the object / of their pursuit, the dogs sniff at the left-overs.

Statues, a philosopher, the embankment, dogs – all this is joined together without any logic and is reminiscent of the frames of a forgotten film. The very city which Peter built as a symbol of the might of Empire, serves the poet as a model for Empire, if not for the whole world. The image of the poet himself remains virtually unchanged: 'an orphan, renegade, son of a bitch, outlaw'.

The inaccessibility of Russia, the impossibility of returning ('you're not a bird who can fly away from here', *Ч.* 91), almost always entails the theme of the senselessness of all that has happened, the absurdity of existence itself:

> "Дорога в тысячу ли начинается с одного
> шага, гласит пословица. Жалко, что от него
> не зависит дорога обратно, превосходящая многократно
> тысячу ли. Особенно отсчитывая от "о".
> Одна ли тысяча ли, две ли тысячи ли –
> тысяча означает, что ты сейчас вдали
> от родимого крова, и *зараза бессмысленности со слова
> перекидывается на цифры; особенно на ноли.*
> . . ."   (*У.* 88)

The road of a thousand li begins with one first / step, according to the proverb. It's a pity that on it / does not depend the road back, which exceeds many times / a thousand li. Particularly counting from 'o'. / Whether it's one thousand li, or two thousand li – / a thousand means that you're now distant/ from your native land, and *the contagion of senselessness from the word / tumbles over on to figures; especially on to the noughts.*

The oft-repeated word 'thousand' occupies all possible positions in the line: the middle, the beginning (twice), and the end. The Chinese measurement of distance, *li*, which is put in the rhyming position, is identified with the Russian *vdali* ('distant', or 'far away') and the supranational *noli* ('noughts', 'zeroes'). The semantics of the absurd are highlighted twice, by mathematical and linguistic signs: *ot 'o'* ('from "o"'), which means both zero and the letter 'o'; and *na noli* ('on to noughts', 'zeroes'); and, equally, by polysyllabic words: превосходящая многократно ('exceeding many times'); бессмысленность ('senselessness'); перекндывается ('tumbles over'). The last word forms a genitive metaphor of comparison of senselessness with an epidemic: *the contagion of senselessness from the word / tumbles over on to figures; especially on to the noughts.* In the original system of rhymes – *aaXabbXb* – the feminine clausulae *mnogokratno* ('many times') and *so slova* ('from the word') remain unrhymed. The meaning of 'o' is made even more ambiguous by a repetition of a stressed 'o', first in rhymes: *s odnogo – ot nego – ot 'o'* ('with one – on it – from "o"'), then in the fifth line of the stanza: *Osobenno otschityvaya ot 'o'* ('Particularly counting from "o"'). This assonance suggests one more meaning to 'o': a sigh 'oh!'. In this way, the poet's experiences are conveyed on the most varied levels of the poem's structure.

The fifth anniversary of exile was marked by two poems dedicated to the 'obliging fatherland'. 'Elaborating Plato' appeared in print first. This is a rarity for Brodsky, in that the first person which appears at the beginning of the poem does not disappear by the end of the narrative. Nonetheless, the central image is the city once more. By virtue of the description of its geographical situation, the historical monuments, the architectural details, one has no difficulty in recognizing the poet's native city:

Я хотел бы жить, Фортунатус, в городе, где река
высовывалась бы из-под моста, как из рукова – рука,

и чтоб она впадала в залив, растопырив пальцы,
как Шопен, никому не показывавший кулака.

Чтобы там была Опера, и чтоб в ней ветеран-
тенор исправно пел арию Марио по вечерам;
   чтоб Тиран ему аплодировал в ложе, а я в партере
бормотал бы, сжав зубы от ненависти: "баран".   (У. 8)

I would like to live, Fortunatus, in a city where the river / would
thrust itself from under the bridge like a hand from a sleeve / and it
would empty itself into a bay opening wide its fingers, / like Chopin,
who never shook a fist at anyone. // There would be an Opera
[House] and, in the evenings, a veteran / tenor would diligently sing
Mario's aria / so that the Tyrant applauds him from his box and I, in
the stalls, / would mutter clenching my teeth with loathing:
'blockhead'.

The poem consists of four parts, in each of which there are four
four-line stanzas, the whole being written in a free *dol'nik* with the
rhyme scheme *aaXa*. The very title contains an ironic allusion to
history's first project for an ideal state, that of Plato, in which the
great philosopher of antiquity saw no place for poets. In the
modern 'ideal' state, the poets are once more banned to the nether
regions, accompanied by the sound of the bestial howling of the
crowd depicted in the last part.

И когда бы меня схватили в итоге за шпионаж,
подрывную активность, бродяжничество, менаж-
   а-труа, и толпа бы, беснуясь вокруг, кричала,
тыча в меня натруженными указательными: "Не наш!" –

я бы в тайне был счастлив, шепча про себя: "Смотри,
это твой шанс узнать, как выглядит изнутри
   то, на что ты так долго глядел снаружи;
запоминай же подробности, восклицая "Vive la Patrie!"

And even if they finally arrested me for espionage, / for subversive activity,
vagrancy, for *ménage / à trois*, the crowd, raging around me, would shout, /
poking at me with overworked forefingers, 'He is not one of us!' // I would
be secretly pleased, whispering to myself, 'Look, / this is your chance to
find out how it looks from the inside / – you've been looking at it long
enough from the outside / – keep in mind every detail while you're
shouting *Vive la Patrie!*'

The real perception of the lyrical hero, how his return to his native
state might end, is overlaid with a nagging desire to go back. The

domination of verbs in the conditional mood, from which the lyrical subject chokes, engenders an unreal atmosphere of reverie or dream: *I would like to live . . . I would mutter . . . I would recognize . . . I would intertwine my voice . . . I would leaf through volumes . . . I would hang about in the Gallery . . . I would follow . . . I would listen impartially to the voice . . . I would know names . . . I would guess . . . I would be secretly pleased . . .*

The next characteristic of this poem lies in the fact that it is full of lexical, semantic, and associative collisons. The first stanza contains a metrical and semantic quotation from a poem by Tsvetaeva: "Я хотела бы жить с Вами / В маленьком городе, / Где вечные сумерки / И вечные колокола" (1. 258: 'I would like to live with you / In a small town, / When there is eternal twilight / And eternal [church' bells'). But whereas Tsvetaeva intensified the lyrical aspect, Brodsky erects a many-tiered image of the despised and beloved 'Patrie'. The poem is addressed to Fortunatus, a lucky man, perhaps one of Brodsky's friends who is still living in his beloved city. The concrete, factual associations with contemporary Leningrad are undermined by the writing of Opera, Library, Station, Gallery with capitals, which hints at the general image of a city as such, of the Empire as such. The text is also heterogeneous in terms of its lexical stock: alongside of obsolete *рядно* ('shroud'), *облекать* ('cover') and slang *жмен* ('couple'), *руб* ('a quid'), are scattered foreign loan-words: *ménage à trois*, *vive la Patrie*. The entire system of images works in this very direction:

II

Там была бы Библиотека, и в залах её пустых
я листал бы тома с таким же количеством запятых,
    как количество скверных слов в ежедневной речи,
не прорвавшихся в прозу. Ни, тем более, в стих.

Там стоял бы большой Вокзал, пострадавший в войне,
с фасадом куда занятней, чем мир вовне.
    Там при виде зелёной пальмы в витрине авиалиний
просыпалась бы обезьяна, дремлющая во мне.

И когда зима, Фортунатус, облекает квартал в рядно,
я б скучал в Галлерее, где каждое полотно
    – особливо Энгра или Давида –
как родимое выглядело бы пятно.   (*У.* 8–9)

There would be a Library there and in its empty halls / I'd leaf through volumes containing as many commas / as there are curses in everyday speech, / words that haven't yet broken into prose. Much less into verse. // There would be a large [Railway] Station which had been damaged during the war, / whose façade would be more amusing than the world outside. / There at the sight of green palms in the airline window / the ape that lies dormant within me would awake. // And when winter, Fortunatus, covers the houses in a shroud / I would hang about in the Gallery, where every canvas, / particularly those of Ingres or of David, / would look like a birthmark.

One is struck by the lack of proportions in the comparisons: the number of commas with the number of curses, the world with the façade of a railway station, masterpieces of world art with a birth-mark. The rhymes, in which substantives dominate (75 per cent), fuse the absurd parallels yet further: *пустых – запятых – в стих* ('empty' – 'commas' – 'into verse'); *рядно – полотно – пятно* ('shroud' – 'canvas' – 'mark'); as in the first stanza: *река – рука – кулака* ('river' – 'hand' – 'fist'), so, too, in the last two: *шпионаж – менаж – не наш* ('espionage' – 'menage' – 'not one of us'); *смотри – изнутри – la Patrie* ('look' – 'from the inside' – 'la Patrie'). It is precisely these semantic rhyme clusters *к губе – к себе – о судьбе* ('to my lip' – 'home' – 'of fate'), which hint that the poet guesses at his own fate no less than the fate of the city's population:

IV

И там были бы памятники. Я бы знал имена
не только бронзовых всадников, всунувших в стремена
    истории свою ногу, но и ихних четвероногих,
    учитывая отпечаток, оставленный ими на

население города. И с присохшей к губе
сигаретою сильно заполночь возвращаясь пешком к себе,
    как цыган по ладони, по трещинам на асфальте
    я гадал бы, икая, вслух о его судьбе.   (*У.* 9–10)

And there would be monuments there. I would know the names, / not only of bronze horsemen who thrust their feet into the stirrups / of history but also those of their four-legged companions / considering the imprint left by them on // the population of the city. And with a cigarette glued to my lip, / long past midnight, returning home on foot, / like a gipsy, reading a palm from the cracks in the pavement, / I would surmise, hiccuping, aloud about its fate.

The allusion to Pushkin's 'The Bronze Horseman' and the hint at the circumstances of one of the poet's arrests, when he too was

returning home on foot after midnight and was detained by the
police, are correlated with the semantics of the rhyme *имена – ими
на* ('names' – 'by them on'), which indicates the depersonalization
and lack of civic rights in the Empire.

The principle of contrastive depiction of the city and Empire is
sustained on the compositional level as well. The repeated adverb
там ('there') indicates the distance and inaccessibility of the desired
place: '*Чтобы там была Опера*...' ('There would be an Opera
there...'); '*Там была бы Библиотека*...' ('There would be a
Library there...')) '*Там стоял бы большой Вокзал*...' ('There
would be a large [Railway] Station there...'); '*Там была бы эта
кофейня*...' ('There would be this coffee house...'); '*Там
должна быть та улица*...' ('There must be that street...'); '*И
там были бы памятники*...' ('And there would be monuments
there...'). The collocation of such spatial localization with the
conditional mood undermines the very reality of the existence of
this city-phantasm.

The adverb *там* ('there') is endowed with an even more gen-
eralizing character in the poem 'Fifth Anniversary'. The country
which is the subject of the poem is not named once, either directly
or by periphrasis, nor is it represented by a metaphor. The
impersonal 'there' removes it in space and time, rationally alienates
it. But neither the emotions nor the language are subordinated to
the voice of reason:

> Падучая звезда, тем паче – астероид
> на резкость без труда твой праздный взгляд настроит.
> Взгляни, взгляни туда, куда смотреть не стоит.
>
> Там хмурые леса стоят в своей рванине.
> Уйдя из точки "А", там поезд на равнине
> стремится в точку " Б". Которой нет в помине.   (*У.* 70)

A falling star, or worse, an asteroid, / incites your idle gaze to
vigilance, without any trouble. / Look, look over there, where it's
not worth looking. // There the sullen forests stand in their rags. /
Departing from point 'A', there a train rushes through the plain / to
point 'B'. Of which there is no trace.

In spite of the fact that the adverb 'there', which serves as the
compositional pivot of the poem, is not capable of marking precise
spatial boundaries, everything that follows it conveys enough
information for us to identify the country. As early as the fourth

stanza there is a reference to the poem by Pushkin, 'Ruslan and Ludmila', with which every Russian child is familiar:

> Там в сумерках рояль бренчит в висках бемолью.
> Пиджак, вися в шкафу, там поедаем молью.
> Оцепеневший дуб кивает лукоморью.   (*У.* 70)

There, in the gloaming, a grand piano jars the temples with the note B flat. / A jacket hanging in the wardrobe is there being made a meal of by the moth. / The enchanted oak nods to the curved seashore.

The image of the oak, which has been aestheticized in Russian poetry, is deliberately made earthy. Lermontov's 'tireless Terek' is also mentioned in a no less ironic context:

> Там лужа во дворе, как площадь двух Америк.
> Там одиночка-мать вывозит дочку в скверик.
> Неугомонный Терек там ищет третий берег.   (*У.* 70)

The pond there in the yard is as big as two Americas. / There the single mother takes her daughter to the public garden. / The tireless Terek there seeks out a third bank.

The poem is written in the most traditional of metres – iambic hexameter with a masculine caesura often on the third foot, with constant feminine rhymes (*AAA*). In Brodsky, the caesura is intensified either by syntactic means – the end of a sentence in mid-line –

> Я вырос в тех краях. Я говорил "закурим"
> их лучшему певцу. Был содержимым тюрем.
> Привык к свинцу небес и к айвазовским бурям   (*У.* 72)

I grew up in those parts. I used to say 'Have you got a fag?' / to their best bard. I was held in prison. / Grew used to leaden skies and Aivazovsky's storms

or by an internal rhyme:

> Там при словах "*я за*" течёт со щёк извёстка.
> Там в церкви *образа* коптит свеча из воска.
> Порой даёт *раза* соседним странам войско,   (*У.* 71)

There at the words 'I'm for' lime flows from the cheeks. / There, in the church, wax candles turn the icons black. / Now and again the army shows the neighbouring lands who is the boss.

The systematic use of caesura not only creates a line symmetry, but also, thanks to the enjambements and internal rhymes, lends the

verse an additional rhythmic source of energy, which is so essential
alongside the monotonous syntactic parallelism. Both these devices
simultaneously rejuvenate the archaic metre. The high style of the
metre is balanced by the 'negative' pathos. In the poem all the
traditional Russian abominations are collected – drunkenness,
sloth, slovenliness, boredom, apathy:

> Там слышен крик совы, ей отвечает филин.
> Овацию листвы унять там вождь бессилен.
> Простую мысль, увы, пугает вид извилин.
>
> Там украшают флаг, обнявшись, серп и молот.
> Но в стенку гвоздь не вбит и огород не полот.
> Там, грубо говоря, великий план запорот.
>
> Других примет там нет – загадок, тайн, диковин.
> Пейзаж лишён примет и горизонт неровен.
> Там в моде серый цвет – цвет времени и брёвен.   (У. 71–2)

There is heard the cry of the owl, the eagle owl answers her. / There
the leader is powerless to repress the leaves' ovation. / The sight of
the brain's windings, alas, frightens simple thought. // There,
embracing sickle and hammer adorn the flag. / But into the wall the
nail is not driven and the vegetable path goes unweeded. / There,
roughly speaking, the great plan has been ruined. // There are no
distinguishing marks there – enigmas, secrets, wonders. / The
landscape is devoid of any marks and the horizon is rugged. / There
the fashion is for grey – the colour of time and of logs.

The tropes and figures of speech have the characteristic feature
either of hyperbolic exaggeration ('the pond there is as big as two
Americas'; 'and the dusty radiator in the entrance has more ribs
than ladies have'), or else of rhetorical diminution ('there the
sunset resembles a cut'; 'there the buzzing of the bee is the main
principle of sound'). On the lexical level, we see a typical feature
of Brodsky's poetics, the transformation of a cliché into a meta-
cliché:[21] 'There they say "It's one of us" in the doorway with a nasty
grin'; 'there in the air hang fragments of old arias'; 'and the
boneless tongue, so fond of intelligible sounds'. The dispiriting
picture of the step-motherland is significantly softened by witty
aphorisms, lightness, brilliance, and self-irony:

> Там, думал, и умру – от скуки, от испуга.
> Когда не от руки, так на руках у друга.
> Видать, не рассчитал. Как квадратуру круга.   (У. 72)

There I thought I was to die – of boredom, of fear. / If not by the
hand of a friend, then in his arms. / You can see I miscalculated.
It's like squaring the circle.

Towards the end of the poem, there is an accumulation of lyricism
which breaks through the mask of the neutral tone and the easy
indifference to his own fate:

> Теперь меня там нет. Означенной пропаже
> дивятся, может быть, лишь вазы в Эрмитаже.
> Отсутствие моё большой дыры в пейзаже
>
> не сделало; пустяк: дыра, – но небольшая.
> Её затянут мох или пучки лишая,
> гармонии тонов и проч. не нарушая.   (У. 72)

I'm no longer there. The aforementioned loss / surprises, perhaps,
only some vases in the Hermitage. / My absence didn't make // a big
hole in the landscape; a trifle: a hole but not a big one. / It will be
covered with moss or a bit of lichen, / the harmony of tones and so
forth wouldn't be ruined.

Behind this seeming calm stands the 'endurer of pain', man, whose
life is riven, as is indicated by the interstrophic enjambement
'большой дыры в пейзаже / не сделало' ('didn't make / a big hole
in the landscape'). Such a reading is suggested by a stanza from the
poem '1972':

> Точно Тезей из пещеры Миноса,
> выйдя на воздух и шкуру вынеся,
> не горизонт вижу я – знак минуса
> к прожитой жизни. Остреи, чем меч его,
> лезвие это, и им отрезана
> лучшая часть.   (Ч. 27)

Just like Theseus, emerging from the Minotaur's lair, / into the air,
carrying out its hide, / I see no horizon, but a minus sign / on the
spent life. / This cutting edge is sharper than his sword / and the
better part / has been shorn off by it.

It is precisely the presence of an agonizing nostalgia (which does
not lessen over the years) for this 'white-eyed monster' (*K*. 60)
which forms the 'nether abyss' of the poet's experience in this
poem. For neither sarcasm nor irony in themselves are capable of
dealing with the situation described: 'For a poet, life is too tragic for
irony to be an adequate response by itself. We all need this kind of

ironic support for our everyday lives. But irony leads you only to its own destination, not deep or profound spheres of spiritual existence.'[22] On to the ambivalent collocation of various aspects of Russo-Soviet reality is projected a no less ambivalent poetic experience. By the end of the poem, not only do the nostalgic notes become more and more clearly distinct, but so does the ambiguous character of the conflict 'poet–state', because it subsumes the classical opposition 'poet–tyrant' and 'poet–crowd':

> Теперь меня там нет. Об этом думать странно.
> Но было бы чудней изображать барана,
> дрожать, но раздражать на склоне дней тирана,
>
> паясничать. Ну что ж! на всё свои законы:
> я не любил жлобства, не целовал иконы,
> и на одном мосту чугунный лик Горгоны
>
> казался в тех краях мне самым честным ликом.
> Зато столкнувшись с ним теперь, в его великом
> варьянте, я своим не подавился криком
>
> и не окаменел. Я слышу Музы лепет.
> Я чувствую нутром, как Парка нитку треплет:
> мой углекислый вздох пока что в вышних терпят. (У. 72–3)

I'm no longer there. It's strange to think of that. / But it would be stranger still to imitate the sheep / to tremble, yet irritate the tyrant in his declining years, // to play the fool. So what! everything has its own law: / I never liked miserliness, haven't kissed the icon, / and on a certain bridge the cast-iron face of the Gorgon // seemed to me the most honest of faces, in those parts. / But seeing it now in its mighty / version I didn't choke with a cry // and did not turn to stone. I hear the murmur of the Muse. / I feel within me how Fate scutches the thread: / my carbon dioxide breath is, for the time, tolerated on high.

The reference to the Muse leads into the main theme of Brodsky's poetry – the theme of the poet and language, fate and time. And here the poet demonstrates his complete humility and his profound inner lack of well-being. He has only one way of disclosing his love for Russia – his love for the language in which he writes:

> и без костей язык, до внятных звуков лаком,
> судьбу благодарит кириллицыным знаком.
> На то она – судьба, чтоб понимать на всяком
>
> наречьи. Передо мной – пространство в чистом виде.
> В нём места нет столпу, фонтану, пирамиде.
> В нём, судя по всему, я не нуждаюсь в гиде.

Скрипи, моё перо, мой коготок, мой посох.
Не подгоняй сих строк: забуксовав в отбросах,
эпоха на колёсах нас не догонит, босых. (У. 73)

and the boneless tongue, so fond of intelligible sounds, / thanks Fate
in the Cyrillic sign. / It is because she is Fate that she will understand
every // dialect. Before me lies space in its pure form. / In it there's no
place for pillar, fountain, pyramid. / In it, to all appearances, I
wouldn't need a guide. // Squeak on, my pen, / my dear claw, my
[shepherd's] crook, / Don't urge these lines: starting to skid through
garbage, / this epoch on wheels will not catch up with us –
barefooted.

The end of the poem is foreshortened in a way that is typical of
Brodsky – stoical solitude:

Мне нечего сказать ни греку, ни варягу.
Зане не знаю я, в какую землю лягу.
Скрипи, скрипи, перо! переводи бумагу. (У. 73)

I have nothing to say, either to a Greek or a Varangian. / For I no
longer know in whose soil I will lie. / Squeak on, squeak on, pen, use
up the paper.

The theme of Russia in Brodsky's poetry is a predominantly
elegiac one. With time, Brodsky says, everything becomes an
object of nostalgia, although certain actions performed by his
'beloved fatherland' drive him to fury, such as the war in Afghanistan, an event which is marked by the poem 'Verses on the Winter
Campaign 1980'. The theme of Russia does not disappear from
Brodsky's poetry; not only because the 'beloved fatherland ... is
always reminding us of itself ... does not allow itself to be
forgotten',[23] but also because the language itself does not allow
forgetfulness, any more than does the poet's feeling of guilt ('I have
abandoned the country that nurtured me', У. 177), that he has
abandoned his readers. The inaccessibility of Brodsky's poetry for
the wider audience in Russia leaves such a hole in its aesthetic and
spiritual landscape that no poetic home-grown plant can, as yet,
cover it.

Speaking into silence

the interlocutor is absent, as is nearly always the case in
poetry.[24]

To the reader brought up on traditional lyric poetry, Brodsky's poetry seems cold and too speculative. There is no romantic celebration of woman, which is characteristic of confessional lyrical poetry. This lack of passion and the refined asceticism of the feelings can be misleading. Thus, despite his having dedicated a whole collection of poetry (146 pages) to a woman, M. B., the Russian reader complains that Brodsky has only a few love poems. And yet it would be difficult to name any other Russian poet who has addressed his love poems to the same woman for the space of a quarter of a century. The secret of the matter is that, whether the topic be love or God, the poet prefers to speak not directly, but obliquely, even with estrangement. It is therefore of particular interest, both poetic and psychological, to examine how emotions find expression in lyric poetry when intellectual control is predominant.

We may find indicators as to how we should read and interpret his lyrics in Brodsky himself. Contrary to the common view, he considers that 'unlike prose, poetry doesn't so much express an emotion as absorb it linguistically'.[25] In his essays on Russian and Western poets, Brodsky highlights lyric features which are characteristic of his own poetry. We have already had occasion to speak of many of these in earlier analyses: restraint, detachment, a dry dispassionate tone as a struggle for objectivity, deliberately monotonous intonation in order 'to make one's voice less theatrical, less *bel canto*-like' (*L.* 46). With time, these devices are cultivated, become refined, or are supplemented by new ones. Brodsky creates a unique lyrical system, in which the feelings are under the control of reason. But, occasionally, either they display disobedience or else they are given their freedom. Suddenly, in mid-line, in the context of everyday psychology and irony, there will ring out genuine lyricism, like classical music, which is just as unexpectedly switched off, and the poet returns to a banal and neutral tone. As a result, we see something akin to anti-climax within the line or within the sentence.

A description and interpretation of Brodsky's anti-lyrical system is only just beginning. A number of interesting articles by Losev, one of the most subtle experts on Brodsky's poetry, merit attention. He has collected and commented on Brodsky's first lyric cycle, 'Songs of a Happy Winter'.[26] In this early cycle (1962–3), which is already completely original, as Losev has noted, we find an initial treatment of many of the leading themes of Brodsky's poetry (faith, language, things, the effect of time on man); the key images are also marked out (mice, birds, scissors, butterflies, moths, mirrors). Brodsky not only overcomes 'melodic banality', but also 'pushes pure lyricism out of its customary mould', moving from a 'romantic depiction of life to a philosophical understanding of it'.[27] On the basis of an analysis of the poem 'I Embraced these Shoulders and Glanced', Losev has shown how the profound inner drama of the poem is formed by a collision between the dispassionate tone and the pathos of the grammatical forms of the verbs, which devour the emotions.[28]

In this section I shall first take a brief look at several poems from the collection *New Stanzas to Augusta* (1962–82), from the point of view of the characteristics of the addressee. Then one poem will be analysed in detail. In the process of a careful reading of separate stanzas, lines, and a short poem, I shall attempt to reveal where the lyricism is hidden, what masks it dons, how de-poeticization of the lyric is achieved, and how far the poet succeeds in going in the direction opposite to himself in his anti-lyrical journey.

'Every utterance', writes Bakhtin, 'always has an addressee (of diverse character, of varying degrees of intimacy, concreteness, awareness etc.), the reciprocal understanding of whom the author of the speech seeks and anticipates.'[29] From Brodsky's very first lyrics, a persistent poetic model is revealed – the addressee is only present metonymically: 'I embraced *these shoulders* and glanced' (*H*. 7); 'I ran from fate . . . *from the arms*, / into which I fell and fell out facing / South' (*H*. 9); 'and I find . . . my reflection *in your eyes* (*H*. 30); '*Her palm* smooths the shawl. / To touch *her hair* or *shoulders*' (*H*. 31). Moreover, not once in twenty-five years is the portrait of a beloved woman given. Often, she is introduced into the poem only via an object that belongs to her: slippers, stockings, socks ('Enigma for an Angel', 'Kellomiaki'). And, not infrequently, the addressee is entirely absent, as if she is squeezed out by the very genre, such as the folk-song: 'Song' (*H*. 8) and 'Song' (*H*. 27). The emotional experiences of the subject of speech himself are hidden behind masks from mythology ('Aeneas and Dido', 'To Lycomedes on Scyros', 'Anno Domini').

The traditional opposition 'I' – 'thou' is substituted by, or identified with, nature: '*You are the wind, my dear. I am your / wood*' (*H*. 13); 'You will flutter out, *robin*' (*H*. 26). The unnamed 'thou' is contained in the imperative of request or wish: 'Never forget / how the water splashes against the pier' (*H*. 21); 'The songs of happy winter / take as a keepsake' (*H*. 24). 'I' and 'thou' are sometimes expelled from the centre of the poem and appear together only in lyrical digressions and then in oblique cases:

> И *тебе* не понять,
> да и *мне* не расслышать, наверное:
> то ли вправду звенит тишина,
> как на Стиксе уключина,
> то ли песня навзрыд сложена
> и посмертно заучена.   (*H*. 29)

and it is not *for you* to understand, / nor *for me* to hear, no doubt: / whether silence really does ring out, / like a rowlock on the Styx, / or else a song is composed while sobbing violently / and learned posthumously.

It is precisely in places like these – on the periphery of the poem, or else on the periphery of the grammar in subordinate and parenthetic clauses – that passion and the loved one herself are concealed: 'Хотя сейчас и ты к моей судьбе / не меньше глуховата, чем потомство' (*H*. 35: 'Although now you too to my fate / are no less deaf than posterity'); 'Чем безнадежней, тем как-то / проще' (*H*. 110: 'The more hopeless, somehow, the / easier it is'); 'с тобой имела общие черты / (шепчу автоматически "о, Боже", / их вспоминая) внешние' (*H*. 120: 'with you she had features in common / (I whisper automatically "Oh, God", / remembering them) external ones').

The rare mergings of 'I' and 'thou' into 'we' and 'our' appear in a context of premonition of the inevitable end: 'и трепещет обрывок / нашей жизни вдвоём' (*H*. 21: 'and a fragment / of our life together trembles'); and after the end, which has begun long ago:

> Неуместней, чем ящур
> в филармонии, *вид*
> *нас вдвоём в настоящем.*
> Тем верней удивит
> обитателей завтра
> разведённая смесь
> сильных чувств диназавра
> и кириллицы смесь.   (*H*. 114)

More inappropriate than a brontosaur / in the Philharmonic Hall is *the sight / of us together in the present.* / All the more surely surprising

/ to the inhabitants of tomorrow / is the diluted mixture / of the strong feelings of a dinosaur / and the mixture of Cyrillic.

The poem is muffled by self-irony. This is one of Brodsky's favourite means of self-protection; it preserves the poet from the 'elevated state of mind' (*L.* 177). Irony also helps him maintain a sense of proportion.

Gradually 'I' and 'thou' are replaced by the more distanced 'he' and 'she' ('Elaborating Krylov'). The grammatically expressed addressee[30] disappears from many of the poems that were written in his northern exile ('The Days Run Over Me'; 'In Autumn from the Nest'; 'Oh, How Dear to Me is the Ring-like Smoke'). In these poems, no answer is expected; the hope even of being heard disappears. When 'the thread snapped', the philosophical understanding of life is intensified: 'В этом мире разлука – / лишь прообраз иной' (*H.* 86: 'In this world one separation – / is only the prototype of another'); 'расставанье заметней, / чем слияние душ' (*H.* 88: 'separation is more visible / than merging of souls'). The 'drying-up' of the lyrics also intensifies, their direction changes. The lyrics move, as it were, in a reverse direction from themselves, towards a neutrality of the feelings, their abstraction. The tendency towards an absolutization of the utterance is also intensified. The boundaries of the inner and outer worlds are eroded. The lyric space may be widened any way at all: from a dacha settlement near Leningrad to the whole world; from contemporary Paris to the Scotland of Mary Stuart.

A whole series of features which are characteristic of Brodsky's lyrics may be uncovered in a small poem addressed to M.B. from the cycle 'A Part of Speech' and dated 1975–6. It has been anthologized in both *A Part of Speech* and *New Stanzas to Augusta*.

1. Ниоткуда с любовью, надцатого мартобря,
2. дорогой уважаемый милая, но неважно
3. даже кто, ибо черт лица, говоря
4. откровенно, не вспомнить уже, не ваш, но
5. и ничей верный друг вас приветствует с одного
6. из пяти континентов, держащегося на ковбоях;
7. я любил тебя больше, чем ангелов и самого,
8. и поэтому дальше теперь от тебя, чем от них обоих;
9. поздно ночью, в уснувшей долине, на самом дне,
10. в городке, занесённом снегом по ручку двери,
11. извиваясь ночью на простыне –
12. как не сказано ниже по крайней мере –

13. я взбиваю подушку мычащим "ты"
14. за морями, которым конца и края,
15. в темноте всем телом твои черты,
16. как безумное зеркало повторяя.   (*H.* 129)

From nowhere with love the enth of Marchember / dear respected
sweet but it's not even important / who for frankly speaking it's hard
to recall / the face's features, not yours or / anyone else's faithful
friend greets you from one / of five continents propped up by
cowboys / I loved you more than angels and Himself / so am farther
off from you now than from both of them / late at night at the very
bottom of a sleeping valley / in the small town buried up to the door
handles in snow / writhing at night upon the sheet / as to say the least
is not stated below / I shake up the pillow by mumbling 'you' / across
the seas which have no end or edge / in the darkness my whole body
is repeating / your features like a mad mirror.

The poem is written in free *dol'nik*, or rather, in a combination of
dol'nik and a traditional metre, the anapaest, which allows the
inclusion of a relatively large percentage of polysyllabic words:
уважаемый ('respected'), *откровенно* ('frankly'), *приветствует* ('greets'), *континента* ('continents'), *держащегося* ('propped up'), *занесённом* ('buried'), *извиваясь* ('writhing'),
безумное ('mad'). Such lexis in its own turn depoeticizes the
verse, brings it closer to prose. The rhyme system is one of alternating masculine and feminine clausulae (*aBaB*). The poem is not
graphically divided into stanzas. The number of syllables per line
varies from ten (lines 11, 15) to eighteen (line 8). Using the schema
devised by G. S. Smith, and which he used to analyse the versification of Brodsky's 'Kellomiaki'[31] we may represent the rhythmical
model of this poem as shown in Table 1.

Of the four-stress lines, only the twelfth and the fourteenth have
an identical rhythmical structure: *как не сказано ниже по
крайней мере* ('as to say the least is not stated below'), and *за
морями, которым конца и края* ('across the seas which have no
end or edge'). The three-stress lines also form pairings: the fourth is
of the same rhythmical type as the sixteenth: *откровенно, не
вспомнить уже, не ваш, но* ('frankly it's hard to recall, not yours
but'), and *как безумное зеркало повторяя* ('like a mad mirror,
repeating'); and so do the eleventh and the fifteenth: *извиваясь
ночью на простыне* ('writhing at night upon the sheet'), and *в
темноте всем телом твои черты* ('in the darkness my whole
body [is repeating] your features').

Table 1. *Rhythmical model for 'Niotkuda s liubovyu'*

Line	Number of stresses	Number of syllables	Pattern of unstressed syllables
1.	4	14	2215
2.	4	15	22241
3.	3	11	2212
4.	3	12	2241
5.	4	14	2224
6.	4	16	22251
7.	4	15	2225
8.	5	18	222241
9.	4	14	2224
10.	5	14	221221
11.	3	10	214
12.	4	12	22211
13.	4	11	2221
14.	4	12	22211
15.	3	10	214
16.	3	12	2241

We may consider the constant characteristic of this poem's versification to be its anapaestic basis, which takes in the first two stressed feet of all the lines, with the exception of the eleventh and fifteenth. The semantic function of using this metre in combination with the free *dol'nik* may be seen to lie in the fact that, firstly, the steady rhythmic principle is shattered every time by the unsteady emotional state of the lyric subject; secondly, in the fact that the anapaestic principle lends the verse a lyrical intonation which, in mid-sentence, is switched off by the neurotic state of mind. It is significant that the eleventh and fifteenth lines which develop the motif of madness are rhythmically highlighted in two ways: by forming a pair, and by forming an exception to the rhythmical pattern of the poem.

Any attempts at rhythmic symmetry within the line are immediately thwarted both by the semantics and by the poem's syntax. The caesura is not metrically regular. It appears sometimes after the first foot (lines 3, 4, 10, 14, 15), now after the second (1, 5, 7, 12, 13,

16), or else it is not present at all, as in the eleventh and fifteenth lines, which have already been highlighted by other metrical means, or, finally, the syntax demands two long pauses within the line (4, 9).

The syntax and rhythm of this poem are consequently brought to a state of extreme conflict. The whole poem becomes one prolonged monster of a sentence, made yet more complex by inversion, enumeration, participial and gerundive turns of speech, subordinate and parenthetic clauses. It is impossible not to notice the grammatical violations. The addressee is defined only by adjectives, of both masculine and feminine genders, without commas or names: the reference may be to one addressee, or to several simultaneously. The reader is offered an answer to this puzzle: 'but it's not even important / who for frankly speaking it's hard to recall / the face's features'. This motif of amnesia is insistently repeated in other poems as well: 'но не вспомнить ни объятья, ни платья' ('but it is impossible to recall either embrace or the dress'); 'Необязательно помнить, как звали тебя, меня' (*H*. 143: 'It's irrelevant to remember your name, or mine').

Grammatical violations can be observed on the level of vocabulary. Twice in the poem a word is omitted – after *самого* the word Бога ('God') is omitted in the line 'я любил тебя больше, чем ангелов и самого' ('I love you more than angels and Himself'); and the negative particle *нет* ('no') is missing in the fourteenth line: 'за морями, которым конца и края' ('across the seas which [have no] end or edge'). As a result, we have before us the sort of syntax which conveys stream of consciousness, and the kind of despair which no grammar can restrain: the sentence breaks off, picks up, and then is broken again. The syntax is shattered both on the horizontal and the vertical planes. On the horizontal, by means of parenthetic words and clauses: 'but it's not even important / who'; 'as to say the least is not stated below'. On the vertical, the tightest semantic groups of words are broken by the poetic line: *но неважно / даже кто* ('but it's not even important / who'); *не ваш, но / и ничей* ('not yours or / anyone else's'); *с одного / из пяти* ('from one / of five'). Such syntactic instability is compensated for, to a certain extent, by the lexical stock of the poem: of 102 words, 25 per cent are nouns and only 7 per cent are verbs, which bears witness to the relatively static character of the poem.

The overall percentage of significant words is very high at 70 per cent. Thus, the lexis creates, as it were, linguistic ground for the existential groundlessness of the poet, forming an opposition to 'from nowhere'.

On top of this lexis is laid an interesting vocal tracery of stressed vowels: of 62 stressed vowels, 'a' is repeated 17 times, 'o' 13, and 'e' 13. Correspondingly, these phonemes dominate in the rhymes, which allows us to divide the poem into four-line strophes. Only in the last quatrain is the alternation 'u – a' repeated. In the feminine clausulae, the unstressed vowels are also strictly organized: 'a – a'; 'i – i'; 'i – i'; 'a – a'.

The tropological aspect of the poem is fairly impoverished: the periphrasis for America contains within it a cliché ('continent, propped up by cowboys'); the metaphor *sleeping valley* can be assigned to poetic phraseology. The only interesting trope is *I shake up the pillow by mumbling 'you'*. And the comparison of the lyric subject with a mad mirror has a staggering effect. An almost unbearable lyricism breaks through.

On the other hand, the alternating masculine and feminine rhymes are almost transformed into metaphorical, associative fields. To make this easier to perceive, we need to switch some of them round: *говоря – мартобря* ('speaking' – 'Marchember'). The next compound rhyme, *не ваш но – неважно* ('not yours but' – 'it's not important'), forms a homonym and hints at the identity between alienation and the absurd; *на ... дне – на простыне* ('at the bottom' – 'upon the sheet'), *ты – черты* ('you' – 'features'), have the semantics of similarity of a part for a whole. The last pair of rhymes, *края – повторяя* ('edge' – 'repeating'), harks back to the first, both in terms of its grammatical structure and in its semantics of the absurd. It is worth noting that there is not a single weak rhyme in the poem.

The absurdity is intensified by references to other writers: 'From nowhere with love' was born from Ian Fleming's *From Russia with Love*. By analogy with Gogol's 'Marchember' from *Diary of a Madman* we have 'the enth of Marchember'. There are also self-references in the poem. The strange illogicality of the seventh and eighth lines, 'I loved you more than angels and Himself / and so I am farther off from you now than from both of them', first appeared in a poem written during Brodsky's Archangel exile: 'Yes, the heart yearns all the more strongly towards you, / and so it

is all the further away' (*H*. 56). In both cases there is no relation
between cause and effect. The comparison of love with madness
can also be found in an early poem: 'thus in nocturnal darkness /
laying bare the toothless hope, / verst by verst) *love steps away
from madness*' (*H*. 28). This is not only a strange logic of love,
which is merely the 'forword to separation' (*O*. 211), but it is also
the inexorable logic of alienation.

Alienation, both physical and psychological, appears before us
in all its facets: the groundless 'from nowhere', by name a foreign
land; the alienation amidst people: 'not yours or anyone / else's
faithful friend'; the inpenetrability of this alienation for the mind:
'I loved you more than angels and Himself / so I am farther off from
you now than from both of them'; and, finally, the pain hidden in
the tropes 'in the darkness my whole body is repeating / your
features like a mad mirror'. This double, triple, multiple alienation
is also conveyed by the choice of lexical terms with negative
semantics: 'from nowhere', 'not important', 'hard to recall', 'not
yours', 'not stated'.

In this way, on all levels of the analysis – rhythmic, phonetic,
syntactical, tropological – we observe the poet making every structural element of the text semantically active. The language of this
poem is not merely motivated by the theme of alienation; it is
insufficient to say even that it embodies it: we are obliged to say
that the language engenders this theme, in accordance with Brodsky's conviction: 'What dictates a poem is the language'
(*L*. 124–5).

The first part creates the greatest degree of alienation: from
place and time, from beloved woman and friends, finally from God
Himself, who is half-named. In the second half, this alienation is
overcome by a lyricism which throws off the dispassionate mask.
The anonymity of pain is expressed in the intensifying image of the
mad mirror, which seems more real than reality itself. We can only
guess at how many other possibilities were rejected. We can be
fairly sure that a traditional elegiac vocabulary was rejected in
favour of a tongue-tied modern Russian. Such a characteristic
feature of Brodsky's poetics as the indiscriminate inclusion of any
lexis could not but have an effect on the choice of metre. It is
revealing how Brodsky gradually departs from classical metres,
more and more frequently giving preference to the free *dol'nik*.
This metre allows Brodsky to satisfy his passion for long words

which, in their turn, accelerate the rhythm, as a second stress will always be cried out for on long words.

More and more, Brodsky 'loosens' his syntax, stretches a sentence to a whole strophe, or, as here, to an entire poem. He increases the weight of the sentence by inversions, makes it more cumbersome by means of subordinate or parenthetic clauses. We may say of him, as of Tsvetaeva, that he is the poet of subordinate clauses. By causing a collison between syntax and metre on the borders of the poetic lines, he deliberately creates semantic and intonational dissonance.[32] Following his grammar, his poetry moves in the direction of prose, from the lyrical monologue to narrative. In this process a peculiar paradox may be observed: the longer the sentence, the more perceptible the poet's striving to reach the end of it as quickly as he can and his inability to stop: 'I cannot finish the tirade' (H. 127). It is as if the language ceases to be obedient. Sometimes the poet almost becomes nauseated by talking so long, for he knows better than the reader that the longer the poet talks, the more tragic he sounds, laying himself bare to a greater number of slings and arrows. But it is precisely this feeling that he strives to place under the control of reason and language. In the very instances where Brodsky succeeds in adopting the position of a clinical observer of everything that is going on in his head and heart as well as around him, he excels himself to the point of self-annihilation. He becomes a voice, a throat, a thing. We hear a voice speaking into silence. In these instances, Brodsky comes close to the poetics of his much-loved Beckett. The discourse is cleansed not only of emotions, but of logic as well. As Kalomirov has noted: 'some of Brodsky's poems end up as merely the expression of a point of view which has been extended and reduced to the point of self-negation'.[33]

But here, too, we observe a paradox. In his lyrics, the poet is a primordial bigamist. The relations between his loved one and his Muse are far from equal. The Muse inevitably transforms her rival into an object for investigation. The very fact of separation from the woman acts as the ideal pretext for writing poetry. Moreover, the safer the distance, the less likely a meeting, the more intense the lyricism. Speaking of Cavafy, the poet himself explains this as follows: 'His sense of loss is much more acute than his sense of gain simply because separation is a more lasting experience than being together' (L. 62). In any event, everything ends to the advantage of the Muse, who always emerges as the victor from any amorous triangle, whether her rival is a woman or the native country. This is reflected in his conception of love: 'Love is essentially an attitude maintained by the infinite towards the finite. The reversal constitutes either faith or poetry' (*L.* 44). The Muse, like faith, demands of the poet that he leave everything behind and follow her.

The image of alienation

Попробуем же отстраннться,
взять век в кавычки.[1]

A stern metaphysical realist

Позволял своим связкам все звуки, помимо воя;
перешёл на шёпот.[2]

The image of a man in exile – physical, political, and existential –
runs through all of Brodsky's works like black and white threads.
The most remarkable fact is that this image appeared in his poetry
long before his exile into the West and even before his northern
exile:

> Слава Богу, чужой.
> Никого я здесь не обвиняю.
> Ничего не узнать,
> Я иду, тороплюсь, обгоняю.
> Как легко мне теперь
> оттого, что ни с кем не расстался.
> Слава Богу, что я на земле без отчизны остался.   (*C.* 84)

Thank God I'm a stranger. / I blame no one here. / There is nothing
recognizable, / I'm going, I'm in a hurry, I'm overtaking. / How
easy it is for me now / because I had no one to part with. / Thank
God that I was left on [this] earth without a homeland.

Perhaps this intensified feeling of destiny is an acute awareness of
time. Yet, when speaking of the future in our time, the poet is
rarely mistaken, especially if he is prophesying what is most
unpleasant for himself or for his nation. When these predictions
were realized, the theme of alienation acquired a new dimension.
The parallel with Dante's fate lent this theme a timeless character.
In the last stanza of 'December in Florence', which was quoted in
the previous chapter, an almost abstract image of exile is created,
despite the concrete details of the native city. The high note of

lyricism is muffled by extreme estrangement, both of the sense of *realia*, and of the poetic concept. *Ipso facto*, the very tragedy of exile is placed under the control of poetic mastery. For the reader, however, it remains understood that the degree of the poet's lack of well-being almost always directly depends on his non-conformism. As Sidney Monas has commented: 'for the most part, the lyrical persona stands so bleakly alone in such a vastly alienated world that the reader, gripped by the power of the verse, nevertheless begins to long for his own "halt in the desert"'.[3]

Brodsky has, more profoundly and more consistently than other contemporary Russian poets, developed the idea of alienation by fusing it with the device of estrangement. On the basis of Shklovsky's definition, this device may be seen to consist of removing the object from its customary context, in presenting the familiar as strange, as if seen for the first time: 'Estrangement is surprise at the world, intensified perception of it.'[4] Brodsky assimilated this device early in his career, thought it through carefully, and consistently realized it both in his poetry and prose. In his autobiographical essay 'Less Than One' Brodsky recalls how early he realized the power of consciousness over existence: 'when I was about ten or eleven it occurred to me that Marx's dictum that "existence conditions consciousness' was true only for as long as it takes consciousness to acquire the art of estrangement; thereafter, consciousness is on its own and can both condition and ignore existence' (*L.* 3).

We have already on numerous occasions observed Brodsky's use of various stylistic resources to create the effect of estrangement. On the lexical level, we can trace the tendency of locating the key words of the poem in an unexpected semantic context. A new semantic field almost inevitably forms a new trope:

> время, упавшее сильно ниже
> нуля, обжигает ваш мозг, как пальчик
> шалуна из русского стихотворенья.   (*У.* 120)

time, falling sharply lower than / zero, scorches your brain, like the little finger / of the naughty boy in the Russian verse.

In this instance, the reification of time which is so characteristic of Brodsky's poetry has occurred. The reification of man, the Spirit, and abstract categories is none other than the realization of the idea of alienation in tropes. Does not this process of transformation of meaning convey the very essence of alienation in our world, where *homo homini res est* (man is a thing to man)? On the syntactic level, the notion of alienation is expressed by the disordering of structural connections by, for example, inversion or ellipsis. The described object, imbued in the trope with qualities which are alien to its nature, is further transposed to new territory by means of frequent enjambement. The close proximity of new stylistic layers simultaneously alters the perspective of perception. Many of Brodsky's poems are constructed on this principle, such as 'Two Hours in the Reservoir', 'Twenty Sonnets to Mary Stuart', and a whole series of others.

A dispassionate tone and the objectification of the perception are cultivated. The music of a poem is either switched on or off without allowing the poem to deviate towards predetermined poetics. A surprise awaits the reader at every stage. It would be difficult to name a structural element of Brodsky's poetry not touched by estrangement, the primary function of which is creation of the sense of distance. As Carl Proffer reports: 'when asked what makes a great writer, Brodsky said the first thing is knowing the dimensions (*Masshtab*) of things, and knowing his place in the chain of things'.[5] It is precisely this aspiration to find the place of every link in the chain of being which explains the constant magnifying of distance right up to the attempt 'to go beyond the brackets of the year' (*K*. 57) and 'to put the century into inverted commas' (*У*. 94). In this process, the distance between the speaker and the addressee sometimes transforms the latter into a barely discernible speck. We hear the voice of a man talking to himself. But he speaks of things which remain of vital interest for the reader of any social system.

As early as 1964, in a poem written during the Archangel exile, 'New Stanzas to Augusta' (*O*. 156–60), the theme of alienation emerges before us in all its diversity. The isolation of the poet from society, from family and friends, is expressed explicitly: 'Тут, захороненный живьём' ('here, buried alive'); 'Я где-то в стороне, за бортом' ('I'm somewhere overboard'); 'И вот бреду я по ничьей земле / и у Небытия прошу аренду' ('And here I wander over no-man's land / and ask rent from non-being'). The absurdity of all that has happened to him is expressed by the objectification of the feelings and memory: 'бреду я от бугра к бугру / без памяти, с одним каким-то звуком' ('I wander from mound to mound / without memory, with just some sort of sound'); 'легла бессмысленности тень / в моих глазах' ('a shadow of senselessness lay in my eyes'). The desire to distance himself and to evaluate the situation and, equally, the failure of this attempt, find a metaphorical formulation:

> Друг Полидевк. Тут всё слилось в пятно.
> Из уст моих не вырвется стенанье.
> Вот я стою в распахнутом пальто
> и мир течёт в глаза сквозь решето,
> сквозь решето непониманья.   (*O.* 159)

Polydeuces, dear friend. Here all merged into a stain. / No groan will escape my lips. / Here I stand with my coat wide open, / and the world flows into my eyes through a sieve, / through a sieve of incomprehension.

In order to comprehend what is happening, the poet exercises to the maximum his ability to distance, to get outside self, to split into two. This is at once a device of depiction and the essence of depiction, a variant of self-alienation:

> И образ мой второй, как человек,
> бежит от красноватых век,
> подскакивает на волне
> под соснами, потом под ивняками,
> мешается с другими двойниками,
> как никогда не затеряться мне.   (*O.* 157)

And my second image, like a man, / runs from the reddish eyelids, / jumps up on a wave / under the pines, then under the osierbeds, / mingles with other doubles, / getting lost in a way I will never be able to.

A poet who is capable of such a degree of self-estrangement must be free of all illusions; he does not suffer from self-pity and may judge others and himself objectively. One may assume that this is one of the aesthetic functions of estrangement. By the same means of estrangement that are used in the metaphors of attribution, alienation extends to the natural world. By this token, nature is not presented as an unreasoning object but, on the contrary, as a thinking being and, hence, more hostile:

> Природа расправляется с былым,
> как водится. Но лик её при этом
> пусть залитый закатным светом
> невольно делается злым.   (*O.* 159)

Nature deals with the past, / as usual. But her face at this, / be it
infused with twilight, / involuntarily becomes spiteful.

It is interesting to remember that in 1964–5 Brodsky was reading a
lot of Frost's poetry: 'As a matter of fact,' he told John Green,
'during this administrative exile I lived 100 per cent Frost poetry.'[6]
Frost, too, notes Brodsky, found his own personal hardship
reflected in nature. On to the alienation of nature is piled the
alienation of life itself. It is ascribed the capability of self-
estrangement so as to understand itself:

> Здесь на холмах, среди пустых небес,
> среди дорог, ведущих только в лес,
> жизнь отступает от самой себя
> и смотрит с изумлением на формы,
> шумящие вокруг.   (*O.* 158)

Here, on the hills, amid the empty heavens, / amid the roads, leading
only into forest, / life steps aside from itself/ and looks with
amazement at the forms / which are roaring around it.

Man's alienation from nature is only a part of the overall complex
canvas of alienation, the inevitability of which, in part, lies in the
fact that, in our times, man is not infrequently placed in circumstances in which his entire previous experience is inadequate. The
degree of alienation increases when it encompasses not only the
social but also the emotional life:

> Да, сердце рвётся всё сильней к тебе,
> и оттого оно – всё дальше.   (*O.* 160)

Yes, my heart yearns all the more towards you, / and so it is all the
more further away.

Over the years, the absurdity of alienation in human relations has
only increased, as we have seen from the poem 'From Nowhere
with Love', in which there is a direct echo of 'New Stanzas for
Augusta':

> я любил тебя больше, чем ангелов и самого,
> и поэтому дальше теперь от тебя, чем от них обоих;   (*Ч.* 77)

I loved you more than angels and Himself / so I am farther off from
you now than from both of them.

In the situation of exile, the degree of alienation of the lyric hero
can be adequately expressed only in the form of the notes of

Gogol's madman: 'the enth of Marchember'. Brodsky has found a witty form of linguistic alienation, which expresses the fact of the poet's alienation from language. The picture of social alienation is supplemented in Brodsky's later poems by various kinds of psychological, aesthetic, and linguistic alienation. It is precisely this last type of alienation that takes the very phenomenon of alienation on to the metaphysical plane.

It is customary to place man at the very centre of alienation and to examine his interrelations with the objective world that is alien to him: with nature, with society, the family, God, and his own 'I'. Everything that deprives man of his liberty and depersonalizes him is inimical to man. All these alienating forces which transform man into a mass being, deprived of individuality, are presented by those who write about them as all-encompassing. These forces take in all classes and all systems, despite the fact that socialist philosophers and sociologists prefer to make an exception for a socialist society. In reality, *homo sovieticus*, spiritually and culturally robbed by the state, is defenceless against cruelty, greed, and hypocrisy, the qualities of which Marx wrote in connection with alienation in a capitalist society and which flourish to this day in socialist society. And if we take into account the fact that in the phenomenon of alienation there intersects a whole series of human psychological conditions, such as fear, despair, and isolation, then socialist society has here, too, broken all records. The viruses of fear, sown by Stalin, have produced such irreversible changes in the organism of socialist man that the condition of inner division, of alienation from oneself, has long since become the norm. Homelessness, unemployment, poverty, ideological and religious persecution – all these have ceased to be the monopoly of the capitalist society.

It is not surprising, therefore, that the notion of alienation has become pervasive in modern sociological, philosophical, and literary discourses and practices. What constitutes the peculiar nature of alienation in Brodsky's poetry is the fact that he makes language part of estrangement, part of the break-up of meaning and communication. As we have seen in the previous chapters, he transmutes man, thing, and word into a state of alienation, using it as a kind of tool for organizing the formal structure of his poetry. In Brodsky, alienation becomes not only content, but form as well. The word is simultaneously estranged from what it denotes and from its semantic essence. An example of this is the alienation of the verb 'said' in the poem 'Gorbunov and Gorchakov'. This allows for the signified and the signifier to be described in an estranged way, in the hope of illuminating the common origins of alienation. The very essence of alienation is transformed by the poet into a means of cognizing the phenomenon of alienation. The alienation of consciousness, language, and creativity from being is, in Brodsky, the theme and method of description of spirit and matter.

As has already been shown in the preceding chapters, the process of reification of all aspects of human activity has in Brodsky the character of a poetic *dominanta*. Things are not so much opposed to man as directly identified with him. This is realized first of all by a whole variety of semantic transformations in the tropes: the de-animation of the animate and the personification of the inanimate world. Several goals are thereby simultaneously attained. Apart from purely poetic objectives, i.e. renovation of old tropes and the creation of new ones, ethical interests are also pursued. By illuminating the depths of alienation, the poet activates our consciousness towards seeking the means of overcoming this negative fact of our time. If he cannot overcome it himself, then he at least neutralizes alienation by according equal rights to the material and the spiritual.

The establishment and reinforcement of the links between ethics and aesthetics constitute one of the fundamental features of Brodsky's work:

we've all been led into a trap, a mental trap, by our civilization. We've all been told by our mother, or nurse, or someone, that life ought to be good, that man is good, that good triumphs over evil, that the big grey wolf never comes. So when we're confronted by something nasty, our initial response is that there must be some mistake – either we've made it, or better still someone else. It would be much better for mothers to tell children that there's a 50 per cent chance of a big grey wolf coming – and that he will look like us.[7]

The poet assumes the responsibility of showing us mercilessly the presence of the evil of alienation both around us and within us. On the other hand, the source of defence against evil also lies within us. For the essence of man consists in his consciousness. Only he himself can make sense of his own existence and purge it of all forms of evil by any means at his disposal: ethical, aesthetic, religious, or political. The poet believes in the last least of all. He said of himself in one of his youthful poems: 'I seek. I make of myself / a man' (*C.* 71). However, he who has sought and found knows that all serious quests lead a man to the path of solitude: 'Solitude teaches the essence of things, for their essence / is solitude' (*Ч.* 101). And in this, perhaps, lies the impossibility of solving the problem of alienation – having overcome one form of alienation, man creates another, more dangerous one. Neither human relations, nor faith, nor creativity is free of this dual nature of alienation.

Poetry itself is its own kind of alienation, for it is the exteriorization of one's own 'I', the objectification of the poet's emotions and thoughts. In this sense any work of art, once finished, is alienated from the creator, irrespective of whether or not it has become a product to be bought and sold on the market: it no longer belongs to its author. Likewise, it is not subject to censorship nor to the tastes of the readers. Clearly, an awareness of the potential for independent life of the work of art has dictated Brodsky's half-humorous encouragement to his students, frozen in silent uncertainty when faced with a new poem by Rilke, Miłosz, or Pasternak which the poet has proposed for analysis: 'Say what you like – nothing will happen to the poem.'[8]

By way of illustrating the alienation of the work from its creator, it is interesting to give a detailed reading of one of Brodsky's poems from the cycle 'A Part of Speech', which was written during 1975–6. The very title of the cycle is a type of linguistic alienation, the dismemberment of language into parts of speech which, on the one hand, expresses the fragmentation of the experience of the world by twentieth-century man, and, on the other, the poet's alienation from language. Operating within what is the most god-like in man – language – the poet, forcibly wrenched from his linguistic environment, submits to an extreme form of alienation from his gift. The efforts expended on overcoming this type of alienation are not, perhaps, within the compass of everyone. In the following poem, alienation is not only the theme but the very essence of the poem, as the poet, with no little success, imparts to the poem itself the qualities of alienation:

Тихотворение моё, моё немое,
однако, тяглое – на страх поводьям,
куда пожалуемся на ярмо и
кому поведаем, как жизнь проводим?
Как поздно заполночь ища глазунию

луны за шторами зажжённой спичкою,
вручную стряхиваешь пыль безумия
с осколков жёлтого оскала в писчую.
Как эту борзопись, что гуще патоки,
там ни размазывай, но с кем в колене и
в локте хотя бы преломить, опять-таки,
ломоть отрезанный, тихотворение?   (Ч. 88)

My quiet creation, my dumb one, / nonetheless, a draught horse to the terror of the bridle, / where can we lodge a complaint against our yoke, and / to whom can we tell the way we spend our life? / Like searching way beyond midnight for the fried egg of / a moon behind the shutters with lighted match, / you brush off, with your hands, the dust of insanity / from the splinters of a yellow grin on writing [paper]. / However much you spread this scribble that is thicker than treacle, / with whom to break on the knee, and on the elbow, once more, / this apportioned slice, my quiet creation?

Here once more we witness the activation of the content on the level of formal structures. The grammatical composition of the poem is highly idiosyncratic. The three sentences thematically reflect the three stages of interrelation between creator and creation. In the first sentence, the unity of the poet and his work is expressed. Their common orphanhood is underlined by syntactic parallelism and by the verbs of the first person plural: 'куда пожалуемся . . . кому поведаем, как жизнь проводим?' ('where can we lodge a complaint . . . to whom can we tell the way we spend our life?). The second sentence, strictly speaking, is not grammatically independent, but is a forcibly wrenched-away subordinate clause of the first. The form of the verb, the second person singular *стряхиваешь* ('you brush off'), breaks the syntactic and psychological parallelism and indicates the poet's isolation. It acts as a formal basis for considering this sentence a separate one. But this disruption is forced and unexpected. In this stanza-sentence is conveyed the culminating moment of the work: the 'insane' poet seeks the moon behind the shutters with the help of a lighted match, and brushes 'the dust of madness' on to a paper. Two genitive metaphors of comparison, of the moon with a fried egg, and the state of insanity with dust, are supported by an infringement in the grammar. In the lines 'вручную стряхиваешь пыль безумия / с осколков жёлтого оскала в *писчую*' ('you brush off, with your hands, the dust of insanity / from the splinters of a yellow grin on *writing*'), the defined word, 'paper', is omitted after the definer, 'on writing'. The metaphor *the dust of insanity* substitutes for inspiration or the state of the creative act, which is an extremely lonely process. The idea of considering inspiration, religious and creative, as insanity was common even in Ancient Greece. The metonymy which replaces the person, *с осколков жёлтого оскала* (*from the splinters of a yellow grin*), is also imbued with the semantics of insanity, which is implied in the colour yellow and in the semantics of the word 'splinter'.

This state is also reflected in the rhyme system. The first four lines have alternating feminine rhymes (*ABAB*), and the remainder are dactylic. These lamenting rhymes seem to suggest that he who experiences pain has three choices – to scream, to weep, or to write poetry. The dactylic rhymes are also retained in the last four lines, which depict the decline of the creative process and the culmination of alienation. We have before us once more two entities, as in the first stanza: the poet and his creation. But this is no longer 'my quiet creation', but an 'apportioned slice', 'this scrawl that is thicker than treacle'. The alienation is also expressed syntactically, by the choice of a concessive construction of a coordinated structure, which usually expresses the quantitative character of limit: 'Как эту борзопись . . . там ни размазывай, но с кем . . . хотя бы преломить. . . ('However much you spread this scrawl . . . with whom to break . . .').

Alienation is also expressed on the level of the compound rhymes: *немое / ярмо и* ('dumb' / 'yoke and'); *в колене и / тихотворение* ('on the knee and' / 'quiet creation'), which are formed at the expense of the non-coincidence of the syntactic and poetic articulation. On the phonetic level, the harmony of vowels and consonants in the first stanza, *моё, моё немое* ('my', 'my dumb one'), gives way to assonances and alliterations: *осколков, оскала, поздно заполночь, за шторами, зажжённой, жёлтого, безумия, борзопись* ('splinters', 'grim', 'way beyond midnight', 'behind the shutters', 'lighted', 'yellow', 'insanity', 'scrawl'). In this way, the rhymes, the syntax, the tropes, the composition of the poem, convey and create the idea of the poem and its formal structure. The poem opens and closes with an authentic *tour de force*: a word *tikhotvorenie*, an abbreviation of *stikhotvorenie* ('a poem'), is formed from the root *tikho* ('still', 'quiet') combined with *stikh*, meaning 'verse', and *tvorenie* ('creation', 'work'). This is one of Brodsky's very few neologisms, as if to show that he is quite capable of creating them, although they are not one of his favourite devices. Thus dumb, quiet creation has turned out to be very daring, a draught horse galloping away from the poet to 'the terror of the bridle' and bearing within itself 'heavy, like chains, feeling, thoughts' (*O.* 24). Hence an apparent contrast in meaning between the first and the last lines: 'Тихотворение моё, моё немое' ('My quiet creation, my dumb one'), and 'ломоть отрезанный, тихотворение' ('the apportioned slice, my quiet creation'). In Russian, the word *немое* ('dumb') also carries an intimation of estrangement, for if divided into its two constituent syllables – *не мое* – it means 'not mine'. The same effect is produced by the inversion contained in both lines. The poet, as it were, starts by persuading himself that the poem is his (*моё, моё немое*), even though it is not really; but in the end it becomes what it is – cut off, no longer his. This colloquial expression, 'apportioned slice', is a periphrasis for the poem; its very essence is a cliché and is transformed by its mere proximity to the author's masterpiece, the 'quiet creation'. Such deliberate mingling of the prosaic and the poetic, the low and the high, lends Brodsky's poem flexibility and not infrequently saves it from hermeticism. By naming the work he has created in silence and solitude with the phrase-cliché 'apportioned slice', the poet offers it for general use. Anyone may slake his spiritual thirst by reading it. And this is indeed the paradox of alienation: in maiming one person, it cures another. The poet's personal experience, his most treasured thoughts and feelings, once objectified in the word, are immediately alienated. And by passing into the hands of the reader they enrich his inner world and, *ipso facto*, protect him against other types of alienation.

The creative process itself is no less a paradox. It is the collocation of the ineffable and what is expressed. In the very conventionality of poetry, in its limited means of expression, there is something that is unlimited and absolute. In this sense, poetry is not only alienation, but also the means of overcoming it. That is why poetry, alongside religion and culture, is proposed by Brodsky as an aesthetic and ethical value which diminishes the effect of alienation. Through poetry the reader finds new contacts with his inner world, finds in it new reserves for the cognizance of the profundity of alienation which exists in the world. Even this cognizance, in itself, the poet insists, is a form of neutralizing alienation.

Fond as he is of paradoxes, Brodsky did not miss the chance of creating yet another paradox. Having declined in his own time to fulfil any 'social demand' in his beloved fatherland, for which he was deprived of the cup at today's feast, he, 'having sampled / two oceans and continents' (Ч. 104), realized that poetry in our times cannot afford to free itself from attending to the problems of humanity. Poetry has an ethical demand: a productive orientation of the personality in our dismembered and dispirited world. He is convinced that 'poetry deals with more essential things than does any other kind of communication. Its job is to provide for people the proper scale of their lives. Only a poet can do this. Philosophers, perhaps, but they use so many words.'[9] Furthermore, in specific socio-cultural conditions, poetry is the sole spiritual support of man. Poetry, along with memory and faith, is proposed by the poet as a means of defence against a force which is no less awesome than alienation, namely time.

Man against time and space

человек есть конец самого себя
и вдаётся во Время.[10]

From Aristotle to Einstein, the category of time has been regarded as something fundamental and unavoidable. Nevertheless, philosophers who have studied the nature, structure, and measurement of time frankly admit that 'for all that science or philosophy have to offer in the way of illumination, time remains profoundly enigmatic'.[11] Following St Augustine, some of them could well repeat: 'What is time then? If nobody asks me, I know: but if I were desirous to explain it to one that should ask me, plainly I know not.'[12] Newton-Smith observes that many definitions of time, either in terms of causation and consciousness or as 'the number of motion' (Aristotle) and 'continued duration', are circular: 'we are accounting for the obscure notion of time in terms of the equally if not more obscure notion of instants, moments, durations'.[13]

Time, involved as it is in the very structure of space, motion, human consciousness, and all changes in the universe, has bewitched not only the philosophers and physicists but writers as well. In Likhachev's view, 'literature to a greater extent than any other art, is becoming the art of time. Time is the object, subject and instrument of representation'.[14] By the instrument of representation, Likhachev has in mind language itself, the rhythm of its words, their phonetics, pauses, the extent of the spoken and written in time. St Augustine named the poetic line as one means of measuring time: 'Thus measure we the spaces of the staves of a poem, by the spaces of the verses; and the spaces of the verses, by the spaces of the feet; and the spaces of the feet, by the spaces of the syllables; and the spaces of long syllables, by the spaces of short syllables. I do not mean measuring by the pages; for that way we should measure places, not time'.[15]

Brodsky, in speaking of the extent to which time permeates all of Mandelstam's poetry, highlights precisely the linguistic-poetic aspect of time: 'It is better, then, to speak not about the theme of time in Mandelstam's poetry, but about the presence of time itself, both as an entity and as a theme, if only because time has its seat within a poem anyway, and it is a caesura' (L. 125).

Time also exists in an artistic work as a compositional and organizing component: the sequence of temporal segments, the perception of their duration, the repeated motifs which, as Bakhtin has observed, are 'by their nature part of the chronotopos'[16] – these are merely some of the self-evident and inevitable means of time's participation in the structure of poetry and prose. But time is also the object of representation. Imitating life, the author conveys the passage of time, he depicts changes in man and his surroundings. In this process, the author pinpoints various types of time – subjective, objective, historical, or biographical, and all these in various combinations.

No less often, time can be the subject of a literary work, a *dramatis persona*. We encounter this kind of instance in Brodsky's poetry. By his own admission, the category of time is one of the central, if not the central, theme of his work: 'I dare to say I write exclusively about one thing: about time and what time does to a person.'[17] In order to show what time does to a person it proved necessary to switch their subject–object roles. In Brodsky's poetry, time not only dons the mask of things, not only sends its metonymic representatives (evening, day, night), but also appears in all its own awesome splendour as a subject of the action:

> а Время
> взирает с неким холодом в кости
> на циферблат колониальной лавки (Ч. 29)

and Time / gazes, with a little cold in its bones, / at the dial of the Colonial store.

пряча лицо, но спиной пленяя,
Время выходит из волн, меняя
стрелку на башне – её одну.   (*Ч*. 41)

concealing the face but captivating by its back / Time emerges from
the waves changing / the clock hand on the tower – just one clock
hand.

'The Guest of Time' began to visit Brodsky from 1961: 'A guest is
coming to see me, / he is coming from the future time' (*C*. 118).
Since then, this guest has become a fixture in Brodsky's poetic
home, as it were, and has required his host to serve and glorify him.
In Brodsky's work, as in Khlebnikov's, we encounter the most
multifarious aspects of the problem of time. And although
Brodsky, unlike his celebrated predecessor, the 'King of Time' as
his friends called Khlebnikov, does not concern himself with the
enumeration of the numerical laws of historical time, he does, like
Khlebnikov, attempt to make sense of the very essence of time.
The paradoxicality of his many definitions of time, the contradictory semantics of his images of time, in which time now comes
close to, now is directly identified with, darkness, light, cold, dust –
all this makes difficult any interpretation of the poet's conception
of time, and so, too, the very possibility of assigning it to any one
of the existing theories of time.

The poet's personal time is conditioned by the antinomy of the
past and future. As such, it may be inscribed in historical time. The
time of the lyrical 'I' correlates now with historical characters, as,
for example, in the 'Imperial' poems, now with the extra-temporal
semantics of mythic heroes ('Aeneas and Dido', 'Odysseus to
Telemachus'). Personal time, which is sometimes made the title of
a poem ('Christmas 1963', 'The Fifth Anniversary', 'Verses on the
Winter Campaign 1980'), can be inscribed in the history of the
country. The many references to other cultures discussed earlier
can also be interpreted as the poet's attempt to establish 'a link
between times' (*L*. 143). Brodsky also touches on the ontological
character of time. The statement 'Time is created by death' (*K*. 59)
was formulated by him as early as 1969. This aphorism contains a
hint at the fact that our conception of time would be different in
principle were we immortal. Time would merge with eternity, while
a man would remain identical with himself. But inasmuch as man
combines within himself the spiritual and corporeal, the immortal
and ephemeral, life itself is a form of time. Beyond time nothing

exists, and time itself is conditioned by material processes. Inasmuch as there is no time beyond the world, and there is no world beyond time, Brodsky continues his quest for time, which constitutes a part of the 'central drama of the characters of the twentieth century'.[18] The very fact of the transition of man and things from being to non-being does not give him rest.

The most interesting action of time is realized in the system of Brodsky's tropes, in which time is completely substituted for by its attributes. Thus things, which can be regarded as masks for time, threaten to assimilate man to themselves. The action of time is associated now with the image of scissors, which cut out emptiness for the poet and all of us (Ч. 116); now with dust, into which, in the final analysis, everything and everybody will turn, for 'dust is the flesh / of time, flesh and blood' (К. 110); now with noughts (О. 174); now with a piece of grey rag (Ч. 69). No less frequently, time is associated with cold. The most consistent identification of time and cold is realized in a poem of 1980, whose title contains a reference to Virgil: 'Fourth Eclogue (Winter)'. The poem opens with an epigraph from Virgil's 'Fourth Eclogue': *Ultima Cumaei uenit iam carminis aetas; / magnus ab integro saeclorum nascitur ordo* ('Now the last age of Cumae's prophecy has come; / The great succession of centuries is born afresh').[19] Virgil's 'Fourth Eclogue' was written circa 40 BC, and has been the subject of much debate concerning the identity of the child in the Cumaean Sibyl's prophecy. But Brodsky's echo of the Latin poet is contrastive. If Virgil sings of the rebirth of a Golden Age, in all probability the age of Christianity, then Brodsky warns us of the onset of a glacial epoch:

> Жизнь моя затянулась. *В речитативе вьюги*
> обострившийся слух различает невольно *тему*
> *оледенения.*   (У. 118)

My life has dragged on. *In the snowstorm's recitative /* the straining ear involuntarily makes out *the theme / of the ice age.*

This theme may be read both metaphorically and literally. The sub-title 'Winter' requires a direct reading, as does the key lexis of the Eclogue: winter, snow, snowstorm, the severe harsh frost, cold hard frost, the cold 'descending from heavens on a parachute' (Ч. 121). A figurative and broader understanding of the theme is suggested by the tropes. Cold, one may say, is the principal *dramatis persona* of the poem. It is directly identified with time in the copula-metaphor in the fifth part:

> *Время есть холод.* Всякое тело, рано
> или поздно, становится пищею телескопа:
> остывает с годами, удаляется от светила.　　　(*У.* 119)

Time is cold. Every body, sooner / or later, becomes food for a telescope, / grows cold with the years, moves away from the luminary.

In the metaphors of identification, time is most commonly objectified: *Time is the meat of a dumb Universe* (*У.* 122). In this metaphor, we can detect a paraphrase of the Marxist definition of time as a form of existence of matter. It is worthy of note that Brodsky uses the most apodeictic metaphors of the grammatical structure *A is B* for the expression of his conception of time. By treating time as cold, he emphasizes the ontological unity of being of man and the earth:

> Сильный мороз суть откровенье телу
> о его грядущей температуре
>
> либо – вздох Земли о её богатом
> галактическом прошлом, о злом морозе.　　　(*У.* 118)

A strong frost is a revelation to the body / of its future temperature // or – a sigh of Earth for its rich / galactic past, for the severe frost.

The theme of glaciation has yet another aspect – the ideological – which is emphasized in the poem of the same year, 'Verses on the Winter Campaign 1980':

> Новое оледененье – оледененье рабства
> наползает на глобус.　　　(*У.* 99)

A new ice age – the ice age of slavery / is creeping across the globe.

If the end of slavery in Europe coincided with the onset of the Christian era, does not the emergence of slavery of a new type signal the end of this era? A similar question, the reader will recall, was put by Brodsky as early as 1966, in the poem 'A Halt in the Wilderness':

> К чему близки мы? Что там, впереди?
> Не ждёт ли нас теперь другая эра?

What are we close to? What's there, up ahead? / Doesn't a new age await us?

The echo of Blok which was discussed in the second chapter is intensified in the 'Fourth Eclogue':

> Как знать, не так ли
> озирал свой труд в день восьмой и после
> Бог?   (У. 119)

Who is to know, wasn't that how, / on the eighth day and after, / God looked upon his labour?

God, who is transposed to the following line, is estranged from his labour, alienated from his creation, by the two thousand years of Christian history. The alienation of man from God and his teaching is conveyed in the 'Eclogue' by metonymic representation of man: instead of the whole personality we are presented with parts of man – a yawn, an eye, brains, fingers, voice, look, expiration, inhalation. A new meaning is lent to these metonymic representatives of man, to his body as part of a more complex whole. If in other poems the technique of *pars pro toto* serves as an expression of man's alienation from his physical 'I', then in the 'Fourth Eclogue', the human body is the sole defence against the cold of time:

> Жизнь моя затянулась. Холод похож на холод,
> время – на время. Единственная преграда –
> тёплое тело. Упрямое, как ослица,
> стоит оно между ними, поднявши ворот,
> как пограничник держась приклада,
> грядущему не позволяя слиться
>
> с прошлым.   (У. 120)

My life has dragged on. Cold resembles cold, / time resembles time. The only barrier – / is the warm body. As stubborn as a she-ass / it stands between them raising its collar, / like a border guard holding the butt of a rifle / not permitting the future to merge // with the past.

This additional ethical meaning does not diminish the poet's profound philosophical pessimism. Nor does the lyrical note which bursts through the 'recitative of the snowstorm':

> Чем больше лютует пурга над кровлей,
> тем жарче требует идеала
> голое тело в тряпичной гуще.   (У. 120)

The more the snowstorm rages above the roofs / the more ardently the naked body in the ragged thicket / demands the ideal.

The lyricism is, however, immediately stifled by the estranged metonymy, 'the body', instead of the lyrical 'I', and by the deliberately 'prosaic' rhymes: *лягушки* / *гуще* ('frogs' / 'thicket'); *одеяло* / *идеала* ('blanket' / 'ideal').

Time in the 'Fourth Eclogue' is subjected to various transformations in the tropes and figures of speech. It is personified in the metonymy 'night':

> Ночь входит в город, будто
> в детскую: застаёт ребёнка под одеялом;   (*У.* 118)

Night enters the city as if it / were a nursery: finds the child under the blanket

and in the simile *Время глядится в зеркало, как певица* (*У.* 120) ('Time looks in the mirror like a singer'). In metaphors, it is identified with the basic components of human existence – light, water, sleep, space:

> Сухая, сгущённая форма света –
> снег – обрекает ольшаник, его засыпав,
> на бессонницу, на доступность глазу
>
> в темноте.   (*У.* 118)

A dry, condensed form of light – / snow – condemns the alder thickets, by covering it, / to sleeplessness, to accessibility to the eye // in the darkness.

As Virgil does in his Third and Fourth Eclogues, Brodsky alternates personal time and ontological, consciously placing side by side the physical and metaphysical:

> Там, где роятся сны, за пределом зренья,
> время, упавшее сильно ниже
> нуля, обжигает ваш мозг, как пальчик
> шалуна из русского стихотворенья.   (*У.* 120)

There, where dreams swarm, beyond the boundaries of sight, / time, falling sharply lower than / zero, scorches your brain, like the little finger / of the naughty boy in the Russian verse.

In this stanza from the fifth part of the 'Eclogue', there are at least two intertextual links: one with Pushkin – 'The naughty boy has frozen his little finger' (*Eugene Onegin*, chap. 5, II, l. 12) – the other, 'beyond the boundaries of sight', resonates with Brodsky's own poem of 1975, 'Lagoon':

> Там, за нигде, за его пределом
> – чёрным, бесцветным, возможно, белым –
> есть какая-то вещь, предмет.					(*Ч.* 43)

There, beyond nowhere, beyond its boundary / – black, colourless, possibly white – / there is a thing, an object.

Into this region beyond the boundary of sight, beyond nowhere, 'where it's possible for thought but not the eye to dwell' (*Ч.* 43), the poet constantly attempts to penetrate. All that he 'sees' there is this ideal of Kazimir Malevich – 'white on white', or the 'hare's dreams' of Khlebnikov (1. 221), that is, light, snow, cold, time in its pure form:

> Вас убивает на внеземной орбите
> отнюдь не отсутствие кислорода,
> но избыток Времени в чистом, то есть
> без примеси вашей жизни виде.					(*У.* 122)

What kills you in extraterrestrial orbit is / really not the absence of oxygen / but an excess of Time in its pure form, that is / minus the admixture of your life.

Brodsky knows full well that time cannot exist without matter and that there is no time in its pure form, which is why he makes the reservation 'minus the admixture of your life'. Equally, this is why he is convinced that there is some kind of thing there, an object. If it is stars, then you can't make them out in daylight, the 'white ones on white'; if they are angels, then they too are invisible. In order to discern these last, man must look upwards more often and with faith:

> В феврале чем позднее, тем меньше ртути.
> Т.е. чем больше времени, тем холоднее. Звёзды
> как разбитый термометр: каждый квадратный метр
> ночи ими усеян, как при салюте.
> Днём, когда небо под стать известке,
> сам Казимир бы их не заметил,
>
> белых на белом. Вот почему незримы
> ангелы. Холод приносит пользу
> ихнему воинству: их, крылатых,
> мы обнаружили бы, воззри мы
> вправду горе́, где они как по льду
> скользят белофинами в маскхалатах.					(*У.* 121)

In February the later it gets the lower the mercury. / I.e. the more time, the colder it is. The stars / are like a broken thermometer: every square metre / of night is sown with them, like at a salute. / During the day when the sky looks like slaked lime / Kazimir himself would not notice them, // white on white. That's why angels are / invisible. The cold is useful / to their host: the winged ones / we would have noticed them if we looked / up in truth, as they skate / like White Finns in their white camouflage.

The comparison of angels with the Finnish soldiers who fought against the Soviet army on the ice of the Gulf of Finland during the Russo-Finnish War of 1940 once more hints at the onset of the age of slavery and the threat to Christianity as the materialistic ideology of the Empire spreads. In likening angels to man, the poet attempts to look at the world from their point of view, but, unlike their view, man's is limited not only by his brows, but also by the duration of his life.

Man is given the possibility of widening his horizons, of lengthening the radius of his purview by the word through the 'all-seeing eye of words' (*K.* 81). Language, be it a private voice, or the voice of the Muse, or the Cyrillic script, can protect man against the coldness of Time:

> Зубы, устав от чечётки стужи,
> не стучат от страха. И голос Музы
> звучит как сдержанный, частный голос.
>
> Так родится эклога. Взамен светила
> загорается лампа: кириллица, грешным делом,
> разбредаясь по прописи вкривь ли, вкось ли,
> знает больше, чем та сивилла,
> о грядущем. О том, как чернеть на белом,
> покуда белое есть, и после.   (*У.* 123)

The teeth exhausted from their tap dance in the cold / do not clatter with fear. And the voice of the Muse / resounds like a restrained, private voice. // That's how an eclogue is born. Instead of a luminary / a lamp lights up: the Cyrillic [letters], (sinful matter) dispersed across the writing at random / know more than that Sybil / about the future. About how to blacken on the white / while white exists, and after.

Such an ending for the 'Fourth Eclogue' from a poet with a Christian world-view is its own kind of answer to the pre-Christian author of the 'Fourth Eclogue'. Faith in God's Word is more powerful than faith in the prophecy of the Sybil. The reference to God himself (Part III) and to angels (Part IX) give the 'private' voice of the Muse and the Cyrillic letters this supplementary sense. We may interpret the domination of the present tense in the poem as an attempt to unite beginnings and endings in the word, this hypostasis of God on earth. Of the 88 verbs in the poem, 75 are in the present tense, that is, 85.5 per cent. Of the remaining 14.5 per cent that are in the past tense, 4 verbs are in the subjunctive mood, e.g. 'Kazimir would not notice them', 'we would have noticed'; these actions are possible, not real. Other verbs in the past tense are imbued with the semantics of the present tense. For example, the thrice-repeated recitative, 'My life has dragged on', signifies that it is still continuing. The semantics of the remaining past-tense verbs either signify a proposition ('wasn't that how, / on the eighth day and after, God looked upon his labour?'), or they are weakened by an indefinite subject: someone, something. Among the verbs of the present tense, we may equally trace a variety of semantic fields. Some of them reflect the continuous present, the habitual: 'Night enters the city', 'snow condemns the alder thickets, by covering them, / to sleeplessness'. The semantics of the surrounding words also either indicate a repeated action, as for example, 'The north . . . repeats to you all life long one and the same thing'; or else a present which is receding into the past: 'in the conversation about death place is playing a more and more important part than time' (У. 123).

Assigning this semantic role to the present tense in the 'Fourth Eclogue' is further justified by the fact that Brodsky interprets the temporal triad very individually. In his work, of the three components of the temporal order, the present is usually entirely absent, or else is reduced to the minimum interval, as, for example, in the sixth part of the 'Eclogue' quoted above, where the future is separated from the past only by the ending of one stanza and the beginning of another, as if to indicate that the duration of the present is equivalent to the duration of the interstrophic interval. In the poem 'Butterfly', the present of a man's life is seen as the fine boundary between the past and the 'coming time', as Brodsky prefers to call the future. Both at one end recede into eternity, and, at the other, squeeze the present like a vice. We may suppose that it is precisely this interpretation that engendered the comparison with prison: 'seeming prison, / the suffocation, / of the past and the future' (*Ч.* 36). In whatever direction the door of the present is opened, it opens into eternity, into nothingness. The past cannot be returned to, the present is unstoppable, while the future encroaches on us with every second: вздрогнув, себя застаёшь в грядущем (*Ч.* 65) ('having started, you find yourself in the future'). This three-faced image of time of 'an astronomical hue' passes through us, moving 'horizontally from Tuesday to Wednesday' (*Ч.* 9), ever in one direction, and transforming us 'into something elongated, like a horse's head' (*Ч.* 89), and into 'future molluscs' (*Ч.* 99). This essentially Bergsonian idea of uni-directional time is conditioned by the fact that on-going physical processes are irreversible.

In Brodsky we can clearly trace a different evaluation of past and future. If his personal past is somewhat romanticized, in that the best part of his life is connected with it, then the historical past is identified with culture. 'In itself,' writes Ivanov, 'an orientation to the past unites cultures of all types.'[20] The future, in reverse, is associated with negative emotions, for it inevitably brings destruction and death: 'The future is a form of darkness' (*K.* 76), where 'a thing acquires not zero, but Chronos' (*K.* 106). It is precisely this destructive feature of time that metaphors of reification are called upon to convey. In attributing the qualities of things to man and his intellectual and spiritual activity, the poet, as it were, imitates the action of time itself:

то Времени, невидимые прежде,
в вещах черты
вдруг проступают, и теснится грудь
от старческих морщин; но этих линий –
их не разгладишь, тающих, как иней,
коснись их чуть. (*K.* 65)

the previously invisible features of Time / in things / suddenly appear, and the chest is oppressed / with the wrinkles of age; but those lines – / you will not smooth them out, melting like hoar frost, / if you scarcely touch them briefly.

The poet himself gives a somewhat different explanation for his preference for the past over the future: 'looking backward is more rewarding than its opposite. Tomorrow is just less attractive than yesterday. For some reason, the past doesn't radiate such immense monotony as the future does. Because of its plenitude, the future is propaganda. So is grass' (*L.* 7). The future is seen by the poet in the contrasting black and white tones of the atomic mushroom, or in the grey colours of the dispirited mass of philistines who are occupied with the material improvement of their private lives. In connection with this, the future seems to him a post-Christian world. Clearly, this is why more and more often 'speech flows from under the pen / not of the future, but of the past' (*K*. 56).

If man possessed an organ for the perception of time, he would notice that into the unstoppable flow of time-eternity are drawn both things and people, and language, which in metaphors is imbued with qualities of both. Mandelstam, in speaking of Dante's metaphors, expressed the proposition that they signify 'the standing-still of time'.[21] Brodsky's metaphors signify the movement of time. They convey that time is unavoidable, it is impersonal and indifferent to man. Our power over it is as nothing. Knowing these truisms, the poet does not offer time Tsvetaeva's challenge: 'Time, I'll pass you!' (III. 75). But Brodsky does something else, 'seizing power over time' (*C*. 205). He objectifies time itself in his metaphors: 'Hammering nails / into past, / into present / into future times' (*C*. 73) as if into a wall, whence has emerged the metaphor *на стену будущего* (*Ч*. 77) (*on to the wall of the future*). However, in reifying time, Brodsky is aware that he cannot alter its nature, for time in its essence is inseparable from the thing, from space, which, in their own turn, do not exist without one another: 'A thing is a space, beyond / which there is no thing' (*K*. 111). In this metaphor, in fact, Wittgenstein's idea is expressed: 'Each thing is, as it were, in a space of possible states of affairs. This space I can imagine empty, but I cannot imagine the thing without the space.'[22]

Space, which exists in Brodsky's poetry as an inalienable part of time – space geodesics – is not imbued with such a complex structure as time. Rather, his conception is deliberately simplified:

"Время больше пространства. Пространство – вещь.
Время же, в сущности, мысль о вещи.
Жизнь – форма времени.   (*Ч*. 106)

Time is bigger than Space. Space is a thing. / Time, though, in essence, is a thought about a thing. / Life is a form of time.

This same idea is repeated in the prose, with the elucidation: 'space to me is, indeed, both lesser and less dear than time. Not because it is lesser but because it is a thing, while time is an idea about a thing. In choosing between a thing and an idea, the latter is always to be preferred, say I' (*L*. 435).

Being a thing, space is often personified by Brodsky: *пусть Время взяток не берёт – / Пространство, друг, сребролюбиво?* (*К.* 57: *though Time doesn't take bribes – / Space, friend, is fond of money!*); *Покуда Время / не поглупеет как Пространство / (что вряд ли)* (*Ч.* 95: *Until Time / does not grow as stupid as Space / (which is unlikely)*). But transformation of meaning in Brodsky's tropes, as we have seen many times, is always moving in two opposite directions. By personifying time and space, Brodsky brings them closer together, as it were. On occasion, almost in correspondence with the theory of relativity, Brodsky uses spatial terms when describing time:

> С точки зрения времени, нет "тогда":
> есть только "там". И "там", напрягая взор,
> память бродит по комнатам в сумерках, точно вор, (*Н.* 140)

From time's point of view, there is no 'then': / only 'there'. And 'there', straining its eyes, / memory prowls about rooms at dusk like a thief.

The spatial adverb 'there' substitutes for the past. In this, we can discern a similarity with the Futurists' conception of time, which was formulated not without the influence of Einstein's theory of relativity, if their fundamentally different interpretation of the present does not contradict this. For the Futurists the present was multilayered. It could accommodate both the past and the future. Jakobson has written of the transformation in Khlebnikov of the present into the sole temporal reality.[23] In Smirnov's view, Khlebnikov's numerous palindromes are directly linked to his conception of time: 'The palindrome signifies the reversal of time in the space of text; in the syntagmatics of the work time flows not only from beginning to end, but in the opposite direction as well; thereby its unidirectionality is neutralized, and is overcome.'[24] In Brodsky, as we discussed earlier, the present is given infinitesimally small significance. It is either not referred to at all, or else it is immediately shifted into the past:

> И подковы сивки или каурки
> в *настоящем прошедшем*, даже достигнув цели,
> не оставляют следов на снегу. Как лошади карусели.
>
> (*У.* 75–6)

And the horse shoes of the dark grey or the light chestnut, / *in the time that it is now passing*, even having reached their goal, / leave no traces on the snow. Like horses on a merry-go-round.

The illusory nature of the present is emphasized either by the semantics of the context, or by the ironic tone, or else by enjambement:

> настоящее в чёрном пальто, чей драп,
> более прочный, нежели шевиот,
> предохранял там *от будущего и от*
> *прошлого* лучше, чем дымным стеклом – буфет.   (*H.* 140)

> *the present in a black overcoat*, the cloth of which / is more durable than cheviot, / protected there *from the future and from* / *the past* better than the buffet by its smoked glass.

Are we not dealing here with yet another of Brodsky's paradoxes: if the past is no more, and the future does not yet exist, while the present is illusory – where, then, is time? Once more, the answer is given in metaphors: time is within ourselves, in the things which surround us, for time is an attribute of being. In his fear of this unseen and elusive entity, man mythologizes time. The ominous, almost mythic image of time with a capital letter is constantly encountered in Brodsky's poetry: 'Время / варварским взглядом обводим форум' (*У.* 112: 'Time. / with a barbarian glance encompasses the forum'). This image of time 'in the form of its own kind of verbal statue, like the statue of Chronos, who devours his own children',[25] for whom 'senility and youth are indistinguishable' (*У.* 167), is opposed by two forces – the image of Creator-Donor and the image of creativity, that is, language. They are constantly present in Brodsky's poetry, if not always in the foreground, as time, then in the background, as forces which neutralize the destructive action of time. He believes that a 'rhyme-mite will pass through Lethe' (*K.* 19), while emptiness which 'is worse than Hell' (*Ч.* 9) is acceptable 'once it is Yours' (*У.* 116).

The tragic pathos of Brodsky's poetry can be felt in his attempt to overcome time and alienation by faith and creativity, and in his awareness of the illusory nature of this attempt. Hence the conflicting image of man in the face of time and space. On the one hand, man is doomed to time, he is 'the end in himself / and flows into Time' (*Ч.* 109). This pessimistic aspect of man is intensified, since for contemporary man such concepts as culture and faith have lost their value. On the other hand, the idea of personality in Brodsky is constantly linked with the problem of historical memory. Man's consciousness is conditioned by language and culture. Both in their own turn are linked with faith. It is worthy of note that all three forces that man has at his disposal to deal with time encompass all three aspects of time. Memory, as the receptacle of the past, that is, the history of mankind, helps man to realize himself as a part of civilization, prepares him for his present life and the future:

> Помни, что прошлому не уложиться
> без остатка в памяти, что ему
> необходимо будущее.   (*У*. 84)

Bear in mind that the past would not fit / into memory without something being left over, that it / needs a future.

Faith illuminates man's path both in the present and the future, which, according to one of Brodsky's definitions, 'is a form of darkness, / comparable with nocturnal rest' (*K*. 76). (There will be a further discussion of faith below.) Creation, which takes place in the present, is based on the culture of the past and includes memory and faith. In its turn, memory, cultural and religious, includes the word as well. As Ivanov observes, the idea of a link between time and memory is itself an ancient one: 'It was embodied in the mythology of Ancient Greece, where the goddess Mnemosyne simultaneously had charge of memory and the passage of time, with which Chronos was later to be concerned.'[26] Mnemosyne appears in Brodsky's poetry in the poem 'Verses in April' (*O*. 136) in her two hypostases at once: as the goddess of memory and time, and as the mother of the nine Muses. The collocation of time and the Muse is seen even earlier, in a sonnet of 1964–5:

> Ты, Муза, недоверчива к любви,
> хотя сама и связана союзом
> со Временем (попробуй, разорви!).
> А Время, недоверчивое к Музам,
> щедрей последних, на беду мою

You, Muse, have no trust in love, / though yourself bound in union / with Time (try to break it!). / But Time, having no trust in the Muses, / is more bountiful than the latter, to my cost.

In Brodsky, the Muses embody language, for the poet the sole reality which embodies all others. In poetry all three forces – memory, faith, and language – are intimately interwoven by means of metaphors, by their polyvalence.

Millennia passed away before man found these forces for overcoming death and time:

Up to a point, all human culture remains a protest against death and destruction, against increasing disorder or the increasing uniformity of entropy. To the extent to which the reality of this threatening destruction increases so should the forces opposite to it become more and more significant. In this lies the principal explanation of the role allotted to the problem of time in contemporary culture, in particular, in art.[27]

In Brodsky's view, 'the only instrument that a human being has at his disposal for coping with time is memory' (*L*. 62).

Credo quia absurdum est

Но пока мне рот не забили глиной,
из него раздаваться будет лишь благодарность.[28]

God, either named or unnamed, has existed in Brodsky's poetry from the very earliest poems. He continually inquires, either naively ('O, God, what moves the world?', *C*. 51), or more intricately ('Who was that jeweller, / who brow serene,/ drew in miniature / on those wings that world, / which drives us mad, / and holds us in its pincers?', *Ч*. 34). It is precisely the presence of God that gives Brodsky's poetry its profound ethical meaning. At the same time, he is sufficiently sensitive not to touch upon religious themes too frequently, not to take the name of God in vain.

In our analysis of such poems as 'A Halt in the Wilderness' and 'Nunc Dimittis', we saw that Brodsky has long been driven to the source of faith. 'Conversation with a Celestial Being' (1970) also deals with spirituality, the essence of faith, the surmounting of alienation through memory, faith, and language. To understand this poem, a discussion of which constitutes the last part of this chapter, we must briefly identify Brodsky's philosophical links.

Indirectly, and sometimes directly, Brodsky's thought lies in the orbit of the ideas of Kierkegaard and Shestov. This is borne out by a poem of 1963, 'Isaac and Abraham', dedicated to the sombre 'riddle of life, given to Abraham by God',[29] over which Kierkegaard agonized in his book, *Fear and Trembling*: 'when I have to think of Abraham, I am as though annihilated. I catch sight every moment of that enormous paradox which is the substance of Abraham's life, every moment I am repelled, and my thought in spite of all its passion cannot get a hair's-breadth further. I strain every muscle to get a view of it – that very instant I am paralyzed.'[30] In striving to unravel this paradox, Kierkegaard glorifies Abraham, who managed to estrange himself not only from the ethical, but from reason itself, managed to 'plunge confidently into the absurd'.[31] This ability to believe when the reason insists it is not possible, the ability to disregard the final end, constitutes a spiritual act of faith in Kierkegaard's system of things.

In his poem, Brodsky alters the perspective of perception in his search for ways of making sense of Abraham's story. The son, not the father, is placed at the centre of the narrative. Just as Abraham trusts God, so Isaac trusts his father. After reading the poem, we begin to surmise that perhaps the secret of God's sombre riddle has long lain on the surface, which is why Kierkegaard did not notice it. After all, all that God demanded of Abraham was what He would have to do Himself – to offer his own son as a sacrifice of faith.

But in essence, during the 1960s Brodsky had still not parted with the basic tenets of the existential philosophy of Kierkegaard and Shestov. Thus, after the trial and northern exile, he had to agree with them that the point at which, on the evidence of experience and reason, all possibilities end and man hits the wall of the impossible, is where true existence begins. Brodsky is sincerely grateful to Fate for making him a convict and not a soldier of the Empire. His life experience and personal philosophical inclinations forced him to assimilate the basic tenets of Shestov's teaching. Man exists, thinks, and feels and must exist in a chasm, over the abyss, without guarantees, without protection, without any certainty that tomorrow will dawn.[32] Hence Brodsky's almost masochistic calls to God in 'Conversation with a Celestial Being':

> Ну что же, рой!
> Рой глубже и, как вывранное с мясом,
> шей сердцу страх пред грустною порой,
> пред смертным часом.
> Шей бездну мук,
> старайся, перебарщивай в усердьи!　　(*K*. 65)

Well, then, dig! / Dig deeper and, as if from the flesh, / sew fear to the heart before the melancholy time, / before the hour of death. / Sew abyss of torment, / strive, let your zeal be boundless!

For Brodsky, an almost stoical resistance to all life's calamities forms the structure of the human soul. Without doubt, this conviction was inspired by his reading of Kierkegaard: 'Only he who has reached the extreme of terror awakens in man his supreme being', notes Kierkegaard in his diary.[33] From this position there emerges in Kierkegaard and Shestov the primacy of faith over knowledge, the absurd over meaning, irrationalism over reason. Perhaps for those for whom 'despair, like a knife, splits the soul in two like a board' (*O.* 185) there remains no option but to 'burst out from the power of the rational and to seek truth in what everyone has become accustomed to consider paradoxical and absurd'.[34] Faith in reason, in Shestov's view, is man's greatest misfortune, as reason is powerless to discover the secret of being. 'What we consider the truth, what we get by our ratiocination turns out to be, in some sense, incommensurate not only with the external world into which we have been plunged since birth, but also with our own inner experiences.'[35]

Brodsky's difference with Kierkegaard and Shestov begins precisely at this point. While not relying on unlimited trust in reason, Brodsky does not feel revulsion from it either. Like Kierkegaard, he does not lack 'the courage to think a thought whole'.[36] But unlike both of them, Brodsky is of the view that only after an idea has been thought through to its logical conclusion may we plunge into the absurd, and not blindly à la Kierkegaard, but with open eyes. The more reason assists us to be conscious of the absurdity of faith, the stronger that faith is. For him, reason and faith are not mutually contradictory. On the contrary, almost following Tixeront, the interpreter of St Augustine, in his *intellige ut credas*, *crede ut intelligas* ('understand in order to believe, and believe in order to understand'),[37] Brodsky frequently uses rationalism to become convinced of the insolubility of the *veritates aeternae*. Through all his poems runs the idea of the absurdity of seeking earthly goods, of the impossibility of keeping anything forever to protect oneself against the cold of alienation. Only a deeply believing person can accept with gratitude all the losses and sufferings which fall to his lot:

> Там, наверху . . .
> услышь одно: благодарю за то, что
> ты отнял всё, чем на своём веку
> владел я. Ибо созданное прочно,
> продукт труда
> есть пища вора и прообраз Рая,
> верней – добыча времени: теряя
> (пусть навсегда)

что-либо, ты
не смей кричать о преданной надежде: (*K*. 64–5)

'There, up above ... / hear just this: I give thanks that / you have taken away everything I possessed / in my lifetime. For what is created well, / the product of labour, / is food for a thief and the prototype of Paradise, / or rather – the spoils of time: losing / (let it be for ever) // something, you / do not dare to scream about betrayed hopes.

There are two years ahead of him before, as if by a sword, 'the best part of life was cut away' (*Ч*. 27) by the horizon of exile, but Brodsky already thanked God for his past and future losses. And after he has lost what was most important – his country, his parents, and his son – he grows to a truly Christian thought: 'Only the degree of loss / makes the mortal equal to God' (*Ч*. 27). We find an analogous idea in Shestov, albeit in a rather different context: 'Only he who has lost everything himself – only he may go to the people as equal to equal.'[38] After the loss of everything, a man can see and hear anew, Shestov insists.

The next departure from Kierkegaard and Shestov begins to be apparent as a result of the quest for something solid and unchanging instead of the ephemeral and transitory, which is 'the booty of Time'. But surely only the Spirit, a profoundly divine category, does not imply the participation of time? What differences could there really be here? Kierkegaard finds his stability, 'the ground under his feet', precisely in faith and in his, deeply personal, experiences. However, Kierkegaard's paradox consists in the fact that, by accomplishing an unusually 'bold onslaught against reason' and logic, by offering a challenge to all ancient and modern philosophy in his counterposing of Abraham and Job to Plato and Hegel, Kierkegaard came to doubt everything except the most central thing – God. Kierkegaard tirelessly repeats that in order to find faith one must repudiate reason, writes Shestov.[39]

The paradox of Shestov himself consists in the fact that, while protesting against all whole philosophical systems, in which everything is explained and all has been explained, Shestov himself explains everything with the help of groundlessness, to which everything is reduced and which gives unity to his *Weltanschauung*. It is striking how rationally Shestov struggles against rationalism, what deep meaning he finds in meaninglessness, what firm ground his groundlessness acquires.

In Brodsky's case, his tendency to go to the extreme limits in his
doubts, quests, and evaluations leaves no room for any exceptions.
In his poetry, reason terrorizes the soul, the emotions, and language, forcing the last to surpass itself. It is precisely through the
test of language and by language that Brodsky finds the ground
beneath his feet in the situation of existential catastrophe – emigration. Finding himself in a socio-psychological vacuum, he came to
the conclusion that the process of survival as a poet outside his
language and people depended on himself alone: 'if a poet cannot
endure the experience of exile he should not shift the blame for his
defeat on circumstances; simply he deserved precisely what he
got'.[40] For him a life which does not have a 'nether abyss', 'an abyss
of torment', that is a life deprived of the deepest dimensions, is
unthinkable. Surely it is from this that the comparison between
himself and Christ comes, as well as the almost blasphemous
declaration that he would have behaved differently on the Cross:

> Там, на кресте
>
> не возоплю: "Почто меня оставил?!"
> Не превращу себя в благую весть?
> Поскольку боль – не нарушенье правил:
>   страданье есть
>   способность тел,
>   и человек есть испытатель боли.
> Но то ли свой ему неведом, то ли
>   её предел.   (*K.* 63)

There, on the cross // I shall not cry out, 'Why hast Thou forsaken
me?!' / I shall not transform myself into glad tidings! / Inasmuch as
pain is not a breaking of the rules: / suffering is / a faculty of bodies /
and a man is an endurer of pain. / But either his limits are unknown
to him or / the limits of pain.[41]

This is the most ambiguous stanza of the whole poem. How are we
to explain this declaration, which is so strange to the usual Christian
way of thinking? It is possible, of course, that there is no direct
parallel here with Christ, but merely a recognition that such a fate
has not been given to him. But even the grammar of the stanza
contradicts this: 'I shall not cry out', as well as the phrase which
precedes 'There, on the cross': 'I don't give a damn about camouflage.' Moreover, in the poem 'Gorbunov and Gorchakov' we also
discover a parallel with the situation of Christ and Judas, in which

Gorbunov, the poet's *alter ego*, clearly associates himself with the image of Christ. In Canto XIII, Gorbunov commits no less a blasphemy, in saying:

> о чём бы и была моя мольба?
> Для слышати умеющего краше
> валов артиллерийская пальба,
> чем слёзное моление о чаше.   (*O.* 214)

And what would my prayer be about? / For he who can listen / the artillery fire of waves is sweeter / than a tearful prayer about this cup.

to which Gorchakov responds: 'But that is a sin!' (*O.* 215). Sin or not, the motif of lonely stoical resistance to all the terrible ordeals of life is characteristic of many of Brodsky's poems.[42] We may also interpret the eighth stanza of 'Conversation with a Celestial Being' as a metaphor, in the sense that it concerns not a physical crucifixion but a figurative one. The poet was figuratively crucified at the shameful court of the Soviet Empire for the same reason as Christ was physically crucified by the Roman Empire – for the Word.

And the Word is present in 'Conversation' from the first to the twenty-eighth and last stanza:

> Здесь, на земле,
> где я впадал то в истовость, то в ересь,
> где жил, в чужих воспоминаньях греясь,
> как мышь в золе,
> где хуже мыши
> глодал петит родного словаря,
> тебе чужого, где, благодаря
> тебе, я на себя взираю свыше,   (*K.* 61)

Here, on earth / where I have fallen sometimes into zealotry, sometimes into heresy, / where I have lived, warming myself on other's memories, / like a mouse in the ashes, / where worse than a mouse / was gnawing the breviary of my native vocabulary, / which is alien to you, where, thanks to you, / I observe myself from on high.

'The breviary of his native vocabulary' is indeed the solitary resource which the poet grasped, gnawing into it like a mouse. The comparison with a mouse immediately supplies several types of interconnections. The meek are with God, thanks to whom man is able to distance himself from himself and look at himself from above, from God's point of view. Relationships with people once more express orphanhood and alienation, and relations with language, as always, are faithful to the point of fanaticism. Through language the image of the mouse is also associated with the Muse, or more precisely with the myth of Apollo, for whom Smintheus assumed the form of a mouse.[43] The reference to the Apollo spring, the Castalian spring in the form of the metonymy 'Castalian moisture', is present in the second stanza. In the same stanza, there is a quotation from Pushkin's 'Prophet', which implicitly points to the link between the poet and God through language. God's emissary, who appears to the poet-prophet in the desert, instructs him:

> Восстань, пророк, и виждь и внемли,
> Исполнись волею Моей,
> И, обходя моря и земли,
> Глаголом жги сердца людей.

Arise, prophet, and see and hear, / Fill yourself with My will, / And, going round the seas and lands, / Burn the hearts of people with your word.

Brodsky complains that the times have changed, or else people have become indifferent to poetry, or they have grown tired of listening to prophets:

> уже ни в ком
> не видя места, коего глаголом
> коснуться мог бы, не владея горлом,
> давясь кивком
> звонкоголосой падали, слюной
> кропя уста взамен кастальской влаги,
> кренясь Пизанской башнею к бумаге
> во тьме ночной,   (*K.* 61)

no longer / seeing a spot where I might touch anyone / with words, not in control of my throat, / choking with a nod / of the ringing/ voiced carrion, with saliva, / instead of Castalian moisture, sprinkling my lips, / listing like the leaning tower of Pisa towards the paper / in the darkness of the night.

The indifference of the reading public or its absence is, undoubtedly, of concern to the poet, although it is not fatal. Let the throat (voice) refuse to obey, but it does not grow silent, as is indicated by the metaphor-rhyme *глаголом* / *горлом* ('with words' / 'throat'). The poet finds opportunities to nurture his Muse, if not from the spring of Apollo, then from the language of the people. Inaccessible to the people (his poetry is banned), the poet sustains a one-way link with it by frequently using popular expressions. Thus *падаль* ('carrion') signifies a seriously ill person, one almost on his death-bed. He is forbidden to moisten his lips with the life-giving 'Castalian moisture'; he is obliged, as Christ did with vinegar, to sprinkle his lips with his own saliva, to choke himself with his own nod. This nod may be deciphered as the resigned acceptance of all that is happening and continued service to the Word of God. It is precisely the service to the Word which holds the poet in the position of the leaning, but not falling, Tower of Pisa in the spiritual darkness of the atheistic Empire. The deliberately understated tropes of this stanza also bear witness to the poet's resignation.

There is also evidence of the religious roots of the poetry in the next stanza. In it is expressed the conviction of the young Brodsky, uttered by him to the face of the Soviet judge Savelyeva, that the gift of the poet, his intensified feeling for language, stems from God:

тебе твой дар
я возвращаю – не зарыл, не пропил;
и, если бы душа имела профиль,
ты б увидал,
что и она
всего лишь слепок с горестного дара,
что более ничем не обладала,
что вместе с ним к тебе обращена.   (*K.* 61)

to you, your gift / I return – I haven't buried it or drunk away; / and if the soul had a profile / you would have seen / that even it / is only a mould of a grievous gift, / it possesses nothing more than that, / together with it is turned towards you.

This stanza contains a quotation from Plotinus, for whom Brodsky had some enthusiasm even in the 1960s:

The soul or mind reaching towards the formless finds itself incompetent to grasp where nothing bounds it or to take impression where the imprinting reality is diffuse; in their dread of holding to nothingness, it slips away. The state is painful; often it seeks relief by retreating from all this vagueness to the reign of sense, there to rest as on solid ground, just as the sight distressed by the minute rests with pleasure on the bold.[44]

The poetic gift, therefore, is realized by Brodsky as a means of giving form not only to the formless, to chaos, but to the soul itself as well. The existence of the Celestial Being lays a particular responsibility on the use of this gift. Admitting his powerlessness to 'burn the hearts of people with his word', the poet set himself the rule not to complain to the Celestial Being about his fate; to ask nothing of him and refuse nothing, seeing in this the virtual ideal of inner freedom:

> Не стану жечь
> тебя глаголом, исповедью, просьбой,
> проклятыми вопросами – той оспой,
> которой речь
> почти с пелён
> заражена – кто знает? – не тобой ли;
> надёжным, то есть, образом от боли
> ты удалён. (*K.* 62)

I will not burn / you, with words, with a confession, with a supplication, / with the accursed questions – that smallpox / with which speech, / almost from the cradle, / is infected – who knows? – perhaps by you; / that is to say, by that sure means, you are distanced from pain.

One of the oppositions of the first three stanzas, between mortal man and the healing Spirit, is given a supplementary aspect which is developed in the already-quoted eighth stanza. If the Spirit is distanced from pain in a reliable way, then 'man is an endurer of pain'. Brodsky had written earlier of pain and suffering being an unavoidable condition of human existence. In particular, this idea runs insistently through the poem 'Gorbunov and Gorchakov': 'стрелы всех / страданий жизни собрались, как в призме, / в моей груди?' (*O.* 182: 'the arrows of all / the sufferings of life gathered, as in a prism, / in my breast'); 'Отчаянье раскраивает мне, / как доску, душу надвое, как нож, но' (*O.* 185: 'despair, like a knife, splits my soul in two like a board, but'). In the same poem, the contradictory effect of pain on man is also spoken of: 'Pain will smash pride,' Gorchakov asserts. 'Not in the slightest,' Gorbunov disagrees, 'pain has watered the tree of pride' (*O.* 182). And if the reader should begin to suspect that perhaps the poet's stoical position is sustained by the pride of pain rather than faith, then he should re-read the third canto of 'Gorbunov in the Night':

> А ежели мне впрямь необходим
> здесь слушатель, то, Господи, не мешкай:
> пошли мне небожителя. Над ним
> ни болью не возвышусь, ни усмешкой,
> поскольку он для них неуязвим. (*O.* 185)

And if I really need / a listener here, then, O Lord, don't delay: / send me a celestial being. Over him / I will not raise myself either by pain or a smirk, / since he is not vulnerable to them.

Another interesting idea in the fourth stanza, that language itself is infected, as if with smallpox, by the 'accursed questions', is developed further in 'Butterfly': 'all God's creatures, / as a sign of kinship / are given a voice, for / communication, for singing: for stretching out a second, / a minute, a day' (*Ч*. 35). Thus, language is programmed with the insolubility of the unchangeable and unsolvable truths. Man is endowed with the gift of speech, not with the aim of solving their mysteries, perhaps, but of communicating with them. Gorbunov also spoke of this:

> Ибо чувствую, что я
> тогда лишь есмь, когда есть собеседник!
> В словах я приобщаюсь бытия!
> Им нужен продолжатель и наследник!   (*O.* 199)

For I feel, that I / only am when there is an interlocutor! / In words I partake of being! / They need a successor and heir!

They equally need a listener. In the Celestial Being the poet finds the ideal listener who never interrupts the speaker. Without waiting for answers, the poet does not curse the Celestial Being; he is almost sure that he does not have any ready answers. Such an interpretation is hinted at by a rhyme-metaphor from 'Nature Morte': *нет / ответ* ('no / answer'), placed in Christ's lips:

> Не стану ждать
> твоих ответов, Ангел, поелику
> столь плохо представляемому лику,
> как твой, под стать,
> должно быть, лишь
> молчанье – столь просторное, что эха
> в нём не сподобятся ни всплески смеха,
> ни вопль: "Услышь!"   (*K.* 62)

I will not await / your answers, Angel, inasmuch as / with a face so poorly visualized / as yours, must be / only silence its match, / silence – so spacious that neither / the splash of laughter / nor the wail: 'Hear!' / will be honoured with an echo.

In this stanza, there is a further allusion to the tenth canto of 'Gorbunov and Gorchakov', where a definition of silence is given through a whole series of metaphors of identification: *Silence is the future of the days . . . Silence is the future of the words . . . Silence is the future of love ... Silence is the present for those, / who lived before us (O.* 206). Life itself is defined as 'a conversation in the face of silence' (*O.* 206). There is also a reference to Pushkin's poem 'Echo': 'И шлёшь ответ: / Тебе же нет отзыва ... Таков / И ты, поэт!' ('You send an answer, / But there is no reply ... Such / are you too, poet!').

All these and other numerous references and allusions to other poets, and in particular to Brodsky's own poetry, sound like an echo of a confession which no one has heard. Brodsky considers poetry to be a very lonely activity. 'The more often a poet takes this next step the more isolated a position he finds himself in' (*L.* 187). Not counting on being heard by anyone, accepting silence as the norm, almost spurred on by it, the poet continues his meditation:

> Вот это мне
> и блазнит слух, привыкший к разнобою,
> и облегчает разговор с тобою
> наедине.
> В Ковчег птенец
> не возвратившись, доказует то, что
> *вся вера есть не более, чем почта*
> *в один конец.*   (*K.* 62)

It's just that / that seduced my ears, accustomed to discord, / and makes conversation with you easier / and private. / The small bird, / not returning to the Ark, proves that / *all faith amounts to no more than / a one-way correspondence.*

It's as if Brodsky, like Shestov, is of the view that the task of poetry (and of philosophy) is 'not to reassure but to disturb people'.[45] The definition of faith as a one-way correspondence is not very reassuring at first sight. But in the light of all that has been said, it is highly logical: I believe, despite the fact that I hear no answers to my requests and pleas; I believe, despite reason and my experience of life; I believe, because it is absurd. *Credo quia absurdum est* is one of Shestov's most cherished *dicta*. It is interesting that both come to the same conclusion, Shestov by unmasking reason and Brodsky by following reason to the furthest limits in his doubts and re-evaluations of commonly accepted philosophical and theological premises.

Stanzas IX, X, and XI develop the theme of 'here, on earth' – the theme of the dead-end and pitch darkness in which man is doomed to live given his powerlessness to solve the mysteries of existence. They are impenetrable for him, which is hinted at by the rhymes for 'earth': *на земле – в золе* ('on earth' – 'in ashes'); *на земле – во мгле* ('on earth' – 'in darkness'); *на сопле – на земле* ('on snot' – 'on earth').

> Здесь, на земле,
> все горы – но в значении их узком –
> кончаются не пиками, но спуском
> в кромешной мгле,
> и, сжав уста,
> стигматы завернув свои в дерюгу,
> идёшь на вещи по второму кругу,
> сойдя с креста.
>
> Здесь, на земле,
> от нежности до умоисступленья
> все формы жизни есть приспособленье.
> И в том числе
> взгляд в потолок
> и жажда слиться с Богом, как с пейзажем,
> в котором нас разыскивает, скажем,
> один стрелок.
>
> Как на сопле,
> всё виснет на крюках своих вопросов,
> как вор трамвайный, бард или философ –
> здесь, на земле,
> из всех углов
> несёт, как рыбой, с одесной и с левой
> слиянием с природой или с девой
> и башней слов!   (*K.* 63)

Here, on earth, / all mountains – in the narrow sense – / end not with a peak but with a descent / into pitch darknes, / and compressing the lips, / wrapping the stigmata in sackcloth, / you encounter things in the Second Circle, / having descended from the cross. // Here, on earth, / from tenderness to delirium, / all forms of life are an adaptation. / This includes / the stare at the ceiling / and the urge to merge with God, as with the landscape, / in which, let us say, one bowman seeks us out. // As if on snot, / everything hangs on the hooks of its own questions / like a tram thief, a bard, or a philosopher – / here, on earth / from all corners / it stinks of fish, from the right and from the left, / of the merger with nature or with a virgin / and with the tower of words!

The poet does not attempt to reduce the complexity of the 'accursed questions' to an apparent solution of them. Thus he deliberately leaves unfinished the definition: 'all forms of life are an adaptation'. One wonders to what? – to death, fate, time, to the categorical imperative? After all, behind the 'Second Circle' lurks not only Dante, but also Kant, in whose opinion the universe is supported on inevitability and on self-propulsion around a circle. The paradox consists in the fact that, whatever object we suggest for the predicate 'to adapt', adaptation in itself denies free will and freedom of choice, of which Brodsky gives such a spiritual defence in his essays. The poet could respond to our bewilderment by saying that there is the freedom of youth and the freedom of maturity. There is the desire to be free of swaddling bands and to gain freedom of movement. This is freedom from something. But there is also freedom for something. Christ said: 'Thou shalt know the truth and the truth shall make thee free.' It is this ineradicable desire to know the truth that obliges the poet to question, resorting now to zealotry, now to heresy, self-contradiction, having recourse to the absurd; and, if necessary, to befriend death, to merge with time.

And all the same, any adaptation is an acknowledgement of the power of necessity to which, perhaps, even God himself must submit. And here, once more, Brodsky shows himself to be the pupil of Shestov, in whose opinion God himself, having once given orders, was later obliged to obey his own orders: 'The will to action which He once manifested has forever exhausted His creative energy and now He is doomed, on the equal footing with the world He created and everything to be found in the world, merely to carry out the instructions, albeit His own, but which are now forever inviolable.'[46] Is this not, then, the reason that 'here, on earth' answers to the 'accursed questions' have still not been found, that man 'as it were is finally and forever cut off from the sources and beginnings of life'? This leads Shestov to the idea that 'either in the world itself not everything is well, or else our approaches to the truth and the demands made on it have some sort of defect at their very root'.[47] Yet one more paradox consists in the fact that, while insisting on the insolubility of the eternal truths, both philosopher and bard continue to inquire; also the universe maintains its silence.

The theme of the dead-end almost always entails the theme of time. Metaphors which substitute for time, either reifying or personifying it, are littered throughout the whole poem: 'I, *from the bottomless Mozer's dishes / stuffed myself with the soup of minutes*'(*K.* 64); 'There are no such embraces that do not part / like *hands [of a clock] at midnight*' (*K.* 64); 'For what is created well, /

the product of labour, / is . . . *the spoils of time*' (*K.* 64). The as yet 'unseen features of Time in things' (*K.* 65) appear so often in Brodsky's poetry that he feels the need to dispel possible accusations that he is possessed not only by the desire to 'merge with nature, with a virgin and with the tower of words', but also with time:

> Ты за утрату
> оразд всё это отомщеньем счесть,
> моим приспособленьем к циферблату,
> борьбой, слияньем с Временем – Бог весть!
> Да полно, мне ль!
> А если так – то с временем неблизким,
> затем что чудится за каждым диском
> в стене – туннель. (*K.* 65)

You are inclined / to think that this is all my vengeance / for my loss, / my conformity to the clock-face, / my struggle, my merger with Time – God knows! / Come on, that's not for me! / And if that is how it is – in a distant time / because, as it seems, behind each dial / in the wall is a tunnel.

This stanza, in essence, is as much about time as it is about the overcoming of time by creativity, which is a tunnel into the future through the darkness of the ages. The idea of fusing with time is thought through to its logical conclusion in the next stanza, where it sounds like an aphorism:

> Но даже мысль о – как его? – бессмертьи
> есть мысль об одиночестве, мой друг. (*K.* 65)

But even the thought of – what's it called! – immortality / is a thought about solitude, my friend.

The intrusion of the colloquial ejaculation 'what's it called!' into such a lofty thought about immortality not only expresses the poet's embarrassment but is also a device characteristic of Brodsky's poetry, namely, the estrangement of lofty themes by deflation of the 'high style'. It is as if he always stumbles, unsure of himself, when he is carried away into lofty spheres.

If creativity will indeed bring immortality to the poet, then it will only be in a distant time, at a cost of suffering and loneliness during his own lifetime. In 'Conversation with a Celestial Being', we again encounter this existentialist idea of the identification of creativity with pain, suffering, and the absurd; in essence, with the components of faith:

И, кажется, уже
не помню толком

о чём с тобой
витийствовал – верней, с одной из кукол,
пересекающих полночный купол.
Теперь отбой
и невдомёк,
зачем *так много чёрного на белом?*
Гортань исходит грифелем и мелом,
и в ней – комок

не слов, не слёз,
но странной мысли о победе снега –
отбросов света, падающих с неба –
почти вопрос.   (*K.* 67)

And, it seems, already / I can't follow the sense / of what I've been
eloquent about / with you – / or rather with one of the dolls, / cross
cutting the midnight cupola. / Now it's time to stop / and ignorance /
why *so much black on white?* / The larynx turns into a slate pencil and
chalk / and in it there is a clod, // not of words, not of tears, / but a
strange thought about the triumph of snow – / light's garbage which
falls from the sky – / almost a question.

This reduction of God's gift to 'black on white' was made earlier:

сумма страданий даёт абсурд;
пусть же абсурд обладает телом!
И да маячит его сосуд
чем-то чёрным на чём-то белом.   (*K.* 33)

the sum total of suffering gives the absurd; / let this absurd possess
the body! / Let its vessel loom / *with something black on something
white.*

In placing the main accent on suffering, a basically Christian
concept, the poet differs from the priest, in that he overcomes the
absurd not only by faith, but also by creation, by the classical device
of estrangement of the process of creation. This estranged image of
'black on white' is insistently repeated in other poems:

Право, чем гуще *россыпь
чёрного на листе,*
тем безразличнее особь
к прошлому, к пустоте
в будущем.   (*H.* 111)

It's true, the thicker *the deposit / of black on the page,* / the more
indifferent the individual is / to the past, to the emptiness / in the
future.

Does such faith in the power of language not overshadow faith in God? No doubt this is why the poet asks the Celestial Being:

> И в этой башне,
> в правнучке вавилонской, в башне слов,
> всё время недостроенной, ты кров
> найти не дашь мне!   (*K.* 64)

And in this tower, / in the great-granddaughter of the Babylonian, in the tower of words, / forever uncompleted, you will not allow me / to find a shelter!

Feeling that he is acquiring firm ground from 'Roman letters' and 'the brevier of [his] native vocabulary', the poet refuses to accept any kind of well-being. He thanks the paradise-dweller for being exiled from the framework of the Russian language, as his poetry remained unpublished in Russia; that, *ipso facto*, he has not been 'passed to the power of petty forms' of happy existence in his homeland, where, one way or another, all poets are given 'odds'; even when they are persecuted their complexes are indulged, and with time they are all turned into the humiliating phenomenon of market-place popularity:

> Благодарю . . .
> Верней, ума последняя крупица
> благодарит, что не дал прилепиться
> к тем кущам, корпусам и словарю,
> что ты не в масть
> моим задаткам, комплексам и форам
> зашёл – и не предал их жалким формам
> меня ва власть.   (*K.* 65)

I give thanks . . . / Or rather my last crumb of intellect / gives thanks, that you didn't allow me to stick / to those dwellings, frameworks, vocabulary / that you did not follow suit / my inclinations, complexes, didn't give odds / and didn't pass me to the power of / their petty forms.

On the other hand, the image of black on white forms a parallel to one of the central oppositions of the poem – darkness and light. In the very nature of this opposition lies a paradox – one cannot exist without the other. They form a *sui generis* closed circle of being itself: faith and lack of belief, good and evil, life and death. The idea of the circle is realized several times in the poem. The last stanza speaks of life and death, of the fusion of the beginning and the end:

Апрель. Страстная. Всё идёт к весне.
Но мир ещё во льду и в белизне.
И взгляд младенца,
ещё не начинавшего шагов,
не допускает таянья снегов.
Но и не деться
от той же мысли – задом наперёд –
в больнице старику в начале года:
он видит снег и знает, что умрёт
до таянья его, до ледохода. (*K*. 68)

April. Holy week. All moves towards spring. / But the world is as yet in ice and whiteness. / And the gaze of the infant, / who has not yet started to walk, / cannot conceive the melting of snow. / And there is no escape / from the same thought – in reverse – / for the old man in the hospital at the year's beginning; / he sees the snow and knows that he will die / before it melts, before the ice breaks.

Death is associated here with the colour white: the old man will die against a background of white snow, this 'light's garbage which falls from the sky' (*K*. 67). With the melting of the snow the black earth will be revealed, onto which a child will step, who will set off around the circle already walked by the old man. But for a long while yet the child will not be able to guess that 'life is bought at the price of the terror of inevitable death'.[48] This payment has already been demanded of the old man.

The idea of the circle is also realized in man's relations with God. Man exists in his mortal body, lives in the memory of posterity and is in God. This circle is closed together by the suffering on the Cross. The opposition 'here, on earth' (stanzas 1, 9, 10, 11, 20, and 25) and 'there, on high' (13, 15) is neutralized by 'there, on the cross' (7, 8), which links them. Christ showed people that God lives in every man and does not exist outside of man. His being in us fills everything with meaning – life, creativity, and time itself.

The poem 'Conversation with a Celestial Being' serves as yet another example of Brodsky's ability to interweave the basic themes of his poetry in the relatively small space of one poem. He is able to condense them into the paradoxical aperçus of metaphors of identification in his attempts to approximate the very bases of being: *the soul . . . is only a copy of a grievous gift; all faith is no more than a one-way correspondence; suffering is a faculty of bodies / and a man is an endurer of pain; the thought of . . . immortality is a thought about solitude.* The similes in the poem are no less unexpected than the other tropes: 'And the taste in the mouth of life in this world / is as if you left your dirty footmarks all over a stranger's flat / and went away' (*K.* 67).

The theme of memory is expressed extremely economically by the joking complaint about the absence of a god of memory in Christianity:

и горько, что не вспомнить основного!
Как жаль, что нету в Христианстве бога –
пуской божка –
воспоминаний, с пригоршней ключей
от старых комнат – идолища с ликом
старьевщика – для коротанья слишком
глухих ночей.   (*K.* 66)

and it's tormenting that one cannot remember the essential! / What a pity that Christianity has no god – even a little one – / of memories with a handful of keys / to the old rooms – an idol with the face / of a rag-and-bone man – for the whiling away of too / lonely nights.

The poem is written in the unusual combination of iambic pentameter (with pyrrhics on the third or, more often, the fourth foot) and iambid dimeter. Twenty-seven of the twenty-eight eight-line stanzas present different rhyme schemes. The most active model is *aBBacDDc*, with the enclosing masculine clausulae: sixteen of the twenty-eight stanzas use it – II–VII, IX–XI, XVI, XII, XXI, XXIII, XXIV, and XXVII. The remaining rhyme schemes have changes either in the first or second part of the stanza: *aBBaCddC* (I, XXV); *AbAbcDDc* (VIII, XVII); *AbbAcDDc* (XII, XIII, XX), *AbbAcDc* (XIV); *aBaBcDDc* (XV, XIX). The last stanza has ten lines (*aaBccBdEdE*). The choice of this metre is not accidental. The short lines create the illusion of breathing spaces from the tyranny of reason for the poet's strained thinking.

Having assimilated Tsvetaeva's 'scholasticism of grief', Brodsky too often listens 'to what he is told by the frightening voice of reason' (*L.* 262). In this process, he is all too well aware that reason's arguments only worsen the position of the sufferer:

The more powerful an individual's thinking, the less comfort it affords its possessor in the event of some tragedy. Grief as experience has two components: one emotional, the other rational. The distinguishing feature of their interrelationship in the case of a highly developed analytical apparatus is that the latter (the apparatus), rather than alleviating the situation of the former, i.e. the emotions, aggravates it. In these cases, instead of being an ally and consoler, the reason of an individual turns into an enemy, and expands the radius of the tragedy to an extent unforeseen by the possessor. (*L.* 261–2)

But, nevertheless, Brodsky seeks answers for the 'accursed questions' in reason no less than in the absurd. And most often he finds them in the Logos. Brodsky is indeed that poet 'who more than most realized that the way to philosophical illumination lies not so much through thesis and anti-thesis as through language itself, stripped of all superfluity'.[49] Brodsky follows this idea to its logical end: if speech is infected with the accursed questions, then the answer must be hidden in language itself. Brodsky's constant preoccupation with language embraces the aesthetic, religious, and philosophical aspects of poetry. The word for Brodsky is the level on which he raises 'the universe on its horn' (*Ч*. 105). It is also a fulcrum. For him, it seems, the opening sentence of the Gospel of St John: 'In the beginning was the Word, and the Word was with God, and the Word was God', has a force which is not metaphorical but axiomatic. In the end, too, there will be the Word; it will not simply be an alienated part of speech or a grammatical abstraction, but will also represent memory, the past, its history and culture. And, finally, it will stand for creativity as a source of immortality. Word just like Spirit exists outside Time. That's why 'Time worships language'. Language worships God. The poet worships both.

Notes

After all, a footnote is where civilization survives.

Brodsky.

PREFACE

1 Brodsky, *Less Than One: Selected Essays* (London, 1986), p. 359. I have deliberately provided footnotes to the epigraphs, as all of them are taken from Brodsky's essays, interviews and poems, in order to indicate the intrinsic link between his poetry and his prose.
2 Eugenio Montale, *Poets in Our Time* (London, 1976), p. 36.
3 Ibid., p. 34.
4 Marina Tsvetaeva, 'Poet i vremia', *Izbrannaya proza v dvukh tomakh* (New York, 1979), vol. I, p. 372.

I. A STEPSON OF THE EMPIRE

1 J. Brodsky, *Less Than One: Selected Essays*, pp. 164–5. Here, Brodsky echoes Auden: 'Biographies of writers, whether written by others or themselves, are always superfluous and usually in bad taste. A writer is a maker, not a man of action. To be sure, some, in a sense all, of his works are transmutations of his personal experiences, but no knowledge of the raw ingredients will explain the peculiar flavour of the verbal dishes he invites the public to taste: his private life is, or should be, of no concern to anybody except himself and his family and his friends.' W. H. Auden, *A Certain World* (London, 1971), p. vii.
2 Brodsky, interviewed by D. M. Thomas, *Quarto*, 24 (December 1981), p. 9.
3 F. Dostoevsky, in *Notes from Underground* (ed. Robert G. Durgy, trans. S. Shishkov (Washington DC, 1969, p. 7) called St Petersburg 'the most abstract and premeditated city on the face of the earth'.
4 Brodsky has also offered his explanations of the flourishing of Russian literature on the shores of the Neva: 'The reason for this sudden outburst of creative power was again mostly geographical. In the context of the Russian life in those days, the emergence of St Petersburg was similar to the discovery of the New World: it gave pensive men of the time a chance to look upon themselves and the nation as though from outside. In other words, this city provided them with the possi-

bility of objectifying the country . . . If it's true that every writer has to estrange himself from his experience to be able to comment upon it, then the city, by rendering this alienating service, saved them a trip', *Less Than One*, p. 79.

5 Brodsky, interviewed by Annie Apelboin, July 1981, Extracts of that interview were published in *Le Monde*, 18 December 1981, p. 21.

6 J. Brodsky, interviewed by Suzanne Massie, *The Living Mirror: Five Young Poets from Leningrad* (London, 1972), p. 223. Brodsky is talking about the Cathedral of the Saviour of Her Imperial Majesty's Transfiguration Battalion, which is situated in the square where the Liteiny Prospect and Pestel Street meet. Brodsky's address was Liteiny Prospect No. 24, Flat No. 28.

7 See the English translation, *The Central Committee Resolution and Zhdanov's Speech on the Journals Zvezda and Leningrad*, Bilingual edition, English translation by Felicity Ashbel and Irina Tidmaksh (Mich., Strathcona, 1978).

8 Mikhail Naritsa, 'Moyo zaveshchanie', *Possev*, 5 (1974), p. 5. On Naritsa, see Yuri Mal'tsev, *Vol'naya russkaya literatura* (Frankfurt am Main, 1976), pp. 40–2.

9 In Etkind's opinion, the preparation for this 'anti-cosmopolitan' campaign began in 1946. See his article, '1946: The Ruin of Hopes', *Vremia i my*, 89 (1986), pp. 173–85.

10 Brodsky, interviewed by Thomas, p. 10.

11 Brodsky, interviewed by Miriam Gross, 'Born in Exile', *The Observer*, 25 October 1981, p. 37.

12 Brodsky, 'A Writer is a Lonely Traveller', *The New York Times Magazine*, 1 October 1972, p. 84.

13 Brodsky, Introduction to Danilo Kis, *A Tomb for Boris Davidovich* (Harmondsworth, 1978), p. xiii.

14 P. Vail and A. Genis, *Sovremennaya russkaya proza* (Ann Arbor, 1982), p. 149. The authors consider that 'the literature of camps has said far more about the victims than the executioners, although it saw its duty as the reverse' (p. 37).

15 Lev Losev, interview with Yury Kublanovsky for the newspaper *Russkaya Mysl'*, 28 July 1983, p. 9.

16 Brodsky, 'Literature and War – A Symposium. The Soviet Union', *The Times Literary Supplement*, 17 May 1985, p. 544.

17 Brodsky, interviewed by Natalya Gorbanevskaya, *Russkaya Mysl'*, 3 February 1983, p. 9. He has repeated this story in the conversation with D. M. Thomas (p. 10) and with S. Birkerts. To the latter Brodsky said that he considered Rein as 'the best poet Russia has today'. 'The Art of Poetry xxviii: Joseph Brodsky', *Paris Review*, 24 (Spring 1982), p. 95.

18 Brodsky, interviewed by Gross, p. 37.

19 Brodsky, interviewed by Thomas, p. 10.

20 Brodsky, interviewed by the author, 20 April 1980 (Ann Arbor, Michigan). A recording is available.

21 Lev Losev, 'Pervyi liricheskii tsykl Brodskogo', *Chast' rechi: Al'ma-nakh literatury i iskusstva*, 2/3 (1981/2), p. 64.
22 Brodsky, interviewed by Thomas, pp. 9–10. The three or four poets Brodsky has mentioned are Yevgeny Rein (1935), Anatoly Naiman (1936) (who was Akhmatova's personal secretary during the last years of her life), both of whom now live in Moscow, and the third one is Dmitry Bobyshev (1936), who has lived in the United States since 1979. It was in fact Rein who introduced Brodsky to Akhmatova.
23 From an unpublished interview by the author.
24 Ibid.
25 Ibid.
26 Brodsky, interviewed by Thomas, p. 9.
27 Brodsky, interviewed by the author.
28 Brodsky, interviewed by Thomas, p. 11.
29 Ibid., p. 9.
30 Mal'tsev, *Vol'naya russkaya literatura*. For the history of *samizdat* in English, see Peter Reddaway, *Uncensored Russia: The Human Rights Movement in the Soviet Union* (London, 1972); M. Meerson-Aksenov and B. Shragin, *The Political, Social and Religious Thought of Russian Samizdat* (Belmont, Mass., 1977); Josephine Woll, *Soviet Dissident Literature: A Critical Guide* (Boston, 1983).
31 This expression belongs to Y. Etkind; see his book, *Zapiski nezago-vorshchika* (London, 1977), p. 354.
32 This 'title' was given to Stalin by his favourite enemy Leo Trotsky, in one of the first interviews to the Western press after he was expelled from Russia to Turkey in 1929.
33 The editor of *Syntax*, Alexander Ginzburg, was arrested after the fourth issue of the journal, tried, and sentenced to five years; he was released in 1971 and emigrated in 1973. The editor of *Phoenix*, Yury Galanskov (1939–72), died in a camp; *Sphinxes* was edited by Valery Tarsis, the author of *Ward 7*. He was allowed to leave the country in 1966. *Boomerang* (1960) was edited by Vladimir Osipov, who was sentenced in 1961 to seven years.
34 'The *Chronicle of Current Events* is one of the most important documents ever to come out of the Soviet Union', writes Peter Reddaway in his introduction: 'An unofficial Moscow journal, its significance can perhaps be compared, in recent years, only with Khrushchev's 'secret speech' of 1956 about Stalin's crimes, or Solzhenitsyn's story of 1962, *A Day in the Life of Ivan Denisovich*, about the Soviet concentration camps.' *Uncensored Russia*, p. 15.
35 Brodsky, interviewed by Gross, p. 39: 'I remember,' he said, 'being absolutely bowled over by Robert Frost. He conveyed a completely new notion of terror. He wasn't a tragic poet ... he was a terrifying poet.'
36 Massie, *The Living Mirror*, p. 222.
37 Brodsky, interviewed by Thomas, p. 9.

38 Ibid.
39 Brodsky, interviewed by the author.
40 O. Mandelstam, 'Word and Culture', *The Complete Critical Prose and Letters*, ed. J. G. Harris, trans. J. G. Harris and C. Link (Ann Arbor, 1979), p. 114.
41 Brodsky, interviewed by the author.
42 Brodsky, interviewed by Thomas, p. 10.
43 Abram Terz (Siniavsky), 'Literaturnyi protsess v Rossii', *Kontinent*, 1 (1974), p. 157.
44 Meanwhile, a poet, Konstantin Kuz'minsky, a connoisseur of poetry, Grigory Kovalev, a writer, Mikhail Kheifets, and others collected everything Brodsky had written before his last arrest. Thanks to them, the first collection of Brodsky's poems appeared in the United States in 1965: *Stikhotvoreniya i poemy* (Inter-Language Literary Associates).
45 'Pesni schastlivoi zimy', afterword by Lev Losev, *Chast' rechi. Al'manakh*, 2/3 (1981/2), pp. 47–68, ed. and pub. G. Poliak (New York).
46 This metaphor can also be found in S. Beckett's *Malone Dies*: 'But I know what *darkness is*, it accumulates, thickens, then suddenly *bursts* and drowns everything.' *The Beckett Trilogy: Molloy. Malone Dies. The Unnamable* (London, 1976), p. 175. This novel is one of Brodsky's favourites, and he probably read it as early as 1961–2.
47 A. Losev, 'Pervyi liricheskii tsykl Brodskogo', *Chast' rechi. Al'manakh*, 2/3, p. 66.
48 S. Dovlatov, 'Kar izdavatsia na Zapade', *The Third Wave: Russian Literature in Emigration*, ed. O. Matich and M. Heim (Ann Arbor, 1984), p. 236.
49 Brodsky, interviewed by James Atlas, 'A Poetic Triumph', *The New York Times Magazine*, 21 December 1980, p. 33.
50 Cited in Etkind's memoir, *Zapiski nezagovorshchika*, p. 151.
51 Khlebnikov defined a police station in one of his poems: 'A station is a great thing! It is the meeting place for me and the state. The state reminds me that it still exists!' *Sobranie sochinenii* (Munich, 1972), vol. v, p. 94.
52 John Green, 'The Underground Life of a Russian Intellectual: Authors in the News – Brodsky', *Biography News*, 1 (1974), p. 61.
53 Brodsky, interviewed by Sven Birkerts, p. 93.
54 Brodsky's translation of Hernández's poem was published in *Zaria nad Kuboi* (Moscow, 1963); and Milan Rakic's poems in *Poety Yugoslavii XIX–XXvv.*, ed. B. Slutsky (Moscow, 1963), pp. 195, 302–3; translations of Gałczyński's poems were published in K. Gałchińsky, *Stikhi* (Moscow, 1967), pp. 70, 106–12, 122–4, 242–4.
55 Losev, 'Pervyi liricheskii tsykl Brodskogo', p. 63.
56 The court proceedings were published in Russian in the West in the almanach *Vozdushnye puti*, 4 (1965), pp. 279–303; in English in *The New Leader*, 31 August 1964, pp. 6–17; and in *Encounter*, vol. 20, no. 9 (9 September 1964), pp. 84–91.

57 N. Mandelstam, *Hope Abandoned: A Memoir*, transl. M. Hayward (London, 1974), p. 377.

58 *Vozdushnye puti*, p. 281.

59 Ibid., p. 303.

60 Brodsky, interviewed by Gross, p. 36.

61 This poem was published in *Kontinent*, 14 (1977), pp. 92–3. Brodsky spells the name of the village 'Norinskaya' as 'Norenskaya'.

62 An English translation of 'The Great Elegy to John Donne' was published in *Tri Quarterly*, 3 (Spring 1965), pp. 87–92; also in *Russian Review*, 24 (1965), pp. 341–53; Italian translation by Giovanni Buttafava in *La fiera litteraria*, 14 (March 1965), pp. 3–4; Polish translation by Józef Lobodovsky in *Kultura*, 3/209 (1965), pp. 30–5.

63 Brodsky's poems, 'The Ballad about the Tugboat' and '13 Points or Verses on Who Discovered America', were published in the children's magazine, *Koster*, 11 (1962). The same magazine in its first number for 1966 published the poem 'In the Middle of Winter' in a somewhat changed form and with a different title, 'January'. The two poems 'Oboz' and 'I obnial eti plechi i vzglianul', saw the light of day in the almanach *Molodoi Leningrad 1966* (Moscow and Leningrad), pp. 120–1. *Den' poezii 1967* included the poems 'Na smert' T. S. Eliota' and 'V derevne Bog...' (Leningrad, 1967), pp. 134–5.

64 G. L. Kline and R. D. Sylvester, 'Brodskii I. A.', *Modern Encyclopaedia of Russian and Soviet Literature*, vol. III (Gulf Breeze, Florida, 1979), pp. 129–37.

65 Brodsky's translation of Donne's poem 'The Apparition' was published in *Renessans. Barokko, Klassitsizm. Problemy stilei v zapadnoevropeiskom iskusstve XV–XVII vekov* (Moscow, 1966), p. 226.

66 Andrei Siniavsky and Yuly Daniel were charged with publishing their 'anti-Soviet' literary work in the West since 1959 under the pseudonyms Abram Terz and Nikolai Arzhak respectively. For a record of their trial, see *Belaya kniga po delu A. Siniavskogo i Yu. Danielia* (Frankfurt, 1967).

67 See Solzhenitsyn's own account of the events between 1961 and 1974 in his book, *The Oak and the Calf: Sketches of Literary Life in the Soviet Union*, trans. H. Willets (London, 1980).

68 N. Gorbanevskaya, *Red Square at Noon* (London, 1972).

69 Brodsky, interviewed by Ian Hamilton for BBC 2 'Bookmark', 2 October 1986.

70 Brodsky, interviewed by Thomas, p. 11; see also 'Poet who sets test for Gorbachov', *The Observer*, 25 October 1987, p. 9.

71 Etkind, *Zapiski nezagovorshchika*.

72 M. Kheifets, 'K istorii napisaniya stat'i: Iosif Brodskii i nashe pokolenie', *Poetika Brodskogo*, ed. Lev Losev (Tenafly, 1986), pp. 230–8.

73 Brodsky, interviewed by Gross, p. 36.

74 Brodsky, 'The Child of Civilization', *Less Than One*, p. 134. Originally, this essay on Mandelstam was written as an introduction to

B. Meares's translation of *Osip Mandelstam: 50 Poems* (New York, 1977), pp. 7–17. Brodsky had formulated the same idea even earlier in 'Notes on Solovyev' ('Zametki o Solovyove', *Russian Literature Triquarterly*, 4, Fall, 1971, pp. 373–5). Speaking of Pushkin's fate, Brodsky wrote: 'The Christian thinker forgets about non-Christian society, about the atmosphere of ignorance and hatred – amongst people, in society, in the demi-monde, in the Tsar's chambers. This is worse than any disgrace and this alone can strike the spark of which Job spoke, but which went unnoticed by the author of the article on "Pushkin's Fate". To put it succinctly, a man who has created a world within himself and who bears this world will sooner or later become an alien body in the sphere he inhabits. And all the physical laws begin to act upon him: compression, displacement, annihilation. Such was Pushkin's fate and he personified it on that cold morning by the Chornaya river' (pp. 374–5).

75 Brodsky, interviewed by Gross, p. 36.
76 Ibid., pp. 39, 41.
77 The first title, 'Joseph Brodsky in Exile', is an article by Susan Jacoby published in *Change*, 5/3 (1973), pp. 58–63. The second is an article-review by Richard Eder, 'Joseph Brodsky in US: Poet and Language in Exile', *The New York Times*, 25 March 1980, p. A2; 'Born in Exile' is an interview by M. Gross; and the last title, 'Conjurer in Exile', is a review of Brodsky's selection of essays, *Less Than One*, by David Bethea, *The New York Times Book Review*, 13 July 1986, pp. 3, 38.
78 Brodsky, interviewed by Ian Hamilton.
79 See, for instance, 'The Art of Poetry xxviii: Joseph Brodsky', by Sven Birkerts.
80 Charles Osborn, *The Life of a Poet* (London, 1980), p. 325.
81 Brodsky, *Selected Poems*, Penguin Modern European Poets (London, 1973), trans. and introd. George Kline, foreword by W. H. Auden, p. 10.
82 S. Spender (ed.), *W. H. Auden: A Tribute* (New York, 1975), p. 243.
83 Birkerts, 'The Art of Poetry', p. 116.
84 Ibid., p. 117.
85 Jacoby, 'Joseph Brodsky in Exile', p. 63.
86 When later (20 May 1987) Yevtushenko was elected to the American Academy of Art and Sciences, Brodsky resigned (20 June 1987).
87 Czesław Miłosz, 'A Struggle against Suffocation', *The New York Times Review*, 14 August 1980, p. 23.
88 A. Kopeikin, 'Zametki o shestoi knige Iosifa Brodskogo', *Kontinent*, 38 (1983), p. 387.
89 These words were torn from the lips of Mikhail Bulgakov by the 'grand inquisitor' Stalin, during a telephone conversation on 18 April 1930: Stalin: 'Perhaps we really should let you go abroad. What is it, have we bored you so very much?' Bulgakov: 'I have thought very much about whether a Russian writer can live outside his motherland, and it seems

to me that he cannot'. Stalin: 'You're right. I don't think so either . . .'
Cited by Ellendea Proffer, *Bulgakov: Life and Work* (Ann Arbor,
1984), p. 322.

90 Brodsky writes about it in his essay, 'A Guide to a Renamed City':
'Unlike both his predecessors and his successors on the Russian
throne, this six-and-a-half-foot-tall monarch didn't suffer from the
traditional Russian malaise – the inferiority complex towards Europe.
He didn't want to imitate Europe: he wanted Russia to be Europe, in
much the same way as he was, at least partly, a European himself.'
Less Than One, p. 72.

91 Brodsky, interviewed by Richard Eder, A2.

92 Steve Aulie, 'Soviets' Suppression of Freedom is Working, Says Exile
Poet Here', *Biography News*, 1 (1974), p. 60.

93 A. Losev, 'Niotkuda s liubovyu . . . (Zametki o stikhakh Iosifa
Brodskogo), *Kontinent*, 14 (1977), p. 323.

94 Brodsky, *V Anglii* (Ann Arbor, 1977).

95 Birkerts, 'The Art of Poetry', p. 124.

96 Ibid.

97 Brodsky, interviewed by D. Savitsky, January 1983 *Emois*, 10 April
1988, pp. 62–3.

98 Henry Gifford, 'The Language of Loneliness', *Times Literary Supplement*, 11 August 1978, p. 903.

99 Brodsky, interviewed by Eder, p. A2.

100 Bethea, 'Conjurer in Exile', p. 3.

101 On Tsvetaeva, Brodsky said in his interview with Sven Birkerts that
she had not only changed his 'idea of poetry, but also . . . perception of
the world . . . I personally feel closer to Tsvetaeva – to her poetics, to
her techniques, which I was never capable of' (p. 104).

102 These are the key statements which are scattered throughout his
prose, see *Less Than One*.

103 Brodsky, 'A Writer Is a Lonely Traveller', p. 78.

104 Brodsky, interviewed by N. Gorbanevskaya, p. 9. This idea of
Brodsky's links up with Mandelstam's remarks 'On the Nature of the
Word': 'Chaadaev, in stating his opinion that Russia has no history,
that is, that Russia belongs to the unorganized, unhistorical world of
cultural phenomena, overlooked one factor – the Russian language.
So highly organized, so organic a language is not merely a door into
history, but is history itself. For Russia, defection from history,
excommunication from the kingdom of historical necessity and continuity, from freedom and theology, would have been defection from its
language.' Mandelstam, *The Complete Critical Prose and Letters*, ed.
J. G. Harris, trans. J. G. Harris and C. Link (Ann Arbor, 1979), p. 122.

2. LONGING FOR WORLD CULTURE

1 Brodsky, *Less Than One*, p. 130.
2 Ibid., p. 30.

3 J. G. von Herder, *Works*, ed. B. Suphan (Berlin, 1877–1913), vol. xiii, p. 4.

4 A. L. Lowell, 'Culture', in *At War with Academic Tradition in America* (Cambridge, Mass., 1934), p. 115.

5 See A. L. Kroeber and C. Kluckhohn, *Culture: A Critical Review of Concepts and Definitions* (Cambridge, Mass., 1952), which contains 164 definitions of culture.

6 This essay was first published in Russian in *Kontinent*, 46 (1985), pp. 6–111, with a slightly different division of 'chapters'. In Alan Myers's authorized translation, we read: 'It is not surprising that the culture we call Greek arose on islands . . . And it is not surprising again that, as its Empire grew, Rome – which was not an island – fled from that culture' (*Less Than One*, p. 410). In Russian, both instances have 'civilization' instead of 'culture'.

7 V. Veidle, 'Iskusstvo pri sovetskoi vlasti', *Mosty* (Munich, 1976), p. 38.

8 Brodsky, *Less Than One*, p. 290. See also Brodsky's introduction to Platonov's *The Foundation Pit* (Ann Arbor, 1973), pp. ix–xii.

9 O. Mandelstam, 'The Word and Culture', *The Complete Critical Prose and Letters*, p. 115.

10 S. Monas, 'Introduction: Friends and enemies of the Word', in *Osip Mandelstam: Selected Essays*, trans. S. Monas (Austin and London, 1977), p. xi.

11 The period known as the 'Silver Age' is usually dated between 1890 and 1917. During this period, creative activity occurred in all spheres of cultural life, which is why it is also called a 'Cultural Renaissance' and a 'new religious consciousness'.

12 Brodsky, 'Beyond Consolation', *The New York Review of Books*, 7 February 1974, p. 14.

13 T. S. Eliot, *Notes towards the Definition of Culture* (New York, 1949), p. 13.

14 N. Mandelstam, *Hope against Hope: A Memoir*, trans. M. Hayward (London, 1971), p. 67. Recently, Academician Dmitry Likhachev devoted an entire article to the problems that are arising as a result of the disappearance of conscience in Soviet society amongst the intelligentsia, party workers, and ordinary people: 'The Anxieties of Conscience', *Literaturnaya Gazeta*, 1 January 1987, p. 11.

15 Brodsky, interviewed by N. Gorbanevskaya, p. 9.

16 For more about the present conditions of the Russian Church, see 'Sem' voprosov i otvetov o russkoi pravoslavnoi tserkvi', by an anonymous author from the USSR, *Sintaksis*, 11 (1983), pp. 3–36.

17 Eliot, *Notes towards the Definition of Culture*, p. 126.

18 Likhachev argues in 'The Anxieties of Conscience' (p. 11): 'Once . . . Dostoevsky's characters rushed to Europe to touch the ancient stones. Is it not time for us, finally, to touch our *own* stones, our *own* memory and our *own* culture?' Brodsky is concerned with both. In the view of Czesław Miłosz, 'the poet's task as Brodsky conceives it is to try to preserve continuity in a world more and more afflicted with a loss of

memory': 'A Struggle against Suffocation', a review of Brodsky's *A Part of Speech*, *The New York Review of Books*, 14 August 1980, p. 23.

19 V. Rozanov, *Russkaya tserkov'* (St Petersburg, 1909), p. 27.

20 Ye. Barabanov, 'Sud'ba khristianskoi kul'tury', *Kontinent*, 6 (1976), p. 295.

21 Brodsky, 'Virgil: Older than Christianity. A Poet for the New Age', *Vogue*, October 1981, p. 178.

22 Brodsky, Author's Reply to Mrs Mark C. Thurlo, *Vogue*, February 1982, p. 121.

23 Ibid.

24 Brodsky, 'A Writer is a Lonely Traveller', p. 79.

25 Brodsky, 'Beyond Consolation', p. 13.

26 Ibid., p. 14.

27 Ibid.

28 D. Likhachev, interviewed by V. Yerofeev, *Voprosy Literatury*, 12 (1986), p. 111.

29 Ibid., pp. 111–12.

30 M. Kreps, *O poezii Iosifa Brodskogo* (Ann Arbor, 1984), p. 123.

31 O. Mandelstam, 'Conversation about Dante', *The Complete Critical Prose and Letters*, p. 401.

32 Brodsky, interviewed by Susan Jacoby, p. 59.

33 Miłosz, 'A Struggle against Suffocation', p. 23.

34 M. Kheifets, 'K istorii napisaniya stat'i', p. 231.

35 Miłosz, 'A Struggle against Suffocation', p. 23.

36 G. S. Smith, 'Brodskii, I. A.', *The Fontana Biographical Companion to Modern Thought*, ed. A. Bullock and R. B. Wooding (London, 1983), p. 105.

37 S. Monas, 'Words Devouring Things: The Poetry of Joseph Brodsky', *World Literature Today*, 57/2 (Spring 1983), p. 215.

38 Smith, 'Brodskii, I. A.', p. 105.

39 Kreps, *O poezii Iosifa Brodskogo*, p. 14.

40 Brodsky, 'On Richard Wilbur', *The American Poetry Review*, January/February 1973, p. 52.

41 A. Losev, 'Iosif Brodskii: Predisloviye', *Ekho*, 1 (1980), p. 30.

42 Miłosz, 'A Struggle against Suffocation', p. 23.

43 K. Verheul, 'Iosif Brodskij's "Aeneas and Dido"', *Russian Literature Triquarterly*, 6 (1973), pp. 490–501. Reprinted in Russian translation in *Poetika Brodskogo*, pp. 121–31.

44 Ibid., p. 314.

45 D.S., 'Pushkin i Brodskii', *Poetika Brodskogo*, p. 213 (first published in *Vestnik russkogo khristianskogo dvizheniya*, 123 (1977), pp. 127–39. D.S. notes a whole series of common features linking the poetics of Brodsky and Pushkin, such as: their ability to imbue a concrete episode with historico-cultural meaning, and to include a concrete hero in the gallery of prototypes; their ways of using 'the other's material', and the

latter's functions in their texts; their naturalness of thought, the free chatter.

46 O. Maksimova, 'O stikhakh Iosifa Brodskogo', *Strana i mir*, 7 (1986), p. 93.

47 Brodsky, interviewed by D. Savitsky, January 1983.

48 V. P. Grigoryev, *Grammatika idiostilia* (Moscow, 1983), p. 3.

49 The definition of poetry as 'the best words in the best order' belongs to Coleridge: see his *Miscellaneous Criticism*, ed. T. M. Raysor (Cambridge, 1936), pp. 403, 422.

50 Brodsky, interviewed by Savitsky.

51 In Viktor Gofman's view, 'The principal hero of Khlebnikov's poetry is language': *Yazyk literatury* (Moscow, 1936), p. 235.

52 Brodsky, interviewed by the author, April 1980, at Ann Arbor. It is interesting that Jakobson said something similar about Pushkin: 'his lyric . . . synthetically summarized the hundred year evolution of Russian Classical poetry, culminated it, and exhausted its creative possibilities'. In his opinion, the Russian Symbolists concluded 'the Romantic melodious lyric (Baratynskij, Lermontov, Tiutchev)': 'Marginal notes on Puskin's Lyrical Poetry', *Pushkin and his Sculptural Myth* (Paris, 1975), pp. 46.

53 B. Pasternak, from his letter to P. N. Medvedev, published by G. G. Superfin in *Trudy po znakovym sistemam*, 5 (Tartu, 1971), p. 529.

54 L. Losev, 'Poetry of Joseph Brodsky' ('Poeziya Iosifa Brodskogo'), a paper delivered at SSEES, London University, 30 March 1984.

55 Yu. Karabchievsky, *Voskreseniye Mayakovskogo* (Munich, 1985), p. 272.

56 Ibid., pp. 273–7.

57 See I. P. Smirnov, *Khudozhestvennyi smysl i evoliutsiya poeticheskikh sistem* (Moscow, 1977).

58 Brodsky's comments on his poetry for the BBC Russian Service, August 1986. I would like to thank Efim Slavinsky for allowing me to listen to Brodsky's new poems and his comments.

59 Brodsky develops this idea in his 'A Commencement Address', *Less Than One*, pp. 384–92.

60 B. P. Scherr, 'Brodsky's Stanzaic Forms' ('Strofika Brodskogo'); G. S. Smith, 'Versifikatsiya v stikhotvorenii Brodskogo "Kellomiaki"', in *Poetika Brodskogo*, pp. 97–120 and 141–59 respectively.

61 Ibid., p. 150.

62 O. Mandelstam, 'Storm and Stress', *The Complete Critical Prose and Letters*, p. 180.

63 According to Irene Steckler, 'the poem reflects one especially significant formal feature of the biblical text. It consists of 18 stanzas – the exact number of verses in Luke's account'. In her unpublished Ph.D. thesis, 'The Poetic Word and the Sacred Word: Biblical Motifs in the Poetry of J. Brodsky' (Bryn Mawr College, 1982), she has provided a comprehensive analysis of this poem; see fols. 51–78.

64 Ibid., fol. 56.
65 Ibid., fol. 70.
66 Brodsky, interviewed by G. L. Kline, 'A Poet's Map of his Poem', p. 228.
67 Ibid., p. 230.
68 B. Bukhshtab, 'The Poetry of Mandelstam', *Russian Literature Triquarterly*, 1 (1971), p. 270.
69 D.S., 'Pushkin i Brodskii', p. 213.
70 Brodsky, interviewed by Kline, p. 230.
71 Yury Mann's paper on Pushkin's poetics presented at 'The Pushkin 150th Anniversary Tribute', at Luton Hoo, 7 February 1987. Quotations are taken from my notes. A recording is available.
72 A. Losev, 'Niotkuda s liubovyu', p. 313.
73 Brodsky, *Less Than One*, p. 358, speaking about W. H. Auden.
74 His unusual technique of translation reveals the heightened interest of the young Brodsky in Donne's poetics. At first he read and translated only the first and last lines. Then he put away the original and tried to imagine what Donne had written in between. His five published translations from Donne ('The Flea', 'The Storm', 'To Mr Christopher Brooke', 'A Valediction: Forbidding Mourning' and 'The Apparition') retain fidelity to the originals, especially as regards metre and the rhyme schemes: to garner exclusively masculine rhymes throughout four whole poems is no mean feat in Russian.
75 Yu. Ivask, 'Literaturnye zametki: Brodskii, Donn i sovremennaya poeziya', *Mosty*, 12 (1966), p. 167.
76 Ibid., p. 168.
77 A similar case can be found in Zabolotsky's poem, 'Merknut znaki zodiaka', where the verb 'to sleep' is repeated 15 times in 61 lines: *Stikhotvoreniya i poemy* (Moscow and Leningrad, 1965), pp. 233–4.
78 Brodsky, interviewed by D. M. Thomas, p. 10. (The 'rotunda' did not, of course exist in Donne's time; but it was part of Brodsky's vision of the cathedral as he was writing the poem.)
79 It is interesting that this metaphor appears in Khlebnikov's prose, in 'The Temptation of a Sinner', which opens with a description of life after death: 'And there were many and many [people] . . . and the face of the old woman in the *kichka* of eternity, and *a vicious dog on the chain of days*, with a tongue of thought, and a path, along which the days run . . . and there was a lake, where instead of stone was time, and instead of reeds, little drops of time make a noise.' *Sobranie sochinenii*, IV, p. 19.
80 Brodsky, in conversation with Solomon Volkov, *Chast' rechi: Al'manakh*, 2/3 (1981–2), pp. 180–1.
81 M. Tsvetaeva, 'Moi Pushkin', *Izbrannaya proza v dvukh tomakh* (New York, 1979), II, p. 263: 'Ибо женщиры *так* читают поэтов, а не иначе.' ('For women read poets *that way* and not otherwise').
82 *W. H. Auden: A Tribute*, ed. S. Spender (New York, 1975), p. 243.

83 From my conversation with Brodsky in Ann Arbor, March 1980.
84 Brodky, in a seminar on 'W. H. Auden as a Modern Poet', University of Keele, 1 May 1985.
85 Kline, 'A Poet's Map of his Poem', p. 228.
86 The close association between time and *lapta* is evidenced by another of Brodsky's poems, 'Sitting in the Shadow': 'Но порок слепоты / время приобрело / в результате лапты, / в которую нам везло' ('But the curse of blindness / time acquired / as a result of *lapta* / we were lucky at) (*У.* 150).
87 Brodsky's lectures on W. H. Auden, Ann Arbor, January–March 1980.
88 W. H. Auden, *A Certain World (A Commonplace Book)* (London, 1971), p. 424.
89 Brodsky's seminars and lectures in Ann Arbor, Spring 1980.
90 I. P. Smirnov, *Porozhdenie interteksta (Elementy intertekstual'nogo analiza s primerami iz tvorchestva Pasternaka)*, Wiener Slawistischer Almanach, 17 (1985), p. 56.

3. THE MASK OF METAPHOR

1 Brodsky, 'On Richard Wilbur', p. 52.
2 Brodsky, 'W. H. Auden as a Modern Poet', Seminar at Keele University, 1 May 1985. The title of this section is borrowed from Miłosz's article 'A Struggle Against Suffocation', p. 23.
3 Brodsky, 'On Richard Wilbur', p. 52.
4 B. Pasternak, 'Zametki k perevodam shekspirovskikh tragedii', *Sochineniya*, vol. III (Ann Arbor, 1961), p. 194.
5 O. Mandelstam, 'Barsuchya nora', *Sobraniye sochinenii*, vol. II (Inter-Language Literary Associates, New York, 1971), p. 271.
6 The research embodied in this and the next chapter was carried out for a PhD. thesis at Keele University (1985). The second volume of the thesis lists all of Brodsky's metaphors from all of his published poems up until December 1984. The metaphors of ten other Russian poets are collected in the third volume. They are taken from the following collections: G. R. Derzhavin, *Stikhotvoreniya* (Leningrad, 1933); G. R. Derzhavin, *Stikhotvoreniya* (Moscow, 1958); E. A. Baratynsky, *Stikhotvoreniya* (Moscow, 1982); K. Bal'mont, *Izbrannoye* (Moscow, 1983); A. Blok, *Stikhotvoreniya* (Leningrad, 1955); V. Khlebnikov, *Sobraniye sochinenii v piati tomakh*, ed. Yu. Tynianov and N. Stepanov, repr. V. Markov, including *Neizdannye proizvedeniya*, ed. N. Khardzhiev and T. Grits (Munich, 1968–71); V. Mayakovsky, *Polnoye sobraniye sochinenii v 13 tomakh* (Moscow, 1955–66); B. Pasternak, *Sochineniya v trekh tomakh*, ed. G. P. Struve and B. A. Filippov (Ann Arbor, 1961); O. Mandelstam, *Sobraniye sochinenii v trekh tomakh*, ed. G. P. Struve and B. A. Filippov (Washington DC, 1967–71), vol. IV (Paris, 1981); M. Tsvetaeva, *Stikhotvoreniya i poemy v piati tomakh*, vols. I–IV (New York, 1980–3); A. Akhmatova, *Sochineniya*,

vols. I–II, ed. G. P. Struve and B. A. Filippov (Munich and Washington DC, 1967–8), vol. III (Paris, 1983).

7 The idea of interaction between meaning in metaphor was proposed in the 1930s by I. A. Richards. In his *Philosophy of Rhetoric* (Oxford, 1971), he writes: 'In the simplest formulation, when we use a metaphor we have two thoughts of different things acting together and supported by a single word, or phrase, whose meaning is resultant of their interaction' (p. 93). Max Black has developed further 'an interaction view of metaphor': see his article 'Metaphor' in *Models and Metaphor. Studies in Language and Philosophy* (Moscow, 1962), pp. 25–47.

8 Albert Henry's book, *Métonymie et métaphore* (1971), and M. Le Guern's, *Sémantique de la métaphore et de la métonymie* (1973), view metaphor as a double metonymy.

9 See one of the most sophisticated studies of metaphor by Group μ, *Rhétorique générale* (Paris, 1970); English trans. by Paul Barrell and Edgar Slotkin, *A General Rhetoric by Group μ*: J. Dubois, F. Edeline, J.-M. Klinkenberg, P. Minquet, F. Pire, H. Trinon (Baltimore and London, 1981).

10 Ted Cohen, 'Metaphor and the Cultivation of Intimacy', *On Metaphor*, ed. A. Sack (Chicago and London, 1970), p. 9.

11 A study of metaphor as a predominantly linguistic manifestation was carried out by Christine Brooke-Rose in 1958. She convincingly demonstrated, on the evidence of a number of English poets, that all the numerous previous classifications of metaphors give way, in logic, to a grammatical classification: 'Whether the figurative use of a word means a transfer from general to particular, from inanimate to animate, from abstract to concrete, whether it is a trope naming the material for the thing made of material or part of the thing for the whole, whether the metaphor is far-fetched, whether the dominant trait common to the two objects justifies the transfer, whether the metaphor is taken from this or that domain of thought, whether it is "smuggled in" from outside or rises within, whether it is true or false, deep or shallow, conscious or unconscious, decorative, sunken, violent or radical, or possessed of any other attributes through which it has been analysed, there should be a way of cutting right across these categories by considering the syntactic groups on which metaphor must, willy nilly be based.' *A Grammar of Metaphor* (London, 1970), p. 16.

12 The term 'metaphor of attribution' has been borrowed from the work of Yury I. Levin. In his article, 'Struktura russkoi metafory', he distinguishes between three types of metaphor: metaphor of comparison; the 'enigmatic' metaphor, a type corresponding to the traditional metaphor of substitution or 'pure metaphor'; and, finally, metaphors 'attributing properties of another object to the depicted object': *Trudy po znakovym sistemam*, vol. II (Tartu, 1965), p. 204. His classification is made 'according to the mode in which the principle of comparison is realised' (p. 204). My suggested classification differs

from Levin's in two ways. Firstly, an additional type of metaphor (identification), which Levin unaccountably omits, is included. Secondly, new principles for the formation of metaphors are considered. Metaphors of attribution are, in my view, rarely built on the principle of analogy between the inanimate with the living, or on the even more arbitrary analogy of the living with the inanimate.

13 In Umberto Eco's opinion, 'of the thousands and thousands of pages written about metaphor, few add anything of substance to the first two or three fundamental concepts stated by Aristotle'. 'The Scandal of Metaphor', *Poetry Today*, 4/2 (1983), pp. 217–18.

14 M. Kreps, *O poezii Iosifa Brodskogo*, pp. 55–69.

15 V. P. Grigoryev, *Poet i slovo. Opyt slovaria* (Moscow, 1975), p. 70.

16 J. Culler, 'Structure of Ideology and Ideology of Structure', *New Literary History*, 4 (1973), p. 223. Elsewhere, Culler pointed out some metaphors which resist Greimas's semantic theory of metaphor: 'In Donne's line "For I am every dead thing", which brings together the animate and the inanimate, we have an effect that cannot be captured by semantic machinery which forces us to select for both subject and predicate either the classeme animate or the classeme inanimate but not both. The identification with the inanimate has point in it only if the "I" retains some of its animate character': *Structural Poetics (Structuralism, Linguistics and Study of Literature)* (London and Henley, 1980), p. 86.

17 I. P. Smirnov, *Khudozhestvennyi smysl i evoliutsiya poeticheskikh sistem* (Moscow, 1977), p. 85.

18 A. Losev, 'Niotkuda s liubovyu', p. 309.

19 A. A. Potebnia, *Iz zapisok po teorii slovesnosti* (The Hague and Paris, 1970), p. 25.

20 V. Gofman, 'Yazykovoye novatorstvo Khlebnikova', *Yazyk literatury* (Leningrad, 1936), p. 221.

21 V. P. Grigoryev, *Grammatika idiostilia* (Moscow, 1983), p. 58.

22 Brodsky, 'A Writer is a Lonely Traveller', p. 78.

23 Brodsky, *Less Than One*, p. 170.

24 Yu. I. Levin, 'Russkaya metafora: sintez, semantika, transformatsiya', *Trudy po znakovym sistemam*, vol. IV (Tartu, 1967), p. 298.

25 In the Soviet Union, several works on genitive metaphors have appeared recently. See, for instance, X. D. Leemets, 'Struktura i funktsii imennoi metafory tipa $N_n N_g$ v yazykt proizvedenii A. A. Bestuzheva-Marlinskogo', *Trudy po russkoi i slavianskoi filologii*, 23 (Tartu, 1975). Leemets considers that the noun metaphors ($N\ N_g$) represent a semantic synthesis of a comparison based on a relation of proportion (p. 221). V. P. Grigoryev dedicated an entire chapter to 'Metaphors of Comparison' in the book *Poetika slova* (Moscow, 1979), in which genitive metaphors alone are discussed, pp. 200–50.

26 As Brodsky's translator, George Kline has pointed out that 'на сплетне себе постели' ('make your bed on gossip') is an allusion to

Pasternak's poem, 'Death of a Poet', written on the occasion of
Mayakovsky's suicide in 1930: 'Ты спал, постлав постель на
сплетне' ('you slept, having made your bed on gossip'): in Brodsky,
Selected Poems, p. 66.

27 J. Deese, 'Mind and Metaphor: A Commentary', *New Literary
History*, 6/1 (Autumn 1974), p. 219.

28 Brodsky, interviewed by the author, 8 March 1980, Ann Arbor.

29 This statement by Buslaev is cited from Potebnia, *Iz zapisok po teorii
slovesnosti*, p. 252.

30 An interesting tendency can be observed: as the use of an adjective in
the attributive metaphor decreases, a participle takes over.

Part of Speech	1st Period	2nd Period	3rd Period
Adjective	58%	45%	34%
Participle	32%	48%	61%
Adverb	10%	7%	5%

31 Smirnov, *Khudozhestvennyi smysl*, p. 137.

32 Ibid., p. 120.

33 Brooke-Rose, *A Grammar of Metaphor*, p. 234.

34 Brodsky, 'W. H. Auden', Keele University Seminar.

35 V. V. Vinogradov, *Poetika russkoi literatury. Izbrannye trudy*
(Moscow, 1976), p. 410.

36 N. D. Arutiunova, 'Yazykovaya metafora (Sintaksis i leksika)',
Lingvistika i poetika (Moscow, 1979), p. 158.

37 The constancy of the expressive energy in copula metaphors is secured
by the physical energy of the type of intonation construction (*IK-3*)
which is usually used in semantically incomplete syntagmas, such as the
first part of the nominal predicative metaphor. The main distinguishing
feature of the *IK-3* is the highest pitch of tone within the centre of this
intonation construction. For more about the semantic and physical
characteristics of Russian intonation, see Bryzgunova, *Zvuki i intonat-
siya russkoi rechi* (Moscow, 1977).

38 Brooke-Rose, *A Grammar of Metaphor*, pp. 128–9.

39 S. Bobrov, 'Zaimstvovaniya i vliyaniya', *Pechat' i revoliutsiya*, 8
1922), p. 72.

40 Smirnov, *Khudozhestvennyi smysl*, p. 117.

41 R. Jakobson, *Selected Writings* (The Hague and Paris, 1979), vol. v,
p. 340.

42 Brodsky, 'Poet i proza', an Introduction to Marina Tsvetaeva, *Izbrannaya proza v dvukh tomakh* (New York, 1979), I, p. 9. This essay is
included in English in *Less Than One*, pp. 176–94.

43 D. Lodge, *The Modes of Modern Writing. Metaphor, Metonymy and
the Typology of Modern Literature* (London, 1977), p. 112.

44 L. Losev, 'Poeziya Iosifa Brodskogo'.

45 Brodsky, Preface to *Modern Russian Poets on Poetry*, ed. Carl R.
Proffer (Ann Arbor, 1977), p. 8.

46 S. T. Coleridge, *Biographia Literaria*, ed. J. Shawcross, vol. 1 (Oxford, 1907), p. 74.

47 Albert Camus, *The Myth of Sisyphus* (Harmondsworth, 1977), p. 16.

48 W. A. Shibles, *Metaphor: An Annotated Bibliography and History* (Wisconsin, 1971), p. 16.

49 Yu. Lotman, *Struktura khudozhestvennogo teksta*, The Brown University Slavic Reprint, IX (Providence, 1971), p. 104.

50 Gerard Genette, 'Métonymie chez Proust', *Figures III* (Paris, 1972), p. 48. English translation by Alan Sheridan, 'Proust and Indirect Language', in G. Genette, *Figures of Literary Discourse* (Oxford, 1982).

51 Paul de Man, *Allegories of Reading* (Yale University Press, 1979), p. 60.

52 Yefim Etkind, *Materiya stikha* (Paris, 1978), pp. 114–19.

53 In a private conversation with me (February 1985), Brodsky admitted that he is deliberately trying to free his poetry not just from metaphors, but from tropes in general.

4. WORDS DEVOURING THINGS

1 Brodsky, *Less Than One*, p. 381.

2 Ibid., p. 265.

3 Limonov, 'Poet-bukhgalter', *Muleta. Semeinyi al'bom, A-1984*, pp. 132–3.

4 Losev, 'Poeziya Iosifa Brodskogo'.

5 Kublanovsky, 'Na predele lirizma', p. 9.

6 Mandelstam, 'Utro akmeizma', *Sobranie sochinenii*, vol. II, p. 324.

7 Shklovsky, Retsenziya na knigu Akhmatovoi *Anno Domini*, Petersburg, No. 2 (1922), p. 18.

8 L. Losev, 'Chekhovskaya tema v poezii Brodskogo', a paper (unpublished) delivered at the Chekhov Symposium, Norwich, Vermont, July 1985.

9 Etkind, *Materiya stikha* (Paris, 1978), pp. 115–19.

10 L. Losev, 'Iosif Brodskii's Poetics of Faith', *Aspects of Modern Russian and Czech Literature*, ed. A. B. McMillin (Columbus, Ohio, forthcoming).

11 Merab Mamardashvili and Aleksandr Piatigorsky, *Simvol i soznanie* (Jerusalem, 1982), p. 27.

12 Etkind, *Materiya stikha*, pp. 116–17.

13 This piece of information is taken from Irene M. Steckler's unpublished PhD thesis, 'The Poetic Word and the Sacred Word: Biblical Motifs in the Poetry of Joseph Brodsky', Bryn Mawr College, 1982. George Kline, her supervisor and Brodsky's translator, told her that Brodsky was in hospital with pernicious anaemia just before he wrote the poem 'Nature morte' and that he thought that he was dying. Ms Steckler also

provides a very thorough but somewhat naive analysis of the poem; see pp. 321–59.

14 See, for instance, Maksimova's article, 'O stikhakh Iosifa Brodskogo'. She perceived on Brodsky's face a smile of contempt for the World (with a capital letter) and a tender regard for things.
15 Losev, 'Iosif Brodskii's Poetics of Faith'.
16 Brodsky, interviewed by the author.
17 The poem 'Midday in the Room' was published in *Vestnik russkogo khristianskogo dvizheniya*, vol. III, no. 126 (1978), pp. 47–52. In the new version which was included in *Uriniya*, all the numbers are replaced by words, parts V, VII and XI are excluded, and four more parts are added. I have used the original text.
18 Brodsky, interviewed by Bella Yezerskaya, 'Esli khochesh poniat' poeta', *Mastera* (Hermitage, Tenafly, N.J., 1982), p. 112.
19 This poem was first published in the almanach *Russica-81* (New York, 1982), p. 30. When including the poem in *Uraniya*, Brodsky removed the epigraph.
20 Cited from Grigoryev, *Grammatika Idiostilia* (Moscow, 1983), p. 121.
21 Ibid., p. 122. 'Khlebnikov was always counting', writes Robin Milner-Gulland: 'numbers, like verbal sounds, were for him never random, but yielded clues to the greater patterns of the universe as of individual lives. Numbers were for him not merely the shorthand of science, but a parallel poetic order: the language of the realm of Time.' *Essays in Poetics*, 12/2 (1987), p. 93.
22 This quotation is from the Khlebnikov manuscripts, which are in the State Archive of Art and Literature in Moscow (CGALI). Quoted from Barbara Lönngvist, *Xlebnikov and Carnival* (Stockholm, 1979), p. 32.
23 My unpublished records of Brodsky's seminars in Ann Arbor, Spring 1980.
24 Aileen Kelly, 'Introduction: A Complex Vision', in Isaiah Berlin, *Russian Thinkers* (London, 1978), p. xvii.
25 Brodsky, interviewed by Gorbanevskaya, p. 9.
26 Mandelstam, 'The Badger Hole', *The Complete Critical Prose and Letters*, ed. Jane Gary Harris, trans. J. G. Harris and C. Link (Ann Arbor, 1979), p. 137.
27 Mandelstam, 'Deviatnadtsatyi vek', in *Sobranie sochinenii*, vol. II, p. 277.
28 Brodsky, 'Preface', Platonov, *The Foundation Pit* (Ann Arbor, 1973), p. ix. Also in *Less Than One*, p. 286.
29 Mamardashvili and Piatigorsky, *Simvol i soznanie*, p. 100.
30 Brodsky, a seminar, Keele University, 7 March 1978. Brodsky tends to ascribe a similar view of language to other poets he writes about: 'He [Walcott] acts out of the belief that language is greater than its masters or its servants, that poetry, being its supreme version, is therefore an instrument of self-bettering for both; i.e. that it is a way to gain an identity superior to the class, race, or ego.' *Less Than One*, p. 171.

31 Brodsky, interviewed by Gorbanevskaya, p. 9.
32 See V. Ivanov's letter to the French critic Charles du Bos, in *Wjatsche-slaw Iwanow und Michael Gerschenson, Briefwechsel zwischen zwei Zimmerwinkeln.* Revidierte u. autorisierte Übersetzung (Vienna, 1949), p. 85.
33 Brodsky, Introduction to Limonov's poems ('Predislovie k stikham Limonova'), *Kontinent*, 15 (1978), p. 153.
34 Brodsky, interviewed by Gorbanevskaya, p. 9.
35 Brodsky, interviewed by the author, 10 March 1980, Ann Arbor.
36 Brodsky, a seminar, Keele University, 7 March 1978. A few years later, asked by Yezerskaya: 'Do you consider yourself an innovator?', Brodsky answered: 'No, I don't think so. Innovation is, in any case, a silly concept. My rhymes sometimes turn out to be quite good, but to consider them "new" is senseless; they're taken from the language in which they have always existed.' Bella Yezerskaya, 'Esli khochesh poniat' poeta', p. 111.
37 See V. Terras's interesting article, 'Osip Mandelstam i ego filosofiya slova', *Slavic Poetics: Essays in Honor of Kiril Taranovsky*, ed. R. Jakobson, C. H. Van Schooneveld and Dean S. Worth (The Hague and Paris, 1973), pp. 455–60.
38 Brodsky, *Less Than One*, p. 261.
39 Kreps, *O poezii Iosifa Brodskogo*, p. 31. Kreps offers an interesting, detailed analysis of the poem 'Butterfly', which encompasses primarily the subject-matter and phonetic level, and only *en passant* touches on other structural elements, such a tropes, rhymes, and syntax. Despite the differences in approach, certain aspects of our analyses intersect and, I hope, complement each other.
40 Ibid., p. 50.
41 Brodsky, 'On Richard Wilbur', p. 52.
42 Kreps, *O poezii*, p. 40.
43 A. Losev, 'Niotkuda s liubov'yu', p. 313.

5. A SONG OF DISOBEDIENCE

1 Brodsky, *Less Than One*, p. 164.
2 Brodsky, 'On Richard Wilbur', p. 52.
3 Brodsky, interviewed by Savitsky, January 1983.
4 A. Losev, 'Niotkuda s liubovyu', p. 324.
5 See *Kontinent*, 36 (1983), pp. 19–20. When Brodsky read this poem for a few friends in London on 17 August 1986, he called it 'Near Alexandria'. In his last collection, *Uraniya*, it is given the title 'On the Outskirts of Alexandria' (pp. 138–9), as an echo not so much to Cavafy's poem 'On the Outskirts of Antioch' as to his Alexandria. The metaphor *a stone syringe* acts as a substitute for the Washington Monument, a stone obelisk which, on its completion in 1884, was the tallest structure in the world.

6 It is interesting that the Voznesensky poem quoted by his critics in *Voprosy yazyka sovremennoi russkoi literatury* (Moscow, 1971, p. 409) is not included in any of his collections.

7 An English reader will recall the last line of T. S. Eliot's 'Gerontion': 'Thoughts of a dry brain in a dry season'. Yet another of Brodsky's 'imperial' poems resonates with this poem of Eliot's, namely *Anno Domini*, which has as its subject-matter the first Christmas in one of the provinces of the Empire.

8 Thomas Venclova, '"Litovskii divertisment" Iosifa Brodskogo', *The Third Wave: Russian Literature in Emigration*, ed. Olga Matich and M. Heim (Ann Arbor, 1984), p. 196.

9 Losev, 'Ironicheskii monument: pyesa Iosifa Brodskogo *Mramor'*, *Russkaya mysl'*, 14 June 1984, p. 10.

10 An English translation of *Marbles*, by Alan Myers with Brodsky, was published in *Comparative Criticism*, ed. E. S. Shaffer, vol. VII (Cambridge, 1985), pp. 199–245. All quotations are given in the English version.

11 Losev, 'Ironicheskii monument', p. 10.

12 Brodsky, 'Why Milan Kundera is Wrong about Dostoevsky', *The New York Times Book Review*, 17 February 1985, p. 33.

13 Brodsky, Preface to Platonov, *The Foundation Pit*, p. ix.

14 Losev, 'Ironicheskii monument', p. 10.

15 Piotr Vail and Aleksandr Genis, 'Ot mira – k Rimu', *Poetika Brodskogo*, pp. 200–1.

16 Brodsky, 'Why Milan Kundera is Wrong', p. 31.

17 Vail and Genis, 'Ot mira – k Rimu', p. 199.

18 Brodsky, interviewed by Savitsky. The title for this section is borrowed from Miłosz's article, 'A Struggle against Suffocation', *The New York Review*, 14 August 1980, p. 24.

19 This direct quotation from *The Tale of Igor's Campaign* is given in Nabokov's translation; see *The Song of Igor's Campaign* (London, 1961), p. 30.

20 Henry Gifford, 'The Language of Loneliness', *Times Literary Supplement*, 11 August 1978, p. 903.

21 This device was noted by Venclova; see 'Materialy k yubileyu Iosifa Brodskogo', *Novy Amerikanets*, 15 May 1980, p. 9.

22 Susan Jacoby, 'Joseph Brodsky in Exile', p. 60.

23 Brodsky, interviewed by Savitsky.

24 Brodsky, *Less Than One*, p. 105.

25 Brodsky, Introduction to Kis, *A Tomb for Boris Davidovich*, p. xvi.

26 The twenty-poem cycle was first published in the almanach *Chast' rechi*, 2/3 (1981/2), pp. 47–62. Four of the poems were included in Brodsky's first collection, *Stikhotvoreniya i poemy*, pp. 226, 230, 231, 234–6; all of them were reprinted in the second anthology, *Ostanovka v pustyne*, with the addition of four more poems, pp. 47, 65, 77, 82. In the collection *Novye stansy k Avguste*, there appeared six more poems from

this cycle, pp. 12, 14, 22, 23, 28, 31. Losev published 'Parable', 'In Winter', 'For the Family Album', 'In the Mastard Wood', 'Christmas 1963', and one more, 'Christmas 1963'.

27 L. Losev, Afterword to 'Pervyi liricheskii tsykl Iosifa Brodskogo', pp. 63–8.

28 L. Losev, paper given at the Chekhov Symposium, Norwich, Vermont, July 1985.

29 Bakhtin, *Estetika slovesnogo tvorchestva* (Moscow, 1979), p. 305.

30 A thorough description of different types of addressee and their grammatical patterns can be found in Kovtunova, *Poeticheskii sintaksis* (Moscow, 1986), pp. 89–146.

31 G. S. Smith, 'Versifikatsiya v stikhotvorenii Iosifa Brodskogo "Kellomyaki"', *Poetika Brodskogo*, pp. 144–5.

32 Kalomirov views the function of suggestibility as being fulfilled by the collision of rhythm and syntax: 'intonation stands in distinct opposition to the syntax and semantics of the text as the irrational elements do to the rationalised creation of forms'. 'Iosif Brodskii (Mesto)', *Poetika Brodskogo*, p. 220.

33 Ibid., p. 228.

6. THE IMAGE OF ALIENATION

1 Brodsky, 'Let us try to estrange ourselves, / put the century into inverted commas', 'Piazza Mattei', *Uraniya* (Ann Arbor, 1987), p. 94.

2 Brodsky, 'Granted my lungs all sounds except the howl; / switched to whisper', 'May 24th, 1980', trans. Brodsky, *Times Literary Supplement*, 29 May 1987, p. 574; *Uraniya*, p. 177. The titles of this and the next section are borrowed from Czesław Miłosz's article, 'A Struggle against Suffocation', *The New York Review*, 14 August 1980, p. 23.

3 Sidney Monas, 'Words Devouring Things: The Poetry of Joseph Brodsky', p. 216.

4 Shklovsky, *Tetiva. O neskhodstve skhodnogo* (Moscow, 1970), p. 230.

5 Carl Proffer, 'A Stop in the Madhouse: Brodsky's "Gorbunov and Gorchakov"', *Russian Literature Triquarterly*, 1 (Fall 1971), p. 350.

6 John Green, 'The Underground Life of a Russian Intellectual', p. 62.

7 Brodsky, interviewed by Miriam Gross, 'Born in Exile', p. 41.

8 Brodsky, unpublished tapes of his seminars, Ann Arbor, Spring 1980.

9 Green, 'The Underground Life of a Russian Intellectual', p. 62.

10 Brodsky, 'Man is his own end / and runs into Time', 'Lullaby of Cape Cod', *Chast' rechi*, p. 109.

11 R. Flood and M. Lockwood (eds.), *The Nature of Time* (Oxford, 1986), p. 2.

12 St Augustine, *Confessions*, with an English translation by William Watts (London, 1912), vol. II, book XI, chap. XIV.

13 W. H. Newton-Smith, *The Structure of Time* (London, 1980), p. 3.

14 D. S. Likhachev, *Poetika drevne-russkoi literatury* (Leningrad, 1967), p. 213.

15 St Augustine, *Confessions*, book XI, chap. XXVI.

16 M. Bakhtin, 'Vremia i prostranstvo v romane', *Voprosy literatury*, 3 (1974), p. 174.

17 Brodsky, interviewed by the author, 10 March 1980.

18 S. M. Eizenshtein, 'Foreword' – Avtobiograficheskie zapiski', *Izbrannye proizvedeniya* (Moscow, 1964), p. 213.

19 Virgil, *Eclogues*, the Latin text with a verse translation and brief notes by Guy Lee (Liverpool, 1980), pp. 26–7. Cumae, with which the Sybil is associated, is one of the early Greek colonies in Italy, near Naples (750 BC).

20 Viacheslav V. Ivanov, 'Kategoriya vremeni v iskusstve i kul'ture XX veka', *Structure of Text and Semiotics of Culture* (The Hague and Paris, 1973), p. 115.

21 Mandelstam, 'Conversation about Dante', *The Complete Critical Prose and Letters*, p. 439.

22 Wittgenstein, *Tractatus Logico-Philosophicus*, trans. D. F. Pears and B. F. McGuinness (London, 1961), 2,013.

23 Jakobson, *Selected Writings*, 'Noveishaya russkaya poesiya' (The Hague and Paris, 1979), vol. V, pp. 316–19.

24 I. P. Smirnov, *Khudozhestvennyi smysl i evoliutsiya poeticheskikh sistem* (Moscow, 1977), p. 125.

25 Losev, 'Ironicheskii monument Iosifa Brodskogo: pyesa *Mramor*', *Russkaya Mysl'*, 14 June 1984, p. 10.

26 Ivanov, 'Kategoriya vremeni v iskusstve i kul'ture XX veka', p. 116.

27 Ibid., pp. 149–50.

28 Brodsky, 'But as long as my mouth has not been stuffed with clay, / only gratitude will sound from it', *Uraniya*, p. 177. See Brodsky's own translation in *Times Literary Supplement*, 29 May 1987, p. 574.

29 Lev Shestov, 'Prorocheskii dar', *Nachala i kontsy*, Sbornik statei (St Petersburg, 1908), p. 89.

30 Soren Kierkegaard, *Fear and Trembling*, trans. W. Lowrie (Princeton, 1945), p. 43.

31 Ibid., p. 44.

32 In 1978, after his first cardiac operation, when I attempted to comfort him by saying that he was now guaranteed ten years of life, Brodsky retorted that there are no guarantees, and good thing too.

33 Quoted from Shestov's *Kierkegaard i ekzistentsial'naya filosofiya* (Paris, 1939), pp. 16–17, since Gerda M. Anderson's translation of Kierkegaard's *The Diary* is incomplete.

34 Shestov, 'Kierkegaard – religioznyi filosof', *Russkie zapiski*, vol. III (1938), p. 201.

35 Shestov, *Skovannyi Parmenid*, p. 7. The book has no publication date, but Shestov's daughter judges that the most likely date is 1932. See N. Baranova-Shestova, *Zhizn' L'va Shestova*, vol. II (Paris, 1983), p. 47.

36 Kierkegaard, *Fear and Trembling*, p. 39.
37 See J. Tixeront, *Histoire des Grogmis*, 3 vols. (Paris, 1906–12).
38 Shestov, *Apofeoz bespochvennosti* (Paris, 1971), p. 78.
39 Shestov, *Kierkegaard i ekzistentsial'naya filosofiya*, p. 63.
40 Brodsky, in conversation with Maksimov, *Novyi Amerikanets*, 15 May 1980, p. 8.
41 We can find an explanation of the last two lines in Brodsky's 'Presentation of Czesław Miłosz to the Jury': 'The existential process of this poet is neither enigma nor explanation, but rather is symbolized by the test tube: the only thing which is unclear is what is being tested – whether it is the endurance of man in terms of applied pain, or the durability of pain itself.' *World Literature Today* (Summer 1978), p. 364.
42 It is significant that Brodsky admires the same quality in Miłosz's poetry: 'In a way, what this poet preaches is an awfully sober version of stoicism which does not ignore reality, however absurd and horrendous, but accepts it as a new norm which a human being has to absorb without giving up any of his fairly compromised values.' Ibid.
43 See Apollo's story in Robert Graves, *The Greek Myths*, vol. I (London: Penguin, 1955), pp. 80–1.
44 Plotinus, *Enneades*, trans. S. MacKenna, VI, 9: vol. III, p. 616 (London, 1956). The reference to Plotinus is more obvious in Russian translation by Shestov: 'Тогда душа колеблется и опасается, что ничем более не обладает.' *Sola Fide – Tol'ko veroyu* (Paris, 1966), p. 144.
45 Shestov, *Apofeoz bespochvennosti*, p. 38.
46 Shestov, *Skovannyi Parmenid*, p. 18.
47 Ibid., p. 7.
48 Shestov, *Sola Fide – Tol'ko veroyu*, p. 13.
49 Brodsky wrote this about Limonov, but in fact had himself in mind. He often most generously attributes qualities to others which more properly should be ascribed to himself. *Kontinent*, 15 (1978), p. 153.

Select bibliography

PRIMARY SOURCES

Works by Brodsky listed chronologically. This bibliography is not exhaustive. It does not include Brodsky's poems published in periodicals, except for those discussed or mentioned in the text.

Stikhotvoreniya i poemy (Short and Long Poems), Inter-Language Literary Associates, Washington and New York, 1965).
Collines et autres poèmes, preface by Pierre Emmanuel, trans. Jean-Jacques Marie (Paris, 1966).
Ausgewählte Gedichte, afterword by Alexander Kaempfe, trans. Heinrich Ost and Alexander Kaempfe (n.p.: Bechtle Verlag, 1966).
Gedichte von Jossif Brodskij. Lyrische Hefte 26, onder redactie van Arnfrid Astel (Cologne, 1966).
Elegy to John Donne and Other Poems, trans. and introd. Nicholas Bethell (London, 1967).
Poesia russa contemporarea; Da Evtusenko a Brodskij, introductory note and trans. by Giovanni Buttafava (Milan, 1967).
Velka elegie. Introd. and trans. Jiri Kovtun (Paris, 1968).
Akedar Yisak (The Binding of Isaac), introd. and Hebrew trans. Ezra Zusman (Tel Aviv, 1969).
Ostanovka v pustyne (A Halt in the Wilderness) (New York, 1970).
Stanica u pustinji, Preface by Milica Nikolic (Biblioteka "Orfej") (Belgrade, 1971).
'A Writer is a Lonely Traveller', *The New York Times Magazine*, 1 October 1972, pp. 11, 78–9, 82–5.
'Zametki o Solovyove', *Russian Literature Triquarterly*, 4 (Fall, 1972), pp. 373–5.
Selected Poems, trans. and introd. George Kline (New York, 1973; Harmondsworth, 1973).
'On Richard Wilbur', *The American Poetry Review*, January/February 1973, p. 52.
'Reflection on a Spawn of Hell', *The New York Times Magazine*, 4 March 1973, p. 10.
Preface to A. Platonov, *The Foundation Pit* (Ann Arbor, 1973), pp. ix–xii.
'Beyond Consolation' (A review of N. Mandelstam, *Hope Abandoned* and

three translations of Mandelstam's poetry), *The New York Review of Books*, 7 February 1974, p. 14.

'Elegy to W. H. Auden', *W. H. Auden: A Tribute*, ed. Stephen Spender (New York, 1975), p. 243.

Postface à A. Platonov, *La Mer de Jouvence* (Paris, 1976), pp. 173–180.

Preface to *Modern Russian Poets on Poetry* (Ann Arbor: Ardis, 1977), pp. 7–9.

'On Cavafy's Side', *The New York Review*, 17 February 1977, pp. 32–4.

'The Art of Montale', *The New York Review of Books*, 9 June 1977, pp. 35–9.

'Akhmadulina, Bella: Why Russian Poets?', *Vogue*, 167 (July 1977), p. 112.

Introduction to *Osip Mandelstam: 50 Poems*, trans. B. Meares (New York, 1977), pp. 7–17.

Konets prekrasnoi epokhi: Stikhotvoreniya 1964–71 (The End of a Beautiful Epoch: Poems 1964–71) (Ann Arbor, 1977).

Chast' rechi: Stikhotvoreniya 1972–6 (A Part of Speech: Poems 1972–6) (Ann Arbor, 1977).

V Anglii (In England) (Ann Arbor, 1977).

'Osen' v Norenskoi' (Autumn in Norenskaya) (1965), *Kontinent*, 14 (1977), pp. 92–3.

'Aqua Vita Nuova' (1970), *Vremia i my*, 17 (1977), p. 135.

Einem alten Architekten in Rom: Ausgewählte Gedichte, trans. by Karl Dedicius, Rolf Fieguth, and Sylvia List (Munich, 1978).

'Questions and Answers after Brodsky's Reading, 21 February 1978', *The Iowa Review*, 9 (1978), pp. 4–9.

Presentation of Czesław Miłosz to the Jury, *World Literature Today*, Summer 1978, p. 364.

'Predislovie k stikham Limonova', *Kontinent*, 15 (1978), p. 153.

'Koliuchei provoloki lira' (Barbed-wire Lyre) (1965), *Ekho*, 1 (1978), p. 11.

'Ty, Muza, nedoverchiva k liubvi' (You, Muse, have no trust in love) (1964–5), *Ekho*, 1 (1978), p. 14.

'Ex Ponto. Poslednee pis'mo Ovidiya v Rim' (Ex Ponto. The Last Letter of Ovid to Rome) (1964–5), *Ekho*, 1 (1978), p. 15.

'Oktiabr' – mesiats grusti i prostud' (October is a month of melancholy and cold) (1967), *Ekho*, 1 (1978), p. 17.

'Zofya' (1962), *Ekho*, 3 (1978), pp. 26–41.

'Leningrad: The City of Mystery', *Vogue*, September 1979, pp. 494–9, 543–7.

'Less Than One', *The New York Review of Books*, 27 September 1979, pp. 32, 41–7.

'Poet i proza', an Introduction to M. Tsvetaeva, *Izbrannaya proza v dvukh tomakh*, 1 (New York, 1979), pp. 7–17.

Fermata nel Deserto, trans. Giovanni Buttafa (Milan, 1979), p. 159.

Introduction to Danilo Kis, *A Tomb for Boris Davidovich* (Harmondsworth, 80), pp. ix–xvii.

A Part of Speech (New York and Oxford, 1980).

'Playing Games' (Olympic Games in Moscow), *The Atlantic Monthly*, 245 (June 1980), pp. 35–9.

'Ob odnom stikhotvorenii (vmesto predisloviya)', in M. Tsvetaeva, *Stikhotvoreniya i poemy v piati tomakh*, II (New York, 1980), pp. 39–80.

'Nadezhda Mandelstam (1899–1980)', *The New York Review of Books*, 5 March 1981, pp. 3–4.

'The Azadovsky Affair', A Letter to *The New York Review*, 8 October 1981, p. 49.

'Virgil: Older than Christianity, a Poet for the New Age', *Vogue*, October 1981, p. 178.

'Pritcha' (Parable) (1962), *Chast' rechi. Al'manakh*, No. 2/3 (1981/2), pp. 51–2.

'Sredi zimy' (In the Middle of Winter' (1963), *Molodoi Leningrad 1966*, pp. 120–1, reprinted in *Chast' rechi. Al'manakh*, 2/3 (1981/2), p. 53.

'V semeinyi Al'bom' (For the Family Album) (1963), *Chast' rechi. Al'manakh*, 2/3 (1981/2), pp. 56–7.

'Pesni schastlivoi zimy', *Chast' rechi. Al'manakh*, 2/3 (1981–2), pp. 47–62.

'V gorchichnom lesu' (In the Mastard Wood) (1963), *Chast' rechi. Al'manakh*, 2/3 (1981–2), pp. 57–60.

'Rozhdestvo 1963 goda' (Christmas 1963), *Chast' rechi. Al'manakh*, 2/3 (1981/2), pp. 60–1.

'Lesnaya idilliya' (Woodland Idyll), *Russica – 1981*, Literaturnyi sbornik pod red. A. Sumerkina (New York, 1982), pp. 25–9.

Author's reply to Mrs Mark C. Thurlo, *Vogue*, February 1982, p. 121.

Rimskie Elegii (Roman Elegies) (New York, 1982).

'O Dostoevskom', *Russica – 81*, pp. 209–13.

'Introduction' to Anna Akhmatova, *Poems*, trans. L. Coffin (New York, 1983).

'On Derek Walcott', *The New York Review*, 10 November 1983, pp. 39–41.

Novye Stansy k Avguste (New Stanzas to Augusta) (Ann Arbor, 1983).

'1983', *Kontinent*, 36 (1983), pp. 20–1.

Mramor (Marbles. A Play in Three Acts) (Ann Arbor, 1984).

'A Commencement Address', *The New York Review*, 16 August 1984, pp. 7–8.

'Viewpoint: Why the Peace Movement Is Wrong', *The Times Literary Supplement*, 24 August 1984, p. 942.

'Predislovie' to Irina Ratushinskaya, *Stikhi* (Ann Arbor, 1984), pp. 7–8.

'Why Milan Kundera Is Wrong about Dostoevsky', *The New York Times Book Review*, 17 February 1985, pp. 31, 33–4.

'Literature and War – A Symposium: The Soviet Union', *The Times Literary Supplement*, 17 May 1985, pp. 543–4.

Select bibliography 307

'Puteshestvie v Stambul', *Kontinent*, 46 (1985), pp. 67–111.
Marbles: A Play in Three Acts, trans. Alan Myers with the author, *Comparative Criticism*, ed. E. S. Shaffer, vol. VII (Cambridge, 1985), pp. 199–243.
Romische Elegien und andere Gedichte, aus dem Russischen von Felix Philipp Ingold, 'Edition Akzente' (Munich and Vienna, 1985).
'In a Room and a Half', *The New York Review*, 27 February 1986, pp. 40–8.
Poesie, trans. Giovanni Buttafava (Milan, 1986).
'Les Trophées', trans. Véronique Schiltz, *Vogue* (Paris), December/ January 1987, pp. 207–12.
'A Cambridge Education', *The Times Literary Supplement*, 30 January 1987, pp. 99–100.
Less Than One: Selected Essays (New York, Toronto, and Harmondsworth: Viking Penguin, 1986; Harmondsworth: Penguin Books, 1987).
Uraniya (Ann Arbor, 1987).
Poèmes 1961–87, trans. M. Aucouturier, J.-M. Bordier, C. Emoult, H. Henry, E. Malleret, A. Marcowicz, G. Nivat, L. Robel, V. Schiltz, J.-P. Sémon (Paris, 1987).
Fuga da Bisanzio, trans. Gilberto Forti (Milan, 1987).
Il Canto del Pendolo, trans. Gilberto Forti (Milan, 1987).

SECONDARY SOURCES

Works devoted to Brodsky, listed alphabetically:
Alloi, Vladimir, 'Proryv v beskonechnost' (chitaya stikhi Iosifa Brodskogo)', *Vremia i my*, 8 (1976), pp. 147–58.
Anonim, 'Pis'mo o russkoi poezii', *Poetika Brodskogo*, Sbornik statei pod red. L. V. Loseva (Tenafly, NJ, 1986), pp. 16–37.
Atlas, James, 'A Poetic Triumph', *The New York Times Magazine*, 21 December 1980, pp. 32–4.
Aulie, Steve, 'Soviet's Suppression of Freedom is working, Says Exiled Poet here', *Biography News*, 1 (1974), p. 60.
Bakhrakh, Aleksandr, 'Konets prekrasnoi epokhi', *Russkaya mysl'*, 3179, 24 November 1977, p. 9.
'Pod znakom Brodskogo', *Russkaya mysl'*, 3331, 23 October 1980, pp. 8–9.
Baranchik, Stanislaw, 'Perevodia Brodskogo', *Kontinent*, 19 (1979), pp. 347–65; reprinted in *Poetika Brodskogo*, pp. 239–51.
Bar-Sella, Zeev (Nazarov, Vladimir), 'Tolkovaniya na...', *Dvadtsat' Dva*, 23 (1982), pp. 214–33.
'Vse tsvety rodstva (iz knigi *Iosif Brodskii. Opyt chteniya*)', *Dvadtsat' dva*, 37 (1984), pp. 192–208.
'Strakh i trepet (iz knigi *Iosif Brodskii. Opyt chteniya*)', *Dvadtsat' Dva*, 41 (1985), pp. 202–13.

Bayley, John, 'The Will to Survive', A review of J. Brodsky's *Selected Poems*, *The Observer*, 6 January 1974, p. 25.

'Sophisticated Razzmazz', *Parnassus: Poetry in Review*, 9 (Spring/ Summer 1981), pp. 83–90.

'Mastering Speech', A Review of Brodsky's *Less Than One; Selected Essays*, *The New York Review*, 12 June 1986, pp. 3–4.

Betaki, Vasily, 'Ostanovis' mgnovenye', *Kontinent*, 35 (1983), pp. 384–8.

Bethea, David, 'Conjurer in Exile', *The New York Times Book Review*, 13 July 1986, pp. 3, 38.

Birkerts, Sven, 'Art of Poetry xxvii: Joseph Brodsky' (Interview), *Paris Review*, 24 (Spring 1982), pp. 82–126.

Blake, P., 'Soviet Literature Goes West', *Time*, 123, 12 March 1984, pp. 78.

Bonnefoy, Yves, 'On the Translation of Form in Poetry', *World Literature Today*, 53/3 (Summer 1979), pp. 374–9.

Bosley, Keith, *Russia's Other Poets*, introd. Janis Sapiets, trans. with D. Pospielovsky and Janis Sapiets (London, 1968), pp. xxii, 18–23.

Bosley, Keith, 'Fit only for Barbarians: The Sound of Translated Poetry', *World Literature Today*, 55/1 (Winter 1981), pp. 52–5.

Bristol, Evelin, 'J. Brodsky', *Handbook of Russian Literature*, ed. V. Terras (Yale University Press, 1985), p. 61.

Brown, Clarence, 'The Best Russian Poetry Written Today', *The New York Times Book Review*, 7 September 1980, pp. 11, 17–18.

Brown, Deming, *Soviet Russian Literature since Stalin* (Cambridge, 1978), pp. 136–44.

Brown, Edward, *Russian Literature since the Revolution* (Harvard University Press, 1982), pp. 340–1, 346, 354–8, 386, 390.

'Russian Literature beyond the Pale', *Slavic and East European Review*, 30/3 (Fall 1986), pp. 380–8.

Carlisle, Olga (ed.), *Poets on Street Corners: Portraits of Fifteen Russian Poets* (New York, 1968), pp. 400, 402–21.

Cohen, Arthur A., A Review of Brodsky's *Selected Poems*, *The New York Times Book Review*, 30 December 1973, pp. 1–2.

Dediulin, Sergei, 'Korotko o knigakh', *Russkaya mysl'*, 4 April 1986, p. 10.

'Novye perevody stikhov Brodskogo', *Russkaya mysl'*, 3622, 22 May 1986, pp. 12–13.

Driver, Sam, Review of Michael Kreps, *O poezii Iosifa Brodskogo*, *World Literature Today*, Winter 1986, pp. 132–3.

Döring-Smirnov, Johanna Renate, 'Uznat', chto budet Ja, kogda...', Vergleichende Anmerkungen zu den Autobiographien von B. Pasternak und Brodskij, *Die Welt der Slaven*, 28 (1983), 2.

D.S. (pseudonym), 'Pushkin i Brodskii', *Vestnik russkogo khristianskogo dvizheniya*, 123 (1977), pp. 127–39; reprinted in *Poetika Brodskogo*, pp. 207–18.

Dunn, Douglas, 'In whom the Language Lives', on Brodsky's *Less Than One, Poetry Review*, 76/3 (1986), pp. 4–6.

Eder, Richard, 'Joseph Brodsky in US: Poet and Language in Exile', *The New York Times*, 25 March 1980, p. 2.

Emmanuel, Pierre, 'A Soviet Metaphysical Poet', *Quest*, 52 (1967), pp. 65–72.

Erlich, Victor, 'A Letter in a Bottle', a Review of Brodsky's *Selected Poems, Partisan Review*, 41 (Fall 1974), p. 617.

Etkind, Yefim, *Zapiski nezagovorshchika* (London, 1977), pp. 51–7, 117–19, 140–81, 364–70, 438–67.

Materiya stikha, Institut d'Etudes Slaves (Paris, 1978), pp. 114–19.

'Vziat' notoi vyshe, ideei vyshe...', *Chast' rechi. Al'manakh*, 1 (1980), pp. 37–41.

Russische Lyrik von der Oktober-Revolution zur Gegenwart. Versuch einer Darstellung (Munich, 1984), pp. 209–16, 254–9.

France, Peter, *Poets of Modern Russia* (Cambridge, 1982.)

Hass, Robert, 'Lost in Translation', a review of *A Part of Speech* by J. Brodsky, *New Republic*, 183, 20 December 1980, pp. 35–7.

Hofmann, Michael, 'Measures of a Poet's Mind', a review of *Less Than One, The Guardian*, 3 October 1986, p. 11.

Garfitt, Roger, 'Near and Far East', a review of Brodsky's *Selected Poems, London Magazine*, June/July 1974, pp. 104–6.

Gifford, Henry, 'The Language of Loneliness', *The Times Literary Supplement*, 11 August 1978, pp. 902–3.

'Idioms in Interfusion'. *The Times Literary Supplement*, 17 October 1980, p. 1159.

'Of Petersburg, Poetry and Human Ties', *The Times Literary Supplement*, 19 September 1986, pp. 1019–20.

Gorbanevskaya, Nataliya, 'Interview with Joseph Brodsky', *Russkaya mysl'*, 3 February 1983, pp. 8–9.

Gould, Tony, 'Out of Russia', a review of *Less Than One, New Society*, 17 (1986), p. 29.

Green, John, 'The Underground Life of a Russian Intellectual: Authors in News: Brodsky', *Biography the News*, 1, June 1974, pp. 61–2.

Gross, Miriam, 'Born in Exile', an interview with Brodsky, *The Observer*, 25 October 1981, pp. 36–41.

Grubishich, Lilia, 'Russkie pisateli v izgnanii: Iosif Brodskii i Sasha Sokolov', *Russkaya mysl'*, 23 May 1985, p. 13.

Innis, Joanne, Review of M. Kreps, *O poezii Iosifa Brodskogo, The Russian Review*, 45/2, pp. 223–4.

Ivask, Yury, Review of Brodsky's *Stikhotvoreniya i poemy, Novy Zhurnal*, 70 (1965), pp. 297–9.

'Literaturnye zametki: Brodskii, Donn i sovremennaya poeziya', *Mosty*, 12 (1966), pp. 161–71.

'Iosif Brodskii. Ostanovka v pustyne', *Novy Zhurnal*, 102 (1071), pp. 294–7.

Jacoby, Susan, 'Joseph Brodsky in Exile', *Change*, 5/3 (1973), pp. 58–63.
Janecek, Gerald, 'Comments on Brodsky's "Stikhi na smert" T. S. Eliota",
    Poetika Brodskogo, pp. 172–84.
Kalomirov, Aleksandr (pseudonym of Viktor Krivulin), 'Iosif Brodskii
    (Mesto)', *Vestnik russkogo khristianskogo dvizheniya*, 123 (1977),
    pp. 140–51; reprinted in *Poetika Brodskogo*, pp. 219–29.
Kalomirov, Aleksandr, 'Dvadtsat' let noveishei russkoi poezii', *Russkaya
    mysl'*, 27 December 1985; reprinted in *Literaturnoe prilozhenie*, 2,
    pp. vi–viii.
Karabchievsky, Yury, *Voskreseniye Mayakovskogo* (Munich, 1985),
    pp. 272–9.
Kasack, Wolfgang, 'Josif Brodski', *Neue Zürcher Zeitung*, 25 June 1972.
'"Das Ende einer schönen Epoche', Josif Brodskis Gedichte auf
    Deutsch. Von Ilma Rakusa', *Neue Zürcher Zeitung*, 16 March 1979.
Kheifets, Mikhail, 'K istorii napisaniya stat'i: "Iosif Brodskii i nashe
    pokolenie"', *Poetika Brodskogo*, ed. Lev Losev (Tendfly, 1986),
    pp. 230–8.
Kline, George L., 'On Brodsky's "Great Elegy to John Donne"', *Russian
    Review*, 24 (1965), pp. 341–53.
'Religious Themes in Soviet Literature', *Aspects of Religion in the Soviet
    Union 1917–67*, ed. R. N. Marshal (The University of Chicago Press,
    1971), pp. 157–86.
'A Poet's Map of his Poem', a personal interview, *Vogue*, 162 (September
    1973), pp. 228, 300.
'A Bibliography of the Published Works of Iosif Aleksandrovich
    Brodsky', in Fred Moody (ed.), *Ten Bibliographies of Twentieth
    Century Russian Literature* (Ann Arbor, 1977), pp. 159–75.
'Russian Posy Throws Curve at American Poet Translator', *Pittsburgh
    Press* (Penn.), October 1974, reprinted in *Authors in the News*, 1 June
    1974, p. 60.
'Working with Brodsky', *Paintbrush*, 4/7–8 (1977), pp. 25–6.
'Iosif Brodsky' in *Columbia Dictionary of Modern European Literature*,
    ed. Jean-Albert Bidé and William B. Edgertont (New York, 1980),
    pp. 121–2.
Kline, George L. and Sylvester, Richard D., 'Brodskii, I. A.', *Modern
    Encyclopedia of Russian and Soviet Literature*, ed. H. B. Weber and
    G. Breeze, vol. III (Gulf Breeze, Florida, 1979), pp. 129–37.
Knox, Jane E., 'Iosif Brodskij's Affinity with Osip Mandel'stam: Cultural
    Links with the Past', Ph.D., University of Texas at Austin, 1978.
'Ierarkhiya drugikh v poezii Brodskogo', *Poetika Brodskogo*,
    pp. 160–71.
Kopeikin, Anatoly, 'Zametki o shestoi knige Iosifa Brodskogo', *Kon-
    tinent*, 38 (1983), pp. 387–93.
'Kak popast' v spetskhran', *Russkaya mysl'*, 9 February 1984, p. 6.
Korolevich, Anna, 'Yerofeev, Brodskii i drugie', *Russkaya mysl'*, 4 April
    1986, p. 12.

Kreps, Mikhail, *O poezii Iosifa Brodskogo* (Ann Arbor, 1984).

Kublanovsky, Yury, 'Na predele lirisma', *Russkaya mysl'*, 11 August 1983, p. 10.

Interview with Lev Losev (pseudonym of Aleksei Lifshits), *Russkaya mysl'*, 28 July 1983, p. 9.

Kustarev, A., 'Kul'tura kruzhka', *Sintaksis*, 17 (1987), pp. 155–60.

Lamont, Rosette C., 'Joseph Brodsky: A Poet's Classroom', *Massachussetts Review*, 15 (1974), pp. 553–77.

Review of Brodsky's *A Part of Speech*, *World Literature Today*, 55/2 (Spring 1981), pp. 341–2.

Langeveld, Arthur, 'Iosif Brodski's "Voor Jalta"', *De Gids*, 146 (1983), pp. 404–12.

Levy, Alan, 'Think it over, Brodsky, but Decide now', Interview with Brodsky, *Saturday Review*, 8 July 1972, pp. 6–8.

Limonov, Eduard, 'Poet-bukhgalter', *Muleta. Semeinyi al'bom*, A-1984 (Paris), pp. 132–3.

Lindsey, Byron, Iosif Brodskij, *Konec prekrasnoj epoxi, Chast' rechi*, *World Literature Today*, Winter 1978, pp. 129–30.

Losev, Aleksei (pseudonym of Aleksei Lifshits), 'Niotkuda s liubovyu ... (Zametki o stikhakh Iosifa Brodskogo)', *Kontinent*, 14 (1977), pp. 307–31.

'Iosif Brodskii: posviashchaetsa logike, *Vestnik russkogo khristianskogo dvizheniya*, 127 (1978), pp. 124–30.

'Iosif Brodskii. Predislovie', *Ekho*, 1 (1980), pp. 23–30.

'Angliiskii Brodskii', *Chast' rechi. Al'manakh*, 1 (1980), pp. 53–60.

'Pervyi liricheskii tsykl Iosifa Brodskogo', *Chast' rechi. Al'manakh*, 2/3 (1981/82), pp. 63–8.

Losev, Lev (pseudonym of Aleksei Lifshits), A paper, 'Poeziya Iosifa Brodskogo', given at SSEES, London University, 30 March 1984, unpublished.

'Ironicheskii monument: pyesa Iosifa Brodskogo *Mramor*', *Russkaya mysl'*, 14 June 1984, p. 10.

'Brodskii: ot poeta k mifu'. Predislovie, *Poetika Brodskogo*, pp. 7–15.

'Chekhovskii lirism u Brodskogo', *Poetika Brodskogo*, pp. 185–97.

(ed.), *Poetika Brodskogo. Sbornik statei* (Tenafly, N.J.; 1986).

'Iosif Brodskii's Poetics of Faith', *Aspects of Modern Russian and Czech Literature* (Columbus, Ohio, in press).

Losev, Lev and Polukhina, Valentina (eds.), *Brodsky's Poetics and Aesthetics* (London, in press).

Lourie, Richard, Review of Brodsky's *Ostanovka v pustyne* (Halt in the Wilderness), *Russian Review*, 30 April 1971, p. 202.

Maksimova, Ol'ga, 'O stikhakh Iosifa Brodskogo', *Strana i mir*, 7 (1986), pp. 89–96.

Massie, Suzanne, *The Living Mirror: Five Young Poets from Leningrad* (London: Gollancz, 1972), pp. 215–99.

'Materialy k yubileyu Brodskogo: pozdravleniya-stat'i V. Maksimova,

312   Select bibliography

S. Kalinskogo, N. Berberovoi, I. Yefimova, T. Venclova, I. Yelagina, S. Dovlatova', *Novy Amerikanets*, 23–9 May 1980, pp. 7–9.

May, Helen, 'Better Writer than Saint', *New York Post*, 24 May 1980, p. 14.

Miłosz, Czesław, 'A Struggle against Suffocation', a review of Brodsky's *A Part of Speech*, *The New York Review*, 14 August 1980, pp. 23–4.

Monas, Sidney, 'Words Devouring Things: The Poetry of Joseph Brodsky', *World Literature Today*, 57/2 (Spring 1983), pp. 214–18.

Iosif Brodskij, *Rimskie elegii*, *World Literature Today*, 57/2 (Spring 1983), pp. 309–10.

Muravnik, Maya, '"Kontinent" No. 51', *Russkaya mysl'*, 7 August 1987, p. 10.

Nikolic, Milica, 'Mutni govor Josifa Brodskog', Preface to Josif Brodski, *Stanica u pustinji* (Belgrade, 1971).

N.N. (pseudonym of Anatoly Naiman), 'Zametki dlia pamiati', Introduction to *Ostanovka v pustyne*, pp. 7–15.

Paramonov, Boris, 'Soglasno Yungu', *Kontinent*, 37 (1983), pp. 275–80.

Pawel, Ernst, 'The Poetry of Joseph Brodsky', *Midstream*, 14, No. 5 (1968), pp. 17–22.

Philips, William, 'Brodsky's *Less Than One*, *Partisan Review*, 1 (1987), pp. 139–45.

Polukhina, Valentina, 'The "Strange Theme" in J. Brodsky's Poetry', *Essays in Poetics*, 4, No. 1 (1979), pp. 35–54.

Interview with Brodsky, 10 April 1980, unpublished.

'The Poetry of Joseph Brodsky: A Study of Metaphor', PhD thesis, Keele University, 1985.

'A Study of Metaphor in Progress. Poetry of Joseph Brodsky', *Wiener Slawistischer Almanach*, 17 (1986), pp. 149–85.

'Grammatika metafory i khudozhestvennyi smysl'', *Poetika Brodskogo*, ed. Lev Losev (Tenafly, 1986), pp. 63–96.

Proffer, Carl R., 'A Stop in the Madhouse: Brodsky's "Gorbunov and Gorchakov"', *Russian Literature Triquarterly*, 1 (Fall 1971), pp. 342–51; reprinted in *Poetika Brodskogo*, pp. 132–40.

Rais, Emanuil, 'Leningradskii Gamlet (O stikhakh I. Brodskogo)', *Grani*, No. 59 (1965), pp. 168–72.

Rannit, Aleksis, 'Zametki o Rossii i Iosife Brodskom', *Chast' rechi. Al'manakh*, 1 (1980), pp. 61–6.

Rayfield, Donald, 'Grist to the Mill', *The Times Higher Education Supplement*, 10 October 1986, p. 18.

Reavey, George (ed. and trans.), *The New Russian Poets: 1953–1966* (New York, 1966), pp. 255–69.

Reeve, F. D., 'Additions and Losses', review of Brodsky's *Selected Poems*, *Poetry*, 127 (October 1975), p. 42.

'On Joseph Brodsky', *American Poetry Review*, July/August 1982, pp. 36–7.

Russell, Noel, Interview with Brodsky, *Literary Review*, January 1986, pp. 10–12.

Rybakov, V., 'Yazyk – edinstvennyi avangard', interview with Brodsky, *Russkaya mysl'*, 26 January 1978, p. 8.

Savitsky, Dmitry, Interview with Brodsky, January 1983, *Emois*, 10 April 1988, pp. 62–3.

Scarpetta, Guy, 'Jossif Brodski: Poésie et Dissidence', *Tel Quel* (1978), pp. 50–5.

Scherr, Barry, 'Strofika Brodskogo', *Poetika Brodskogo*, pp. 97–120.

Schmidt, Michael, 'Time of Cold', *New Statesman*, 17 October 1980, p. 13.

Serke, Jürgen, 'Die verbanneten Dichter', *Stern*, 1981, pp. 137–8, 140–1, 144–8.

Shargorodsky, Sergei, 'Igry v sadu (Ob odnom stikhotvorenii Brodskogo)', *Dvadtsat' dva*, 40 (1985), pp. 205–13.

Sheppard, R. Z., 'Notes from a Poet in his Prime', review of Brodsky's *Less Than One*, *Time*, 7 April 1986.

Shtein, Emmanuil, 'Peremena vetra', *Novy Amerikanets*, 65, 10–16 May 1981, pp. 38–9.

Smith, Gerald, 'Brodskii, I. A.', *The Fontana Biographical Companion to Modern Thought*, ed. Alan Bullock and R. B. Woodings (London, 1983), pp. 104–5.

'Versifikatsiyav stikhotvorenii Brodskogo "Kellomiaki"', *Poetika Brodskogo*, pp. 141–59.

'More than Brodsky', *The New York Times Book Review*, 7 September 1986, p. 37.

'Another Time, Another Place', *The Times Literary Supplement*, 26 June 1987, pp. 692–4.

'Russian Poetry outside Russia since 1970: A Survey', *Aspects of Modern Russian and Czech Literature* (Columbus, Ohio, in press).

Solovyov, Vladimir, 'Iz "romana" s epigrafami. Dve glavy ob Iosife Brodskom', *Novy Amerikanets*, 12–14 March 1981, p. 6.

Soprovsky, Aleksandr, 'Konets prekrasnoi epokhi', *Kontinent*, 32 (1982), pp. 335–54.

Spender, Stephen, 'Bread of Affliction', A review of Brodsky's *Selected Poems*, *New Statesman*, 14 December 1973, pp. 915–16.

Steckler, Irene M., 'The Poetic Word and the Sacred Word: Biblical Motifs in the Poetry of Joseph Brodsky', unpublished Ph.D. thesis, Bryn Mawr College, 1982.

Stern, M., A review of Brodsky's *Selected Poems*, *Midstream*, June/July 1976, p. 87.

Stukov, Georgy (pseudonym of Gleb Struve), 'Poet – "tuneyadets" – Iosif Brodsky', Introduction to *Stikhotvoreniya i poemy*, Inter-Language Associates (New York, 1965), pp. 5–15.

Sylvester, Richard D., 'The Poem as Scapegoat: An Introduction to Joseph Brodsky's *Halt in the Wilderness*', *Texas Studies in Literature and Language*, 17 (1975), pp. 303–25.

Ternovsky, Yevgeny, 'Soimennik i imiarek', *Grani*, 100 (1976), pp. 430–8.

Thomas, D. M., Review of Brodsky's *A Part of Speech*, *Poetry Review*, 70, No. 4 (1981), pp. 47–50.

Interview with Brodsky, *Quarto*, 24 (December 1981), pp. 9–11.
Timmer, Charles B., 'Russische Notities', *Torade*, 27 (January/February 1983, pp. 44–59.
Vail, Piotr, and Genis, Aleksandr, 'Ot mira – k Rimu', *Poetika Brodskogo*, pp. 198–206.
Venclova, Thomas, '"Litovskii divertisment" Iosifa Brodskogo', *The Third Wave: Russian Literature in Emigration*, ed. Olga Matich and M. Heim (Ann Arbor, 1984), pp. 181–201.
Verheul, Kees, 'Iosif Brodskij's "Aeneas and Dido"', *Russian Literature Triquarterly*, 6 (1973), pp. 490–501; reprinted in *Poetika Brodskogo*, pp. 121–31.
'Het persoonlijkt konflikt van Iosif Brodski', *Verlaat debuut* (Amsterdam, 1976), pp. 53–8.
Vigdorova Frida, 'Zasedanie Dzerzhinskogo raiona goroda Leningrada'. Sud nad Iosifom Brodskim, *Vozdushnye puti. Al'manakh*, 4 (New York, 1965), pp. 279–303.
Vitale, Serena, 'La voce di Brodskij contro un mondo di uomini-fossili', review of Iosif Brodskij, *Poesie*, Bibliotecca Adelphi, 165 (1986), trans. G. Buttafava, *Stampa*, 5 April 1986, p. 5.
Volkov, Solomon, 'New York: peizazh poeta', intervyu s Iosifom Brodskim', *Chast' rechi. Al'manakh*, 1 (1980), pp. 27–36.
'Venitsiya glazami stikhotvortsa. Dialog s Iosifom Brodskim', *Chast' rechi: Al'manakh*, 2/3 (1981/2), pp. 175–87.
'Vospominaya Annu Akhmatovu: Razgovor s Iosofom Brodskim', *Kontinent*, 53 (1987), pp. 337–82.
Wainwright, Jeffrey, 'The Art of Estrangement', *Poetry Nation Review*, 14, No. 2 (1987), pp. 36–8.
Wu, Duncan, 'Translation as Exile', review of Brodsky's *Less Than One*, *Literary Review*, October 1986, pp. 38–9.
Yezerskaya, Bella, Interview with Brodsky, *Mastera* (Tenafly, NJ, 1982), pp. 103–12.
Zeeman, Peter, 'Leegte en Licht: Josif Brodski', *De Gids*, 146 (1983), pp. 392–9.
'Kees Verheul over Josef Brodski', *De Gids*, 146 (1983), pp. 400–4.
Zholkovsky, Aleksandr, 'Writing in the Wilderness: On Brodskij and a Sonnet', *Slavic and East European Journal*, 30, No. 3 (Fall 1986), pp. 404–19.
'"Ya vas liubil..." Brodskogo: interteksty, invarianty, tematika i struktury', *Poetika Brodskogo*, pp. 36–62.

Index

315

INDEX TO WORKS BY BRODSKY DISCUSSED OR NOTED IN THE TEXT;
TITLES IN ENGLISH TRANSLATION

GENERAL INDEX

Walcott, Derek, 38, 112, 298 n. 30
Wilbur, Richard, 102, 290 n. 40, 293 n.
1, n. 3, 299 n. 41
Wittgenstein, Ludwig, 259, 302 n. 22

Yeats, W. B., 81, 90, 128, 197
Yesenin, Sergei, 11
Yevtushenko, Yevgeny, 4, 15, 287 n. 86

Zabolotsky, Nikolai, 5, 292 n. 77
Zamiatin, Yevgeny, 208
Zhdanov, Andrei, 3
Zhukovsky, Vasily, 73
Zinovyev, Aleksandr, 30, 36
Zoshchenko, Mikhail, 3